IDEA AND FORM

Karin Wilhelm

IDEA AND FORM

Häuser von Houses by SZYSZKOWITZ+KOWALSKI

mit Seitenblicken von with sideways glances by
Johann Sauer

Vorwort Preface
Peter Blundell Jones

Birkhäuser – Verlag für Architektur Publishers for Architecture
Basel · Berlin · Boston

Layout und Umschlaggestaltung Layout and cover design:
Silke Nalbach, Stuttgart

Übersetzung Translation:
Michael Robinson, London

Bearbeitung des Buches im Büro Szyszkowitz+Kowalski Coordination
at office Szyszkowitz+Kowalski:
Ingrid Frisch, Graz

A CIP catalogue record for this book is available from the Library
of Congress, Washington D.C., USA

Bibliographic information published by Die Deutsche Bibliothek
Die Deutsche Bibliothek lists this publication in the Deutsche
Nationalbibliografie; detailed bibliographic data is available in the
Internet at <http://dnb.ddb.de>.
This work is subject to copyright. All rights are reserved, whether
the whole or part of the material is concerned, specifically the rights
of translation, reprinting, re-use of illustrations, recitation, broadcasting,
reproduction on microfilms or in other ways, and storage in data
banks. For any kind of use, permission of the copyright owner must be
obtained.

© 2003 Birkhäuser – Publishers for Architecture, P.O.Box 133,
CH-4010 Basel, Switzerland
A member of the BertelsmannSpringer Publishing Group
Printed on acid-free paper produced from chlorine-free pulp. TCF ∞
Printed in Germany
ISBN 3-7643-6927-2

9 8 7 6 5 4 3 2 1   www.birkhauser.ch

Inhalt Contents

6	Vorwort
6	Preface
	Peter Blundell Jones
10	Das Einfamilienhaus als „Territorialkunst"
10	The detached house as "territorial art"
	Karin Wilhelm
90	Annäherung an Graz
90	Approaching Graz
94	Das Architekturbüro Szyszkowitz+Kowalski
94	Szyszkowitz+Kowalski's practice
100	Ein Hausbesuch
100	A home visit
	Johann Sauer
96	Wichtigste Realisierungen
97	Most important realizations
98	Biographien Szyszkowitz+Kowalski
98	Biographies Szyszkowitz+Kowalski

Häuser Houses
Karin Wilhelm

104	Haus über Graz House above Graz
110	Grünes Haus Green House
114	Haus Zusertal House in Zusertal
120	Rotes Haus Red House
124	Haus am Hohenrain House on Hohenrain
128	Graues Haus Grey House
132	Haus Harmisch Harmisch House
140	Häuser in Wien/Hietzing – Unteres Haus
	Houses in Hietzing, Vienna – Lower House
146	Häuser in Wien/Hietzing – Oberes Haus
	Houses in Hietzing, Vienna – Upper House
156	Haus in Bad Mergentheim
	House in Bad Mergentheim
164	Haus in Maria Enzersdorf House in Maria Enzersdorf
170	Haus am Plattenweg House on Plattenweg
180	Turm Fölling Tower in Fölling
184	Designhaus Design House
188	Haus in Moosburg House in Moosburg
196	Stadtvillen Mariagrün Urban villas in Mariagrün
206	Haus am Ruckerlberg House on Ruckerlberg
214	Haus in Kumberg House in Kumberg
220	Preise und Auszeichnungen
220	Prizes and awards
220	Publikationen
220	Publications
224	Bildnachweis
224	Illustration credits

Vorwort Preface

PETER BLUNDELL JONES

Die Zeit, in der Michael Szyszkowitz und Karla Kowalski ihre Tätigkeit aufnahmen, stand im Zeichen verbreiteter Desillusionierung angesichts einer modernen Architektur, die sich in der Wiederholung eines schmalen Formenkanons erschöpfte. Gegen Ende der sechziger Jahre wuchs die Erkenntnis, daß der enge verwissenschaftlichte Funktionalismus, der zur architektonischen Regel geworden war, nicht nur langweilige, farblose Gebäude hervorbrachte, sondern auch seinen eigenen Ansprüchen kaum gerecht wurde. Schlimmer noch, er unterwarf die kreativen Möglichkeiten dieser Kunst bürokratischen Normen und Techniken der Massenproduktion. Daß die beiden Architekten einander im Münchner Büro Behnisch & Partner kennenlernten, die damals gerade ihr größtes und ambitioniertestes Projekt, die Olympiabauten für 1972, angingen, ist vielleicht kein Zufall, denn Behnisch und sein Team hatten dem standardisierten Bauen soeben den Rücken gekehrt und sich bewußt auf eine „Situationsarchitektur" eingelassen, eine Bauweise, die nicht die wiederholbaren Aspekte eines Projekts, sondern dessen Besonderheit in den Mittelpunkt stellte. Kowalski kam als Mitarbeiterin von Behnisch, Szyszkowitz zusammen mit Domenig und Huth, die gerade ein Restaurantprojekt bearbeiteten. Auch die beiden Österreicher waren entschlossen, den Beweis dafür zu erbringen, daß die Architektur einem kreativen, ja absichtsvoll künstlerischen Vorgehen Raum bietet, und wurden die Gründer der „Grazer Schule" oder, wie ich sie nenne,

Michael Szyszkowitz and Karla Kowalski began their practice at a time of widespread disillusion about the narrow and repetitive formula that modern architecture had become. Towards the end of the 1960s architects began to recognize that the narrow scientific functionalism regarded as the normal way of working not only produced dull and colourless buildings, but did not even really work in its own terms. Worst of all, it subordinated the creative possibilities of the art to bureaucratic norms and mass-production techniques. It is perhaps no accident that the two architects met in the Munich office of Günter Behnisch & Partner, who were then just embarking on their largest and most ambitious project, the Olympic complex for 1972; for the Behnisch office had just turned their backs on prefabrication to indulge in a consciously "situational" architecture, which concentrated not on the repeatable aspects of projects but instead on what was specific to each case. Kowalski arrived as part of Behnisch's team: Szyszkowitz came with Domenig and Huth who were working on a restaurant. The two Austrians were also determined to prove that there remained room in architecture for a creative and even self-consciously artistic approach, and became the founders of the "Grazer Schule", or as I call it the New Graz Architecture*, Domenig as the figurehead of creative individualism, Huth as pioneer of participation.

In the architectural renaissance of the early 1970s, it is hard to separate the new concerns with image, place, and personal expression. Szyszkowitz+Kowalski excelled at all three. Distinctly impatient with standard forms, they launched into an architecture that was intensely three-dimensional and

Peter Blundell Jones, Dialogues in Time: New Graz Architecture, Haus der Architektur (HDA) (Hg.), Graz 1998
Dialogues in Time: New Graz Architecture by Peter Blundell Jones, Haus der Architektur (HDA) (ed.), Graz 1998.

der Neuen Grazer Architektur* – Domenig als Schlüsselfigur eines schöpferischen Individualismus, Huth als Pionier der Partizipation.

In der architektonischen Renaissance der frühen siebziger Jahre sind die neuen Fixpunkte Bildhaftigkeit, Ort und persönlicher Ausdruck kaum voneinander zu trennen. Szyszkowitz+Kowalski brillierten in allen drei Dimensionen. Der standardisierten Formen überdrüssig, wandten sie sich einer betont dreidimensionalen, farbigen Bauweise zu. Die neuartigen Bauten, die in schwungvollen Skizzen festgehalten waren, ließen sich darüber hinaus gut fotografieren, und die zwei jungen Architekten beeindruckten von Anfang an durch einen kreativen Umgang mit Gelände und Kontext sowie ein Faible für die Behandlung von Stirnseiten und Ecken, den oft schwierigsten Teilen eines Projekts. Außerdem bewiesen sie großes Geschick darin, den Bau und die Detailbehandlung ihrer komplexen Arbeiten innerhalb des normalen Kostenrahmens zu halten, indem sie die zentralen Ideen während der Ausführungsplanung deutlich markierten, statt sie abzuschwächen. Doch ihre weltweite Reputation verdankt sich vor allem einer künstlerischen Handschrift, die in der internationalen Architekturszene zum Markenzeichen wurde.

Die stilistische Signatur von Szyszkowitz+Kowalski war Segen und Fluch zugleich. Sie sicherte den beiden in den achtziger und neunziger Jahren zwar den Erfolg, brachte es aber auch mit sich, daß das eigentliche Originelle ihrer Arbeit oft aus dem Blick geriet. Die fotografischen Umsetzungen bestechen, doch in der Realität sind die Arbeiten häufig besser; sie erscheinen dem Betrachter ausgeglichener und haben ihm mehr zu bieten. Die Formen wirken zurückhaltender, die Größenverhältnisse harmonischer.

Weil in den frühen Darstellungen der modernen Architektur der Expressionismus zum Funktionalismus, die Subjektivität zur vielgeliebten Sachlichkeit in Opposition gesetzt wurde,

colourful. It photographed well, backed up by fluent sketches, and the two young architects showed from the start a creative use of site and context, including a penchant for dealing with ends and corners, often the most difficult parts of a project. They also showed considerable skill in their ability to build and detail their complex works within normal price limits, enhancing the main ideas in the constructive phase rather than letting them be reduced. But their world-wide reputation was above all due to an artistic signature which became a recognizable brand within architecture's star system.

Their recognizable style has been both a blessing and a curse, for it carried them high in the 80s and 90s, while much of the time it distracted attention from the real ingenuity in the work. The photographs which carry it are certainly striking, but the work is in real life often better, appearing less mannered and offering more to the visitor. The shapes seem less outspoken, the changes in scale more appropriate.

Because the early histories of modern architecture opposed the idea of Expressionism to that of Functionalism, and subjectivity to the beloved objectivity (Sachlichkeit), there is a continuing tendency to return to this classification, which over-emphasizes the personal and makes Expressionism seem rather a selfish position. All too often this prejudice is also naively shape-bound, assuming that anything rectangular and answerable to a geometric grid must be "rational" while irregular things are necessarily "irrational". In practice there are many reasons why buildings may need to be irregular, such as sloping and irregular sites and lop-sided programmes of accommodation. Far from being destructive, these irregularities can tie a building to the place and give it specific character. In contrast, the purveyors of supposedly "rigorous" puritanical boxes can be more selfish, obsessed with their own aesthetic concerns. This shows most on the inside, where "minimalism" means exclusion, and a living room must be

bleibt man auch weiterhin gerne bei dieser Klassifizierung, die das persönliche Element übermäßig betont und den Expressionismus als ausgesprochen selbstbezogene Haltung erscheinen läßt. Allzuoft ist dieses Vorurteil auch von naiven Formvorstellungen geprägt; es wird vorausgesetzt, daß alles Rechteckige, alles, was in einem geometrischen Raster aufgeht, „rational" sein müsse, Unregelmäßiges dagegen zwangsläufig „irrational". In der Praxis allerdings gibt es zahlreiche Gründe für die Unregelmäßigkeit eines Gebäudes, etwa ein abschüssiges oder ungleichmäßig begrenztes Grundstück oder ein asymmetrisches Raumkonzept. Solche Unregelmäßigkeiten sind keineswegs destruktiv – sie können ein Gebäude mit dem Standort verklammern und ihm ein besonderes Profil geben. Die Schöpfer vermeintlich „rigoroser" puritanischer Kuben können in ihrer obsessiven Verfolgung der eigenen ästhetischen Interessen weitaus selbstbezogener sein. Sichtbar wird das meist im Gebäudeinneren, wo „Minimalismus" Ausschluß bedeutet und ein Wohnzimmer die asketische Reinheit einer Kapelle aufweisen muß. Es sind paradoxerweise also die Architekten mit reichem Vokabular, die in der Lage sind, auf Gegebenes einzugehen und Vielfalt zu schaffen. Wenn in diese Entwicklung dann auch expressive Elemente einfließen, ist das nicht unbedingt schlecht und vielleicht auch kaum vermeidbar. Jeder Architekt bildet eine persönliche Handschrift aus, auch diejenigen, die alles daran setzen, sich nicht zu wiederholen.

Szyszkowitz+Kowalski sind weithin bekannt für ihre organischen, genauer vielleicht: zoomorphen Formen. Die Natur dient seit jeher als Quelle für künstlerisches Schaffen jeder Art und als ständige Bezugsebene. Uns fasziniert unsere animalische Natur und unsere Körperlichkeit. Wir können nicht umhin, uns in die biologischen Vettern im Reich der Pflanzen und Tiere einzufühlen, ihre Erscheinung zu betrachten, über ihr Wesen nachzusinnen. Es scheint uns daher natürlich, die Ausdehnung von Bauwerken in den Raum als Landschaft zu erleben, in baulichen Formen und Profilen Körper zu sehen, Fassaden als Gesicht des Gebäudes wahrzunehmen. Eine allzu buchstäbliche Ausprägung solcher Analogien allerdings läßt keinen Raum für Deutung. In Szyszkowitz+Kowalskis klug gestalteten Fassaden und Formen sind sie nur als Anspielung und Verweis enthalten, sie werden nahe gelegt, drängen sich nie auf. Sie sind da, ohne das Raumkonzept oder den

as ascetically pure as a chapel. Paradoxically then, it is the architects with rich vocabularies who are able to respond to the given and to develop variety. If in the process they also express themselves, it may be no bad thing, and is perhaps inevitable. Every architect develops some signature vocabulary: even those most concerned not to repeat themselves.

Szyszkowitz+Kowalski's works are widely recognized for their organic or perhaps more accurately zoomorphic imagery. Nature has always been a source for art of all kinds and a constant reference point, for we are fascinated by our animal nature and bodily being. We cannot help empathizing with our biological cousins in the plant and animal kingdoms, looking at their forms and considering their identities. It therefore comes naturally to us to find landscapes in the way buildings unfold, bodies in forms and profiles, faces in façades. But too literal a presentation of these things does not leave room for interpretation. The cleverness of Szyszkowitz+Kowalski's façades and forms is that they are merely hinted at, quietly suggestive, not overstated. They exist without disrupting the spatial programme or the building process, and without making the buildings too expensive. It is fascinating to discover that Kowalski has privately created a whole menagerie of curious creatures. Are they mythical beasts or caricatures?

Bauprozeß zu sprengen und ohne die Gebäude allzu kostspielig zu machen. Man entdeckt fasziniert, daß Kowalski ihre private Menagerie seltsamer Kreaturen geschaffen hat. Sind es mythische Wesen oder Karikaturen? Spiegeln sie Elemente des Bauwerks? Die Verbindung wird leicht übertrieben, leugnen läßt sie sich nicht. Als paralleler kreativer Kosmos reflektieren die Skulpturen zwar dieselbe Sensibilität, aber Andeutungen sind besser als eine vordergründige „Erklärung". Karla Kowalskis Wurzeln liegen in Deutschland, doch spielte das Duo eine Schlüsselrolle in der Bewegung der Neuen Grazer Architektur. Sein Einfluß verdankt sich nicht nur dem Beispiel der eigenen Werke; eine erstaunliche Anzahl von Architekten, die später für diese Strömung wichtig wurden, haben dem Büro zeitweilig als Mitarbeiter angehört, sogar Riegler/Riewe, die führenden Grazer Minimalisten. Daß die Arbeitsgemeinschaft Szyszkowitz+Kowalski auch für junge Kollegen, die sich in andere Richtungen entwickelten, ein so gutes Übungsfeld darstellt, belegt die Breite ihres Ansatzes und die Gründlichkeit ihrer Methoden. Ein Blick auf die Gesamtheit der Projekte zeigt die erstaunliche thematische Vielfalt: Auseinandersetzung mit dem Kontext, Neuinterpretation des Daches, Wiederentdeckung und Neuformulierung des symmetrischen Grundrisses, Material- und Farbkontraste, Fassadenschichtung, die Mitbestimmung des Nutzers und selbst die Behandlung ökologischer Themen. Für eines aber sollten wir vor allem dankbar sein: Sie führen uns vor Augen, daß Architektur auch heute noch einfallsreich, überraschend, persönlich, mitreißend und irritierend sein kann – alles, nur nicht öde.

And do they reflect something in the architectural work? The connection is easily overstated, yet it cannot wholly be denied. Even as an parallel creative realm, the sculptures reflect the same sensibility, but hints are better than a facile 'explanation'.
Although Karla Kowalski's roots are in Germany, Szyszkowitz+Kowalski played a key role in the movement of the New Graz Architecture. Their influence has spread not only through the example set by their own work. An astonishing number of architects who were later significant for the movement passed through their office, even the leading Graz minimalists Riegler/Riewe. That their office has proved such a good training ground for others departing in different directions shows the breadth of their approach and the thoroughness of their methods. Looking across the range of their work there is a wealth of themes: responding to the site, reinterpreting the roof, rediscovering and reinterpreting the symmetrical plan, contrasting materials and colours, layering façades, accepting participation, even dealing with ecological themes. Above all, though, we should thank them for showing us that architecture can still be inventive, surprising, personal, delightful, annoying – anything but dull.

Karin Wilhelm

Das Einfamilienhaus als „Territorialkunst"

The detached house as "territorial art"

Zuweilen gibt es das: Das erste gebaute Haus als Manifestation, das erste tatsächlich realisierte Bauprojekt als Demonstration einer Architekturprogrammatik, mit der sich der unvergleichliche Charakter eines künftigen architektonischen Oeuvres ankündigt. Für die seit 1973 in Österreich ansässige Architektin Karla Kowalski und den in Graz geborenen Architekten Michael Szyszkowitz trifft dieser Sachverhalt zu. Ihr erstes Projekt, das mit der Gründung des gemeinsamen Architekturbüros im steiermärkischen Graz zwischen 1973 und 1974 entstanden ist, darf aus der Sicht auf eine dreißigjährige gemeinsame Büropraxis als ein programmatischer Bau dieser Art gelten. Zum einen deshalb, weil mit dem *Haus über Graz* der Typus des freistehenden Einfamilienhauses am Beginn steht, der wie ein roter Faden die Entwurfsarbeit von Szyszkowitz+Kowalski durchwirkt. Und zum anderen, weil jenes Haus für eine fünfköpfige Familie bereits als Experimentierfeld für eine differenzierte Raumkonzeption angesehen werden darf, in dem sich der Eigen-Sinn eines konzeptionellen Denkens zu erkennen gibt, das nicht nur die zuweilen fragile, dann wieder kraftvoll geäußerte Gestik der architektonischen Formensprache begründet, sondern bereits den Grundsatz der Architektur als hohe Kunst des Behausens bestimmt hat. Daß das Bauen als eine Praxis der Sinngebung aufzufassen sei, die das Leben der Menschen als einen Akt der Gewißheit des In-der-Welt-Seins zu bestärken vermag, teilen die beiden Architekten mit einigen jener Konzeptionäre des modernen Einfamilienhauses, die in bezug auf das Werk des Architektenpaares immer wieder genannt werden, seien dies Hugo Häring, Hans Scharoun oder Frank Lloyd Wright.[1] Und in der Tat ist der Gleichklang vor allem mit den konzeptionellen und theoretischen Aussagen der Altmeister der Moderne nicht zu überhören. Auch der Nachhall jenes berühmt gewordenen und häufig im Zusammenhang mit den Fragen des menschlichen Wohnens genannten Vortrages „Bauen, Wohnen, Denken", den Martin Heidegger anläßlich der legendären „Darmstädter Gespräche" 1951 in der ehemaligen hessischen Residenzstadt gehalten hat, sollte durchaus vernommen werden.

Anläßlich der Ausstellung „Standpunkte '94", die das Forum Stadtpark in seinem im idyllischen Grünraum des Grazer Stadtparkes gelegenen Domizil 1994 präsentierte, formulierten Szyszkowitz+Kowalski ihr Architekturprogramm bereits aus der Rückschau auf ein Werk, das damals neben größeren und kleineren Privathäusern einige Siedlungs-

It does happen sometimes: the very first building, the first project actually realized, unveils an architectural repertoire announcing the incomparable character of the subsequent architectural oeuvre. This is the case for Karla Kowalski, an architect resident in Austria since 1973, and the Graz-born architect Michael Szyszkowitz. They built their first project at the same time as they founded their joint practice in the Styrian town of Graz between 1973 and 1974. It is a piece of work that announces a vision in the manner described above, a fitting start for their thirty years of work together. This is partly because the *House above Graz* establishes from the outset that the detached family home is a building type that will run through their work as the central thread. And partly because that house for a family of five can already be identified as a test-bed for handling space in a sophisticated way. It demonstrates the kind of obstinate conceptual thinking that inaugurates the gestures of their architectural language, sometimes fragile, sometimes powerfully expressed. It also defines from the beginning the high art of providing accommodation – a "housing" – as the fundamental basis of their architecture. Szyszkowitz+Kowalski feel that building should make human lives mean something, should make people more certain of their actual existence in the world. They share this idea with some of their predecessors who conceived the modern house for a single family, and who are constantly mentioned in relation to their own work: Hugo Häring, Hans Scharoun or Frank Lloyd Wright.[1] And in fact it is impossible not to sense their harmony with the conceptual and theoretical old masters of Modernism in particular. We should also catch an echo of Martin Heidegger's now famous lecture "Bauen, Wohnen, Denken" (Building, Dwelling, Thinking) that is mentioned so often in the context of human habitation. Heidegger delivered it in 1951 on the occasion of the legendary "Darmstädter Gespräche" in the former Hessian residence city.

The Forum Stadtpark presented the "Standpunkte '94" exhibition in its home in the idyllic green space of the municipal park in Graz in 1994. Here Szyszkowitz+Kowalski were able to formulate their architectural vision looking back to a body of work including, at that time, large and small private houses, some housing estate units of various sizes, and also large conference buildings, church centres and university and school

> 1
Haus über Graz, Graz 1972–1974, Luftaufnahme   House above Graz, Graz 1972–1974, aerial photograph

[1] *Diese Bezüge sind mehrfach hergestellt worden. Siehe dazu: Peter Blundell Jones, Dialogues in Time. New Graz Architecture, Haus der Architektur (Hg.), Graz 1998, S. 73. Eine umfassende Darstellung der Architektur von Szyszkowitz+Kowalski hat erstmals Andrea Gleininger vorgelegt. Andrea Gleininger, Szyszkowitz+Kowalski 1973–1993, Tübingen, Berlin 1994.* These connections have been made many times over. Cf.: Peter Blundell Jones, Dialogues in Time. New Graz Architecture, Haus der Architektur (ed.), Graz 1998, p. 73. Andrea Gleininger was the first author to produce a full account of Szyszkowitz+Kowalski's architecture. Andrea Gleininger, Szyszkowitz+Kowalski 1973–1993, Tübingen, Berlin 1994.
[2] *Karla Kowalski/Michael Szyszkowitz in: Standpunkte '94, Forum Stadtpark Architektur (Hg.), Graz 1994.* Karla Kowalski/ Michael Szyszkowitz in: Forum Stadtpark Architektur (ed.), Standpunkte '94, Graz 1994.
[3] *Der Begriff ist einem Vortrag von Karla Kowalski entnommen.* This concept is taken from a lecture by Karla Kowalski.
[4] *Martin Heidegger, Bauen, Wohnen, Denken, in: Mensch und Raum. Das Darmstädter Gespräch 1951, Ulrich Conrads/Peter Neitzke (Hg.), Braunschweig 1991, S. 90.* Martin Heidegger, Bauen, Wohnen, Denken, in: Ulrich Conrads/Peter Neitzke (ed.), Mensch und Raum. Das Darmstädter Gespräch 1951, Braunschweig 1991, p. 90.

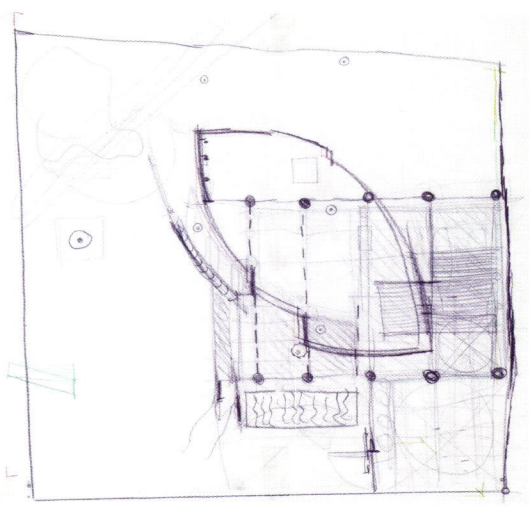

>2
Haus am Ruckerlberg, Graz 1998–2002, Entwurfsskizze des linsenförmigen Grundrisses House on Ruckerlberg, Graz 1998–2002, design sketch for the lenticular plan

einheiten von unterschiedlicher Größe sowie großzügige Tagungsgebäude, Kirchenzentren, Universitäts- und Schulbauten umfaßte: „… (es) mehrt sich aber das tiefe Bewußtsein, daß es nicht um Verpackung, sondern um Identität mit dem Leben schlechthin geht, und daß die Sehnsucht nach dem Paradies in dem Phänomen Architektur eingeschlossen werden kann und dort dann sinnbildhaft fortzuwirken vermag … man erkennt zunehmend, daß diese eingewebte Zuneigung zu einem Stück erahnten Lebens und zu dem kaum zu erklärenden Begriff Schönheit auf den Benutzer und Betrachter aus dem Gebauten heraus zu wirken versteht, und daß der so umschriebene geistige Inhalt der Architektur das eigentliche lohnenswerte Ziel aller Anstrengungen ist."[2] Wenn Karla Kowalski daher heute die Architektur als „Territorialkunst"[3] beschreibt, der die „Zuneigung zu einem Stück Leben" inhärent sei, dann lebt in diesem Architekturverständnis, wenn auch unausgesprochen, jener umfassende Begriff des Bauens fort, den Martin Heidegger während der Darmstädter Tagung, mit dem Thema „Mensch und Raum", als Antwort auf die einleitende Fragestellung: „Inwiefern … das Bauen in das Wohnen?" gehöre, gegeben hat. Seine Differenzierung, daß jedes Bauen zugleich ein *aedificare* (errichten) und *colere* (pflegen) sei, mithin eine Aussage enthalte über die „… Art wie du bist und ich bin, die Weise, nach der wir Menschen auf der Erde *sind*", verlieh dem Verständnis des Bauens existentielle Bedeutung. Heideggers Auffassung: „Mensch sein heißt: als Sterblicher auf der Erde sein, heißt: wohnen"[4], darf durchaus als ideeller Bezugs-

buildings: "… we are increasingly profoundly aware that the issue is not packaging, but identifying with life. Our longing for paradise can be built into in the phenomenon of architecture, and can then continue to make its effect symbolically … People increasingly recognize that this built-in inclination towards a piece of imagined life and towards the scarcely explicable concept of beauty can affect the user and the viewer as something coming from within the built structure, and that the spiritual content of architecture, when defined in this way, is the actual worthwhile aim of all our efforts."[2] Karla Kowalski now describes architecture as "territorial art"[3] with an "inclination towards a piece of life within it". Thriving within this view of architecture – though unspoken – is the comprehensive concept of architecture that Martin Heidegger produced at the Darmstadt conference under the heading of "Mankind and Space", as a response to the introductory question: "To what extent … [can] building [be said to be part of] dwelling?". He made a distinction that introduced an existential level into the understanding of building: he said that every act of building involves both *aedificare* (constructing) and *colere* (cultivating), and therefore contains a statement about the "… way you are and I am, the way in which we human beings *are* on earth." Heidegger's view: "Being human means: being on earth as a mortal, means: dwelling",[4] is entirely suitable as a conceptual framework for Szyszkowitz+Kowalski's architectural vision.

rahmen für das Architekturprogramm der Grazer Architekten genannt werden.

Keine Bauaufgabe verhandelt diese Idee naturgemäß zwingender als der Wohnbau und nirgendwo darf das Gelingen eines auf Verantwortlichkeit ausgerichteten Wohnens auf einen höheren Respekt hoffen als im Einfamilienhausbau – eben deshalb erfreut sich dieser Gebäudetypus einer hohen sozialen Akzeptanz und gilt als *die* schichtenübergreifende, auf die Kleinfamilie hin orientierte Wohnform, die sich, trotz der Vereinzelung spätmoderner Lebensstile, einer ungebrochen hohen Wertschätzung erfreut. Das Einfamilienhaus erscheint mithin bis heute als jene Form der Behausung, in der das Zusammenspiel von Individualisierungswünschen und Anpassungszwängen, die Vermittlung zwischen dem Ich und dem Du auf sehr individuelle Weise gelingen soll.

Wie jene Ontologie des Wohnens in den Häusern von Szyszkowitz+Kowalski architektonisch interpretiert wird, ist bei aller ideellen Nähe zu den genannten Positionen der organi-

Of course housing is the natural field for developing these ideas compellingly. Within that field it is the family house that is most likely to produce a sense of living devoted to responsibility and careful cultivation. This is why this type of building is so acceptable socially, and is considered to be *the* most classless dwelling for the nuclear family, and why it is still valued as such despite the fragmentation of late-modern life-styles. So the family house still seems to be the accommodation form most likely to reconcile desires for individuality and the necessity to adapt, in other words to mediate between "I" and "you" in a very individual way.

Despite being theoretically close to the named positions taken up by organic architecture, there is still something quite particular about how the ontology of dwelling is interpreted in Szyszkowitz+Kowalski's houses. Ultimately neither the architectural form nor the formal language of the architecture is predetermined by the above intellectual framework; the language of architecture can interpret the idea of cultivating living in an enormous number of ways. This is precisely what happens in Szyszkowitz+Kowalski's work. They achieve this by analysing the objective conditions and due to factors that are closely linked with the personality of the two architects. Above all, it is important to acknowledge the extraordinary drawing and sculptural skills that shape the expressive power of their buildings and details, along with the artistic preferences and experience-related criteria that apply in each case (figs. 5, 12, 13). This artistic ambition is an essential component of the design decisions reached when analysing objectifiable factors and functional requirements. The process begins with a search for the client's own ideas about home life. This addresses the space that is definitely needed, but above all examines the deeper matter of individual wishes.

> 3
Haus in Moosburg, Moosburg bei Klagenfurt 1995–1996, Entwurfsskizze der Gebäudesilhouette House in Moosburg, Moosburg near Klagenfurt 1995–1996, design sketch of the building silhouette

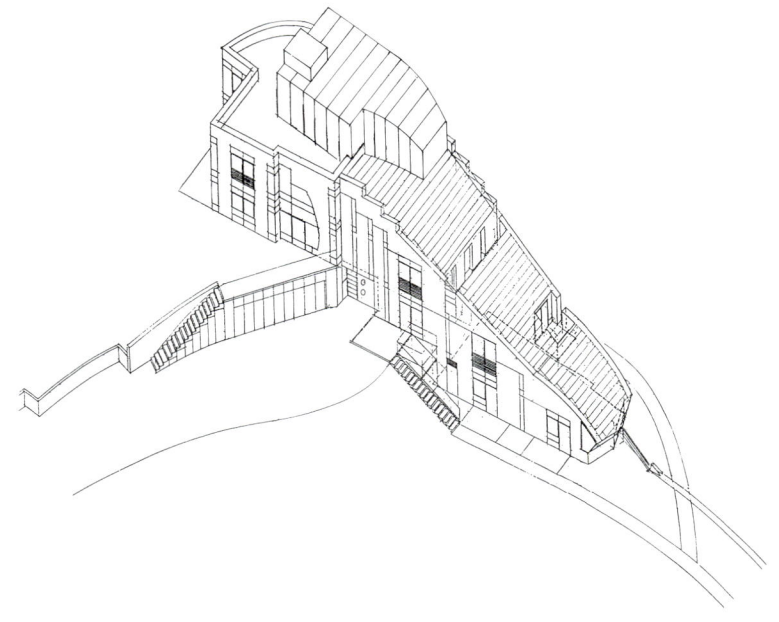

> 4
Haus am Plattenweg, Graz 1994–1996, Axonometrie
House on Plattenweg, Graz 1994–1996, axonometric view

schen Architektur von dezidierter Eigentümlichkeit. Schließlich ist die architektonische Gestaltung grundsätzlich nicht und die Formensprache dieser Architektur schon gar nicht durch den angesprochenen gedanklichen Rahmen präformiert und festgelegt; die Sprache der Architektur kann die Idee des pflegenden Wohnens vielmehr ungemein vielgestaltig interpretieren und eben dies geschieht im Werk von Szyszkowitz+Kowalski auf der Basis einer Analytik von objektiven Bedingungen und auf der Grundlage von Faktoren, die eng mit der Persönlichkeit dieser beiden Architekten verbunden sind. Es gilt vor allem die außergewöhnlichen zeichnerischen und skulpturalen Begabungen zu beachten, die, im Verbund mit den jeweiligen künstlerischen Vorlieben und erfahrungsgebundenen Maßstäben, die Ausdruckskraft ihrer Bauten und Details prägen (Abb. 5, 12, 13). Diese künstlerische Ambition ist ein wesentlicher Bestandteil der Entwurfsentscheidungen, die in der Auseinandersetzung mit objektivierbaren Faktoren und sachlichen Voraussetzungen getroffen werden. Das entwurfsleitende Motiv des Beginnens besteht in der Suche nach den Wohnvorstellungen der Bauherren, die, neben dem definierten Raumbedarf, vor allem die Tiefenschichten der individuellen Wünsche zu entschlüsseln bestrebt ist. So entsteht im Verbund mit einer Analytik der unmittelbaren Umgebung, sodann in der Bestandsaufnahme der atmosphärischen Dichte der vorgefundenen Topographie und einer Art Psychogramm der jeweiligen Auftraggeber allmählich jenes Entscheidungspotential, das dem Haus seinen Platz im Gelände zuweist und die Besonderheit der Grundrißformation sowie die Entscheidung für die jeweiligen Konstruktionen der Gebäudekörper bedingt. Auf der Grundlage des Zusammenwirkens jener Faktoren entfaltet sich schließlich die formale Variabilität der Oberfläche in Fassadenbildern, die diese Architektur der territorialen Verortung mit spielerisch anmutenden, ornamentalen Zeichen anreichert, die die archetypische Symbolik des Raum-Ergreifens zwischen Himmel und Erde nicht allein den Gebäudekörpern überträgt, sondern mit der formalen Ausdeutung der Konstruktionen und Materialien verbindet.

Dieses Spannungsfeld wurde mit dem ersten Wohnhaus in Graz (Abb. 1) beziehungsreich eröffnet, und seither wirkt es in jede Bauaufgabe hinein, die das Büro später zu bearbeiten hat; ob dies, wie häufig im Siedlungsbau, auf „freiem Felde"

They start by analysing the immediate vicinity, and also look at the atmospheric density of the site topography and draw up a kind of psychogram of the particular client. Thus a certain decision-making potential starts to emerge according to which the building is placed on the site, the particular ground plan is drawn, and decisions are taken about the structure of the building volumes. These factors ultimately work together to indicate formal variations within the façade image with seemingly playful ornamental signs, variations that enrich this architecture of territorial location. Thus the archetypal symbolism of seizing space between heaven and earth is transferred to the various parts of the building, and also tied into the formal interpretation of the structures and materials.

This field of tension was set up highly allusively by the first house in Graz (fig.1), and since then it has affected every commission that the practice has worked on. These have been on "green-field sites", as frequently happen in housing estates, or were part of an existing development, where projects had to be planned as extensions to high calibre historic building stock (fig. 6), or in an town planning context. The architects have always made their desire to produce individual and unmistakable architecture – which can achieve paradigm

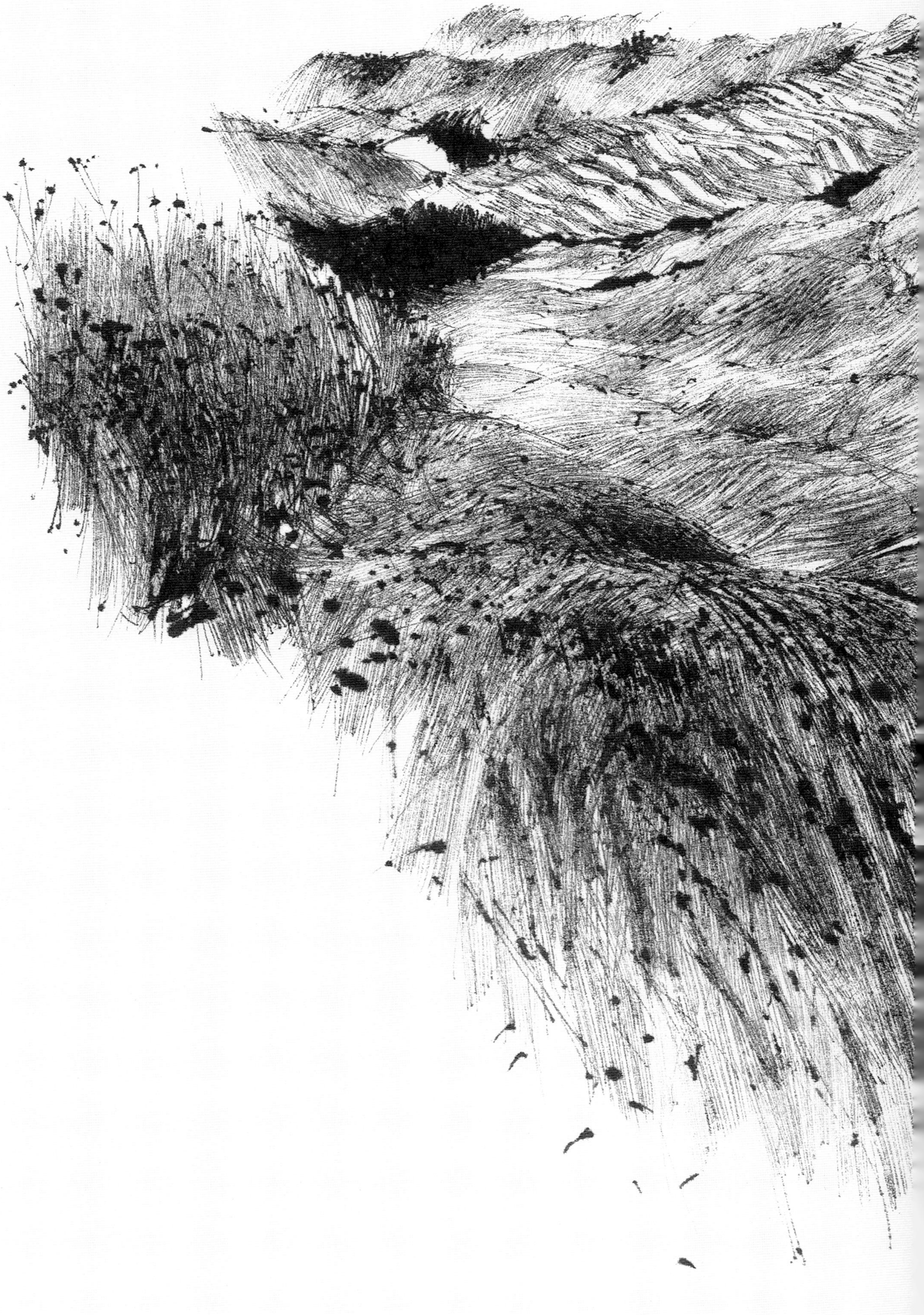

THE DETACHED HOUSE AS "TERRITORIAL ART" · DAS EINFAMILIENHAUS ALS "TERRITORIALKUNST"

16 | 17

> 5
Karla Kowalski, Federzeichnung Karla Kowalski, pen drawing

> 6
Schloß Großlobming, Großlobming (Steiermark), Hauswirtschaftsschule mit Internat 1979–1981,
Volksschule 1996–1997, Luftbild der Gesamtanlage Großlobming castle, Großlobming (Styria),
home economics school with boarding-house 1979–1981, primary school 1996–1997, aerial photograph
of the whole complex

[5] Siehe dazu: Die Kunst zu Hause zu sein, Hans Paul Bardt u.a., München 1962
Cf.: Hans Paul Bardt et al., Die Kunst zu Hause zu sein, Munich 1962.

> 7
Haus in Moosburg, Moosburg bei Klagenfurt 1995–1996, Ansicht von Süden   House in Moosburg, Moosburg near Klagenfurt 1995–1996, view from the south

geschieht oder im Kontext einer vorhandenen Bebauung wie bei jenen Projekten, die als Anbauten eines architektonisch außerordentlich qualitätvollen, historischen Bestandes zu planen sind (Abb. 6) oder im Kontext der Stadt entstehen. Stets haben die Architekten den Wunsch nach Individualität und Unverwechselbarkeit der Architektur, wie er nun einmal im Einfamilienhausbau paradigmatisch erscheinen darf, zum Signum ihrer zugleich auf strukturelle Systematik bedachten Formfindung gemacht. Daß sich allerdings der „Wunsch zu Hause zu sein"[5] mit dem Bedürfnis nach ausdrucksstarken Raumzeichen für Individuationen und Identifikationen nirgendwo kunstvoller entäußern kann als im frei in die Landschaft gesetzten Privathausbau, kommt den künstlerischen Intentionen dieser Entwurfshaltung ungemein entgegen.

Zugleich aber ist den Architekten die Folie der damit verbundenen Problemlagen bewußt, denn daß diese Wohnform dem Landschaftsverbrauch oder, wie sie es gerne nennen, der „Verklecksung" Vorschub leistet, stellt eine ökologische Herausforderung dar, die ebenso bedacht werden will wie die Tatsache, daß das private Wohnhaus immer als ein Akt der Vermittlung zwischen Privatheit und Öffentlichkeit aufgefaßt werden muß. In dieser medialen Wirkung liegt auch die Verantwortlichkeit für eine akzentuierte Architektur begründet, die in ihrer Individuationsgestik die Umweltgebundenheit nicht verlieren soll. Im Spektrum dieser Anforderungen erhält das Einfamilienhaus seine Komplexität, die es im weiten Aufgabenfeld der Architektur so ungemein attraktiv macht.

quality in the family house – a symbolic part of the way they determine forms, which also entails structural systematics. The artistic aims of this design approach are greatly furthered by the fact that the "desire to be at home"[5] can never be reconciled more artfully with the need to deliver expressive signs for individuation and identification than by constructing a private house, freely placed in the landscape. But the architects are also aware of the associated problems: this form of housing uses up the countryside or causes more "blots on the landscape", as they like to call it. This represents an architectural challenge that has to be addressed, along with the fact that a private house has always to be seen as an act of mediation between privacy and public space. This mediation also requires them to take responsibility for a kind of accentuated architecture that is determined not to let its individual gestures break its ties with the environment. It is this spectrum of demands that makes the family house so attractively complex within the broad field of architectural challenges.

Raumsprachen des Wohnens

Das *Haus über Graz* (Abb. S. 104–109) ist ein Auftrag gewesen, der, wie so häufig in der Architekturgeschichte, durch private Kontakte an das junge Architektenteam herangetragen wurde. Der Bauplatz im Weichbild von Graz liegt im östlichen Teil der Stadt, eingebunden in eine weitläufige, liebliche Hügellandschaft, die mit ihren alten Villenbauten aus der Spätphase des Historismus bereits in den siebziger Jahren des 20. Jahrhunderts zu den begehrtesten Wohngebieten zählte. Was einst der landwirtschaftlichen Nutzung diente, war inzwischen zu einer Parklandschaft mutiert, in der das Grundstück, von einem wertvollen alten Baumbestand begrenzt, dem Landschaftsraum seine eigenen Konturen aufprägt. Leicht abfallend eröffnet es den Blick auf die im Tal liegende Altstadt mit dem dominanten Schloßberg und führt die Sicht bei gutem Wetter bis weit in das nahe Slowenien mit der Bergkette des Pachern hinüber. Diesem topographischen Gefälle nachspürend liegt das Haus ein wenig zurückgesetzt am höchsten Punkt des Geländes, dann fällt es senkrecht zum Hang ab, indem der Höhenlinienverlauf mitvollzogen wird. Gleichsam als Widerhall der natürlichen Geländemodulation reagiert die Grundriß- und Geschoßentwicklung, indem ein kompakter, zweigeschossiger Baukörper mit vorgelagerten Garagen den undurchdringlichen Auftakt bildet, um zur Gartenseite hin den Wohnbereich als eingeschossigen Annex in das Gelände vorzuschieben und das Haus in ein dreigeschossiges Raumkontinuum zu überführen. Das in den Hang eingefügte Untergeschoß erweitert die Orientierung des Lebensraumes in den Garten hinein und nimmt hangseitig die notwendigen Kellerräume auf, so daß das Haus eine dynamische Linearität erhält, die in den vier parallel verlaufenden, pergolagleichen Holzbindern in den Außenraum hinein verlängert wird. Gleich einem Wasserlauf scheinen die derart ineinandergefügten Raumkörper in die Ebene zu fließen und vermitteln in ihrem Strukturgerüst und der stereometrischen Klarheit doch zugleich die notwendige Stabilität.

Die konzeptionelle Entscheidung, das Haus auf die höchste Stelle des Bauplatzes unweit des öffentlichen Straßenraumes zu setzen und in seiner Binnenerschließung auf den Landschaftsraum mit der von Obstbäumen bestandenen Wiese und den Park hin auszurichten, ist mit dem Verzicht auf Inszenierungsgesten der öffentlichen Repräsentation eng verbunden. Das Haus verfügt über keine auf den Außenraum bezogene Dominanz der Eingangs- und Empfangssituation,

Spatial language in the home

The *House above Graz* (figs. p. 104–109) was a commission that came to the young team of architects through private contacts, as so frequently happens in architectural history. The site is on the outskirts of Graz, in the eastern part of the city, set in a sweep of pleasingly hilly countryside. Its old, late historicist villas made it one of the most desirable residential areas even in the 1970s. Here, former agricultural land had changed into parkland. The site is surrounded by fine old trees and gently imposes its own outlines on the surrounding landscape. The plot slopes slightly to open up a view of the old town in the valley with its dominant castle hill. In good weather the eye is taken far into nearby Slovenia and the Pachern mountain range. Following this topographical incline, the house is set slightly back at the topmost point of the site; the building then drops vertically to the slope, following the contour line. The development of the floors and ground plan is almost an echo of the natural modulation of the land. A compact, two-storey volume with garages in front of it makes an impenetrable start. Then, on the garden side it thrusts the living area into the terrain as a single-storey annexe, shifting the house as a whole into a three-storey spatial continuum. The basement storey, which is built into the slope, extends the orientation of the living space into the garden and accommodates the necessary cellars on the slope side. This gives the house a dynamic linear quality that is extended into the exterior space by the four parallel, pergola-like timber trusses. The volumes fitted together in this way seem to flow into the plane like a watercourse, and yet their structural framework and stereometric lucidity convey the necessary stability at the same time.

The decision to place the house on the highest point of the site not far from the open street and to face the interior access areas towards the landscape of grassy orchards and parkland is closely linked with an abstention from public manifestations of prestige. The entrance and reception areas make no dominant impact on the outside world; instead they are built into the side façade, so that the house at first sight seems reticent and not particularly eloquent. How the family's living space is actually organized, how the spaces are accessed and fit together remains concealed from the public. The house insists that you walk round it and into it to see what cannot be seen from the outside and to find out how the spatial compartments link up so that the family's communal areas can flow into each other. Here the *House above Graz* is deliberately adopting a distinctive feature of old Japanese houses that had fascinated the modern architects of the early 20th century. It is a quality of being closed to visitors that Karin

[6] Karin Kirsch, Die neue Wohnung und das alte Japan. Architekten planen für sich selbst, Stuttgart 1996, S. 64. *Karin Kirsch, Die neue Wohnung und das alte Japan. Architekten planen für sich selbst, Stuttgart 1996, p. 64.*

> 8
Haus über Graz, Graz 1972–1974, Ansichten *House above Graz, Graz 1972–1974, views*

die ist vielmehr zurückhaltend in die Seitenfront integriert, so daß das Haus dem Besucher zunächst verschlossen und wenig beredt erscheint. Wie der Lebensraum der Familie tatsächlich organisiert ist, wie die Raumerschließung und die Raumfolgen ineinandergreifen, bleibt den Blicken der Öffentlichkeit verschlossen. Das Haus will vielmehr umschritten sein, es will betreten werden, damit das Unsichtbare sichtbar wird und das Ineinandergreifen der Raumkompartimente als kalkuliertes Ineinanderfließen der familiären Kommunikationsbereiche erfahren werden kann. Damit greift das *Haus über Graz* intentional eine Eigenheit des alten japanischen Hauses auf, das bereits die modernen Architekten im frühen 20. Jahrhundert faszinierte. Es ist jene Verschlossenheit gegenüber den Besuchern, die Karin Kirsch mit dem Hinweis auf den amerikanischen Völkerkundler E. S. Morse, der sich bereits im 19. Jahrhundert dem Kulturraum Japans zugewandt hatte, beschrieben hat, daß nämlich „ … die Straßenseite des japanischen Hauses belanglos anmutete und die Qualität der Wohnung sich erst im inneren Teil offenbarte, wo es vom Garten aus betrachtet ‚kunstvoll und malerisch' wirkte."[6] Dieses Prinzip der Innenorientierung, die Ausrichtung auf den Binnenbereich des Gartens hat die

Kirsch described with reference to the American ethnologist E. S. Morse, who had addressed Japanese culture in the 19th century: "… the street side of the Japanese house seemed to be of no importance, and the quality of the dwelling was revealed only in the interior, which seen from the garden looked 'artistic and picturesque'".[6] Modern private house architecture has enjoyed paraphrasing this internal orientation principle, the notion of facing the inner garden area, ever since Japanese architecture was discovered. One of the most impressive examples is still the Tugendhat House, also on a sloping site, designed by Mies van der Rohe in Brno, Czechia, in 1928/30. The lower main floor of the house is "hermeti-

Architektur des modernen Privathauses seit der Entdeckung der Architektur Japans gerne paraphrasiert. Eines der beeindruckendsten Beispiele ist nach wie vor das Haus der Familie Tugendhat, das Ludwig Mies van der Rohe 1928/1930 im tschechischen Brno gleichfalls an einem Hanggrundstück geplant hat. Das untere Hauptgeschoß des Hauses erscheint in seiner „hermetischen Verschlossenheit"[7] zur Straße hin in der Tat belanglos, denn der Baukörper läßt in seiner Undurchdringlichkeit Rückschlüsse auf die Binnenstruktur des Hauses nicht zu, er hält mit Bedacht die Belange des Privaten verschlossen. Wenngleich das *Haus über Graz* ganz anders als die Mies van der Rohe-Villa in Brno nicht unmittelbar an der Straße liegt, sondern in den Landschaftsraum zurückgesetzt ist, und der Baumbestand den Architekturpart eines natürlichen Vestibüls übernimmt, so bleibt auch diese Fassade dem Besucher gegenüber verschwiegen. Zudem mag der Hinweis auf das Tugendhathaus im Zusammenhang mit der Architektur von Karla Kowalski und Michael Szyszkowitz auf den ersten Blick gewagt erscheinen, denn die ausdrucksstarke Formensprache des Grazer Hauses ist gegenüber der formalen Strenge der Tugendhat Villa wirklich unvergleichlich. Doch dem zweiten, dem Grundsätzlichen geltenden Blick offenbart sich das gemeinsame Prinzip des nach Innen gerichteten, zum Garten orientierten Lebensraumes, dem ein repräsentativer Vermittlungsgestus gegenüber dem öffentlichen Raum untersagt wird. Viele Häuser der Moderne haben diese Bescheidenheit thematisiert, weil sie jenem neuen bürgerlichen Selbstbewußtsein der Jahre nach dem Ersten Weltkrieg entsprach, das sich zumindest in der Außendarstellung architektonische Verweise auf eine soziale Distinktion zunehmend verbat.

Dem Erbe der Moderne gegenüber, die, wie Christian Norberg-Schulz zu Recht betont hat, mehr war als reiner Funktionalismus[8], erweist das *Haus über Graz* in vielerlei Bezügen seine, wenn auch eigenwillige Reverenz, die jedoch in der als „vital" und „anarchistisch"[9] apostrophierten Formensprache

cally sealed",[7] and does seem utterly unimportant when viewed from the street. This part of the building is so impenetrable that it reveals nothing at all about the internal structure of the house; it keeps private interests carefully hidden away. Although the *House above Graz*, unlike the Mies van der Rohe villa in Brno, is not right on the road, but set back a little from it into the landscape, the existing trees taking on the role of a natural vestibule, its façade is reticent to visitors as well. Mentioning the Tugendhat House in the context of Karla Kowalski and Michael Szyszkowitz's architecture may seem risky at first glance: the expressive formal language of the *House above Graz* has absolutely nothing in common with the formal austerity of the Tugendhat villa. But a second, more fundamental look reveals the shared principle of an inward-looking living space facing the garden, disallowing any gestures conveying prestige to the public. Many Modern houses embraced this kind of modesty. It was appropriate to the new self-awareness of the middle classes after the First World War. This increasingly ruled out architectural indications of social distinction, at least as far as the exterior was concerned.

Christian Norberg-Schulz has correctly pointed out that the legacy of Modernism was more than mere functionalism.[8] The *House above Graz* acknowledges that legacy in many ways, some of them perhaps even wilfully, and not immediately apparent in the formal language of Szyszkowitz+Kowalski's architecture, which has been described as "vital" and "anarchic".[9] But on closer examination the signs are clearly, if secretly, in place. For example, the structure of the interlinking sections of the building is based on a structural principle that draws on experience with the steel skeleton structures of Modernist building, though in the case of the *House above Graz* the framework architecture of reinforced concrete construction, as fashionable then in Britain and in Dutch Structuralism, is taken back, one might say, to timber construction. The structural basis of the *House above Graz* is a system of self-supporting prefabricated wooden sections placed on concrete floors. This material was chosen because the clients wanted to bring a little souvenir of the United States back to Austria after several years in America. They wanted to live in a wooden house in their old home country, just as they had in the USA. The architects accommodated this

[7] Wolf Tegethoff, Im Brennpunkt der Moderne: Mies van der Rohe und das Haus Tugendhat in Brünn, München 1998, S. 31. *Wolf Tegethoff, Im Brennpunkt der Moderne: Mies van der Rohe und das Haus Tugendhat in Brünn, Munich 1998, p. 31.*
[8] Siehe dazu: Christian Norberg-Schulz, Architecture: Presence, Language, Place, Milano 2000, S. 106. *Cf.: Christian Norberg-Schulz, Architecture: Presence, Language Place, Milan 2000, p. 106.*
[9] Frank Werner, „Arche-Tektonik pur" – Szyszkowitz/Kowalski 5 Bauten – 5 Projekte 1985–1990, in: Architektur- und Bauforum Nr. 139, 1990, S. 19. *Frank Werner, "Arche-Tektonik pur" – Szyszkowitz/Kowalski 5 Bauten – 5 Projekte 1985–1990, in: Architektur- und Bauforum no. 139, 1990, p. 19.*

> 9
Haus über Graz, Graz 1972–1974, Entwurfsskizzen zur Grundidee des Hauses „Hügel+Bäume+Haus" *House above Graz, Graz 1972–1974, design sketches for the basic idea behind the house "hill+trees+house"*

> 10
Haus über Graz, Graz 1972–1974, Ansicht von Südwesten
House above Graz, Graz 1972–1974, view from the south-west

> 11
Haus über Graz, Blick von der Talseite, Südwesten House above Graz, view from the valley side, south-west

der Architektur von Szyszkowitz+Kowalski nicht unmittelbar zu sehen ist. Bei genauerer Betrachtung aber kommt man jener Erbschaft durchaus auf die Spur, denn sie wirkt im Geheimen. So basiert die Konstruktion der ineinander verschränkten Gebäudekörper auf einem Strukturprinzip, das auf den Erfahrungen mit den Stahlskelettkonstruktionen des modernen Bauens beruht, wenngleich im *Haus über Graz* die zu Beginn der siebziger Jahre weiterentwickelte Framework-Architektur des Stahlbetonbaus, wie er in England und im holländischen Strukturalismus damals en vogue war, in den Holzbau, man möchte sagen, rückgeführt wird. Die konstruktive Struktur des Grazer Hauses beruht auf einem System aus selbsttragenden Holzfertigteilen, die auf Betondecken aufgesetzt wurden. Die Wahl dieses Materials resultierte aus dem Wunsch der Bauherren, nach einem mehrjährigen Amerikaaufenthalt ein Stückchen Erinnerung an die Vereinigten Staaten von Amerika nach Österreich zu transferieren. Wie in den USA, so wünschten sie auch in der alten Heimat ein Holzhaus als Domizil.

Diesem Wunsch sind die Architekten nachgekommen, wenngleich in einer eigenwilligen Ausdeutung jenes Begehrens. Indem sie nämlich die Holzpaneele nur in einigen Wandfeldern sichtbar ließen, um sie in weiten Bereichen und in der Bedachung mit einer zweiten, farbigen Hülle aus rosa-violet-

request, though they treated in their own way. They left the wooden panels visible only in some fields of the walls, covering up all the others and the roof with a second, coloured envelope of pinky-purple, plastic-coated steel sheets. In this way they provided a new interpretation of the relationship between structure and filling, thus creating a bridge between tradition and the present, regional and international building. What can be seen is a timber-frame structure that does not deny the prefabrication, and yet still allows the craft tectonics of timber construction to make its presence felt; then individual wall compartments being clad in an industrial material that hides the nature of the natural wood, while at the same time ostentatiously stressing its presence. This is an apparent paradox that underlines the character of this architecture and its calculatedly confusing tactics. The double outer skin seems all the more lively because of the contrasting materials. The interplay of colour between the warm wood and the colder-seeming light pur-

> 12, 13
Karla Kowalski, Federzeichnungen Karla Kowalski, pen drawings

> 14
Aufbahrungshalle in Schwarzach/Pongau, Salzburg 1977–1978, Weg aus dem Ort Mortuary in Schwarzach/Pongau, Salzburg 1977–1978, path out of the town

ten, kunststoffbeschichteten Stahlblechtafeln zu verkleiden, deuteten sie das Verhältnis von Struktur und Füllung neu und schlugen derart eine Brücke zwischen Tradition und Gegenwart, regionalem und internationalem Bauen. Man sieht ein Fachwerk, das den Charakter der Präfabrikation nicht verleugnet und doch die Attribute der handwerklichen Tektonik des Holzbaues noch mitschwingen läßt; man erkennt eine weitere Umhüllung einzelner Wandkompartimente mit einem industriell gefertigten Material, das den Charakter des aus der Natur gewonnenen Baumaterials kaschiert und es doch eben dadurch zugleich demonstrativ betont, eine scheinbare Paradoxie, die den Charakter dieser Architektur und deren kalkuliertes Verwirrspiel unterstreicht. So erscheint die zweischalige Aussenhaut im Materialkontrast umso belebter, und im Farbenspiel zwischen dem warmen Holz und dem kälter wirkenden, hellen Violett der Stahlbleche verwandelt sich die Haut des Baukörpers in eine atmosphärisch schimmernde Oberfläche, die ihre Farbigkeit wie von Zauberhand mit den Jahreszeiten und dem Lichteinfall wie ein Chamäleon zu verändern scheint.

In diesem Konstruktionsprinzip und der gewählten Wandschichtung, deren Material jeglichen Anspruch auf Exklu-

ple of the steel sheets transforms the skin of the building into an atmospherically shimmering surface that seems to change colour with the seasons and the incident light like a chameleon as though a magic hand were at work.

This construction principle, and the layered wall cladding, using materials that avoid any sort of claim to exclusivity, can definitely be identified as a variant on the "dressing principle" that Gottfried Semper, who lived in Vienna for a short time, in the 19th century considered to be part of the *initium topos* of architecture. Semper's idea also helped to create a particular style and played an incomparably luxurious role in Otto Wagner's and Joseph Hoffmann's Austrian Modernism around 1900. Although this effect is studiously avoided in the *House above Graz*, it still suggests the possibility of taking another look at the functionalist renunciation of ornament and a move towards a symbolic interpretation of construction as practised by Otto Wagner, who provided a theoretical basis for this in his much-read book "Moderne Architektur".[10] This

[10] Otto Wagner, Moderne Architektur, Wien 1896. Das Buch wurde innerhalb weniger Jahre mehrfach aufgelegt. *Otto Wagner, Moderne Architektur, Vienna 1896. The book ran through several editions within a short period.*

> 15
Rotes Haus, Graz 1982–1984, Ansicht von Osten Red House, Graz 1982–1984, view from the east

sivität vermeidet, darf man durchaus eine Variante jenes „Bekleidungsprinzips" erkennen, das der kurzzeitig in Wien ansässige Gottfried Semper im 19. Jahrhundert zum *initium topos* der Architektur zählte und das in der österreichischen Moderne um 1900, im Werk von Otto Wagner oder Joseph Hoffmann einst eine stilbildende, unvergleichlich luxurierende Rolle gespielt hat. Obwohl diese Wirkung im *Haus über Graz* mit Bedacht vermieden worden ist, deutete sich darin doch die Möglichkeit einer Revision des funktionalistischen Ornamentverzichtes an und die Hinwendung zu einer symbolischen Ausdeutung der Konstruktion, wie sie Otto Wagner praktiziert und in seinem vielgelesenen Buch über die „Moderne Architektur"[10] theoretisch begründet hatte. Im *Haus über Graz* findet sich dieser Ansatz noch im Geburtsstadium, doch deuten die Holzträger der beiden Pergolen in den kräftigen Betonverankerungen bereits an, daß dieses Anliegen der Wiener Moderne in den kommenden Bauaufgaben immer wieder aufgegriffen werden sollte. Schon in der *Aufbahrungshalle in Schwarzach* (Abb. 14) bei Salzburg kam dieser Ansatz 1977 zum Tragen, um im *Roten Haus* (Abb. 15, Abb. S. 120–123), dem *Haus am Hohenrain* (Abb. 19, Abb. S. 124–127) und schließlich im *Grauen Haus* (Abb. 18, Abb. S. 128–131), die alle drei zwischen 1983 und 1986 in der Grazer Umgebung errichtet wurden, weitergeführt zu werden.

Der Wunsch der Architekten, eine neue Ausdrucksstärke der Architektur mithilfe der Materialbehandlung und einer vielschichtigen Oberflächentextur zu erreichen, hat in einem weiteren Orientierungsfeld bereichernde Anregungen erfahren, die in der prägnanten Physiognomie des *Grauen Hauses* ihren eindeutigsten Niederschlag fanden. Die Schüler Frank Lloyd Wrights hatten zu Beginn der sechziger Jahre in der „vernacular high-art architecture" das Konzept eines program-

approach is still in its early stages in the *House above Graz*, but the timber supports for the two pergolas with their massive concrete anchoring points already suggest that this aspect of Viennese Modernism was to recur frequently in future commissions. A start was made as early as the *Mortuary in Schwarzach* near Salzburg in 1977 (fig. 14), and was then continued in the *Red House* (fig. 15, figs. p. 120–123), the *House on Hohenrain* (fig. 19, figs. p. 124–127) and finally in the *Grey House* (fig. 18, figs. p. 128–131), all three built around Graz between 1983 and 1986.

The architects' desire to make architecture more expressive through the treatment of materials and complex surface textures was much enriched by ideas from another field. The effect of these is shown most clearly in the succinct physiognomy of the *Grey House*. In the early sixties, Frank Lloyd Wright's disciples had presented the notion of programmatic anti-classicism in "vernacular high-art architecture". Herb(ert) Greene demonstrated the principles of this very skilfully in his Prairie House in Oklahoma in 1961 (fig. 17). Greene overlapped timber planks of different lengths to show the wall as a layer and as layering. This apparently random arrangement of shingles or larger areas of cladding made the amorphous building look as though it had been roughly cobbled together. And so this was how craft-based "bricolage" was presented, with a touch of coquetry. Szyszkowitz+Kowalski have always avoided this characteristic style, though the idea of also using timber ornamentally as part of a new face for architecture was applied in some buildings dating from those years. Here

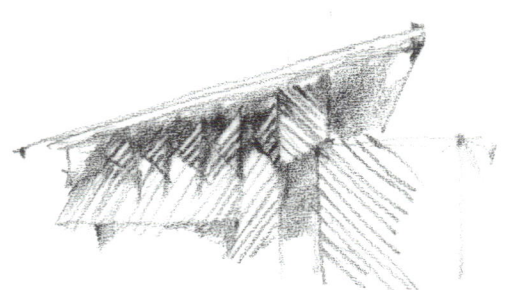

> 16
Bruce Goff, Helen Unseth House, Park Ridge, Illinois 1940 Bruce Goff, Helen Unseth House, Park Ridge, Illinois 1940

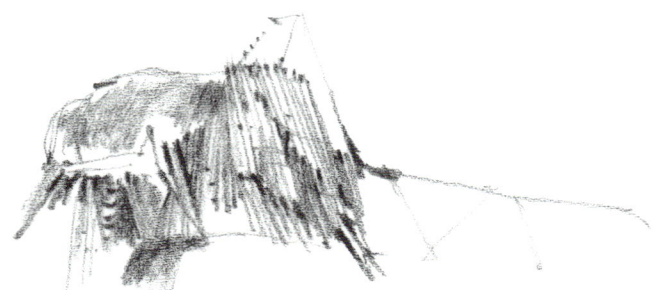

> 17
Herb Greene, Greene Residence, Norman, Oklahoma 1961 Herb Greene, Greene Residence, Norman, Oklahoma 1961

matischen Antiklassizismus vorgelegt. Deren Gestaltungsprinzipien waren von Herb(ert) Greene 1961 in seinem „Prairie House" in Oklahoma (Abb. 17) mit großer Kunstfertigkeit demonstriert worden. In der Überlagerung unterschiedlich langer Holzlatten zeigte Greene die Wand als Schicht und Schichtung, deren scheinbar zufällige Anordnung aus Schindeln oder großflächigeren Schalungen den amorphen Baukörper wie roh zusammengezimmert erscheinen ließ. Ein wenig kokett wurde derart die handwerkliche „bricolage" gekonnt in Szene gesetzt. Diesen Duktus haben Szyszkowitz+Kowalski jedoch stets vermieden, wenngleich die Idee, das Holz auch ornamental als Bestandteil einer neuen Physiognomik der Architektur zu nutzen, in einigen Bauten jener Jahre umgesetzt worden ist. Sie folgten darin vielmehr den Spuren von Bruce Goff, dem bewunderten Lehrer Greenes, der im 1940 entstandenen Helen Unseth House (Abb. 16) die Schalung durch streng diagonal gesetzte Holzlatten gefügt hatte, wodurch der Akt der bewußten Gestaltung betont worden war.[11] Diese Haltung, den Esprit des Gestaltungsprozesses von Formen und Materialien dem Erscheinungsbild der Gebäude zeichenhaft einzuprägen, haben sich Szyszkowitz+Kowalski zueigen gemacht; dessen beeindruckendste Beispiele sind das *Katholische Pfarrzentrum* in Graz-Ragnitz (1982–1987) (Abb. 22) und das *Institut für Biochemie und Biotechnologie* (1984–1991) der Technischen Universität Graz (Abb. 21). In diesem Bau vor allem besannen sich die Architekten zudem auf eine andere Gestaltungsmöglichkeit der Fassade, wie sie Otto Wagner in dem Wiener Amtsge-

they were much more influenced by Bruce Goff, Greene's much-admired teacher. In his 1940 Helen Unseth House (fig. 16), Goff had assembled his cladding by placing wooden planks strictly on the diagonal, stressing that this was a consciously creative act.[11] This is an approach that Szyszkowitz+Kowalski have very much made their own: stamping the spirit of the process by which forms and materials have been created into the outward appearance of the building symbolically. The most impressive examples are the *Catholic Parish Centre* in Ragnitz, Graz (1982–1987) (fig. 22), and the *Institute of Biochemistry and Biotechnology* (1994–1991) at the Technical University in Graz (fig. 21). In the latter building in particular the architects also remembered another possible façade design, as used by Otto Wagner for his Post Office Savings Bank in Vienna (1903–1910), where the arrangement of metal bolts was visible as dressing for the wall (fig. 20). Karla Kowalski later linked the envelope character of the *House above Graz* with another primordial architectural motif: the light structures used by the American settlers, as remembered by their clients at the time, "… and for a long time afterwards they were still longing for light, mobile timber structures that don't pinch like solid leather shoes, they wanted a

[11] Siehe dazu: The Architectue of Bruce Goff 1904–1982. Design for the Continuous Present, Chicago, München, New York, S. 50. Und: Dennis Sharp, A Visual History of Twentieth-Century Architecture, Norwich 1972, S. 248 ff. Cf.: The Architecture of Bruce Goff 1904–1982. Design for the Continuous Present, Chicago, Munich, New York, p. 50. And: Dennis Sharp, A Visual History of Twentieth-Century Architecture, Norwich 1972, p. 248 ff.

18 >>>
Graues Haus, Graz 1984–1986, Ansicht von Süden, (s. S. 128) Grey House, Graz 1984–1986, view from the south (see p. 128)

> 19
Haus am Hohenrain, Graz 1983–1985, Seitenansicht mit Eingang House on Hohenrain, Graz 1983–1985, side view with entrance

> 20
Otto Wagner, K.K. Postsparkassen-Amtsgebäude,
Wien 1903–1910, Fassade mit Platten und Bolzen
Otto Wagner, K.K. Post Office Savings Bank,
Vienna 1903–1910, façade with slabs and bolts

> 21
Institut für Biochemie und Biotechnologie der Technischen Universität Graz, Graz 1985–1991, Detail der Gebäudehaut Institute of Biochemistry and Biotechnology at the Graz Technical University, Graz 1985–1991, detail of cladding

bäude der K. K. Postsparkasse (1903–1910) in der Anordnung der Metallbolzen als Bekleidung der Wand gezeigt hatte (Abb. 20).
Karla Kowalski hat den Hüllencharakter des *Hauses über Graz* später mit einem weiteren Ursprungsmotiv der Architektur in Verbindung gebracht, mit jenen leichten Konstruktionen der amerikanischen Siedlergeschichte, an die sich ihre Bauherren damals erinnert hatten „ ... und noch lange danach galt ihre Sehnsucht leichten, beweglichen Holzbauten, die nicht drückten wie es zu feste Lederschuhe tun, sie wünschten einen kleinen, sanft bewegten Duktus, eine irgendwie unmanifeste, weiche, leicht-warme geästartige Umwebung."[12] Dieser sanft bewegte Duktus zeigt sich vor allem in der Grundrißkonzeption und in der Raumabwicklung, die im *Haus über Graz* entlang einer zentralen Längsachse erfolgt, die einem Rückgrat gleich, dem höhengestuften Baukörper Halt verleiht. Obwohl die einzelnen Räume ineinander übergehen, das Familienleben im Erdgeschoß also in einem offenen System von Küche, Eßplatz, Wohnraum und kleiner Bibliothek erfolgt, sie daher ineinander zu verfließen scheinen, so lassen sich auch hier konzeptionelle Varianten erkennen, die wir gewohnt sind, dem klassischen Kanon der Architekturgeschichte zuzuordnen. Im Grundriß reproduziert sich nämlich das modulare System der Konstruktion, und man erkennt, daß der Erdgeschoßbereich einer geometrischen Dominanz unterworfen und aus dem Quadrat entwickelt ist (Abb. S. 109). Damit wird ein Modul variiert, das seit der Renaissance in der Entwurfsgeschichte Europas immer wieder aufgegriffen wurde und das auch im modernen Wohnhaus eine lange Zeit unterschätzte Rolle gespielt hat; man denke an das Projekt des Wiener Architekten Adolf Loos, der in den Variationen zum Konzept des Letzten Hauses 1933 nach der

small-scale, gently moving line, woven around them in some way that was not clearly manifest, soft, slightly warm, like branches."[12] This gently moving line appears above all in the ground plan concept, and in the way the space develops. In the case of the *House above Graz* this is handled along a central longitudinal axis that supports the building like a backbone and holds its terraced levels. Here too we can make out conceptual variants that are usually ascribed to the classical canons of the history of architecture, even though the individual rooms run into each other and family life on the ground floor takes place in an open system consisting of kitchen, dining area, living room and a small library that all seem to flow into each other. In fact the modular construction system is reproduced in the ground plan, and it is clear that the ground floor area is dominated by geometrical figures derived from a square (fig. p. 109). This is a variant on a module that has been used in European design history since the Renaissance, and that has played a role in modern domestic architecture undervalued for a long time; one has only to think of the Viennese architect Adolf Loos's project – he tried to break through

[12] *Karla Kowalski, Materialität, unveröffentlichtes Manuskript 1996/97, S. 174.*
Karla Kowalski, Materialität, unpublished manuscript 1996/97, p. 174.

> 22
Katholisches Pfarrzentrum Ragnitz, Graz, Ragnitzstraße 1984–1987, aufgefächerte Holzkonstruktion des Kirchenraumes   Catholic Priests' Centre in Ragnitz, Graz, Ragnitzstraße 1984–1987, fanned timber structure in the church

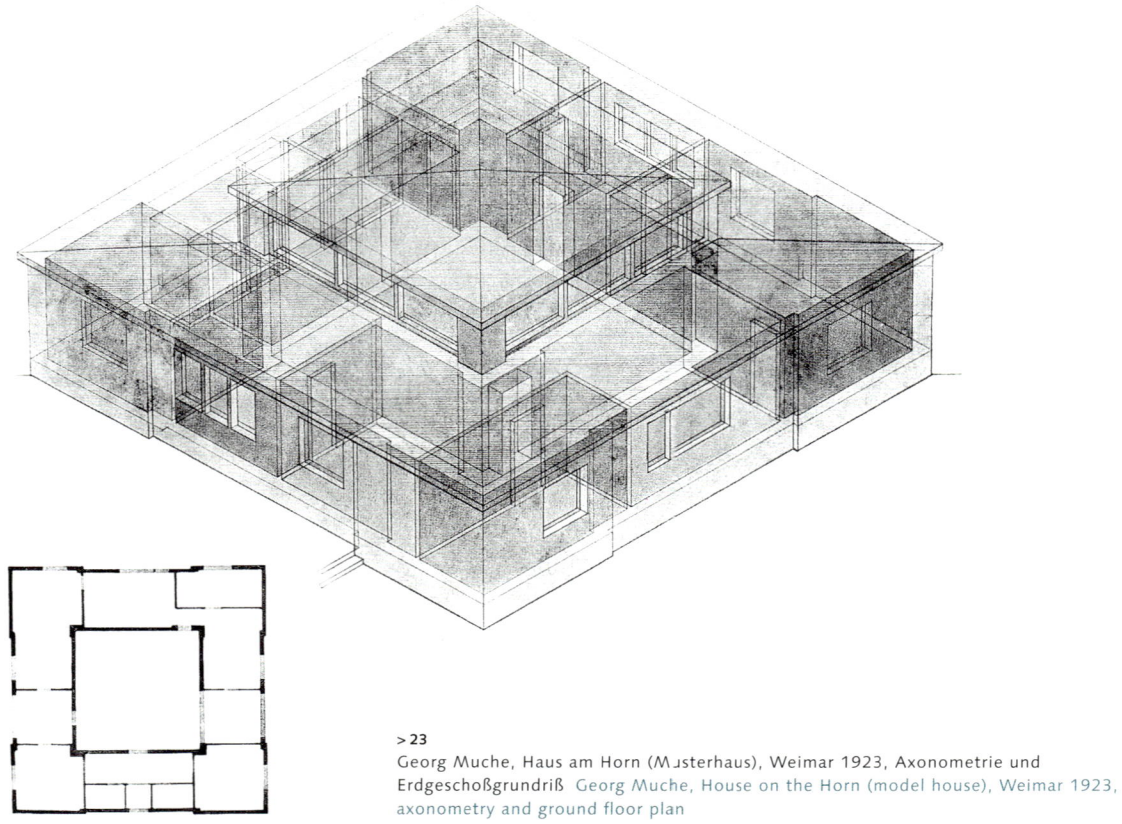

> 23
Georg Muche, Haus am Horn (Musterhaus), Weimar 1923, Axonometrie und Erdgeschoßgrundriß   Georg Muche, House on the Horn (model house), Weimar 1923, axonometry and ground floor plan

letztgültigen Lösung eines elementaren Raumes vorzudringen trachtete, oder an das Musterhaus in Weimar (Abb. 23), das der Maler Georg Muche 1923 zur Bauhausausstellung realisieren durfte. Loos und Muche übertrugen diese Geometrie in die Stereometrie des Würfels, der die Innenraumerschließung unter die Dominanz der Mitte und der Vertikalen stellte. Von dieser Konsequenz und deren Starrheit aber ist das *Haus über Graz* weit entfernt, obwohl Szyszkowitz+Kowalski auch diesen naheliegenden Schritt in einigen Häusern später in Ansätzen vollziehen sollten. Im *Haus über Graz* ist vielmehr der Gedanke des Aufbrechens dieser Figur und deren Ausweitung in kleine, angelagerte Raumeinheiten prägend, die wie die Bibliothek, der Wohnraum oder das Mädchenzimmer aus der Primärgeometrie des Erdgeschoßgrundrisses ausgelagert werden, um als eigenständige Kompartimente, die dem äußeren Erscheinungsbild des Hauses Prägnanz und Variabilität in der Höhenstaffelung verleihen, neue Bedeutungsebenen wie die des Erkers zu erschließen. Das Erkermotiv haben Szyszkowitz+Kowalski denn auch im nachfolgenden Hausprojekt, dem 1978/79 auf einem kleinen Plateau in der Nähe von Graz errichteten *Grünen Haus* (Abb. S. 110–113), geradezu zelebriert. Der auf das Quadrat konzentrierte Grundriß des ursprünglich als Sommerhaus konzipierten Volumens greift mit den auskragenden Eckrisaliten in den Außenraum ein, wobei die betrachtenden Augen durch die Fenster in der rahmenden konstruktiven Hülle gleichsam wie in einem Landschaftsgemälde auf die Natur gelenkt werden (Abb. 29). Auch hier, wie im *Haus über Graz*, ist das Leitbild des auf das Familienleben konzentrierten Wohnens wirksam, das in der geometrischen Grundfigur den adäquaten

to an ultimately valid solution for an elemental space in his 1933 variations on the Last House concept –, or of the model house in Weimar realized for the 1923 Bauhaus exhibition by the painter Georg Muche (fig. 23). Loos and Muche transferred this geometry into the stereometry of the cube, thus subjecting internal access to dominance by the centre and the vertical. But the *House above Graz* is a far cry from this degree of logic and rigidity, even though Szyszkowitz+ Kowalski were to take this obvious step to an extent in some of their later buildings. In the *House above Graz* the key is much more the idea of breaking up this figure and extending it into small, attached spatial units. The library, the living room and the nanny's room are shifted out of the primary geometry of the ground floor plan to become independent compartments. These make the house's elevation look concise and variable from the outside and allow the architects to explore new planes of meaning, as do the bay window, for example.

In fact Szyszkowitz+Kowalski practically celebrated the bay window motif in their next house, the *Green House* (figs. p. 110–113), built on a little plateau near Graz in 1978/79. The volume, originally conceived as a holiday home, has a ground plan concentrated on the square. Its corner projections thrust out into the exterior space, which means that the eye is directed at nature through the windows in the framing structural envelope, with almost the same effect as in landscape painting (fig. 29). Here, as in the *House above Graz*, the model is living focused on family life. The appropriate expres-

24, 25 >>>
Grünes Haus, Graz 1977–1979, isometrische Entwurfsskizze (s.S.111)
Green House, Graz 1977–1979, isometric design sketch (see p.111)

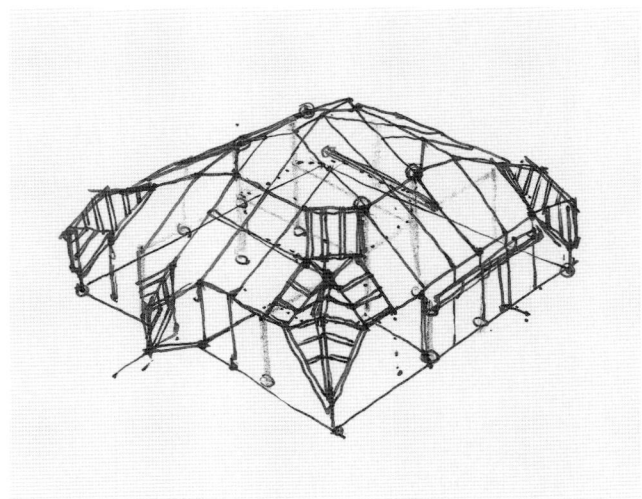
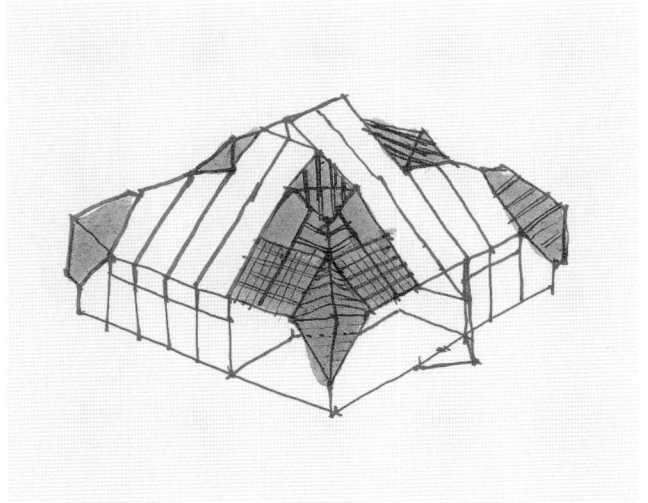

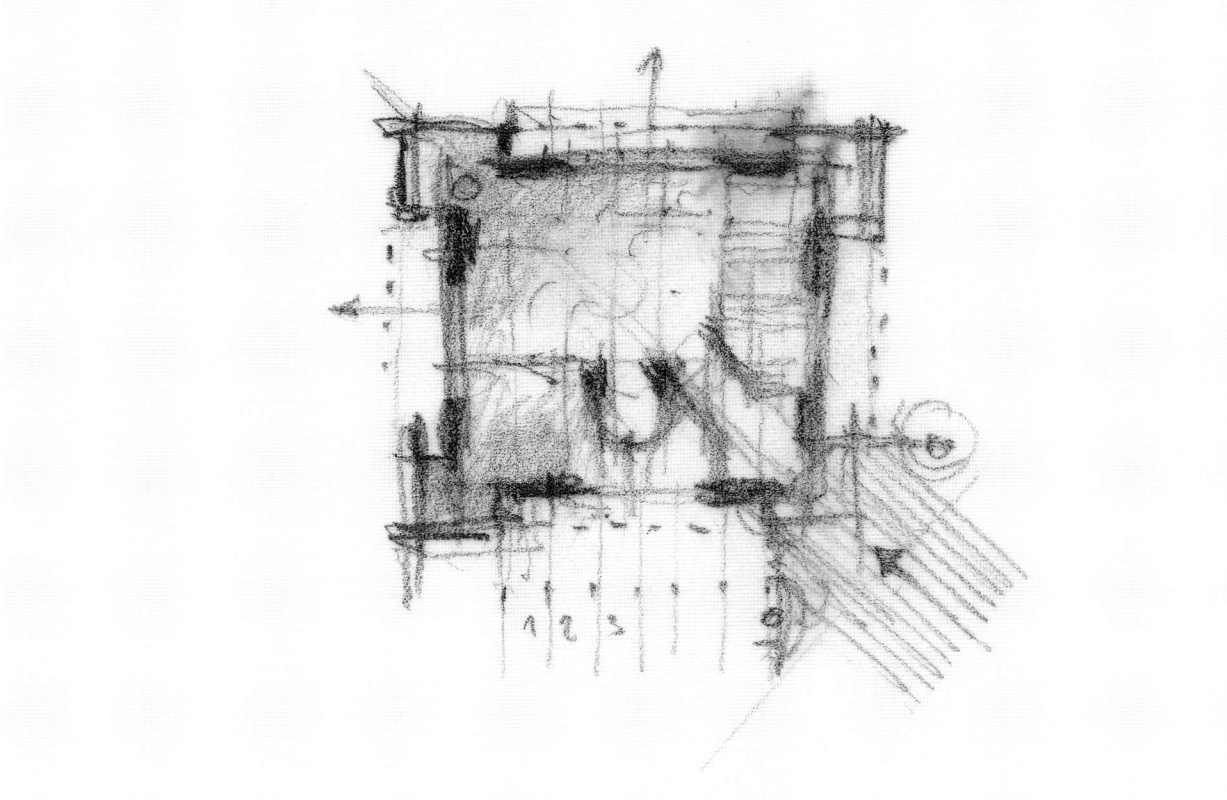

> 26
Grünes Haus, Graz 1977–1979, Entwurfsskizze des Grundrisses
Green House, Graz 1977–1979, floor plan design sketch

> 27
Designhaus, Projekt 1997, Entwurfsskizze des Grundrisses mit Nutzungskonzept Design House, project 1997, floor plan design sketch with use concept

 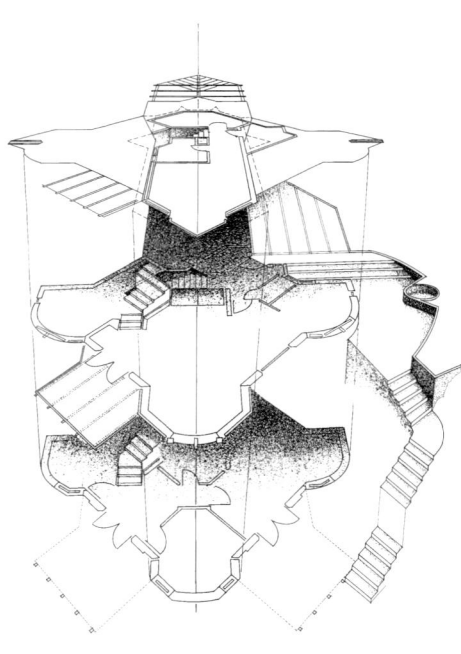

> 28
Graues Haus, Graz 1984–1986, Entwurfsskizze und übereinanderliegende Grundrisse
Grey House, Graz 1984–1986, design sketch and superimposed floor plans

>29
Grünes Haus, Graz 1977–1979, Blick durch den Erker Green House, Graz 1977–1979, view through the bay

30 >>>
Grünes Haus, Graz 1977–1979, Ansicht mit Regenrinnenkonstruktion, (s. S. 111)
Green House, Graz 1977–1979, view with gutter structure, (see p. 111)

Ausdruck für ein kommunikatives, gelebtes Miteinander gefunden hat. In beiden Häusern befinden sich daher die privaten Räume der Schlaf- und Kinderzimmer im oberen Geschoß und verfügen über jene Abgeschlossenheit, die den Bereich des Intimen für jedes Familienmitglied garantiert.

In den Privathäusern, die dem *Haus über Graz* und dem *Grünen Haus* gefolgt sind, werden die dort entwickelten Raumformationen immer wieder unter unterschiedlichen Gewichtungen paraphrasiert und den jeweiligen Anforderungen gemäß assimiliert. So finden wir die dynamischen Kaskadenhäuser am Hang neben den kleineren, auf Zentralität konzentrierten Wohnhäusern in der Ebene und auch die opulente Villenarchitektur hat ihren Platz im Werk der Architekten gefunden. Im Villenbau gibt es schließlich jenen Variantenreichtum im Raumgefüge und im architektonischen Detail, eben jene Exklusivität im Material, die dieser Bauaufgabe inhärent ist. Das Feuerwerk aus Phantasie und kalkuliertem Einsatz der Mittel, das der Begabung von Karla Kowalski und Michael Szyszkowitz entspricht, hat sich an dieser Bauaufgabe ohne Restriktionen entzünden dürfen. Es erscheint nur konsequent, wenn in diesen Häusern auch das Spektrum des repräsentativen Bauens als Anspruch auf Distinktion der Besitzer nicht nur im Inneren, sondern auch im Außenraum in Erscheinung getreten ist.

Doch bei aller Unterschiedlichkeit der Häuser, die dem kleineren oder größeren finanziellen Rahmen und den verschiedenen Bedürfnissen der Auftraggeber zu entsprechen hatten, alle sind sie gleichermaßen von einem Gedanken durchdrungen: Das Wohnen in seiner existentiellen Dimension für das unvergleichliche Individuum in Architektur zu übersetzen, die das geschützte In-der-Welt-Sein erfahrbar machen kann, das sich in ganz alltäglichen Verrichtungen im Kreis der

sion for living together and communicating has been found in the basic geometrical figure. Thus in both houses the private bedrooms and children's rooms are on the top floor and enjoy the seclusion that guarantees an intimate area for every member of the family.

In the private houses that followed the *House above Graz* and the *Green House*, the spatial formations developed there are paraphrased with various different emphases and assimilated according to the particular demands. So we find dynamic cascade houses on the slope with smaller, essentially centralized homes on the plain. Opulent villa architecture finds a place in the architects' work as well. Ultimately, villa construction offers the rich variety of spatial structure and architectural detail and precisely that exclusivity in terms of materials that is inherent in this building brief. Michael Szyszkowitz's and Karla Kowalski's talents made them capable of unrestrained firework displays of imagination and calculated resource use, and these have been ignited unreservedly in this particular brief. And so it seems only logical that the spectrum of prestigious building as an expression of the owner's claim to distinction should appear outside as well as inside these buildings.

These houses are all very different, as they had to accommodate larger or smaller budgets and the various clients' needs, but they are all equally driven by the same idea: translating the existential dimension of living into architecture for each distinct individual. This will be architecture that can make it possible to feel in-the-world and protected, as expressed in

31>>>
Haus am Ruckerlberg, Graz 1998–2002, Wohnraum mit Blick in den Garten und den Wintergarten (noch nicht ausgeführt) (s. S. 213) House on Ruckerlberg, Graz 1998–2002, living room with view into garden and conservatory (not yet realized) (see p. 213)

Familie ebenso wie mit Freunden und Bekannten in umgrenzten Territorien vollzieht. Gemessen an der jeweiligen Besonderheit des familiären Alltags will diese Architektur Orte definieren, sie architektonisch interpretieren und in Raumatmosphären übertragen, die die Selbstgewißheit der Benutzerpersönlichkeit zu tragen verstehen. „Das ‚Einen-Ort-Schaffen' ist … der Versuch," so Michael Szyszkowitz, „das Wesen unserer Existenz zu interpretieren."[13] Diese Anschauung der Architekten begründet den motivischen Gleichklang in den Grundrißkonzeptionen der einzelnen Häuser, sie ist die Basis einer Architektur der charaktervollen, schützenden Baukörper. Deshalb ist jedes Haus auf den Innenraum bedacht, der zwar zum Außenraum mit dem gestalteten Garten ebenso wie mit der umgebenden Landschaft in Kontakt tritt, aber niemals den einen mit dem anderen verschmelzen läßt. Immer werden die Raumeinheiten des Innen und Außen deutlich begrenzt, und doch darf das Auge den Blick auf das nahe Grün, die ferne Bergkette oder den unweit gelegenen Aussichtspunkt suchen. Im ausgewogenen Wechsel von verschließenden Wandeinheiten und öffnenden Fenstern wird der Blick, so erscheint es zuweilen, gleichsam auf Umwegen zum Aussichtspunkt geführt, denn die Wände dieser Häuser werden nicht zu gläsernen Hüllen, die den Weitblick auf den gesamten Horizont eröffnen, ein Faszinosum, dem die Architektur der Moderne huldigte. Das ideale Haus dieser Architekturauffassung gerinnt vielmehr zu einem Netzwerk aus gewiesenen Blickrichtungen und binnenräumlichen Wegeführungen, aus Niveausprüngen und Grenzlinien, die, wie in einer Stadtlandschaft, die Wirkpunkte im Raumgefüge betonen (Abb. 32).

quite ordinary tasks and events in the family circle, and also with friends and relatives in territories with boundaries. This architecture intends to define locations, interpret them architecturally and translate them into spatial atmospheres that do justice to the self-confidence of the users' personalities. All this is measured against the particular features of everyday family life in each case. "'Creating a location' is … an attempt," says Michael Szyszkowitz, "to interpret the essence of our existence."[13] This approach taken by the architects is the basis for the similarity of motifs within the ground plan concepts of the individual houses, for an architecture of characterful, protecting building volumes. For this reason each house focuses on the interior, which does make contact with the exterior and its designed garden and also with the surrounding landscape, but never allows one to blend in with the other. The interior and exterior spatial units always have clear borders, which still allow the eye to see the nearby green areas, the distant mountain chain or a landmark not too distant. It sometimes seems as though the eye is guided via detours within this balanced interplay of closing walls and opening windows. The walls in these houses do not become glazed envelopes opening up a broad view of the whole horizon, a fascinating element that Modernism clung to with great devotion. Instead, within this view of architecture, the ideal house tends to become a network of indicated sight angles and interior pathways, changes of level and borderlines, all emphasizing the effective points in the spatial structure, as in an urban landscape (fig. 32).

[13] *Michael Szyszkowitz, Der Ort und die Form (bezogen auf „Das Zentrum und die Peripherie"), in: Karin Wilhelm/Gregor Langenbrinck (Hg.), City-Lights. Zentren, Peripherien, Regionen. Interdisziplinäre Positionen für eine urbane Kultur, Wien, Köln, Weimar 2002, S. 140 ff.* Michael Szyszkowitz, Der Ort und die Form (with regard to "Das Zentrum und die Peripherie"), in: Karin Wilhelm/Gregor Langenbrinck (ed.), City-Lights. Zentren, Peripherien, Regionen. Interdisziplinäre Positionen für eine urbane Kultur, Vienna, Cologne, Weimar 2002, p. 140 ff.

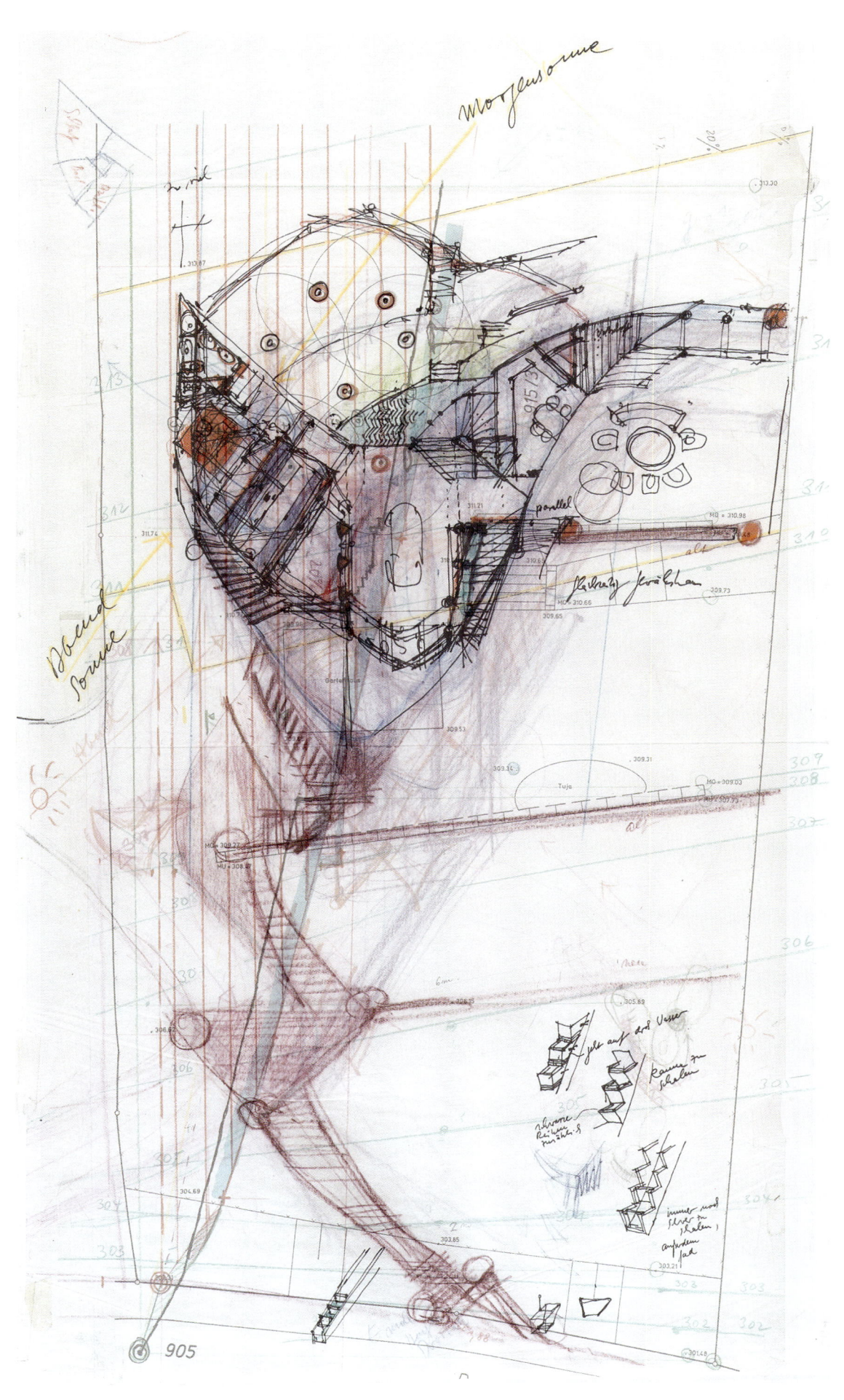

> 32
Haus in Bad Mergentheim, Bad Mergentheim 1991–1993, Entwurfsskizze mit Wegeführung und Nutzungskonzept House in Bad Mergentheim, Bad Mergentheim 1991–1993, design sketch with pathways and use concept

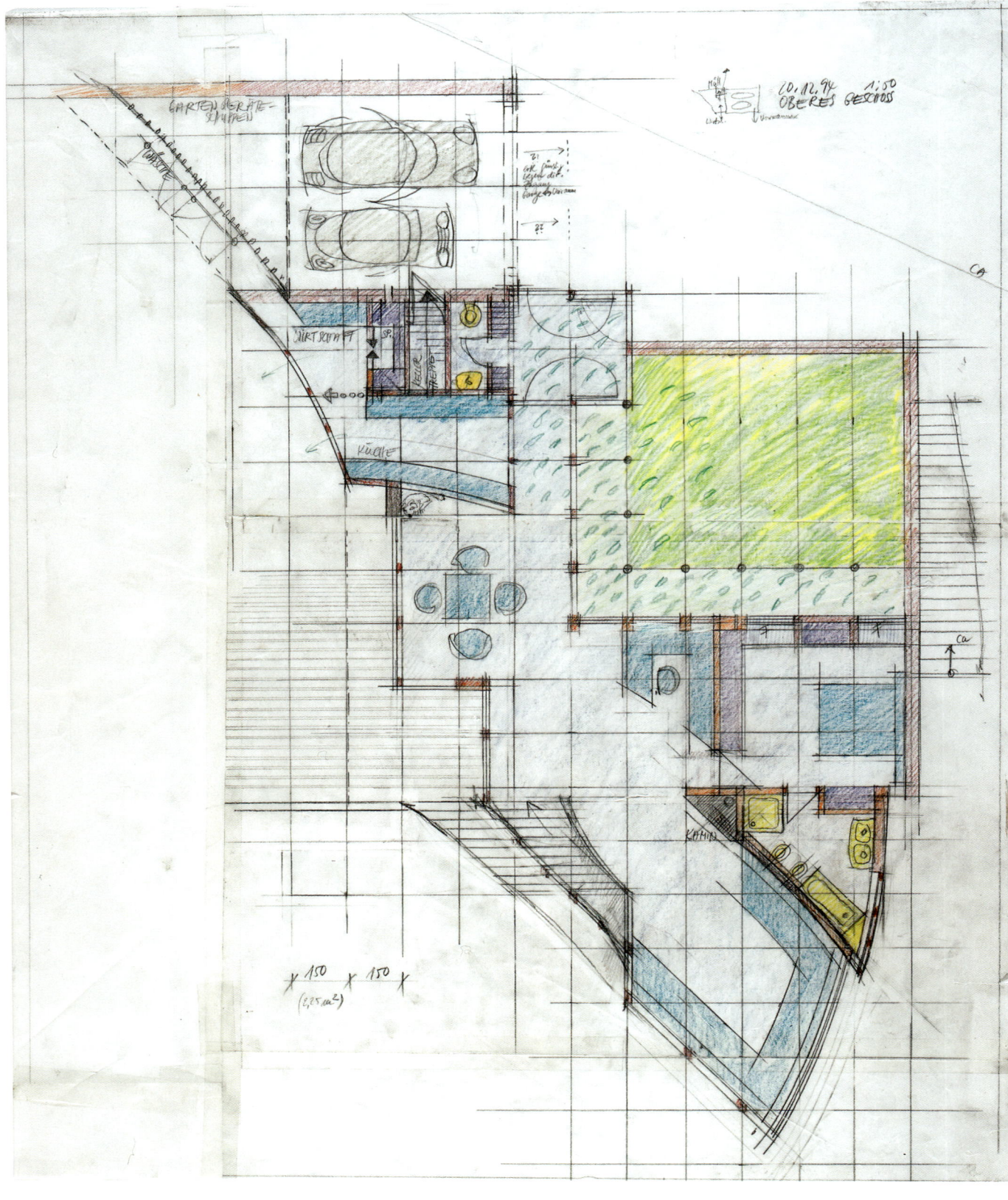

> 33
Haus in Moosburg, Moosburg bei Klagenfurt 1995–1996, Erdgeschoßgrundriß mit Innenhof House in Moosburg, Moosburg near Klagenfurt 1995–1996, ground floor plan with courtyard

[14] Josef Frank, Das Haus als Weg und Platz, in: Der Baumeister, 29. Jg., Aug. 1931, Heft 8, S. 316 ff. Josef Frank, Das Haus als Weg und Platz, in: Der Baumeister, vol. 29, Aug. 1931, issue 8, p. 316 ff.
[15] op. cit. Anm.: 14, S. 316/319. Op. cit. note: 14, pp. 316/319.
[16] Jürgen Joedicke, Zum Werk Hugo Härings, in: Jürgen Joedicke/Heinrich Lauterbach, Hugo Häring. Schriften, Entwürfe, Bauten, Stuttgart/Zürich, 2001, S. 152 ff. Jürgen Joedicke, Zum Werk Hugo Härings, in: Jürgen Joedicke/Heinrich Lauterbach, Hugo Häring. Schriften, Entwürfe, Bauten, Stuttgart/ Zurich, 2001, p. 152 ff.
[17] op. cit. Anm.: 16, S. 153. Op. cit. note: 16, p. 153.
[18] op. cit. Anm.: 14, S. 319 ff. Op. cit. note: 14, p. 319 ff.

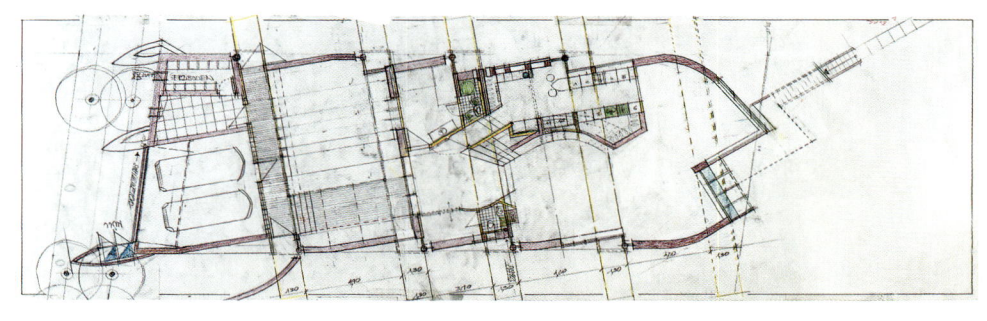

> 34
Haus in Maria Enzersdorf, Maria Enzersdorf bei Wien 1991–1994, Erdgeschoßgrundriß mit Innenhof House in Maria Enzersdorf, Maria Enzersdorf near Vienna 1991–1994, ground floor plan with courtyard

Welt – Stadt – Haus

Die Idee einer Kongruenz zwischen der Anlage einer Stadt und der eines privaten Wohnhauses hat in der Architektur des 20. Jahrhunderts zahlreiche Varianten aufzuweisen. Die wohl prominenteste ist vermutlich die des österreichischen Architekten Josef Frank geworden, die er 1931 in der Zeitschrift „Der Baumeister" unter dem programmatischen Titel: „Das Haus als Weg und Platz"[14] veröffentlichte. „Ein gut organisiertes Haus ist wie eine Stadt anzulegen mit Straßen und Wegen, die zwangsläufig zu Plätzen führen, welche vom Verkehr ausgeschaltet sind, so daß man auf ihnen ausruhen kann … Ein gut angelegtes Haus gleicht jenen schönen alten Städten, in denen sich selbst der Fremde sofort auskennt und, ohne danach zu fragen, Rathaus und Marktplatz findet."[15] Ganz ähnlich hatte zehn Jahre zuvor Hugo Häring einen Entwurf zum Empfangsgebäude des Leipziger Hauptbahnhofes charakterisiert, indem er in einer Bleistiftnotiz die Lesart seiner Zeichnung beifügte: „Grundriss lösen wie stadtplan…wege, straßenführung, plätze."[16]

Diese Vorstellung hat Häring, wie Jürgen Joedicke schrieb, in die Grundrisse seiner ersten Privathäuser übertragen, indem er „gekurvte und polygonal gebrochene Raumbegrenzungen"[17] entwickelte. Für Frank lag im Verzicht auf die Rechteckigkeit von Zimmern überhaupt erst die Möglichkeit, um zu charaktervollen Raumgestaltungen im Wohnbau vordringen zu können.

„Ich glaube", so Frank, „daß, wenn man ein Polygon wahllos aufzeichnet, sei es mit rechten oder stumpfen Winkeln, dieses, als Grundriß eines Zimmers betrachtet, viel geeigneter ist als der regelmäßig-rechteckige."[18] Die Umsetzung dieser Erkenntnis findet sich in den Häusern von Szyszkowitz+Kowalski wieder ein.

World – town – house

20th century architecture has seen numerous variants on the idea that there is a congruency between the layouts of towns and of private houses. Probably the most distinguished is the one put forward by the Austrian architect Josef Frank, published in the magazine "Der Baumeister" in 1931 under the programmatic title "Das Haus als Weg und Platz" (The House as Pathway and Square).[14] "A well organized house should be laid out like a town, with streets and pathways leading inevitably to squares from which traffic has been eliminated, so that it is possible to rest and relax there … A well laid out house is like those beautiful old towns that strangers know their way about immediately, finding the town hall and the market place without having to ask."[15] Ten years before, Hugo Häring was making a very similar point about a design for the reception building in the main station at Leipzig when he added a pencil note about how to read his drawing: "Solve ground plan like town plan … paths, lines of streets, squares."[16] As Jürgen Joedicke pointed out, Häring applied this idea in the ground plans for his first private houses by developing "spatial boundaries with curves and polygonal breaks".[17] Frank thought that abandoning right angles in rooms was the only way to achieve characterful spatial designs for housing. "I believe," said Frank, "that if you draw a polygon at random, whether it has right or obtuse angles, it will be much more suitable as the ground plan of a room than the regular rectangle."[18] This insight recurs in Szyszkowitz+ Kowalski's houses.

> 35
Haus in Bad Mergentheim, Bad Mergentheim 1991–1993, Ansicht von Südosten, Dachkonstruktion House in Bad Mergentheim, Bad Mergentheim 1991–1993, view from the the south-east, roof structure

Will man aber den Wurzeln ihrer Architektur in der Baugeschichte sinnvoll auf die Spur kommen, so sind es darüber hinaus vielerlei Verästelungen, denen zu folgen ist. Sie berühren sich durchaus mit den genannten Positionen und sind im Konzept der „promenade architecturale", wie es Le Corbusier in seinen Villenbauten als Spazierweg der Wahrnehmung inszeniert hat, zu finden. Auch Frank Lloyd Wrights „fließender Grundriss", jene „Kontinuität" der Raumabwicklung, die eine „lebendige Architektur" oder das, was er die „organische Architektur" nannte, „die einzige, die es erlaubt, zu leben und leben zu lassen",[19] hat seine Auswirkungen gezeitigt. Noch Wrights Bekenntnis: „Das *Gefühl des Schützenden* im Aussehen (eines) Gebäudes gefiel mir", lebt hier weiter. Doch bei allem Respekt diesen Positionen gegenüber: Die Gestalt ihrer Häuser, die Fassadenbildungen und die Materialbehandlung beruhen wesentlich auf persönlichen Erfahrungen mit der experimentellen Architektur ihrer Studienzeit und auf der eigenen ästhetischen Position, die in der Architektur eine Symbolierungsarbeit sieht, das Bemühen um den „charactère" in der architektonischen Form, die als Zeichen „psychischer Verankerungen"[20] spürbar werden kann. Die Entwicklung ihrer Architektur muß auf diesen

But there are a lot more ramifications to be followed if we are to trace the roots of their architecture meaningfully in architectural history. They definitely touch upon the positions that have been mentioned and are to be found in Le Corbusier's concept of the "promenade architecturale", presented in his villas as a pathway of perception. And Frank Lloyd Wright's "open plan", that "continuity" of spatial development that he called "living architecture" or "organic architecture", the only kind that makes it possible to live and let live, as he said,[19] made an impact as well. And Wright's declaration that "the *feeling of protection* in the appearance of a building appealed to me," lives on here too. But although they undoubtedly respect these positions, the form of their houses, the façades and the treatment of materials are essentially based on personal experiences with the experimental architecture of their college days and their own aesthetic position, which allots a symbolic task to architecture: a striving for "caractère" in architectural form that can be discerned as signs of "psychological embodiment".[20] The development of their architecture has to be traced back to this impulse. It should be inter-

[19] Frank Lloyd Wright, Das natürliche Haus, München 1954, S. 21. *Frank Lloyd Wright, The Natural House, New York 1954.*
[20] Karla Kowalski, Territorien, unveröffentlichtes Manuskript, o. S. *Karla Kowalski, Territorien, unpublished manuscript, no p.*

36 >>>
Haus in Maria Enzersdorf, Maria Enzersdorf bei Wien 1991–1994, Seitenansicht mit Abfolge der Dachträgerkonstruktion und Innenhof, (s. S. 168–169) *House in Maria Enzersdorf, Maria Enzersdorf near Vienna 1991–1994, side view of roof support structure sequence and courtyard, (see p. 168–169)*

> 37
Haus am Hohenrain, Graz 1983–1985, Luftbild *House on Hohenrain, Graz 1983–1985, aerial photograph*

> 38
Behnisch & Partner, Olympiagelände München, München 1968–1972,
Landschaftsraum mit transluzider Zeltdachkonstruktion
Behnisch & Partner, Munich Olympics site, Munich 1968–1972,
landscape space with translucent tent roof structure

Impuls zurückgeführt werden, den wir als eine Spielart der „Architecture parlante" interpretieren dürfen, deren Symbolik allerdings nicht der klaren Analogie verpflichtet bleibt, wie wir sie in der Revolutionsarchitektur vor 1800 vor Augen haben, sondern die in einer hieroglyphengleichen Bildersetzung eher raunend zu vernehmen ist.

Als Karla Kowalski und Michael Szyszkowitz ihre Bürotätigkeit aufnahmen, hatten sie bereits gemeinsam an der Realisierung der Olympiabauten in München (1967–1972) (Abb. 38–40) gearbeitet, Karla Kowalski als Mitarbeiterin im Büro von Günter Behnisch und Michael Szyszkowitz als Diplomand im jungen Grazer Gemeinschaftsbüro von Günther Domenig und Eilfried Huth. In dieser Konstellation trafen zwei Mentalitäten aufeinander, die zum einen durch Behnischs grundlegende Idee einer landschaftsbezogen, demokratischen Architektur geprägt war, die selbst wie eine Landschaft „Sensationen" in sich bergen sollte und zum anderen durch eine Architektur, die mit neuen Konstruktionen und Materialien dem kybernetischen Paradigma auf der Spur war. Norbert Wieners Entdeckung von der Gleichartigkeit der Informationsübertragung und -verarbeitung in den Organismen und in der Technik, hatte seit den fünfziger Jahren eine Experimentierfreudigkeit der jungen Architekten weltweit angeregt, die Domenig und Huth schon seit geraumer Zeit teilten. Ihr Pavillon in der Schwimmhalle des Münchener Olympiaparks (Abb. 40) war in diesem Umfeld entwickelt worden, ein transluzides Gebilde, das wie eine biomorphe, gleichsam atmende Haut wirkte, unter der die Tragkonstruktion mit der Gebäudetechnik sichtbar gelassen worden war und derart die Analogie zwischen lebendem und artifiziellem Organismus

preted as a variety of "architecture parlante", though not one whose symbolism is based on clear analogies of the kind familiar from Revolutionary Architecture before 1800. It is much more to be apprehended as a whispered rumour with hieroglyph-like figures slipping in to replace the images.

When Karla Kowalski and Michael Szyszkowitz started their joint practice they had already worked together on the buildings for the Olympic Games in Munich (1967–1972) (figs. 38–40). Karla Kowalski was employed in Günter Behnisch's office and Michael Szyszkowitz was a diploma student in the young Graz practice of Günther Domenig and Eilfried Huth. So two mentalities met within this constellation which was shaped by Behnisch's basic idea of landscape-related, democratic architecture intended to conceal "sensations" within itself like a landscape, and also by an architecture that was on the track of the cybernetic paradigm with its new constructions and materials. Ever since the 1950s, Norbert Wiener's discovery that organisms and technology convey and process information in the same way had stimulated young architects to experiment all over the world, and Domenig and Huth had been among their number for some time. Their pavilion in the swimming hall in the Olympic Park in Munich had been developed in this context (fig. 40). It was a translucent structure, looking like a biomorphic skin that

> 40
Günther Domenig/Eilfried Huth, Pavillon in der Schwimmhalle des Olympiageländes München von Behnisch+Partner, München 1968–1972, Konstruktion und Hülle der Galerien und Rampen Günther Domenig/Eilfried Huth, pavilion in the indoor swimming pool in Behnisch+Partner's Munich Olympics site, Munich 1968–1972, construction and covering for the galleries and ramps

> 39
Karla Kowalski, Zeichnung vom Münchner Olympiadach nach Entwurfsskizzen aus dem Büro Behnisch & Partner (aus einem Vortrag 1993) Karla Kowalski, drawing of the Munich Olympics roof from design sketches by Behnisch & Partner (from a lecture in 1993)

unmißverständlich visualisierte. Das Farbkonzept der tragenden Elemente und Klimaschläuche, das zwischen Pink und Hellblau die Pop-Art-Palette variierte und gleichsam den Knochenbau vom Blutkreislauf unterschied, stellte diesen Ansatz demonstrativ zur Schau. Damit war die Zeit gekommen, in der man sich allmählich von der Ausdrucksstärke des „béton brut", wie er in Le Corbusiers Nachkriegsarchitektur gepflegt wurde, verabschiedete und in der man dennoch aufmerksam beobachtete, welcher Formenreichtum und welche Plastizität diesem Material in den Projekten eines Jørn Utzon, Eero Saarinen oder Oskar Niemeyer innewohnte. Mit gleichem Interesse aber verfolgte man gleichzeitig die andere, durch Günter Behnisch und Frei Otto repräsentierte Architekturauffassung, die sich soeben in der Seilnetzkonstruktion des Olympiadaches zeigte: „Landschaft + Zelt = das war's." (Abb. 39), so Kowalskis knapp gefaßte Analyse. Frei Ottos forschende Suche nach den „Natürlichen Konstruktionen", seine Idee der temporären, zeltgleichen Architekturen, schließlich die Rezeption des „nativen Bauens" und der durch Otto in Deutschland wieder ins Bewußtsein gerückten, außereu-

seemed to be breathing. The load-bearing structure and the building services had been left visible underneath this, and so the analogy between a living and an artificial organism was unmistakably visible. The colour scheme for the load-bearing elements and the air-conditioning ducts, which varied the Pop Art palette from pink to light blue, distinguishing bone structure from the circulation of the blood, as it were, was a vivid demonstration of this approach. And so the time had come to start saying a gradual goodbye to the expressive qualities of "béton brut" as cultivated in Le Corbusier's post-war architecture. Nevertheless, a careful eye was kept on the formal richness and sculptural quality of this material inherent in projects by architects like Jørn Utzon, Eero Saarinen or Oskar Niemeyer. But at the same time one also looked at the other view of architecture, represented by Günther Behnisch and Frei Otto and reflected in the tent-roof construction of the Olympic roof: "Landscape + tent = that was it," (fig. 39) was Kowalski's terse analysis. Frei Otto was searching intently for "natural constructions" and exploring the idea of temporary, tent-like architecture. This, and with it the response to

ropäischen Architektur mit ihrem ornamentalen Reichtum eröffnete vielen eine neue, unbefangene Sicht auf die Qualität und den Reichtum des Entwerfens. Hier konnten Karla Kowalski und Michael Szyszkowitz die eigenen Ambitionen bestätigt finden, die während der Auslandsaufenthalte in Frankreich und England gewachsen waren, wenngleich das temporäre Bauen, sieht man einmal von Ausstellungsgestaltungen ab, niemals ein Thema ihrer Arbeit geworden ist. In den Stuttgarter Vorlesungen hat Karla Kowalski die Bedeutsamkeit jener Neuorientierung in der Architektur der Bundesrepublik Deutschland beschrieben: „*Eigentlich* ist es ... doch erstaunlich, daß ausgerechnet 20, 25 Jahre nach dem Krieg mit seinem Grauen und der ‚Wiederaufbauzeit' mit ihrer Nutzarchitektur, die notwendigerweise vornehmlich an Nutzwohnraum dachte, (wieder) an Stadtzwischenraum als dem eigentlich ...phantasiefüllenden (Raum) gedacht (wurde), daß also just nach dieser Zeit sich eine Lücke der Sehnsucht auftat nach etwas anderem ... Es stieg offensichtlich aus einem steinernen Erwerbsdenken, wie ein lange vergessener Bestandteil, so etwas hervor wie der Wunsch nach Poesie, auch nach Erde, nach Luft, nach melodischem Leichternehmen ... "[21]

Diesem Potential einer neuen poetischen Architekturauffassung war Karla Kowalski bereits während ihres Studiums an der Technischen Hochschule in Darmstadt begegnet. Ausgerechnet der damalige Assistent Ernst Neuferts, der mit der Pragmatik seiner „Bauentwurfslehre" der Architektur jede metaphorische Dimension genommen hatte, bestärkte die jungen Studentinnen und Studenten, weniger den maßre-

"native" building and the lavish ornament found in architecture outside Europe that Otto had introduced to Germany again, opened up a new, uninhibited view of the quality and richness of design for many people. This confirmed Karla Kowalski's and Michael Szyszkowitz's own ambitions, which had emerged during their stays in France and England, though temporary buildings never became a subject they addressed, with the exception of exhibition designs. Karla Kowalski described the importance of this new architectural direction in Western Germany in her Stuttgart lectures: "*Actually* it is astonishing ... that at all times 20, 25 years after the war with all its horrors, and the 'reconstruction period' with its functional architecture that was necessarily concerned mainly with functional living space, thoughts turned to urban gaps (again) as the actual (space) ... to occupy our imaginations, in other words that just after this period a sense of longing for something different emerged ... it seemed that something like a desire for poetry was rising from stony acquisitive thinking like a long-forgotten component, and also a desire for earth, for air, for a tuneful way of taking things more easily ..."[21]

Karla Kowalski had come across this potential for a new and poetic view of architecture while studying at the Technical University in Darmstadt. While Ernst Neufert's pragmatic "construction design theory" had removed any metaphorical dimension for architecture, it was somewhat surprisingly his assistant at the time who encouraged the young students to trust their own creative powers rather than disciplined processes. Jochem Jourdan's wealth of ideas and tolerance established the necessary climate for new thinking, in which Karla Kowalski was able to develop her individual pleasure in the formal wealth of architecture, a quality that was unusually well promoted in the drawing training by Jourdan and Peter Färber, two "stars" (Karla Kowalski) in the dark sky of post-war German architectural education.

Szyszkowitz+Kowalski's approach to architecture grew up on the basis of their shared delight in the constructive and their joint wish for an expressively aware, artistic architecture paying homage to the natural surroundings. This was their contribution to the fundamental changes in architectural thinking that were taking place at the time. Both also

[21] *Karla Kowalski, Raumkonzepte, unveröffentlichtes Manuskript 1997, S. 209.*
Karla Kowalski, Raumkonzepte, unpublished manuscript 1997, p. 209.

[22] *Candilis-Josic-Woods, Ein Jahrzehnt Architektur und Stadtplanung, in: Dokumente der modernen Architektur, Jürgen Joedicke (Hg.), Stuttgart 1968, S. 15. Über die städtebaulichen Intentionen schrieben die Architekten: „Wir versuchen für die Stadt ein Rückgrat zu schaffen, ... Es besteht aus: dem Sektor der Konzentration der Aktivitäten und der hohen Dichte des Gemeinschaftslebens: der Zentrumsstrasse; dem System der Wegverbindungen, den durchlaufenden Grünzonen." Georges Candilis, Alexis Josic, Sharach Woods, Toulouse le Mirail. Geburt einer neuen Stadt, in: Dokumente der modernen Architektur, Jürgen Joedicke (Hg.), Stuttgart 1975, S. 18.*
Candilis-Josic-Woods, Ein Jahrzehnt Architektur und Stadtplanung, in: Dokumente der modernen Architektur, Jürgen Joedicke (ed.), Stuttgart 1968, p. 15. The architects wrote as follows about their urban development intentions: "We are trying to create a backbone for the city. ... It consists of: the sector with concentrated activities and a high density of community life: the centre street; the pathway connection system, the continuous green zones." Georges Candilis, Alexis Josic, Sharach Woods, Toulouse le Mirail. Geburt einer neuen Stadt, in: Dokumente der modernen Architektur, Jürgen Joedicke (ed.), Stuttgart 1975, p. 18.

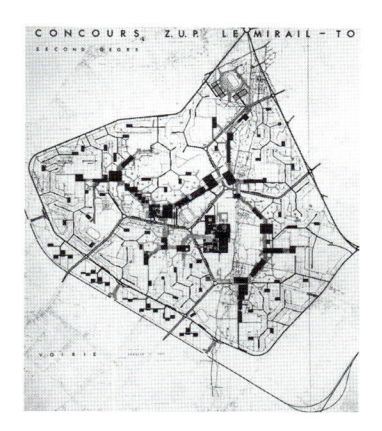

>41
Georges Candilis/Alexis Josic/Shadrach Woods, Toulouse le Mirail, 1963–1971, Wegesystem
Georges Candilis/Alexis Josic/Shadrach Woods, Toulouse le Mirail, 1963–1971, path system

gelnden Verfahren als vielmehr der eigenen schöpferischen Kraft zu vertrauen. Jochem Jourdan nämlich verbreitete mit seinem Ideenreichtum und seiner Toleranz das notwendige Klima für ein neues Denken, in dem Karla Kowalski ihre individuelle Lust am Formenreichtum der Architektur entwickeln konnte, eine Qualität, die in der zeichnerischen Ausbildung durch Jourdan und Peter Färber, zwei „Sternen" (Karla Kowalski) am dunklen Firmament nachkriegsdeutscher Architekturpädagogik, ungemein gefördert wurde. Das Architekturprogramm von Szyszkowitz+Kowalski wuchs auf der Basis dieser großen Lust am Konstruktiven und dem gemeinsamen Wunsch nach einer ausdrucksbewußten, künstlerischen, landschaftbezogenen Architektur, womit sie die damalige Zeitenwende im architektonischen Denken begleiteten. Beide brachten zudem Potentiale ein, die im Ausland geschult worden waren. Karla Kowalski war 1966/67 nach Paris gegangen, um als junge Mitarbeiterin im damals hochgeschätzten Büro von Georges Candilis, Alexis Josic und Shadrach Woods die „Geburt einer neuen Stadt" mitzuerleben. Toulouse le Mirail (Abb. 41) war ein Großprojekt mit nahezu 23 000 Wohneinheiten, das nicht mehr dem CIAM-Dogma einer funktionalen Gliederung der Stadträume folgte, aber aus Großstrukturen bestand, die auf dem „linearen System" basierten, an das die einzelnen, gleichwertig gestalteten „Wohneinheiten angeschlossen"[22] waren. Michael Szyszkowitz besuchte während seiner Studienzeit mehrfach die Städtebauseminare der Salzburger Sommerakademie unter J. B. Bakema und Georges Candilis, somit war auch er mit den Konzepten der Holländer und den Gedanken des ehemaligen Mitarbeiters Le Corbusiers wohl vertraut. Gleichermaßen hatten sie sich also mit einem Architekturbegriff auseinandergesetzt, der die Architektur und den Städtebau als sich bedingende Einheit ansah. Ihre eigene Position wuchs mithin auf der Basis des kontextuellen Denkens, das der Wahrnehmung für die landschaftliche und urbane Umgebung ebensoviel Aufmerksamkeit schenkte, wie den sozialen Anforderungen des Wohnens. Zugleich bewegte der Städtebau und die Wiederaufbauarbeit der kriegsdemolierten Städte wie Rotterdam oder des in einer Bombennacht zerstörten Darmstadt die Gemüter und öffnete die Augen für die räumliche Einbindung neu zu errichtender Gebäude. Daß der Blick dabei auch auf die Strukturen der alten Städte mit ihrer

introduced capacities acquired from training abroad. Karla Kowalski had gone to Paris in 1966/67 to experience the "birth of a new city" in the practice of Georges Candilis, Alexis Josip and Shadrach Woods, which (Fig. 41) was very highly thought of at the time. Toulouse Le Mirail was a major project involving almost 23,000 residential units. It no longer followed the CIAM dogma of structuring urban spaces functionally, but was made up of large structures based on the "linear system" to which the individual "living units", all designed to the same standard, were "attached".[22] Michael Szsyszkowitz frequently attended urban development seminars at the Salzburg Summer Academy under J. B. Bakema and Georges Candilis while he was a student. This made him extremely familiar with current concepts in Holland and the ideas of Le Corbusier's former colleague. They had also come to terms with the view that saw architecture andurban development as mutually dependent units. Thus their own position developed on the basis of contextual thinking that paid as much attention to landscape and the urban surroundings as to the social requirements of housing. At the same time, urban development and the reconstruction of cities like Rotterdam that had been wiped out by the war, or Darmstadt, which had been destroyed in a single night airraid, were occupying people's minds and opening their eyes to tying necessary new buildings into existing spaces. So one of the unspectacular side effects of the time the two

> 42
Antoni Gaudí, Park Güell, Barcelona 1900–1914, Haupteingang mit Treppenführung Antoni Gaudí, Güell Park, Barcelona 1900–1914, main entrance with steps

„Artenvielfalt" des Historischen gelenkt wurde, auf ihre Schönheiten und lebendigen Lebensqualitäten, war in Paris ebenso wie in London, wo Karla Kowalski sich ebenfalls für ein Jahr der Städtebaulehre an der Architectural Association School widmete, ein unspektakulärer Nebeneffekt des Aufenthaltes. Michael Szyszkowitz, der in der steirischen Landeshauptstadt aufgewachsen war, genoß diesen Vorzug gleichsam naturwüchsig, denn Graz war mit der barocken Bausubstanz und dem bourgeoisen Flair vom Weltenlauf des Krieges relativ unberührt geblieben. Auch und gerade aus diesem subjektiven Erfahrungshorizont speiste sich der allmählich wachsende Unmut an den Großstrukturen eines ökonomieversessenen Bauwirtschaftsfunktionalismus im Städtebau, so daß sich die Aufmerksamkeit neugierig dem Verlorengegangenen, dem Atmosphärischen der Räume des einzelnen Hauses und seiner Umgebung zuwenden konnte – dem Reichtum des Jugendstils etwa, der auf der Darmstädter Mathildenhöhe mit den Wohnhäusern von Josef Maria Olbrich oder Peter Behrens (1901) in seiner strengen Variante studiert werden konnte oder dessen ungemein reichhaltigere Spielart, die im Park Güell (Abb. 42) des Antoni Gaudí in Barcelona die Sinne elektrisierte. Zur Jahrhundertwende, zeitgleich mit der Veröffentlichung von Sigmund Freuds „Traumdeutung" 1900 als „Garten-Vorort" geplant, wenn auch derart nie realisiert, vermittelten dessen Rudimente immerhin die Vision des lebensfrohen Wohnens in einer „gelungenen Synthese von Architektur, Skulptur und Farbigkeit, Natur, Raum und Licht"[23] als Widerschein des verlorenen Paradieses und Sehnsucht der Seele.

Die Suche nach vergleichbaren und dennoch zeitgemäßen Ausdruckswerten erhielt zudem in der aufmerksam betriebenen Lektüre der ausländischen Architekturzeitschriften weitere Anregungen. In „Architecture d'aujourd'hui" konnte man die kritischen Städtebaudiskurse der französischen Marxisten ebenso verfolgen wie die metabolistischen Stadtutopien, und in „The Architectural Review" waren neben den neuesten Projekten aus aller Welt immer wieder Berichte über die historischen Städte und Gebäude ferner Konti-

spent abroad was that their attention was attracted to the structures of old towns, with all their historical "diversity of species", their beauty and their sense of life. This applied to Paris, but also to London, where Karla Kowalski also devoted herself to urban development theory for a year at the Architectural Association School. Michael Szyszkowitz, who grew up in the Sytrian capital, enjoyed this advantage quite naturally: Graz, with its Baroque buildings and bourgeois atmosphere had remained relatively untouched by the toils of war. This subjective horizon of experience also made a key contribution to their unease about the large-scale structures currently used in urban development by finance-obsessed functionalism in the building industry. This meant that their attention could turn to curiosity about what had been lost, the atmospheric quality of rooms in a particular building and its surroundings – the rich textures of Jugendstil, for instance, which could be studied in its austere variant in the buildings by Joseph Maria Olbrich or Peter Behrens (1901) on the Mathildenhöhe in Darmstadt, or the infinitely more lavish variety that sent a tingle through the senses in Antoni Gaudí's Park Güell in Barcelona (fig. 42). Planned as a garden suburb at the turn of the century, at the same time as Sigmund Freud's "Interpretation of Dreams" was published in 1900. It was never realized in this form, but its rudiments still conveyed a vision of zestful living in a "successful synthesis of architecture, sculpture and colour, nature, space and light"[23] as a reflection of a lost paradise and the yearnings of the soul.

[23] Gabriele Sterner, Barcelona. Antoni Gaudí. Architektur als Ereignis, Köln 1979, S. 77.
Gabriele Sterner, Barcelona. Antoni Gaudí. Architektur als Ereignis, Cologne 1979, p. 77.

>43
Haus Bad Mergentheim, Bad Mergentheim 1991–1993, Ansicht von der Auffahrt mit Treppenführung und Pflanzenschiffen House in Bad Mergentheim, Bad Mergentheim 1991–1993, view of the drive with stairs and plant containers

nente zu finden, die im Mutterland des Commenwealth wie der Bestand der eigenen (Architektur-) Geschichte gegenwärtig gehalten wurden. Dieser Reichtum der Weltarchitektur beflügelte den Willen, eine neue, umgebungsbewußte Architektur zu entwickeln, um eine „Architekturerfindung, jedes Eck, jeden Raum so zu machen, wie es bestimmt vorher nicht war ... Es ist (aber) ... schwer, wirklich ‚neu' zu sein, denn selbst in der Negation liegt soviel Wissen davon, wie es vorher einmal war."[24]

Mit diesem Vor-Wissen haben Szyszkowitz+Kowalski den Weg zur eigenen Architektur seitdem beschritten. Er ist durch Spuren jener konstruktiven Lust geprägt, die Michael Szyszkowitz im Büro Domenig/Huth erlebt hatte. Dieser Kompetenz frönt er heute auch im kleinen, experimentellen Maßstab, wenn er den „Monstern"[25] (Abb. 58), diesen animalischen Wunder- und Fabelwesen aus Ton von Karla Kowalski jenes filigrane Stützwerk unterlegt, das mit schwindelnder Leichtigkeit die Schwerkraft der Objekte zu widerlegen scheint. Ihr gemeinsamer Weg wurde zudem vom Wissen um die strukturellen Überlagerungen der Haus- und Stadtfiguren geleitet, ging es doch gleichermaßen um die räumliche Organisation sozialer Beziehungen im Hinblick auf die individuelle Existenz. In dieser Komplexität erscheint das einzelne Haus abermals als *nucleus* der Vergesellschaftung und als Raum für die Sozialisierungsarbeit der Subjekte. Daß dem Privathaus damit für den Siedlungsbau und für das Wohnen in der Gemeinschaft in städtischen Arealen Vorbild- und Experimentalfunktion zugewiesen wird, zeigen die vielfältigen Einflüsse, die zwischen den stadträumlichen Raumanordnungen der Siedlungen und den Privathäusern immer wieder zu beobachten sind (Abb. 2, 87, 90). So gesehen ist das Privathaus kein asozialer Luxus, sondern das Feld, in dem der Anspruch auf einen definierten, großzügigen Lebensraum ausprobiert werden kann. Daß dieses Konzept eine besondere ästhetische Option in sich trägt, die im Typus und im architektonischen Detail dem Symbolischen sich zuneigt, gehört zum Credo eines Denkens, das die Architektur nicht als Funktion diagrammatischer Entscheidungen auffaßt, sondern als ein Zeichensystem von Empfindungen, Stimmungen und Erinnerungen.

Michael Szyszkowitz and Karla Kowalski's search for comparable expressive values that were also appropriate to their own times was also helped along by carefully reading foreign architecture magazines. "L'architecture d'aujourd'hui" enabled them to follow the French Marxists' critical urban development discourses and also the metabolist urban utopias. "The Architectural Review" contained reports on the most recent projects from all over the world, along with accounts of historical towns and buildings in distant continents, which the motherland of the Commonwealth saw as part of its own (architectural) history at that time. This rich vein of world architecture inspired them with the will to develop a new architecture that was aware of its surroundings, to look for "architectural invention that would make every corner, every room something that it had certainly not been before ...(But) it is ... difficult to be really new, as there is so much knowledge of how things used to be even in negating them."[24] From then on, Szyszkowitz+Kowalski moved towards their own architecture with this prior knowledge in mind. The sense of revelling in construction that Michael Szyszkowitz had experienced in the Domenig/Huth practice helped to show them the way. He also indulges himself in this aspect on a small, experimental scale when working on Karla Kowalski's "Monsters"[25] (fig. 58). He gives these miraculous and fabulous creatures filigree support systems whose deceptive lightness seems to deny the objects' gravity. Their journey together was also guided by knowledge of how building and urban figures can overlap structurally, a key to their concern about the spatial organization of social relationships in terms of individual lives. Within all this complexity, the house appears once again as the nucleus of the social order, and as a space in which the people involved can adapt to that order. A whole range of influences flow between the treatment of urban space in housing estates and in private houses. This is a regularly observed phenomenon, and it indicates that the private house has acquired the status of model and experimental field for housing estate construction and for living in society in urban areas (figs. 2, 87, 90). Seen in this way, a private house is not an antisocial luxury, but a field in which the right to have a defined, generous space in which to live can be tested. This concept carries a particular aesthetic option within it, one that inclines towards symbolism in type and in architectural detail. This is part of an intellectual credo that does not see architecture as a function of diagrammatic decisions, but as a sign system made up of sensations, moods and memories.

[24] *Karla Kowalski, unveröffentlichtes Manuskript, o. S.* Karla Kowalski, unpublished manuscript, no p.
[25] *Siehe dazu: Walter Jens, in: Monster. Kowalskis Tiere mit Gestellen von Szyszkowitz, Berlin 1996.* Cf.: Walter Jens, in: Monster. Kowalskis Tiere mit Gestellen von Szyszkowitz, Berlin 1996.

> 44
Haus Bad Mergentheim, Bad Mergentheim 1991–1993, Entwurfsskizzen zum Hausduktus mit Wege- und Treppenführung House in Bad Mergentheim, Bad Mergentheim 1991–1993, design sketches for the outline of the house with paths and stairs

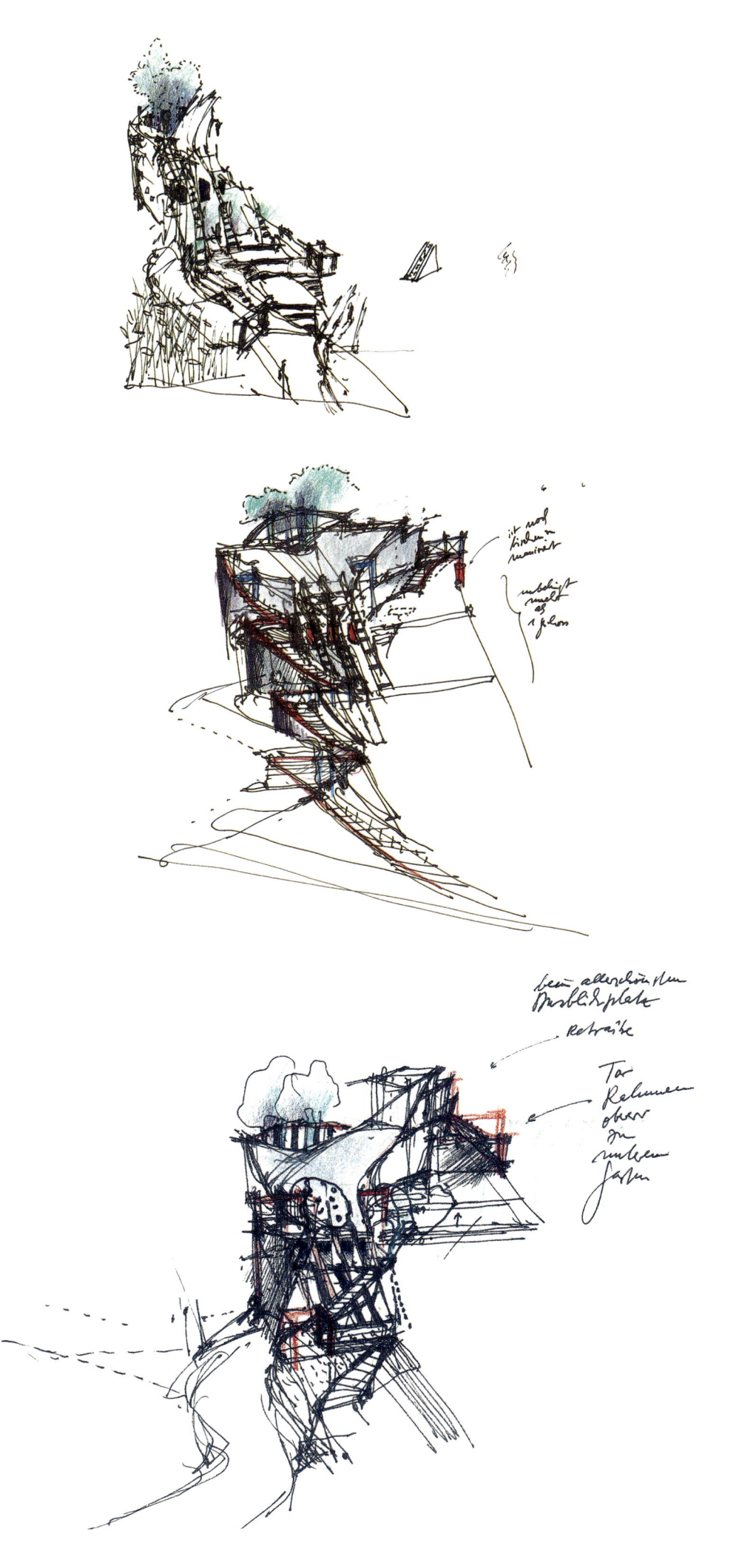

> 45
Haus Zusertal, Graz 1979–1981, Luftbild House in Zusertal, Graz 1979–1981, aerial photograph

[26] zit. nach Bauwelt 1983, Heft 30/31, S. 1224 (Haus Zusertal. Bauen in Landschaftsschutzgebieten). Quoted from Bauwelt, Heft 30/31, p. 1224 (Haus Zusertal. Bauen in Landschaftsschutzgebieten).

46 >>>
Haus Zusertal, Ansicht der Eingangsfassade, (s. S. 114) House in Zusertal, view of the entrance façade, (see p. 114)

Bühne und (T)Raum

Unweit des *Hauses über Graz* entsteht in den Jahren 1980/81 das *Haus Zusertal* (Abb. S. 114–119) auf einem landschaftlich ebenso reizvollen Areal wie das erste Haus sieben Jahre zuvor. Szyszkowitz+Kowalski müssen sich dort mit den Auflagen auseinandersetzen, die für Landschaftsgebiete dieser Art in der Steiermark gelten. Nach einem langwierigen Baugenehmigungsverfahren können sie ihren Entwurf durchsetzen, denn die zuständige Berufungsbehörde stellt fest: „Es darf daran erinnert werden, daß das Bild einer naturhaften Landschaft weder das Steildach, noch das Flachdach als wesentlichen Gestaltungsfaktor von Gebäuden verlangt oder ausschließt ... Ein typisches Villenviertel einer Stadt erfährt seine Prägung meistens durch die Individualität seiner Einzelobjekte, d. h. es ist der rechte Ort für Innovation."[26] Das viergeschossige Haus für einen Grazer Chirurgen und dessen Familie erscheint in der Tat ungewöhnlich, denn weder das Steil- noch das Flachdach schließt das Gebäude nach oben hin ab, vielmehr geschieht dies durch eine höhengestaffelte Dachlandschaft aus zwei auseinanderstrebenden Vierteltonnen mit dazwischenliegenden steilen Giebeldächern. Diese bewegte Dachformation reagiert auf die nahegelegene Gründerzeitvilla, die mit ihren Turmaufsätzen und herausgehoben Giebelelementen über die Baumspitzen lugt und in diesem differenzierten Schauspiel den *genius loci* bereits mitgeprägt hat (Abb. 47). Ihm erweist das *Zusertalhaus* in seiner prägnanten Dachsilhouette freundlich Reverenz. Der Leitgedanke dieser Figuration resultiert zudem aus der Anlage der Innenräume, die wie um die Mitte eines städtischen Zentrums gruppiert sind, dessen Mittelpunkt durch die zwei sich schneidenden Orientierungsachsen in Nord-Süd- und Ost-West-Ausrichtung definiert wird. Er tritt allerdings, so wie man es von der Vierung der sich kreuzenden Kirchenschiffe kennt, erst im Dachfirst in Erscheinung (Abb. 45). So wird in luftiger Höhe sichtbar, was als Konzentrationspunkt des darunterliegenden Baukörpers verborgen ist, eine offene Halle, die über zwei Stockwerke in die Höhe ragt und von einer u-förmig umlaufenden Galerie umfangen wird. Als Hohlkörper steckt sie

Stage space and dream space

The *House in Zusertal* (figs. 114–119) was built not far from the *House above Graz* in 1980/81 in a setting that is just as attractive as the one for the first house seven years before. Szyszkowitz+Kowalski had to deal with the rules that apply to landscapes of this kind in Styria. They managed to get their design accepted, after a long-drawn-out planning permission process. The relevant authorities stated: "It should be pointed out that the setting of a natural landscape neither demands nor rules out either a pitched roof or a flat roof as an essential design factor for buildings ... A typical villa quarter in a town usually acquires its character from the individuality of the single items in it, i.e. it is the appropriate place for innovation."[26] This four-storey house for a Graz surgeon and his family certainly does seem unusual, as it has neither a flat nor a pitched roof. Instead there is a roof landscape with various staggered heights, made up of two quarter barrels thrusting away from each other with steep gable roofs between them. This animated roof formation responds to the nearby 1870s villa, which peeps over the treetops with its towers and

> 47
Haus Zusertal, Blick über die Dachgeometrie zur benachbarten Villa House in Zusertal, view towards the neighbouring villa across the roof geometry

zwischen den Geschossen und eröffnet mit einer maximalen Höhe von 7.50 Metern im gläsernen Giebel den Blick in den Himmel (Abb. S. 115 rechts unten). Diese Halle erfüllt im Erdgeschoß die Verteilerfunktion zu den angelagerten Raumkompartimenten, zur abgeschlossenen Küche und dem offenen Raumfluß aus Eßplatz, Sitzecke und Musikzimmer. Die Schlafräume des Ehepaares und der vier Kinder liegen im oberen Geschoß. Mit dem Motiv der hohen, geschoßdurchstoßenden Halle führen Szyszkowitz+Kowalski einen Typus des Villenbaus in die Nachmoderne ein, der mit der Rezeption des antiken Atriumhauses und der palladianischen Villa im bürgerlichen Wohnen des 19. Jahrhunderts die Konzeption der zentralen Diele als dem „idealen Familienraum"[27] ausgebildet hatte. Im Haus Zusertal klingt dieser Raum des Familiären jedoch nur noch als Erinnerungspartikel an, er ist ephemer geworden und im offenen Grundriß zu einem Handlungsgefüge der Gleichzeitigkeiten im Familienverband transformiert. Dies ist nicht länger ein von patriarchalen Mustern durchzogener, zentraler Raum der Familie wie noch im 19. Jahrhundert, vielmehr symbolisiert dieser Hohlraum wie ein Innenhof die Idee des gemeinschaftlichen Lebens und aktiviert Assoziationen an die ehemals soziale Funktion des Zen-

emphasized gable elements, already making its own mark on the *genius loci* in this sophisticated play (fig. 47). The succinct roof silhouette of the *House in Zusertal* pays friendly homage to it. The guiding idea behind this figuration results from the arrangement of the rooms inside, which are grouped as if they were around the centre of a town, as defined by the two intersecting orientation axes running north-south and east-west. But this idea can only be discerned in the roof ridge, in a way we are familiar with from the crossing in a church (fig. 45). And so at a lofty height we see the concealed focal point of section of the building underneath, an open hall rising up through two storeys and contained by a U-shaped gallery. It fits between the floors as a cavity, and opens up a view of the sky at its maximum height of 7.5 metres in the glazed gable (fig. p. 115 right below). On the ground floor, this hall acts as a distributor for the attached spatial compartments, giving

[27] Wolfgang Brönner, Die bürgerliche Villa in Deutschland 1830–1890, Worms 1994, S. 47. Wolfgang Brönner, Die bürgerliche Villa in Deutschland 1830–1890, Worms 1994, p. 47.

> 48
Haus Zusertal, Blick in die Oberlichtkonstruktion der Terrasse House in Zusertal, view of the terrace skylight structure

49 >>>
Haus Zusertal, Innenansicht der Halle mit Blick in den Eßbereich und Garten, (s. S. 119) House in Zusertal, interior view of the hall looking into the dining area and garden (see p. 119)

> 50
Haus Zusertal, Erkerfenster mit Blick in den Garten House in Zusertal, Bay window with view into the garden

trums im gemeinschaftsbildenden Herd aus der Urgeschichte des menschlichen Wohnens.

In dieser Architekturkonzeption hat der leere Raum aber eine weiterreichende psychologische Wertigkeit, die in seiner beeindruckenden Höhe deutlich wird. Denn die Architekten verbinden mit dem gefaßten, hohen, leeren Raum die Vorstellung des „Gedankenluftraumes", der der schweifenden Phantasie im Blick zum Himmel das Gefühl des Unermeßlichen zurückgibt. Im *Haus im Zusertal* wird damit zum ersten Mal eine Architekturauffassung sichtbar und ein Wohnkonzept anschaulich, das zwar schon im *Grünen Haus* von 1978/79 angeklungen war, aber auf Grund des bescheideneren Wohnbedarfs jener Auftraggeber noch nicht ausgereift in Erscheinung treten konnte. Es ist die Idee der Verbindung einer „Psychologie des Hauses" mit einer Symbol- und Archetypenlehre, die der Architektur von Szyszkowitz+Kowalski seitdem das unvergleichliche Gepräge gegeben hat. Gaston Bachelards in den siebziger Jahren des 20. Jahrhunderts erstmals in deutscher Sprache erschienene und inzwischen zum Standardwerk einer Phänomenlogie der poetischen Einbildungskraft avancierte „Poetik des Raumes" führt uns heute wie ein Ciceronetext durch die Semantik dieser Häuser. Anhand dieser Schrift läßt sich die Poesie erschließen, die Karla Kowalski und Michael Szyszkowitz mit ihrem theoretischen Rückgriff auf die Psychologie C.G. Jungs Raum und Gestalt werden lassen. Mit Jung teilen sie nämlich die

access to the enclosed kitchen and the open spatial flow of dining area, sitting corner and music room. The master bedroom and the four children's bedrooms are on the upper floor. By choosing to use a high hall thrusting up through both floors, Szyszkowitz+Kowalski are introducing a villa type to late Modernism that started in middle class living in the 19th century with its response to the ancient house with atrium and the Palladian villa and the concept of the central hall as the "ideal family space".[27] But in the *House in Zusertal* this family space is merely an echoing fragment of memory. It has become ephemeral, transformed into a structure within the open ground plan where the family unit can act out its simultaneous events. It is no longer a central family space shot through with patriarchal patterns, as it still was in the 19th century. This cavity, like an inner courtyard, symbolizes the idea of communal life and triggers associations with the former social function of life centred around the hearth, the cradle of community and an echo of the primeval history of human habitation.

But this empty space is of more far-reaching psychological importance in this architectural conception, as its impressive height shows. The architects associate the idea of "air space for the mind" with this contained, high empty space, restoring a sense of the immeasurable to the soaring imagination as it looks towards heaven. So the *House in Zusertal* is the first visible demonstration of a view of architecture and a living concept that was hinted at in the 1978/79 *Green House* but did not mature fully because of the clients' more modest needs for their home. It is the idea of combining a "psychology of the house" with a theory of symbols and archetypes that has made Szyszkowitz+Kowalski's architecture unique ever since.

> 51
Haus Harmisch, Harmisch-Kohfidisch (Burgenland) 1986–1988, Ansicht von Nordwesten Harmisch House, Harmisch-Kohfidisch (Burgenland) 1986–1988, view from the north-west

> 52
Haus Harmisch, Blick von der Galerie ins Erdgeschoß und in die Oberlichtkonstruktion der Halle Harmisch House, view of the ground floor and hall skylight structure from the gallery

Auffassung, daß die symbolische Bilderwelt in unseren Erinnerungen und Träumen angelegt sei, die in der Interpretationsarbeit der Architekten vom Tagträumerischen in die Helligkeit des Bewußtseins gelangen.[28] Mit dem Hinweis auf die Sehnsuchtsmetaphorik der Romantiker, die im Bild der blauen Blume des Novalis den Primat der selbstbezogenen Vernunft relativierten, richtet sich ihr Blick auf den Raum der Architekturgeschichte wie auf einen Fundus an vieldeutigen kulturellen Symbolen. Es ist mithin der Versuch, die „verwischten Bilder" wie ein Analytiker interpretierend zu aktivieren, um sie in der Symbolik von Archetypen anschaulich werden zu lassen. Als ein solcher Interpretationsversuch muß das Motiv der Halle auch gelesen werden, denn sie symbolisiert das Haus als „vertikales Wesen" zwischen Keller und Dach, worin „der Raum der Innerlichkeit"[29] zur Grenze des Unermeßlichen erhoben erscheint. Die Bedeutung dieses erhabenen Grenzwertes hat Bachelard benannt: „Das eigentliche *Produkt* auf diesem Wege der Unermeßlichkeitsträumerei ist das Bewußtsein des Größerwerdens. Wir fühlen uns zum Range eines bewundernden Wesens erhoben."[30]

Dem individualpsychologischen Effekt jenes „Gedankenluftraumes" ist darüberhinaus eine sozialpsychologische Komponente zueigen, der man im *Haus Harmisch* (Abb. S. 132–139), das auf einem leicht ansteigenden, offenen Gelände im Burgenland 1988 errichtet wurde, abermals begegnet. Diese großzügige, dreigeschossige Villa weist im ersten Geschoß gleichfalls eine zentrale, über zwei Geschosse geführte, galeriegesäumte Halle auf, die durch eine Glaskonstruktion geschlossen ist und an der höchsten Stelle auf die beeindruckende Höhe von 9.00 Metern emporragt (Abb. 52).

Gaston Bachelard's "The Poetics of Space" (Orion Press, 1964), published in German in the 1970s, has since become the standard work on the phenomenology of the poetic imagination. It now serves as our cicerone through the semantics of these houses, giving us access to the poetry that Karla Kowalski and Michael Szyszkowitz endowed with form by their theoretical recourse to the psychology of C. G. Jung. They share Jung's view that the symbolic world of images is embedded in our memories and dreams. The architects as interpreters move them from the realm of daydreams into the bright light of consciousness.[28] They turn their attention to the expanse of architectural history as a fund of ambiguous cultural symbols, alluding to the metaphorical system of longing created by the Romantics, who introduced a subtly changed view of the primacy of self-referential reason in Novalis's image of the "Blaue Blume". Thus they are attempting to activate and interpret the "blurred images" analytically, bringing them to life in the symbolism of archetypes. The hall motif should also be read as an interpretative attempt of this kind, as it symbolizes the house as a vertical being between cellar and roof, in which the space of inwardness[29] seems raised to the limits of the immeasurable. Bachelard identified the significance of this sublime limit: The actual product on this dream path to immeasurability is the awareness of becoming greater. We feel ourselves raised to the rank of an admiring being.[30]

Harmisch House (figs. p. 132–139) was built in 1988 on a slightly rising, open site in Burgenland. Here again we come across an additional socio-psychological component, over and above the individual psychological effect of the "air-space

[28] Siehe dazu: C.G. Jungs Buch: Der Mensch und seine Symbole, das er mit Koautoren erstmals 1964 veröffentlicht hat. Es gehört zu den erfolgreichsten Büchern seiner Sparte, das in deutscher Übersetzung inzwischen in der 15. Auflage vorliegt. Zürich, Düsseldorf 1999. „Das, was wir Symbol nennen, ist ein Ausdruck, ein Name oder auch ein Bild, das uns im täglichen Leben vertraut sein kann, das aber zusätzlich zu seinem konventionellen Sinn noch besondere Nebenbedeutungen hat." C.G.Jung, Symbole und Traumdeutung. Ein erster Zugang zum Unbewußten, Düsseldorf, Zürich 1998, S.13. Zur Explikation des Archetypus und zum Begriff des „kollektiven Unbewußten" siehe: Cf. C.G.Jung, Archetypen, München 2001. C.G. Jung's book: Der Mensch und seine Symbole, which he published with co-authors for the first time in 1964, is one of the most successful books of its kind. The German version already runs to 15 editions, Zurich, Düsseldorf 1999. "What we call a symbol is an expression, a name or also an image that can be familiar to us in everyday life, but in addition to its conventional meaning it also has special additional meanings." C.G.Jung, Symbole und Traumdeutung. Ein erster Zugang zum Unbewußten, Düsseldorf, Zurich 1998, p.13.
[29] Gaston Bachelard, Poetik des Raumes, München 1975, S. 233. Gaston Bachelard, The Poetics of Space, Boston 1994.
[30] Gaston Bachelard, Poetik des Raumes, München 1975, S. 224. Op. cit.

> 53
Haus Harmisch, Luftbild Harmisch House, aerial photograph

> 54
Haus am Ruckerlberg, Graz 1998–2002, Luftbild House on Ruckerlberg, Graz 1998–2002, aerial view

> 55
Haus am Plattenweg, Graz 1994–1996, Blick durch die Raumfolgen des Wohngeschosses mit Galerie House on Plattenweg, Graz 1994–1996, view through the flowing space in the living area with gallery

Dieser zentrale Lebensbereich des Hauses wird dergestalt zum Ereignisraum, der den repräsentativen Effekt einer bel étage in der Weitläufigkeit der Höhen- und Tiefenentwicklung des Hauses geradezu dramaturgisch in Szene setzt. Der „Rang des bewundernden Wesens" wird vom Gestus der gesellschaftlichen Würde der Bewohner berührt, so daß die räumliche Gebärde in die Harmonie eines räumlichen Handlungsgefüges aus distanzierender Großzügigkeit und ungezwungener Privatheit einführt.

Das Wechselspiel von repräsentativer Distanz und privater Nähe innerhalb eines Hauses hat seit diesem Projekt die Villenarchitektur von Szyszkowitz+Kowalski begleitet. Auch im *Haus am Plattenweg* (Abb. 4), das in den neunziger Jahren wieder im Weichbild von Graz entstanden ist und in dem wie in keinem anderen ihrer Kaskadenhäuser die Linearität der Raumfolgen in schwingende, dem Gelände folgende Stufen aufgelöst erscheint, gibt es diesen hohen, jenen Hallen vergleichbaren Raum, denn der Wohnraum dieses Hauses reicht gleichfalls über zwei Geschosse und schwingt sich zu einer lichten Höhe von 5.70 Metern auf (Abb. 55). Allerdings dominiert in der Höhenentwicklung dieses Innenraumes nicht mehr das Thema der ausgeschiedenen Halle, vielmehr nähert er sich dem Zentralraumgedanken an, denn die unterschiedlichen, gemeinschaftlichen Funktionen gehen ineinander über, und nur die Küche bleibt den Blicken der Besucher verborgen.

Daß gerade dieser Raum der häuslichen Arbeit zu einem integralen Bestandteil der kommunikativen Nähe avancieren könnte, um gleichsam als Akteur auf der Bühne des alltäglichen Lebens die Rolle des dienstbaren Geistes in aller Öffentlichkeit zu spielen, diese häufig diskutierte Idee haben Szyszkowitz+Kowalski jüngst im *Haus am Ruckerlberg* (Abb. S. 206–213) realisiert. Dem linsenförmigen Grundriß des Hauses ist nämlich ein Zentralraum eingeschrieben, der mit sei-

of the mind". This spacious, three-storey villa also has a central hall fringed with galleries, rising in this case from the first to the second floor. It is covered by a glass structure and at it the highest point reaches an impressive 9 metres (fig. 52). This central living area becomes an eventful space. It produces the prestigious effect of a *bel étage*, staged almost theatrically within the house's sweeping height and depth. The "rank of an admiring being" is touched by the occupants' social dignity. The spatial gesture thus leads into the harmony of a spatial structure combining dispassionate generosity and informal privacy.

The interplay of prestigious aloofness and private proximity within a house has been part of Szyszkowitz+Kowalski's architecture every since this project. The *Haus on Plattenweg* (fig. 4) was built in the 1990s, again on the outskirts of Graz. Here as in no other of their cascade houses the linear quality of the spatial sequences is dissolved into curving steps following the lines of the terrain. Again there is a high space, comparable with the halls: the living room in this house also rises through two floors, soaring to a headroom of 5.7 metres (fig. 55). But the idea of the separate hall no longer dominates the elevation of this interior, which is much closer to the notion of a central space. The different social functions in fact merge, and only the kitchen is hidden away.

There has been much discussion about whether the kitchen, as a space for domestic work, could become an integral component within a scheme of communicative proximity – an actor in the theatre of everyday life, playing the part of the servant spirit, fully exposed to public gaze. Szyszkowitz+ Kowalski put this concept into practice recently in their *House*

> 58
Turm Fölling, Graz 1994–1996, Gartenansicht Tower in Fölling, Graz 1994–1996, garden view

ner beeindruckenden, maximalen Höhe von 6.10 Metern die von einander abgegrenzten Funktionen der dienenden Hausarbeit und des bedienten Wohnens ohne trennende Wände in sich vereint. Die Flächengröße und die Höhe dieses Zentralraumes verhindert im Zusammenspiel mit den Möglichkeiten der Querlüftung olfaktorische Belästigungen und eröffnet im Wechsel der breiten und sehr schmalen hohen Fensterflächen zugleich den visuellen Kontakt zum Garten. In der Höhe des Zentralraumes mit der geschlossenen, undurchdringlichen Decke ist die Beziehung zum Unermeßlichen gewissermaßen in das Innere des Hauses selbst zurückgekehrt.

Das Fremde und die Konvention

Kein Bautypus repräsentiert diesen metaphysischen Überhang eindrücklicher als der Turm, und tatsächlich haben Szyszkowitz+Kowalski nahezu gleichzeitig mit dem *Haus am Plattenweg* in Graz-Mariatrost ein solches Bauwerk errichtet. Als Anbau zu einem Einfamilienhaus aus den sechziger Jahren konzipierten sie einen *Bibliotheksturm* (Abb. S. 180–183), der nicht nur der stattlichen Sammlung der Bücher, sondern auch den privaten Arbeitsräumen der Autraggeber Platz geben mußte. Die vertikale Erschließung über die großzügige Treppe mit Richtungswechsel bildet die zentrale Bewegungsfigur zwischen den Geschossen, die vom Rund der Decken-

on Ruckerlberg (figs. p. 206–213). The lenticular ground plan of this house has a central space inscribed into it. It is an impressive 6.1 metres high, and brings together the separate functions of servant space for domestic work and served space for living without any separating walls. The large area and height of this central space, along with the possibility of transverse ventilation, make it possible to avoid unpleasant smells, and the alternating wide and very narrow windows make the garden part of the visual experience. The height of this central space with its closed, impenetrable ceiling means that contact with the immeasurable has returned to the interior of the house to a certain extent.

The alien and convention

There is no building type that presents this metaphysical surplus more impressively than the tower, and Szyszkowitz+ Kowalski did indeed build one at almost the same time they built their *House on Plattenweg* in Mariatrost, Graz. They devised a *library tower* (figs. p. 180–183) as an extension to a sixties family house, intended to house an imposing collection of books and also the clients' private workrooms. Vertical access via the generous staircase, turning back in itself once, establishes the central figure for movement between the floors, which conclude in the circle of the ceiling vaulting. "What a great dream principle for intimacy – a vaulted

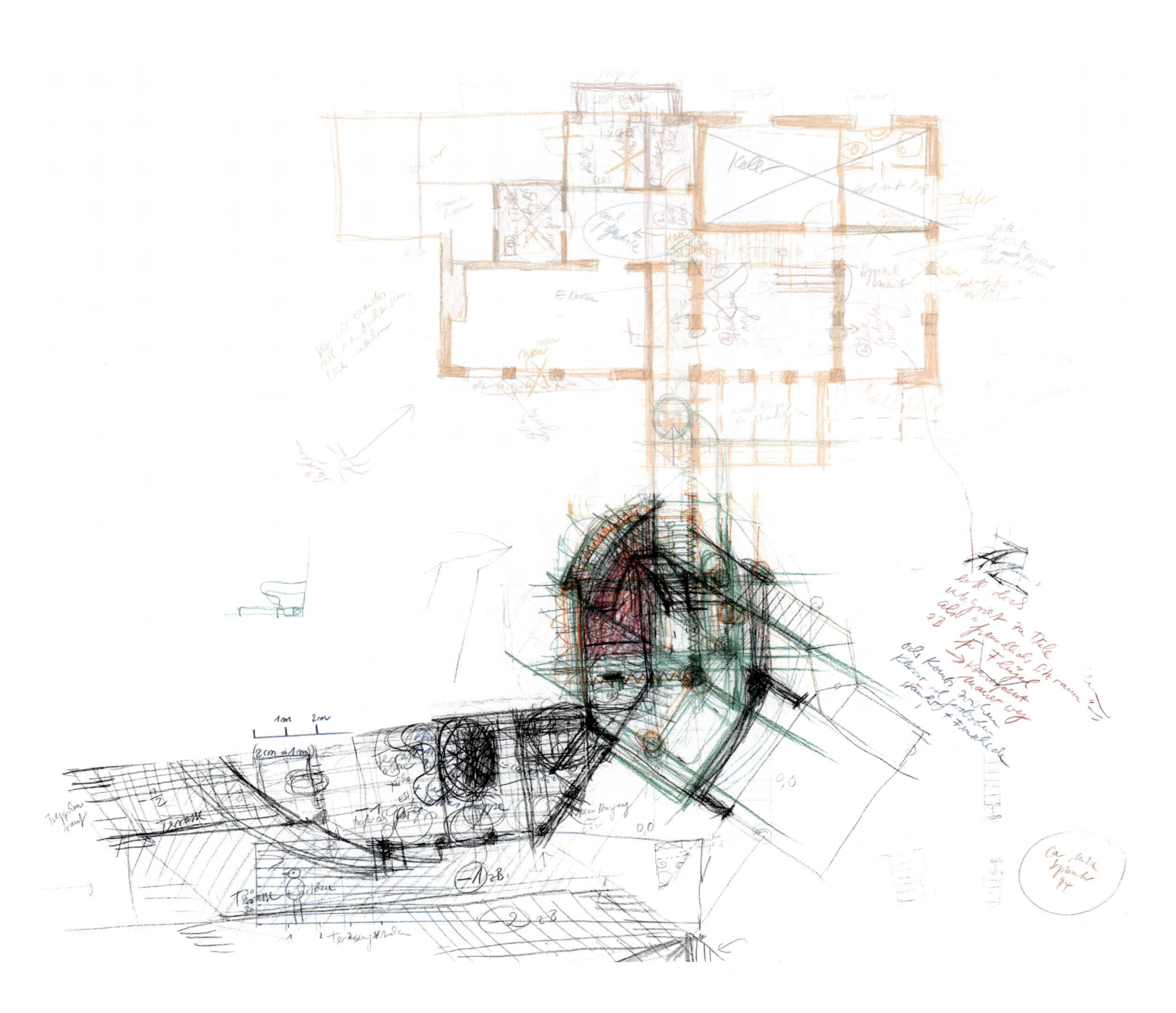

> 57
Turm Fölling, Graz 1994–1996, Entwurfsskizze mit Einliegerwohnung Tower in Fölling,
Graz 1994–1996, design sketch with granny flat

58 >>>
Turm Fölling, Innenansicht mit „Monster oder Kleinem Schwein" von Kowalski auf einem Gestell von Szyszkowitz (s. S. 180) Tower in Fölling, interior view with "Monster or Little Pig" by Kowalski on a stand by Szyszkowitz (see p. 180)

[31] op. cit. Anm. 29, S. 55. *Op. cit. see ref. 29, p. 55*

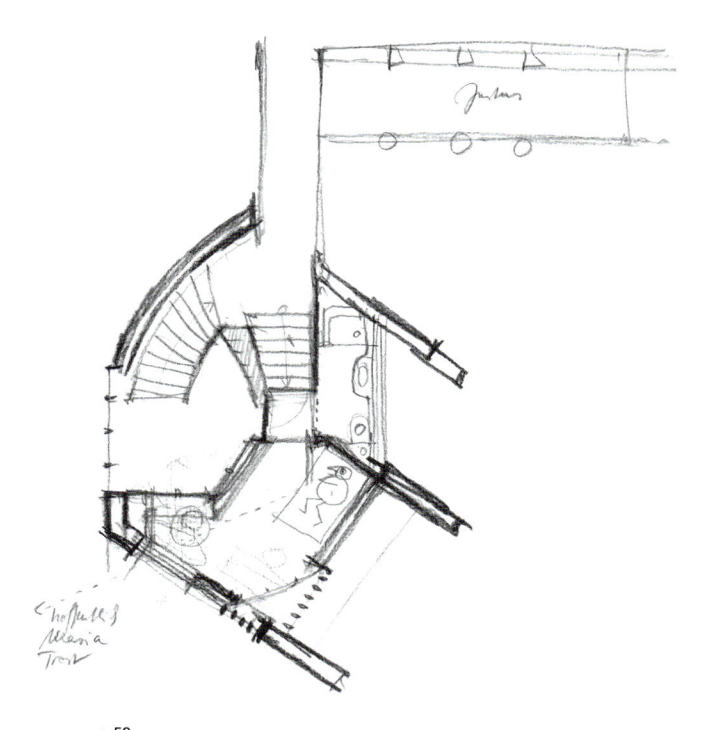

> 59
Turm Fölling, Grundrißskizze des Obergeschosses mit Schlafplatz und Bad Tower in Fölling, upper floor plan sketch with sleeping area and bathroom

wölbung abgeschlossen werden. „Welches große Traumprinzip der Intimität – eine gewölbte Decke. Ohne Ende reflektiert sie die Innerlichkeit in ihrem Zentrum"[31], so Bachelard, dem im Typus des Turmes die „Vertikalität des Menschlichen" zum poetischen Bild ohnegleichen wird. Der Gestus des Introvertierten prägt die Architektur des Gebäudes, denn zur Straße hin ist es nur durch schmale, umlaufende Fensterbänder belichtet, so daß der Turm nahezu uneinsehbar verschlossen erscheint. Zum Garten ist das Gebäude hingegen über die gesamte Höhe in Glas aufgelöst, eine transluzide Wand, die das Sonnenlicht in den Raum fließen läßt. So erscheint der *Bibliotheksturm in Fölling* nicht nur als Symbol der kontemplativen Konzentration, sondern ebenso als ausdrucksstarke Umfriedung der Bewohner, die im Schutzraum des Turmes die Distanz zur Umgebung der Kleinhaussiedlung suchten und im Blick über den Garten die Ferne, um ihren Fluchtgedanken freien Lauf zu lassen. Mit der gebotenen Ironie haben Szyszkowitz+Kowalski diesem Wunsch nach dem anderen, fernen Ort einen Orientierungspunkt der Nähe eröffnet, denn ein kleiner Balkon im Dachbereich lenkt den Blick über das schmale Tal zur gegenüberliegenden barocken Wallfahrtskirche, die mit ihrem Namen, Maria Trost, Versöhnung verspricht (Abb. 59).

Das Haus mit dem schützenden Giebel, die zum Himmel geöffnete Halle, das gewölbte Dach des Turmes, es sind dies wahrlich archetypische Elemente der Architektur, die der Traumarbeit mit ihren Raumsymbolen entsprechen. Aber wie variantenreich wird diese eindeutige, kanonisierte Syntax in eine neue Architektursprache überführt, wenn, wie im *Zusertalhaus* (Abb. S. 114), das Sprossenfenster mit der Verglasung der Fußbodenecken im Obergeschoß des Hauses verknüpft wird, wenn der Giebel hoch oben eingezwängt zwi-

ceiling. It is an infinite reflection of the inwardness at its centre,"[31] says Bachelard, for whom the tower as a type becomes an unparalleled, poetic image of the "vertical quality of humanity". The whole building is imbued with the gestures of introversion. On the street side it is lit only by narrow, ribbon windows, so that its looks as though it is entirely impossible to look into from the outside. But on the garden side the whole height of the building dissolves into glass, a translucent wall that allows the sunlight to pour into the space. This means that the *tower* is not just a symbol of contemplative concentration, but also an impressive enclosure for the occupants. They can distance themselves from the surroundings of this estate of little houses in the protective space of the tower, and by looking far out over the garden they can allow their thoughts to soar freely. Deploying the appropriate irony, Szyszkowitz+Kowalski have confronted this desire for a different, distant place with a nearby landmark: a small balcony in the roof area directs the eye across the narrow valley to the Baroque pilgrimage church opposite. Its name, Maria Trost, offers a promise of reconciliation (fig. 59).

A house with a protecting gable, a hall that is open to the sky, a tower with a vaulted roof: all these truly are archetypal elements of architecture appropriate to dream-work, with its spatial symbols. But the architects translate this unambiguous, canonized syntax into a new architectural language using a great range of variety: In the *House in Zusertal* (fig. p. 114), for example, when the window with glazing bars is linked with the glass in the corners of the floor in the upper storey

> 60
Turm Fölling, Graz 1994–1996, Gartenansicht mit Wandscheiben
Tower in Föllig, Graz 1994–1996, garden view with walls

61 >>>
Haus in Maria Enzersdorf, Maria Enzersdorf bei Wien 1991–1994, Gartenansicht mit gerundeten Wandscheiben (s. S. 165)   House in Maria Enzersdorf, Maria Enzersdorf near Vienna 1991–1994, garden view with rounded walls (see p. 165)

schen Tonnen die Fassade des Hauses zwar akzentuiert, aber als Zeichen des traditionellen Bauens in Österreich nicht mehr lesbar bleibt (Abb. S. 114), wenn die Baukörper und Dächer, wie *im Haus in Maria Enzersdorf* (Abb. S. 164–169) bei Wien fragmentiert sind oder wie im *Moosburger Haus* (Abb. S. 189 oben) in Kärnten gar zu flattern scheinen! Wieviel Erinnerungswert bleibt erhalten, wenn die schützenden Wände in rhythmisch kantige Bewegungsfolgen versetzt werden, wie dies im *Bad Mergentheimer Haus* (Abb. 66) der Fall ist, und was bleibt identifizierbar, wenn Fassaden einen konvexen Baukörper umfassen, der, wie im *Haus am Ruckerlberg* (Abb. S. 207), ein „Wohlgefallen" düpiert, das gewohnt ist, *das* Haus als ein rechteckiges Volumen mit vier, statt zwei Schauseiten aufzufassen?[32]

Man kann diese Auflösungen und Brüche der klassischen *kanonices* mit den Dynamisierungsformeln der Barockarchitektur vergleichen, doch bliebe diese Parallelisierung in einer formalisierten Analogie befangen, wenngleich Szyszkowitz+Kowalski dieser Epoche durchaus gewogen sind. Ihre Architektur ist vielmehr ein kalkuliertes Spiel mit Überlagerungen unterschiedlicher Motivlagen und Bedeutungsebenen, in denen vertraute Typologien zwar aufgegriffen werden und auch identifizierbar bleiben, aber immer so, daß sie als Konventionen zugleich außer Kraft gesetzt werden. Denn der Kon-

of the house, when the gable, crammed in up at the top between the barrels does accentuate the façade of the house, but is no longer intelligible as a sign of traditional building in Austria (fig. p. 114), when, as in the *House in Maria Enzersdorf* (figs. p. 164–169) near Vienna, the sections of the building and the roofs are fragmented or even seem to flutter, as in the *House in Moosburg* (fig. p. 189) in Kärnten! How much memory survives when the protecting walls are shifted in rhythmically angular sequences of movement, as in the *House in Bad Mergentheim* (fig. 66), and what remains identifiable when façades enclose a convex building volume that, as in the *House on Ruckerlberg* (fig. p. 207), refuses to fulfill the promise of an aesthetic satisfaction that is based on seeing the house as a rectangular volume with four rather than two show sides?[32]

It is possible to compare these dissolutions and transgressions of the classical canons with the formulas for greater dynamism Baroque architecture devised, but this parallel remains a mere formal analogy, even though Szyszkowitz+Kowalski are favourably inclined towards this period. It is much more that their architecture is a calculated game in which different layers of motifs and planes of meaning overlap. Familiar typologies are adopted and also remain identifiable, but always in such a way that they at the same time lose their power as conventions. The context in which the architectural elements and detailed forms have to assert their

[32] *Szyszkowitz+Kowalski hatten im Baugenehmigungsverfahren Schwierigkeiten diesen Entwurf durchzusetzen, da man sich nur schwer darauf einzulassen verstand, daß das Haus nicht vier, sondern nur zwei Fassaden hat.* Szyszkowitz+Kowalski had trouble in getting planning permission for this design, as the authorities found it very difficult to accept that the house has only two façades, and not four.

63 >>>
Haus am Ruckerlberg, Graz 1998–2002, Wandrundung (s. S. 207) House on Ruckerlberg, Graz 1998–2002, rounded wall (see p. 207)

> 62
Haus am Plattenweg, Graz 1994–1996, Wandrundung mit Fensterband zur Küche House on Plattenweg, Graz 1994–1996, rounded wall with continuous windows to the kitchen

> 64
Stadtvillen Mariagrün, Graz 1993–1997, Gartenansicht mit Wandscheiben Town houses in Mariagrün, Graz 1993–1997, garden view with walls

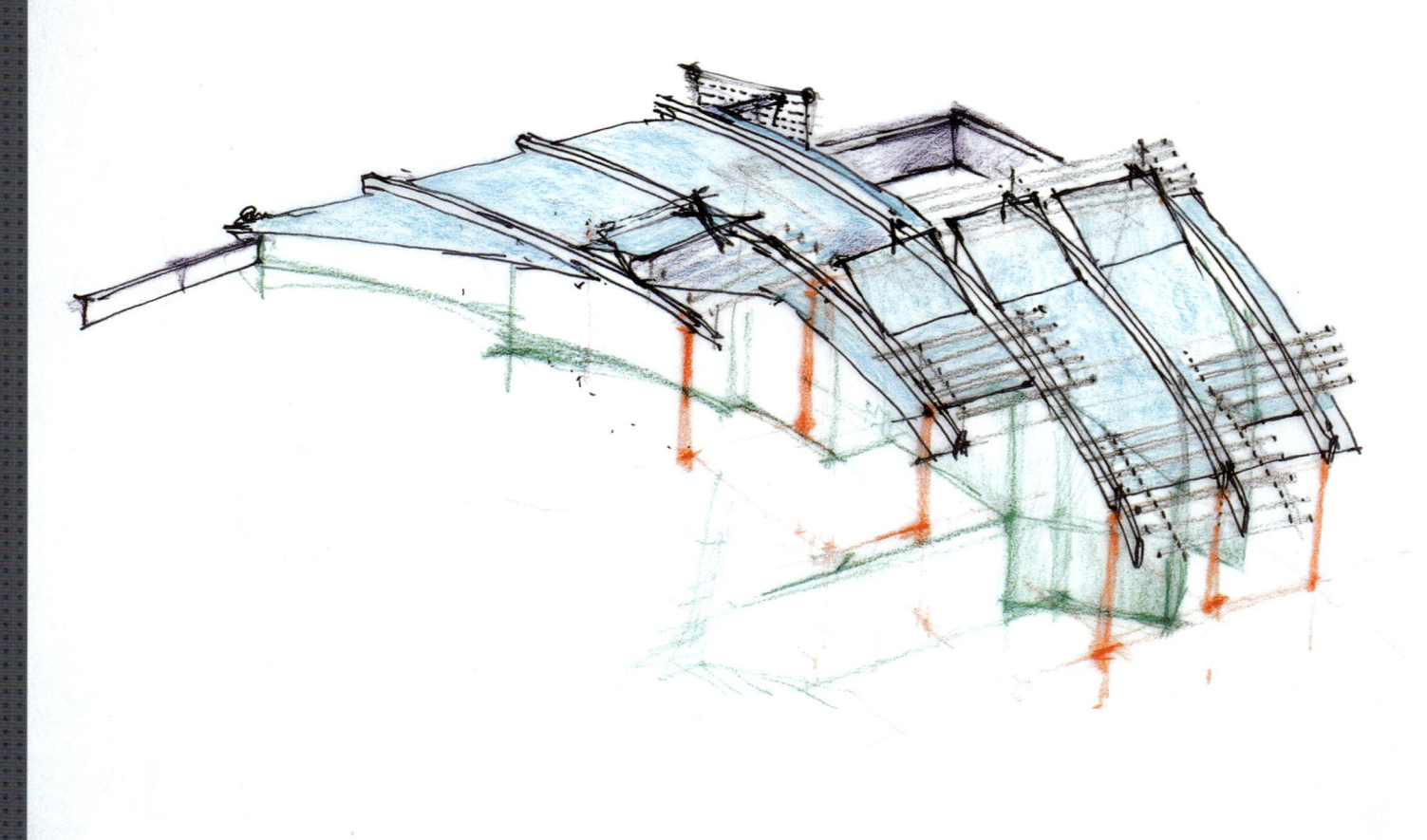

> 65
Haus in Moosburg, Moosburg bei Klagenfurt 1995–1996, isometrische Skizze der Dachkonstruktion House in Moosburg, Moosburg near Klagenfurt 1995–1996, isometric sketch of the roof structure

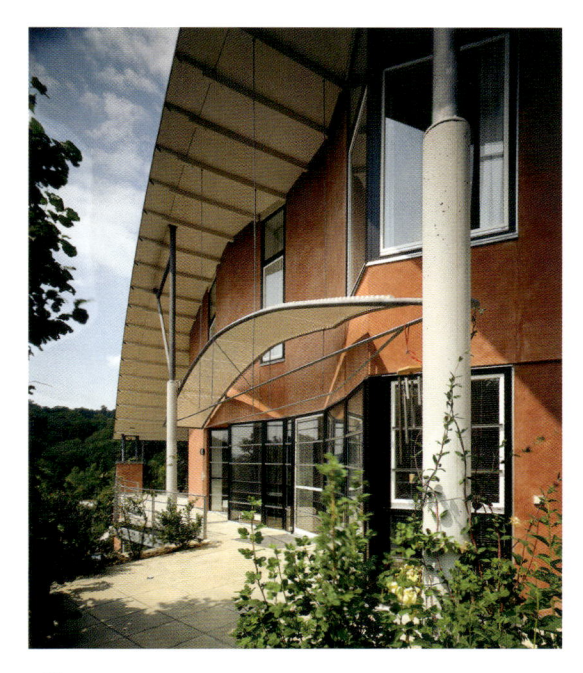

> 66
Haus in Bad Mergentheim, Bad Mergentheim 1991–1993, Ansicht der Terrassenfassade mit abgehängtem Vordach House in Bad Mergentheim, Bad Mergentheim 1991–1993, view of the terrace façade with suspended canopy

text, in dem die architektonischen Elemente und Detailformen ihre Position behaupten müssen, widerspricht sowohl in der Gestaltung als auch in der Materialverwendung den traditionellen Verfahren. Erkennbar bleiben einzig Facetten von Typologien und Bruchstücke archetypischer Bilder, die ihre Semantik allein im Erinnerungsvermögen des Betrachters realisieren. Deshalb gibt es in ihren Häusern auch jene zuweilen verblüffende Gleichzeitigkeit von Ordnungsmustern, die, wie die Symmetrie, der klassischen Tradition zugeschrieben werden, und einer Symbolik, die dieses Ordnungsgefüge sogleich zu konterkarieren scheint. Der Betrachter dieser Bauten erkennt Vertrautes und wird ihm doch zugleich entfremdet; so wird, wie im *Föllinger Turm*, geheimnisvoll, was eindeutig zu sein schien.

Dieses Verfahren ist in den Bauten aus den neunziger Jahren vielfach durchgespielt worden und hat im *Haus am Plattenweg* (Abb. S. 170–179) eine geradezu idealtypische Lösung gefunden. Auf Wunsch der Bauherren ist dieses Haus ein Backsteinbau, es liegt auf einem sanft abfallenden Gelände mit einem herrlichen alten Baumbestand. Um den großartigen Eindruck des über viele Jahre kultivierten Parks zu erhalten, haben die Architekten das Haus an die seitliche Grundstücksgrenze gerückt. Wie im *Haus über Graz* und im unteren Wiener *Haus in Hietzing*, folgt auch hier das Gebäude dem sanft abfallenden Hang und vollführt darin eine Assimilation mit der Landschaft, die die Konvention des orthogonal definierten Volumens nun weitgehend durchbricht. Die Diagonale der Wände steigert die Dramatik des Gefälles und die Modulation der Dachhaut mit den eingeschnittenen Terrassen verleihen dem Haus eine Dynamik, die es im Wechsel mit diesen Plateaus gleichsam zum Spiegel der Geländekonturen werden läßt. Das *Haus am Plattenweg* reagiert auf den Hang,

position contradicts the traditional processes both in terms of design and in the materials used. All that can still be recognized are facets of typologies and fragments of archetypal images whose semantics come into play only in the observer's memory. For this reason, there is in their houses often an astonishing simultaneity of ordering patterns, which, like symmetry, are ascribed to the classical tradition, and of a symbolism that seems to immediately run counter to this ordering structure. Anyone looking at these buildings recognizes something familiar, but is alienated from it at the same time; thus, as in the case of the *Tower in Fölling*, things which seemed unequivocal become mysterious.

This process went through a number of versions in the nineties' buildings, finding an almost ideal-typical solution in the *House on Plattenweg* (figs. p. 170–179). This house is in brick, at the client's request. It is set on a gently sloping site, with splendid old trees. To maintain the magnificent impression given by this park, which has been cultivated for many years, the architects have shifted the house to the very edge of the plot. As in the *House above Graz* and the lower *House in Hietzing* in Vienna, here too the building follows the gentle slope. It is thus assimilated with the landscape in a way that largely breaks through the convention of a volume defined by right angles. The diagonal of the walls intensifies the drama of the slope, and the modulation of the roof skin with incised terraces gives the house in the interplay with these plateaux a dynamic quality that makes it reflect the contours of the plot. The *House on Plattenweg* responds to the

> 67
Haus am Plattenweg, Graz 1994–1996, Luftbild House on Plattenweg, Graz 1994–1996, aerial photograph

> 68
Haus am Plattenweg, Graz 1994–1996, Dachaufbau der Sauna
House on Plattenweg, Graz 1994–1996, sauna as rooftop structure

es wird zur Landschaft und wie diese bebaubar ist, so auch das „Gelände" des Hauses (Abb. 67): Den Wunsch des Bauherrn, einen Rekreationsbereich mit Sauna zur Verfügung zu haben, interpretierten Szyszkowitz+Kowalski in diesem Sinne. Auf die höchste Erhebung des Gebäudes, gleichsam auf dessen Kuppe, haben die Architekten ein kleines, hell abgesetztes Volumen gesetzt, das von der Straße aus unscheinbar bleibt, aber vom Innenbereich des Parks als eigenständiger Baukörper sichtbar wird (Abb. 68). Wie ein kleines Häuschen steht es auf dem künstlichen Plateau des Gebäudes, ein Solitär, der die Konturen eines Giebeldaches aufgreift, wie es dem kollektiven Bewußtsein von Kinderhand gezeichnet durchaus vertraut und im Sinne C. G. Jungs als Archetypus lebendig ist. Man erreicht diesen Aufbau über einen internen Aufzug und tritt auf eine große Terrasse, die wie die Aussichtsplattform eines Berggipfels das Panorama der Südsteiermark eröffnet.

Dieses Verfahren, bekannte Muster der Architektur zwar aufzugreifen und sie durch eine ungewöhnliche Kontextualisierung gleichzeitig fremd erscheinen zu lassen, ist in diesem repräsentativen Einfamilienhaus zu wahrer Meisterschaft entwickelt worden. So ruft das Haus in der Mauerrundung der Wand zur Straße hin das Bild des undurchdringlichen Turmes ab, sobald man sich jedoch der Villa über die Zufahrt nähert, verfliegt der Charakter des Verschlossenen in einem wohldosierten Kontrast von vertikalen Fensterformen. Man erblickt Wände, deren Schichtung die Tektonik des Mauerwerksbaus demonstrieren und, wie in der nordöstlichen Fassade, sogar das Treppengiebelmotiv der nordeuropäischen Backsteingotik andeuten (Abb. 70). Doch dieser Wandver-

slope, it becomes landscape, and just as this can be cultivated, so can the "terrain" of the house (fig. 67): Szyszkowitz+Kowalski interpreted the client's request for a recreation area with sauna in this spirit. The architects placed a small volume, distinct in its lightness, at the highest point of the building, on its hilltop, as it were. This volume is inconspicuous when seen from the street, but it is visible as an independent entity from the inner area of the park (fig. 68). It stands on the building's artificial plateau like a little cottage, a solitaire adopting the outline of a gable roof, familiar to the collective consciousness from children's drawings, and flourishing as an archetype as identified by C. G. Jung. This additional building is reached by an internal lift and a large terrace that opens up the panorama of southern Styria like a viewing platform on a mountaintop.

This process of taking up familiar architectural patterns while at the same time alienating them by placing them in an unusual context has been developed to the point of true mastery in this impressive family house. The rounded wall on the street side evokes the image of an impregnable tower, but as soon as you move up the drive to the villa the feeling of being shut out evaporates in the carefully judged contrast made by vertical windows. You start to see walls whose layering demonstrates the tectonics of brickwork, and on the north-eastern façade even hint at the stepped gables of northern European brick Gothic (fig. 70). But this wall for-

> 69
Haus am Plattenweg, Dachterrasse mit Blick in die nordwestliche Steiermark
House on Plattenweg, roof terrace with view of north-western Styria

[33] Frank Werner, Wolkenkuckucksheim in Gelsenkrichen. Anmerkungen zu einer „unmöglichen" Wohnsiedlung der Architekten Szyszkowitz+Kowalski im Rahmen der IBA Emscher Park, Haus der Architektur Baudokumentation 16, Graz 1999, S. 32. *Frank Werner, Wolkenkuckucksheim in Gelsenkrichen. Anmerkungen zu einer 'unmöglichen' Wohnsiedlung der Architekten Szyszkowitz+Kowalski im Rahmen der IBA Emscher Park, Haus der Architektur Baudokumentation 16, Graz 1999, p. 32.*

70 >>>
Haus am Plattenweg, Seitenansicht von Nordosten (s. S. 171)   House on Plattenweg, side view from the north-east (see p. 171)

>71
Curzio Malaparte mit Alberto Libera, Casa Malaparte, Capri 1938–1942, Ansicht bzw. Aufsicht mit Treppengiebel   Curzio Malaparte with Alberto Libera, Casa Malaparte, Capri 1938–1942, view/top view with stepped gable

band weist eine eigensinnige Struktur auf, denn großflächige Verglasungen zur Belichtung der inneren Treppenführung zwischen den Geschossen brechen die Massivität der Steinfläche auf, die von einem bestimmten Blickpunkt hinter dem dichten Grün der Bäume wiederum als undurchdringliche Stufenformation erscheint, eben so wie man sie aus der archaischen Baukunst kennt. Die betrachtenden Augen können derart einem weit gesteckten Assoziationsimpuls folgen, der auch zur Villa Malaparte (Abb. 71) auf einem Felsenplateau Capris führen darf, zum Haus des italienischen Schriftstellers Curzio Malaparte vom Ende der dreißiger Jahre, das seine Konturierung einer großzügigen Freitreppe verdankt. Das

Haus auf der Platte verfolgt allerdings ganz andere Intentionen als der kompakte, begehbare Baukörper der Casa Malaparte. Das Grazer Haus ist kein felsengleicher Monolith, der Wind und Wetter trotzen will, sondern ein Schutzraum, der in der Landschaft als künstliche Landschaft mitschwingt und das Elementare der Elemente freundlich domestiziert in Szene setzt. Das im Dach abgeführte Regenwasser wird nämlich in einer nach außen geführten Blechrinne „sichtbar inszeniert"[33], die derart die virtuelle Mittelachse des Gebäudes akzentuiert und das ordnende Strukturelement des longitudinalen Hauskörpers im Inneren, die Achsialität, gestisch in den Außenraum überführt.

mation has a very wilful structure: large areas of glass providing light for the arrangement of the interior steps between the floors break down the solid quality of the stone surfaces. But from a particular viewpoint behind the dense green of the trees they look like an impenetrable arrangement of steps, again of the kind familiar from archaic architecture. So the eye can follow a wide-ranging set of triggered associations. These may even lead to the Villa Malaparte (fig. 71) on a rocky plateau in Capri, the house of the Italian author Curzio Malaparte, dating from the late thirties, which derives its contours from the lines of a lavish outside staircase. But the *House on*

Plattenweg has quite different intentions from the compact, accessible Casa Malaparte. The Graz house is not a rocky monolith, defying wind and weather, but a protective space, sounding its note as an artificial landscape within the general landscape, and presenting the elemental quality of the elements in friendly domesticity. The rainwater from the roof is in fact "staged visibly"[33] in an external sheet metal gutter accentuating the virtual central axis of the building, picking the ordering structural element of the longitudinal interior, the axial quality, and showing it to the outside world as a gesture.

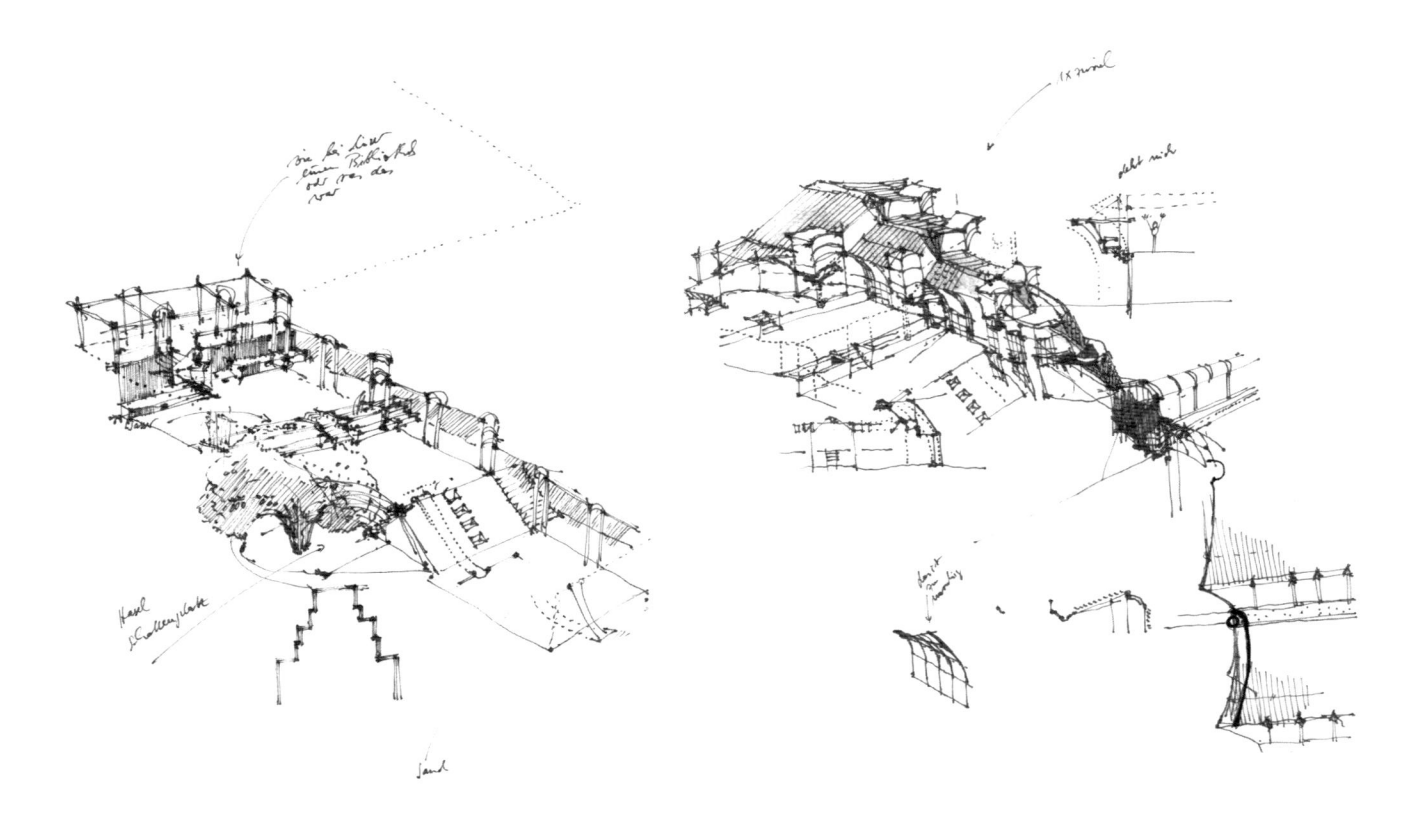

> 72
Häuser in Wien/Hietzing (Unteres Haus), Wien 1986–1989, Entwurfsskizze zur parallelen Entwicklung der Bodenhöhen im Inneren und Äußeren
Houses in Hietzing, Vienna (Lower house), Vienna 1986–1989, design sketch for parallel development of the internal and external surface heights

Natur und Atmosphären

Nahezu alle Häuser sind durch derartige Achsenführungen, die zum Außenraum überleiten, organisiert. Immer wieder geschieht dies durch Vermittlungsräume, die das Innen und Außen des Hauses mit dem Gefühl des Introvertierten und Extrovertierten zu verbinden suchen. Je nach Lage der Häuser variieren allerdings die Konzepte. Sind es in den früheren Wohnhäusern häufig bewachsene Pergolen, die in die kultivierte Landschaft vordringen (Abb. 18) oder stählerne Rankgerüste, die die Pflanzen in die Nähe des Hauses bringen (Abb. S. 115 links unten), so findet man in unwirtlichen Lagen, die der Witterung ungeschützt preisgegeben sind, eingefriedete Höfe, in denen die Idee vom *hortus conclusus* auflebt. Im *Haus am Hohenrain* (Abb. S. 127) ist dieser Außenraum 1985 geplant, aber nicht realisiert worden. Drei Jahre später, im burgenländischen *Haus Harmisch* hingegen können die Architekten dieses Paradiesgärtlein, das in den Sommermonaten die Funktion eines Patio übernimmt, verwirklichen (Abb. S. 135, 136). Auch der Wunsch, den architektonischen Raum mit der Natur zu verbinden, ihre Schönheiten also nicht nur in Ausblicken zu präsentieren, sondern als Pflanzenkultur dem Haus zu integrieren, wird mit der Fertigstellung der *Villa im Burgenland* erfüllbar.

1988 erhalten Szyszkowitz+Kowalski den Auftrag für *zwei Einzelhäuser in Wien-Hietzing* (Abb. S. 140–155), die zwei Familien auf einem gemeinsamen nicht sehr breiten, aber langen Grundstück errichten wollen. Diesen Voraussetzungen tragen die Architekten insofern Rechnung, als sie die leichte

Nature and atmospheres

Almost all these houses are organized by axes of this kind, providing a transition to the exterior space. This is often done by means of mediating spaces that try to link the inside and the outside of the house with the feeling of introversion and extroversion. But the concepts vary according to the position of the houses. In the earlier dwellings there are often pergolas with plants growing over them that thrust into the cultivated landscape (fig. 18) or steel trellises to bring the plants close to the house (fig. p. 115 below left). But in less hospitable locations that are exposed to wind and weather unprotected there are enclosed courtyards, reviving the idea of the *hortus conclusus*. This kind of external area was planned for the *Haus am Hohenrain* (fig. p. 127) in 1985, but not realized. Three years later, in the *Harmisch House* in Burgenland, the architects were able to construct such a little paradise garden, which functions as a patio in the summer (fig. p. 135, 136). And the desire to link the architectural space with nature was also fulfilled when the *Villa im Burgenland* was completed, the desire to make the beauty of nature part of the house as plant culture, rather than featuring only in outside views.

In 1988, Szyszkowitz+Kowalski were commissioned to design two detached *Houses in Hietzing, Vienna* (see figs. p. 140–155), which two families wanted to build on a joint plot that was

> 73
Häuser in Wien/Hietzing (Oberes Haus), Wien 1987–1990, Blick vom Erdgeschoß auf die Treppenspindel   Houses in Hietzing, Vienna (Upper house), Vienna 1987–1990, view from the ground floor of the staircase newel

> 74
Häuser in Wien/Hietzing (Oberes Haus), Blick durch den Kern der Treppenspindel zum Oberlicht   Houses in Hietzing, Vienna (Upper house), view through the staircase newel core to the skylight

Hanglage wieder achsial definieren und die beiden Häuser voneinander durch einen hofartigen Freiraum separieren, die doch durch diesen gemeinsamen Zwischenraum in Beziehung gesetzt sind (Abb. 75). Zur hinteren Hangseite ist das obere Haus durch die Rundung des tief nach unten gezogenen Daches geschützt und nach Süden durch einen die Mittelachse betonenden, vom Dach bis zum Boden aus gestuften Wintergarten weit geöffnet. Durch die kräftige Stahl-Glas-Konstruktion dringt das Licht ins Innere des Hauses und dramatisiert derart den Bereich zwischen dem Natur- und Kunstraum der Pflanzen. Bereits in den sechziger Jahren hatte Frei Otto in seinem eigenen Wohnhaus in Warmbronn bei Stuttgart den breit gelagerten Hauskörper ganz ähnlich durch einen Wintergarten in der Mitte akzentuiert, doch war hier die konstruktive gläserne Hülle als Atelier und Wohnbereich nutzbar.[34] Demgegenüber bleibt der Wiener Wintergarten dem Charakter der Orangerie verpflichtet, dessen luftiger Schutzraum für die Pflanzen durch eine Wandverglasung vom dahinterliegenden Kompaktraum der Wohnbereiche abgetrennt ist. Es ergibt sich derart eine indirekte und diffuse Lichtführung für den dahinter liegenden großen Raum, die den Charakter des Verborgenen mit der Atmosphäre einer natürlichen Lichtung erfüllt (Abb. 76). Das gestreute Licht erzeugt in Verbindung mit den kühlen Materialien, dem Edelstahl, dem Marmor und im Zusammenklang mit den zurückhaltenden Grautönen eine Atmosphäre aus Eleganz und Gediegen-

not very wide, but quite long. The architects met these requirements by defining the slightly sloping situation axially again and separating the two houses by a courtyard-like open space that also relates them to each other, as it is shared (fig. 75). The upper house is protected on the rear side of the slope by the rounded roof, which comes down very low, then opened up on the south side by a conservatory, stepped from roof to floor, which also emphasizes the central axis. This powerful steel and glass structure allows light into the interior of the house, thus dramatizing the area between the natural and artificial locations for the plants. Frei Otto had accentuated the breadth of the building similarly in his own house in Warmbronn near Stuttgart with a central conservatory in the sixties, but here the structural glass envelope could be used as a studio and living area.[34] In contrast with this, the Viennese conservatory owes more to the nature of an orangery, where the airy protected space for the plants is separated from the compact living space behind it by a glazed

> 75
Häuser in Wien/Hietzing, (Oberes und unteres Haus), Entwurfszeichnung zur Höhenentwicklung beider Häuser im Gelände mit Zwischenraum
Houses in Hietzing, Vienna, (Upper and Lower houses), design drawing for the height development of the two houses on the site with gap

34 Siehe dazu: Karin Wilhelm, Porträt Frei
Otto. Architekten heute, Bd.2, Berlin 1985,
S. 101 ff. *Cf.: Karin Wilhelm, Porträt Frei
Otto. Architekten heute, vol.2, Berlin 1985,
p. 101 ff.*

> 76
Häuser in Wien/Hietzing (Oberes Haus), Blick vom Wohnbereich in den Wintergarten *Houses in Hietzing, Vienna (Upper house), view from the living area into the conservatory*

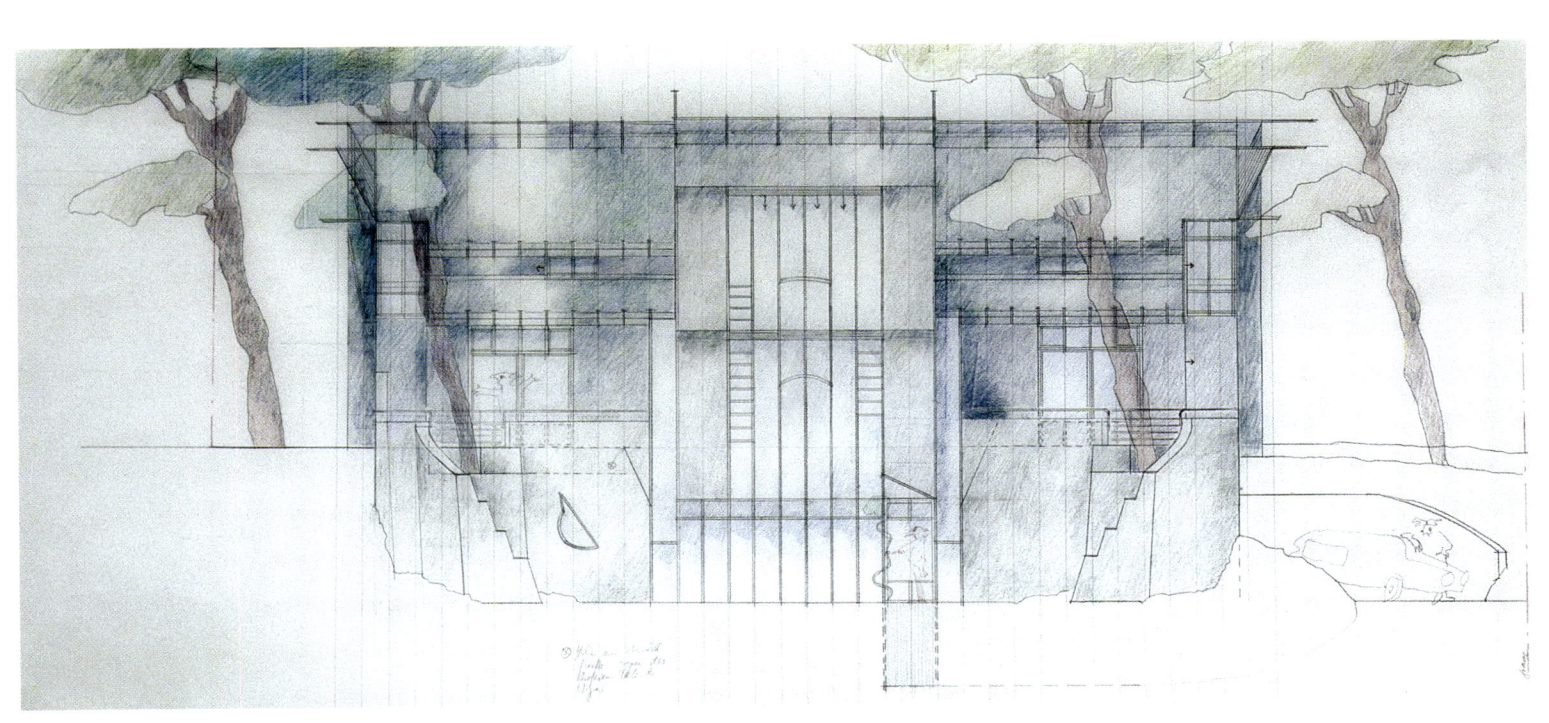

> 77
Häuser in Wien/Hietzing (Oberes Haus), Zeichnung der Außenfassade mit Wintergarten und hochliegenden Terrassen *Houses in Hietzing, Vienna (Upper house), drawing of the outer façade with conservatory and high terraces*

heit, die den Wohnbereich mit seinen Möbeln gleichsam auratisch umhüllt. Allein in den Treppenführungen greift die Architektur auf eine prononcierte inszenatorische Gestik zurück, die, in der Modulation durch das Licht, den Körper der geschlossenen Treppenspirale in eine gleichsam kinetische Schwingung versetzt (Abb. 73, 74). Auch das untere Kaskadenhaus, dessen nach unten gestaffelter Baukörper seitlich belichtet wird, ist von vergleichbarer Eleganz und führt über Treppenniveaus durch den Wohnraum zu einem Fenster im Scheitelpunkt des Gebäudes, das den Blick in einen kleinen Hof mit seitlichen Mauereinfassungen freigibt. Im kürzlich fertiggestellten *Haus am Ruckerlberg* haben Szyszkowitz+Kowalski abermals einen Wintergarten geplant, der an der Spitze des linsenförmigen Grundrisses über die gesamte Höhe des Gebäudes führen wird und dergestalt den imponierenden Raumeindruck der Palmenhäuser aus Glas und Eisen des 19. Jahrhunderts en miniature in einem Privathaus nochmals aufleben läßt.

Das Bestreben der Architekten, den Räumen der Häuser bereits in der Planung charaktervolle Atmosphären zu verleihen, ist ein integraler Bestandteil ihres Entwerfens. Die vielen Skizzen und Zeichnungen (Abb. 32), die häufig mit Buntstiften in wunderschöne, farbenfrohe Bildwerke verwandelt werden, übermitteln schon im Vorfeld der konkreten Ausführungsplanungen außerordentlich anschaulich die gewünschten Wirkungen, sie sind das Medium der räumlichen Phantasie und der möglichen Gestaltungsvarianten, die zugleich der Kommunikation untereinander dienen. Schon in den ersten Skizzen erhalten Ideen Konturen, die häufig bis zur Ausführungsplanung Bestand behalten, und Linien umreißen bereits Bewegungsabläufe, die, ineinander verwirbelt, auf künftige Konzentrationspunkte innerhalb und außerhalb der

wall. This provides indirect and diffused light for the large space behind, which meets the criterion of concealment with the atmosphere of a natural clearing (fig. 76). In combination with the cool materials, the stainless steel and marble, and in harmony with the reticent grey tones, the diffused light creates an atmosphere of elegance and solidity that seems to invest the living area and its furniture with an auratic quality. The architecture only resorts to theatrical gestures in the line of the stairs, where modulation through light sets the body of the closed spiral of steps into something like kinetic motion (fig. 73, 74). The lower cascade house, whose downward staggered structure is illuminated from the side, is comparably elegant and leads via the level of the stairs through the living room to a window at the apex of the building, revealing a view of a small courtyard framed by side walls. Szyszkowitz+Kowalski have also planned a conservatory for the recent *House on Ruckerlberg*, completed in 2002. This will be placed at the point of the lenticular ground plan and will lead across the full height of the building, reviving the impressive spatial impression of 19th century glass-and-iron palm houses in miniature, in a private house.

The architects' efforts to give the rooms in their houses a characterful atmosphere even at the planning stage is an integral part of the design process for them. They produce a large number of sketches and drawings (fig. 32), which they frequently transform into wonderful, colourful pictures using coloured crayons. Even in the preliminary stages of the concrete planning for realization they convey the desired effect extraordinarily vividly. They are the medium for spatial imagination and the possible design variants, and they also help

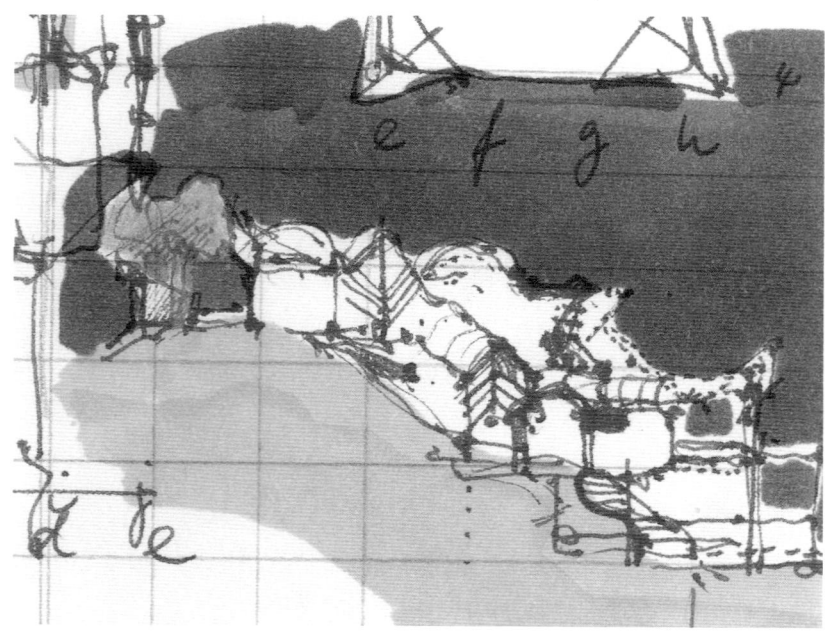

> 78
Weißes Haus, Projekt in Graz, 1980, Entwurfsskizze White House, project in Graz, 1980, design sketch

> 79
Haus in Moosburg, Moosburg bei Klagenfurt 1995–1996,
Detail der Dachkonstruktion mit gelben Stahlmanschetten
House in Moosburg, Moosburg near Klagenfurt 1995–1996,
detail of the roof structure with yellow steel jackets

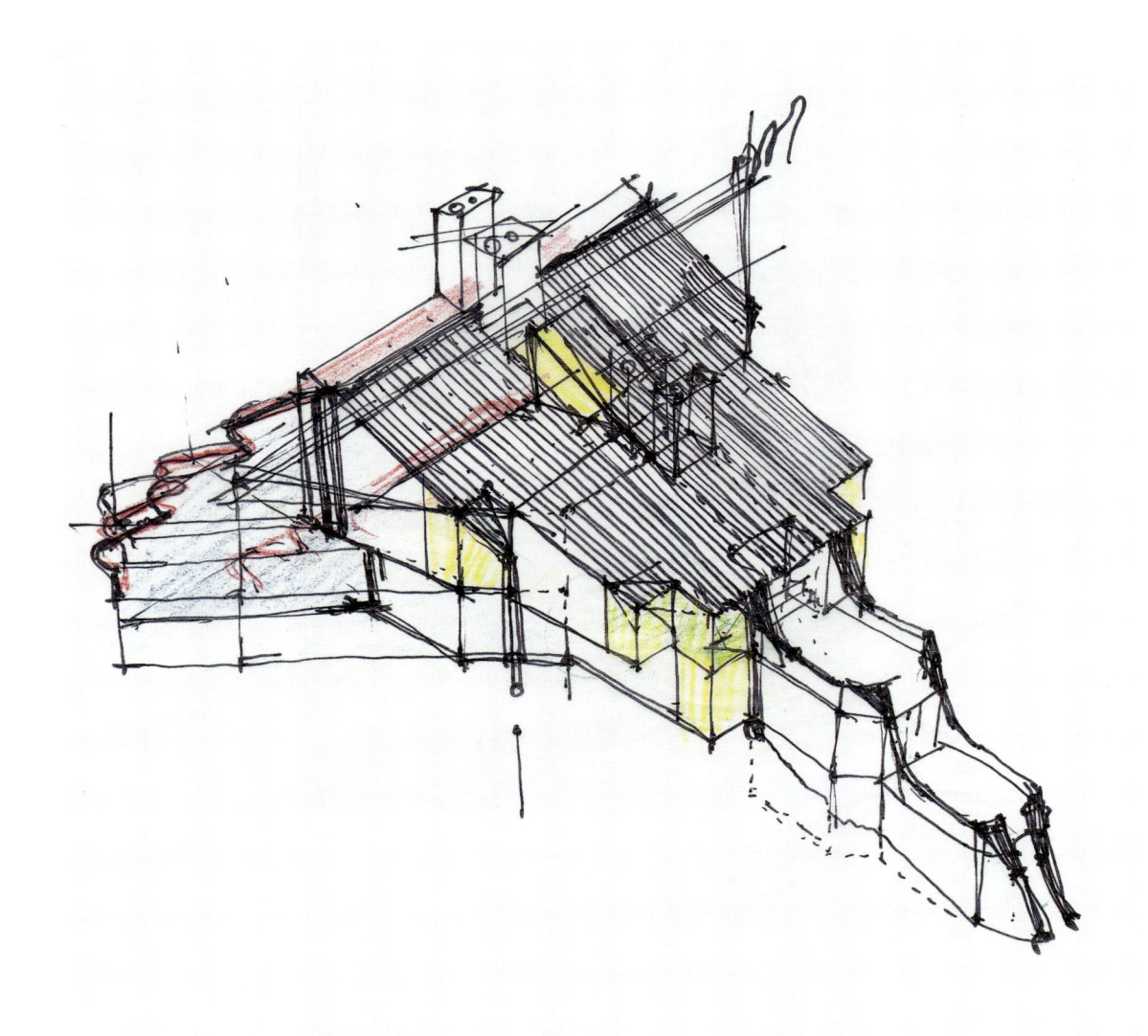

> 80
Häuser in Wien/Hietzing (Unteres Haus), Wien 1986–1989, isometrische Entwurfsskizze Houses in Hietzing, Vienna (Lower house), Vienna 1986–1989, isometric
design sketch

> 81
Designhaus, Projekt 1997 Design House, project 1997

Gebäude hinweisen (Abb. 57, 78). Farben erzeugen Stimmungen und unterstützen auf dem Papier die optischen Sensationen, die die Räume prägen sollen. Selbst die Oberflächentexturen von Materialien meint man zuweilen in der Zeichnung zu spüren, die im Zusammenspiel mit der Beleuchtung, dem Hell und Dunkel des Lichtes, dem gebauten Haus eben jene spezifische „Physiognomie (verleihen werden), von der eine Atmosphäre ausgeht."[35] Als Mittlerin des Wohlgefühls übernimmt die Integration der Natur neben der Schaffung von Kleinklimata gleichfalls die Aufgabe, ästhetische Atmosphären zu erzeugen, die dem „merkfähigen Ambiente"[36] der Architektur dienlich sind. Daß Szyszkowitz+Kowalski dieses Fluidum, wie einst Frank Lloyd Wright, immer wieder in der farbigen Zeichnung evozieren und nicht der Glätte einer Computergraphik anvertrauen (Abb. 81), stellt sie zugleich in die Tradition jener zeichnerisch begabten Heroen ihrer Zunft, die seit den Wunderbildern der „Gläsernen Kette" viele prominente Namen kennt.

Mit den Wiener Häusern, die 1990 fertiggestellt wurden, liegt diese Entwurfsprogrammatik ausgereift vor. Die reiche Palette der Farben früherer Häuser, deren Namensgebung bis in die achtziger Jahre hinein mit den jeweils dominierenden Farbtönen verbunden wurde, die Kontrastierung unterschiedlicher Materialien und deren atmosphärische Haptik ist in den Wiener Häusern einer ruhigen, verputzten Oberflächenbehandlung und einer zurückhaltenden Farbgebung gewichen: Ein ins Grau changierendes Aubergine bestimmt den Charakter des oberen und ein Türkis den des unteren Hauses. Zumeist sind es Farbmischungen, mit denen die Architekten auf die Umgebung der jeweiligen Häuser zu reagieren suchen, häufig findet man Türkistöne, die entweder, wie im Haus Harmisch, ins Grau sich neigen oder den Anteil von Blau betonen, wie im Föllinger Turm.

In den Hietzinger Häuser haben die Architekten aber keinesfalls einen unwiderruflichen künstlerischen Schlußpunkt gesetzt und keine Rezeptur für einen konsumierbaren déjà vu-Effekt gegeben. Noch im Jahr der Fertigstellung der Wiener Häuser 1990 greifen sie im Haus in Bad Mergentheim (Abb. S. 156–163) auf die Vielfalt der farbigen Stimmungswerte zurück. Das zwei Jahre später fertiggestellte Wohnhaus mit Praxisräumen für ein Psychotherapeutenehepaar erstrahlt in einem warmen Siena-Rot, und die schwarzen Fensterlaibungen im Inneren kontrastieren mit dem Weiß der Wände, so daß, wie in einem Gemälde Piet Mondrians, ein optisches Flächengitter entsteht (Abb. 82). Auch die Lust an der im Detail deutungsfähigen Konstruktion taucht im Bogen des großen, metallverkleideten Daches wieder auf und wird in der Holzleimbinderkonstruktion

them to communicate with each other. Ideas acquire outlines even in the first sketches, and these frequently hold until the realization stage. Lines are already defining sequences of movement that whirl around in complex patterns and identify future concentration points inside and outside the building (figs. 57, 78). Colours create moods, and support on paper the visual sensations that will ultimately be created in the rooms. Sometimes the drawings even give a sense of the surfaces textures of materials whose interplay with the lighting, the light and dark areas, will give the house that specific "physiognomy, from which an atmosphere emerges."[35] Nature is integrated in order to convey a sense of well-being, and also creates a micro-climate, fulfilling its task of providing aesthetic atmospheres that serve the "memorable ambience" of the architecture.[36] Szyszkowitz+Kowalski, like Frank Lloyd Wright before them, regularly evoke this aura in a coloured drawing, rather than entrusting it to a bland computer graphic (fig. 81). This places them in the tradition of the talented draughtsman heroes of their guild, which boasts many distinguished names since the miraculous images of the "Gläserne Kette".

This approach to design is present in full maturity in the Houses in Vienna completed in 1990. The rich colour range of earlier buildings, whose names alluded to the dominant colour shade until well into the eighties, the contrast between different materials and their atmospheric tactile qualities has given way to a calm, rendered treatment of surfaces and reticent colour schemes in the Houses in Vienna: aubergine shading into grey established the character of the upper house and a shade of turquoise that of the lower one. Usually the architects choose mixtures of colours that respond to the surroundings of the particular buildings. Shades of turquoise

[35] Gernot Böhme, Atmosphäre. Essays zur neuen Ästhetik, Frankfurt a.M. 1995, S. 97.
Gernot Böhme, Atmosphäre. Essays zur neuen Ästhetik, Frankfurt am Main 1995, p. 97.
[36] Op. cit. Anm.: 20, o. S. Op. cit. note 20, no p.

des *Hauses in Moosburg* (Abb. S. 188–195) zur dominanten, plastischen Silhouette. Hier ruhen die gebogenen Holzbinder von unterschiedlicher Länge und großer Spannweite auf runden Stahlbetonstützen und die Dächer sind zwischen die Holzbinder gespannt. Die Farbmischung aus Altrosa und Magenta der schräg, in Zacken geschnittenen Binder trifft auf ein fahles Zitronengelb der Stahlmanschetten, so daß die Stütze-Last-Relation, das Tragen und Getragenwerden in diesem farblichen Kontrast optisch überhöht wird (Abb. 79). Sichtbeton und grau verputzte Wandscheiben strukturieren den zur Talseite zweigeschossigen Baukörper, der in den schwarzgerahmten, die Vertikale betonenden Fenstern synkopisch gebrochen erscheint. Der Raumfluß des Wohnbereiches wird derart großzügig belichtet und die bekannte Rhetorik des Wohnens tritt mit neuen Gebärden in Erscheinung. Doch nach wie vor wird der Kontakt zur umgebenden Landschaft erhalten und das Wasser in den weit in den Garten ausgreifenden Regenwasserrinnen abermals als ein atmosphärisches Element der Architektur zelebriert (Abb. 7).

are frequently found, either inclining towards grey, as in the *Harmisch House*, or emphasizing the blue element, as in the *Tower in Fölling*.

But in the *Houses in Hitzing* the architects were certainly not placing an irrevocable artistic full stop, nor were they giving a recipe for a consumable *déjà vu* effect. Even in the year the *Houses in Hitzing* were completed, 1990, they went back to a range of atmospheric colouring for the *House in Bad Mergentheim* (figs. p. 156–163), a home with consulting rooms for a psychotherapist couple, completed two years later, whose exterior is coloured in a warm red Sienna. Inside, the black window reveals form a contrast with the white of the walls, creating a visual grid, as in a painting by Piet Mondrian (fig. 82). The pleasure to create a construction that is open to detailed interpretation crops up again in the sweep of the large, metal-clad roof and becomes a dominant sculptural silhouette in the bonded timber frame structure of the *House in Moosburg* (figs. p. 188–195). Here the curved timber trusses of various lengths and extending over a broad span rest on round reinforced concrete supports, and the roofs are fitted in between the timber frames. The colour mixture, old rose and magenta, chosen for the trusses, which are obliquely cut in zig-zags, meets the dull lemon-yellow of the steel sleeves, so that the support-load ratio, the notion of bearing and being borne, is visually heightened by this colour contrast (fig. 79). Exposed concrete and grey-rendered walls articulate the building, which has two storeys on the valley side. The black-framed windows emphasizing the vertical break up the volume and give it a sense of syncopation. The spatial flow of the living area is generously lit and the familiar rhetoric of living acquires some new gestures. But contact with the surrounding landscape is maintained as before, and the water in the rainwater gutters, which run out far into the garden, is once again celebrated as an atmospheric element of the architecture (fig. 7).

82 >>>
Haus in Bad Mergentheim, Bad Mergentheim 1991–1993, Innenansicht des Wohnraumes mit Blick ins Tal (s. S. 163)
House in Bad Mergentheim, Bad Mergentheim 1991–1993, interior of the living room with view into the valley (see p. 163)

Häuser und Siedlungen: Raumformen zwischen Individualität und Gemeinschaft

Sigfried Giedion veröffentlichte 1956 einen Aufsatzband mit dem Titel „Architektur und Gemeinschaft". Diese kleine Schrift gilt als ein Selbstverständigungstext für die Neuorientierung der CIAM nach 1945. Die Texte Giedions repräsentieren jenen Umbruch in der Nachkriegsarchitektur, die den Zweifel an der kulturellen Eindeutigkeit der modernen Paradigmen in ein weitaus demütiger formuliertes „Humanisierungsprogramm"[37] begleitet haben. Angesichts der unübersehbar gewordenen Widerständigkeit kultureller Eigenarten in den einzelnen Regionen der Welt, lenkte Giedion den Blick auf Differenzen in der Architektur, die offensichtlich aus der Ungleichzeitigkeit der jeweiligen Lebensstile entsprungen waren, die also nach wie vor der Behauptung zuwiderliefen, daß sich in den modernen Zeiten die Lebensformen und damit die Lebens- und Wohnbedürfnisse der Menschen notwendiger Weise allmählich anglichen. Klimatische, lebenspraktische und produktionsbedingte Voraussetzungen hatten gegenüber dieser behaupteten Angleichung

Houses and housing estates: spatial forms between individuality and community

Sigfried Giedion published a volume of essays called "Architektur und Gemeinschaft" (Architecture and Community) in 1956. This little publication is seen as an explanation for the new direction taken by CIAM after 1945. Giedion's essays articulate the upheaval in post-war architecture, whereby doubts in the total cultural unambiguity of the modern paradigms were transmuted into a humanization programme[37] that was much more modestly formulated. Given resistant cultural features that could no longer be ignored in the individual regions of the world, Giedion drew attention to differences in architecture that obviously derived from the lack of simultaneity in the various life-styles. This tended to refute the assertion that in modern times life-forms, and thus people's living and housing needs, were necessarily all gradually becoming the same. Requirements imposed by climate, the way life is led and production, had led to building traditions that ran counter to this suggestion of increasing similarity. These had apparently been taken up by architects operating

> 83
Stadtvillen Mariagrün, Graz, Haignitzhofweg 1993–1997, Luftaufnahme mit Blick auf den verbindenden Corso, die Gärten und Dachterrassen Urban villas in Mariagrün, Graz, Haignitzhofweg 1993–1997, aerial photograph with view of the linking avenue, the gardens and roof terraces

[37] Sokratis Georgiadis, Sigfried Giedion. Eine intellektuelle Biographie, Zürich 1989, S. 182. *Sokratis Georgiadis, Sigfried Giedion: An Intellectual Biography, Edinburgh 1993.*
[38] Sigfried Giedion, Architektur und Gemeinschaft. Tagebuch einer Entwicklung, Hamburg 1956, S. 90. *Sigfried Giedion, Architektur und Gemeinschaft. Tagebuch einer Entwicklung, Hamburg 1956, p. 90.*
[39] Op. cit., S. 92. *Op. cit., p. 92.*

> 84
Wohnsiedlung Alte Poststraße-Eggenberg, Graz 1982–1984, Luftaufnahme mit Blick in den zentralen, inneren Hofbereich
Housing estate in Alte Poststraße-Eggenberg, Graz 1982–1984, aerial photograph with view of the central inner courtyard area

resistente Bautraditionen ausgeprägt, die, nach den kollektiven Destruktionsorgien in Europa, offensichtlich von den international agierenden Architekten neuerlich aufgegriffen worden waren und die tendentielle Rigidität des „International Style" aufzuweichen begonnen hatten. Giedion jedenfalls bemerkte diesen Wandel mit feinem Gespür: „Die modernen Bewegungen, soweit sie wirklich konstitutiv sind, versuchen wieder, nach dem langen rationalistischen Interregnum, auf die Urphänomene des menschlichen Wesens einzugehen … Diese Einstellung, die von den besten heutigen Architekten befolgt wird, um den regionalen Bedingungen gerecht zu werden, sei es in den Tropen oder sei es in den polaren Gegenden, sei es im Osten, oder sei es im Westen, könnte man als den *neuen Regionalismus* bezeichnen."[38] Mit diesem Verständnis des Regionalen lieferte Giedion ein Stichwort, dem er so unterschiedliche Architekten wie Alvar Aalto, Jørn Utzon und Georges Candilis zuordnete, die seiner Einschätzung nach, bei aller Unterschiedlichkeit jedoch ähnliche Ziele verfolgten, indem sie entweder regional bedingte, handwerkliche Bautraditionen aufgriffen, oder an typologische Eigenarten anknüpften, die in dem jeweiligen Kulturraum mit seinen spezifischen Lebensformen über Jahrhunderte hinweg ausgebildet worden waren. In diesem Kontext des Zweifels an wesentlichen Dogmen der modernen Bewegung, unterzog Giedion auch die Vorherrschaft des rechtwinkligen Hauses einer Revision, die sich auf ethnologische Befunde besann. Nicht das rechtwinklige Haus, „sondern das Kurvenhaus" sei in der Urzeit des Bauens die Regel gewesen. Was ihn damals nachdenklich stimmte, war die Tatsache, daß „… es (das Kurvenhaus, K.W.) in dem industriell höchst entwickelten Land, den USA, …"[39] wieder aufgetaucht war und damit die funktionalistische Gleichung von moderner Fortschrittlichkeit und industriell gefertigter 90 Grad-Standardisierung offensichtlich außer Kraft zu setzten begonnen hatte. Giedion dachte bei seiner Analyse an die Bauten Frank Lloyd Wrights, dessen Wohnhäuser aus

internationally after the collective orgies of destruction in Europe, and had started to soften the "International Style's" tendency to be rigid. Giedion certainly has a fine sense of this change: "The modern movements, to the extent that they are really constitutive, are again trying, after the long rationalist interregnum, to address the primal phenomena of human nature … This attitude, which is adopted by the best contemporary architects so that they can do justice to regional conditions, whether in the tropics or in the polar regions, the East or the West, could be defined as the new regionalism."[38] Giedion placed architects as different as Alvar Aalto, Jørn Utzon and Georges Candilis under this heading. In his view, despite all the differences, they were pursuing similar aims, either by taking up regionally determined craft building traditions or went back to typological peculiarities that had been formed over the centuries in their respective culture with its specific life-forms. When raising these doubts about crucial dogmas of the Modern movement, Giedion was also taking an ethnologically based fresh look at the dominance of the rectangular building. It was not the rectangular building "but the curved building" that had been the rule in the primal days of building. What made him think about the idea at that time was the fact that "… it (the curved house, K.W.) (had cropped up again) in the country that was most developed industrially, the USA",[39] and had thus obviously started to erode the functionalist equation of modern progress and industrially prefabricated 90 degree standardization. In his analysis, Giedion was thinking of Frank Lloyd Wright's build-

> 86
Katholisches Pfarrzentrum Ragnitz, Graz, Ragnitzstraße
1984–1987, Luftaufnahme mit Blick auf den zentralen, inneren
Platz (3seitig geschlossene Gesamtanlage geplant) Catholic
parish centre in Ragnitz, Graz, Ragnitzstraße 1984–1987, aerial
photograph with view of the central inner square (projected
complex closed on three sides)

> 85
Wohnsiedlung Eisbach-Rein, Eisbach-Rein (Steiermark)
1984–1986, Luftaufnahme mit Blick auf den hufeisenförmigen
Platzraum Housing estate in Eisbach-Rein, Eisbach-Rein
(Styria) 1984–1986, aerial photograph with view of the horse-
shoe-shaped square

den vierziger und fünfziger Jahren, wie er meinte, dem „minoischen Farmhaus so merkwürdig gleichen", und die sich just in diesem Rückgriff von der „Tyrannei des Rechtecks"[40] frei gemacht hatten. Es war mithin unübersehbar geworden, daß sich der Anschauungshorizont der Architekten in der Nachkriegszeit erweitert hatte, um fortan in zunehmend kritischer Distanz einige Kerngedanken der funktionalistischen Moderne zu befragen und zu verwerfen. Die folgende Entwicklung sollte sich allerdings keineswegs eindimensional und widerspruchsfrei vollziehen, vielmehr verlief dieser Prozeß nach dialektischen Mustern, die in einer Art Echternacher Springprozession die Progression der Architektur vorantrieb. Im Namen des Stilphänomens der retrospektiv ausgerichteten Postmoderne wurde schließlich in den achtziger Jahren triumphierend behauptet, daß die Moderne an ihr historisches Ende gekommen und damit radikal überwunden sei.

Schon die französischen Situationisten hatten zu Beginn der fünfziger Jahre, gleichfalls mit dem Blick auf Frank Lloyd Wright, „leidenschaftliche Häuser"[41] gefordert, und waren sich keineswegs darüber einig, ob denn Le Corbusiers Konzept des Hauses als „machine à émouvoir" in dieser Hinsicht als ein gelungenes Projekt zu werten sei. Als die in Österreich ungemein wirkungsvolle englische Gruppe ARCHIGRAM in den sechziger Jahren des 20. Jahrhunderts das Wohnmodell des „Plug-in" entwickelte, mit dem der antibourgeoise, nomadische Lebensstil der Jugend emphatisch gefeiert wurde, so durfte man sicher sein, daß anderswo bereits Einspruchs-

ings. Giedion felt that the houses Wright built in the forties and fifties were "remarkably similar to Minoan houses", and had liberated themselves from the "tyranny of the rectangle"[40] by precisely this recourse. It had thus become impossible to ignore the fact that architects' horizons had broadened considerably in the post-war period, and they had gone on to question and reject some core ideas of functionalistic Modernism as they adopted an increasingly critical distance. But the subsequent development was not to be at all one-dimensional and free of contradictions. The evolution of architecture would follow dialectical and contradictory patterns, and thus take place in forward and backward moves. Finally, in the eighties, it was triumphantly asserted in the name of retrospective Postmodernism as a stylistic phenomenon that Modernism had reached its historical conclusion and had thus been radically defeated.

The French Situationists, also with an eye on Frank Lloyd Wright, had demanded "passionate buildings"[41] as early as the fifties. They were not able to agree among themselves whether Le Corbusier's concept of the building as a "machine à émouvoir" could be said to be successful in this respect. The English group ARCHIGRAM, which had an amazing impact on Austria in the 1960s, developed the "Plug-in" as a housing model. This celebrated the anti-middle class, nomadic life-style of young people, and so it was of course not long before objections were heard from people who remained

[40] Op. cit. Op. cit.
[41] Guy Debord (Hg.), Potlach. Informationsbulletin der Lettristischen Internationale, Berlin 2002, S. 21. Guy Debord (ed.), Potlach. Informationsbulletin der Lettristischen Internationale, Berlin 2002, p. 21.

diskurse laut wurden, die dieser Haltung etwa in Anlehnung an Alison und Robert Smithon skeptisch gegenüber blieben, weil sie weiterhin dem Sozialkonzept in der Architektur den Vorrang geben und politisch Einspruch erheben wollten. Meinten die holländischen Strukturalisten noch die Idee der Egalität sozialverträglich definiert zu haben, schlossen sich schon die ersten Engagierten zusammen, die demgegenüber im Partizipationsgedanken die Akzeptanz der individuellen Wohnbedürfnisse propagierten. Als schließlich Hans Hollein in Österreich erklärte, daß „alles Architektur" sei und in den Vereingten Staaten von Amerika durch Robert Venturi und Denise Scott Brown die populäre Kultur geadelt wurde, durfte man sicher sein, daß im Namen der „Anderen Moderne"

Einspruch erhoben wurde gegen eine allzu leichtfertige Akzeptanz konsumistischer Tendenzen. Hatten sich in den achtziger Jahren die verschiedenen Spielarten der Postmoderne ins Rampenlicht der Debatten gestellt, so tauchten bereits ihre Widersacher auf, die im Namen einer „Zweiten Moderne" die Traditionen der Moderne hochhielten. Längst schon gab es jene, die in Anlehnung an die Vernunftkritik der französischen Philosophen oder aus der neuerlichen Rezeption des russischen „Konstruktivismus" das Konzept des „Dekonstruktivismus" in die Architektur einbrachten oder die, wie Coop Himmelb(l)au, mit der provokanten These, daß „Architektur brennen" müsse, nochmals den Wert der Leidenschaften priesen.

sceptical about this attitude, citing the views of Alison and Robert Smithson. They wanted to continue to keep the social concept to the fore in architecture, and raise political objections. No sooner had the Dutch Structuralists defined the idea of equality in terms of the social contract than the first committed groups were coming together to speak up for the acceptance of individual housing requirements in a spirit of participation. Finally Hans Hollein declared in Austria that "everything (is) architecture", and popular culture was talked up in America by Robert Venturi and Denise Scott Brown. So it was certain that there would soon be objections in the name

of the "Other Modernism" to an all too ready acceptance of consumerist tendencies. In the eighties the various varieties of Postmodernism had thrust themselves into the limelight of the debate, but opponents were already coming forward and upholding Modern traditions in the name of a "Second Modernism". Of course there had long since been people who borrowed from the French philosophers' critique of reason or the recent response to Russian "Constructivism" to bring the concept of "Deconstructivism" into architecture, or who like Coop Himmelb(l)au were again lauding the value of passion with the provocative thesis that "architecture (has to) burn."

> 87
Wohnsiedlung auf dem Küppersbuschgelände in Gelsenkirchen, IBA Emscher Park, Gelsenkirchen 1994–1998, Blick in den linsenförmigen Platzraum mit hochgelegten Aquädukten für das Regenwasser Housing estate on the Küppersbusch site in Gelsenkirchen, IBA Emscher Park, Gelsenkirchen 1994–1998, view of the lenticular square with high rainwater aqueducts

> 88
Institut für Biochemie und Biotechnologie der Technischen Universität Graz, Graz 1985–1991, Luftaufnahme mit Blick auf den zentralen, inneren Platzraum   Institute of Biochemistry and Biotechnology at the Graz Technical University, Graz 1985–1991, aerial photograph with view of the central, inner square

[42] Kenneth Frampton, Die Architektur der Moderne. Eine kritische Baugeschichte, Stuttgart 1997, S. 263. Kenneth Frampton, Modern Architecture. A Critical History, third edition, London 1992, p. 314.
[43] Karla Kowalski muß in diesem Rahmen als eine Ausnahmeerscheinung insofern betrachtet werden, als ihre architektonischen und ideellen Bezugspunkte außerhalb Österreichs zu finden sind. Friedrich Achleitner schrieb 1982 über Szyszkowitz+Kowalskis Architektur: „Das künstlerische Engagement auf einer generell expressiven Basis, mit der Vorliebe für freie, assoziative Formen mit Grenzüberschreitungen ins ‚organische' Bauen, das teilweise Auftreten von Collage-Effekten, auch die Betonung graphischer Werte in der Umschreibung von Räumen, in der Bestimmung von Baukörpern, alles dies hat in seiner Signifikanz fast schulbildenden Charakter." Friedrich Achleitner, Die Widerspiegelung des Abwesenden, in: Aufforderung zum Vertrauen. Aufsätze zur Architektur, Wien 1987, S. 200 ff. Karla Kowalski has to be seen as an exception in this context, as her architectural and intellectual reference points came from outside Austria. Friedrich Achleitner wrote in 1982 of Szyszkowitz+Kowalski's architecture: "Their artistic commitment on a generally expressive basis, showing a preference for free, associative forms with forays across the border into 'organic' building, occasional collage effects, and also the emphasis placed on graphic values when defining spaces and building volumes, all this has a significance that adds up to the sort of character that establishes a school." Friedrich Achleitner, Die Widerspiegelung des Abwesenden, in: Aufforderung zum Vertrauen. Aufsätze zur Architektur, Vienna 1987, p. 200 ff.

Als Kenneth Frampton diese neue Unübersichtlichkeit 1980 abermals im Zusammenhang mit den regionalen Eigenheiten diskutierte und den Begriff Giedions vom „neuen Regionalismus" im Verständnis des „Kritischen Regionalismus" adaptierte und neu interpretierte, erhielt der Versuch, das Eigene im Kontext globaler Entwicklungen architektonisch zu behaupten, eine theoretische Klarheit, die der philosophischen Postmoderne mit ihrem Anspruch, das Pluralitätsprinzip durchzusetzen, zu entsprechen vermochte. Für Frampton rekurierte der „Kritische Regionalismus" nämlich nicht auf einen „regionalen Stil", sondern bezog sich auf neuere, regionale „... ‚Schulen', deren Ziel es ist, die begrenzten Gesellschaften, in denen sie begründet sind, im kritischen Sinne zu repräsentieren und zu bedienen ... Zu den Vorbedingungen für regionale Ausdrucksformen gehört ... eine dezentralistische Einstellung – ein Streben nach kultureller, ökonomischer und politischer Unabhängigkeit." [42]

Für die „Grazer Schule", eine unglückliche Wortschöpfung, welche die erstaunliche Konzentration hochbegabter junger Architekten in der steirischen Landeshauptstadt am Beginn der siebziger Jahre nur unzureichend beschreibt, trifft die Aussage Framptons insofern zu, als ein Großteil ihrer frühen Bauten in Graz und seiner Umgebung errichtet worden sind. Zudem traf ihre Arbeit wie die der Kollegen bereits in den siebziger Jahren auf eine außerordentlich aufgeschlossene Kulturpolitik der damaligen Landesregierung, die eine allgemeine Aufbruchsstimmung in den Künsten beflügelt hatte und damit auch die Durchsetzung innovativer Architekturkonzepte förderte. Wenngleich die Exponenten der „Grazer Schule" schon in der Phase ihrer Positionierung in den siebziger und achtziger Jahren keineswegs einheitliche Konzepte vertraten und sich vielmehr im Individualitätsgestus der jeweiligen Architektur vereint fanden – inzwischen sind sie ganz unterschiedliche Wege gegangen –, so schuf vor allem eine Bauaufgabe die Basis für ein koordiniertes Handeln, das die Rede von der „Grazer Schule" rechtfertigt. [43] Es war der Siedlungsbau, der im Rahmen des „Modells Steiermark" eine besondere Bedeutung erlangte, weil in dieser Bauaufgabe die kulturelle Dominanz einer auf die Familie orientierten Gesellschaft erfüllt und gleichzeitig mit alternativen Vorstellungen über gemeinschaftliche Lebensformen angereichert werden konnte. Diese Bewegung hat den Ruf der Grazer

When Kenneth Frampton was discussing this new lack of a complete overview again in the context of distinctive regional features in 1980 he changed Giedion's concept of "new regionalism" to "Critical Regionalism" and reinterpreted it. This gave theoretical clarity to the attempt to assert what is one's own architecturally, in the context of global developments. It was thus able to stand up to theoretical Postmodernism with its claim to be implementing the plurality principle. For Frampton, "Critical Regionalism" was not intended to identify "a vernacular", but related to "those recent regional 'schools' whose primary aim has been to reflect and serve the limited constituencies in which they are grounded. Among other factors contributing to the emergence of a regionalism of this order is ... some kind of anti-centrist consensus – an aspiration at least to some form of cultural, economic and political independence." [42]

For the "Graz School" – an unfortunate coinage providing a less than adequate description of the astonishing concentration of highly talented young architects in the Styrian capital in the early seventies – Frampton's statement applies insofar as most of their early buildings were built in and around Graz. As well as this, their work, like that of their colleagues, benefited from the exceptionally enlightened cultural policies of the then Land government, which had inspired a general sense of a new beginning in the arts, and thus also promoted the implementation of innovative architectural concepts. The exponents of the "Graz School" did not share uniform concepts even when they were establishing themselves in the seventies and eighties, in fact they were brought together by the individuality of their approaches, and have now all gone off in quite different directions. But there was one building commission that created a basis for co-ordinated action and that justifies talking about a "Graz School". [43] Estate building acquired particular significance in the context of the "Styrian model", because it was in this sphere that the dominance of a family-oriented society could be acknowledged and at the same time enriched with alternative ideas about ways of living together in a community. This movement helped to establish the reputation of Graz architecture in general and Szyszkowitz+Kowalski's in particular. Constructing housing estates and homes has become a key point within Szyszkowitz+Kowalski's theoretical work. It

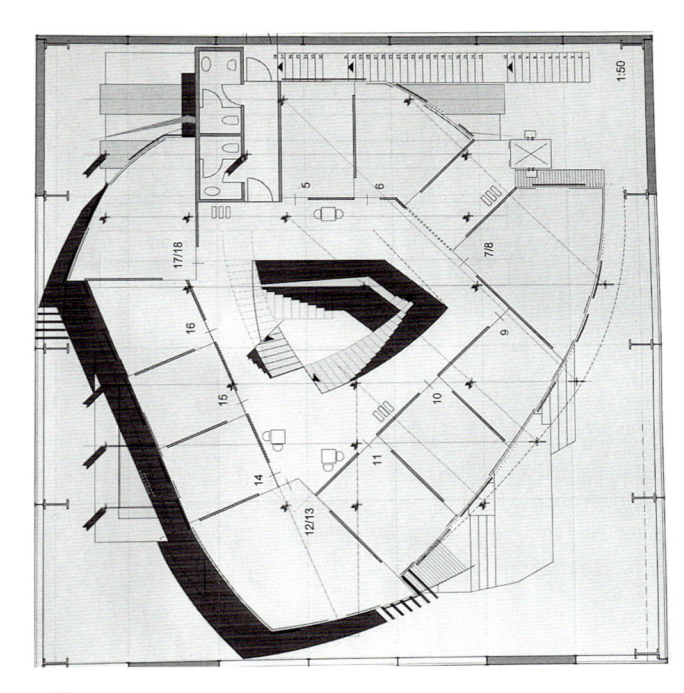

> 89
Büro- und Ausstellungsgebäude der Zeche Zollverein Essen, Projekt innerhalb der historischen Halle 2000–2001 Office and exhibition building for the Zeche Zollverein Essen, project 2000–2001 within the historic hall

Architektur im allgemeinen und den Szyszkowitz+Kowalskis im besonderen international mitbegründet.
Siedlungs- und Wohnbau ist ein Schwerpunkt der konzeptionellen Arbeit von Szyszkowitz+Kowalski geworden. Daß diese Siedlungen durch die Erfahrungen im Privathausbau geprägt wurden, daß die ideelle Konzeption des Wohnens auch in den ungleich strikteren Programmvorgaben des gemeinschaftlichen Lebens und Bauens zum Tragen kommen konnte, erscheint naheliegend, wenn auch nicht selbstverständlich. Die Grundlage der Angleichung zwischen den Siedlungshäusern und dem Privathaus bildet die Auffassung der Architekten, daß die Menschen differenzierte Wohnwünsche haben, die sie auch im Kontext einer Siedlungsgemeinschaft realisieren wollen. Wie in einem Familienverband geht es auch hier um die Ausdifferenzierung privater Räume, halbprivater Zwischenzonen und öffentlicher Gemeinschaftsräume, die ganz ähnlich wie in den fließenden Grundrissen der Privathäuser organisiert werden. Immer formt die Idee der definierten Gemeinschaft unter der Maßgabe größtmöglicher Individualisierung die Bebauungsstruktur eines Siedlungverbandes. So gibt es, wie in der Wohnbebauung der *Alte Poststraße* in Graz (Abb. 84), die 1984 im Industriegürtel der Stadt hinter dem Bahnhof entstand, eine gestaffelte Blockrandbebauung, die einen Innenhof umschließt oder, wie in der auf freiem Feld errichteten *Wohnanlage in Eisbach-Rein* (Abb. 85), einen hufeisenförmigen zentralen Innenbereich, um den die Siedlungshäuser wie eine Zweiflügelanlage gruppiert sind. Das Symbol der Gemeinschaft, wie es Bruno Taut in der Hufeisensiedlung in Berlin-Britz (1925–1931) gestaltet hatte, zeigte noch einmal seine kulturelle Prägung. Die Überlagerung von großräumlichen Erschließungsfiguren einer Wohnanlage und kleinräumlichen Hausgrundrissen ist in be-

seems likely, but it cannot be taken for granted, that the housing estates were shaped by their experience in building private houses, and also the fact that their intellectual concepts relating to home life could also make an impact when faced with the much stricter programme requirements of community life and building. The estate houses and the private houses work along the same lines because the architects feel strongly that people have different ideas about how they want to live, and need to be able to realize these in the context of social housing as well. As in a family unit, here too private spaces, semi-private intermediate zones and communal public spaces have to be separated out and organized in a very similar way to the fluid ground plans in the private houses. The idea of a defined community with the greatest possible individualization always defines the development structure for a housing estate. For example, it can take the form of a staggered block periphery development surrounding an inner courtyard, as in the *Alte Postraße housing estate* in Graz (fig. 84), which was built in 1984 in the city's industrial belt behind the station, or a horseshoe-shaped central inner area with the estate houses grouped around it like a complex with two wings, as in the *estate in Eisbach-Rein*, built on a green-field site (fig. 85). The symbol of community, as created by Bruno Taut in the Hufeisensiedlung in Britz, Berlin (1925–1931), showed its cultural character once again. The idea of overlapping large-scale access figures and small-scale house ground plans in a housing complex showed up particularly clearly in the *estate on the*

sonderem Maße in der *Wohnsiedlung auf dem Küppersbuschgelände in Gelsenkirchen* (Abb. 87), die im Rahmen der IBA Emscher Park seit 1990 entstand, zum Tragen gekommen. Die zur Straße hin verdichteten Wohneinheiten dieser Siedlung sind um Innenbereiche gruppiert, die zu den ovalen Platzräumen eine geringere Dichte und eine eher verschachtelte Raumorganisation halböffentlicher und öffentlicher Zonen aufweisen. Die zentrale Figur der Siedlung bildet neben diesen nach innen orientierten Höfen ein großer linsenförmiger, öffentlicher Platz. Die räumliche Dominanz dieser geometrischen Figur hat später auch dem Grundriß des *Hauses am Ruckerlberg* das unverwechselbare Gepräge gegeben und klingt als Raumfigur der Kommunikation in einigen Projekten der Architekten an (Abb. 86, 88, 89). Die in den neunziger Jahren im Privathausbau vielfach und variantenreich durchgespielte Einbindung der Natur in den unmittelbaren Lebensbereich der Bewohner und die Transformation ökologischer Vorgaben in symbolische Formen ist gerade in der Gelsenkirchener Siedlung in einzigartiger Weise demonstriert worden: „… Blech-Aquädukte sammeln das Regenwasser der Dächer, um es … am tiefsten Punkt der Geländewanne sichtbar in die ‚Linse' einzuleiten."[44]

Das Wohnhaus, das Szyszkowitz+Kowalski 1991/92 anläßlich der IGA (Internationale Gartenschau und experimenteller Wohnbau) in Stuttgart errichtet haben, hatte die Architekten bereits für die Probleme des ökologischen Bauens sensibilisiert, so daß das Stuttgarter Projekt als Experiment für die Anforderungen im Rahmen der IBA Emscher Park gelten kann. Wenngleich der symbolische Duktus ihres ökologischen Wasserspiels im Zentrum der Gelsenkirchner Wohnanlage

Küppersbuschgelände in Gelsenkirchen, which came into being in 1990 as part of IBA Emscher Park (fig. 87). The residential units in this estate become denser towards the street. They are grouped around internal areas that towards the oval squares show lower density and an essentially encapsulated spatial organization of semi-public and public zones. A large lenticular public square alongside these inner-facing courtyards forms the central figure of the estate. The spatial dominance of this geometrical figure also gave unmistakable form to the ground plan of the *House on Ruckerlberg*, and is present as a communication figure in some of the architects' projects (figs. 86, 88, 89). In the nineties, nature was included in the occupants' immediate living area in many different ways in private houses, and ecological requirements were transformed into symbolic forms. This was demonstrated uniquely in the Gelsenkirchen estate: "… sheet-metal aqueducts collect the rainwater from the roofs, in order to … direct it into the 'lens' at the lowest point in the site trough."[44]

The private house built by Szyszkowitz+Kowalski in 1991/92 for IGA (International Horticultural Show and experimental housing construction) in Stuttgart had already made the architects aware of the problems of ecological building, so the Stuttgart project can be seen as an experiment with the requirements in the context of IBA Emscher Park. Even though the symbolic lines of their ecological water feature

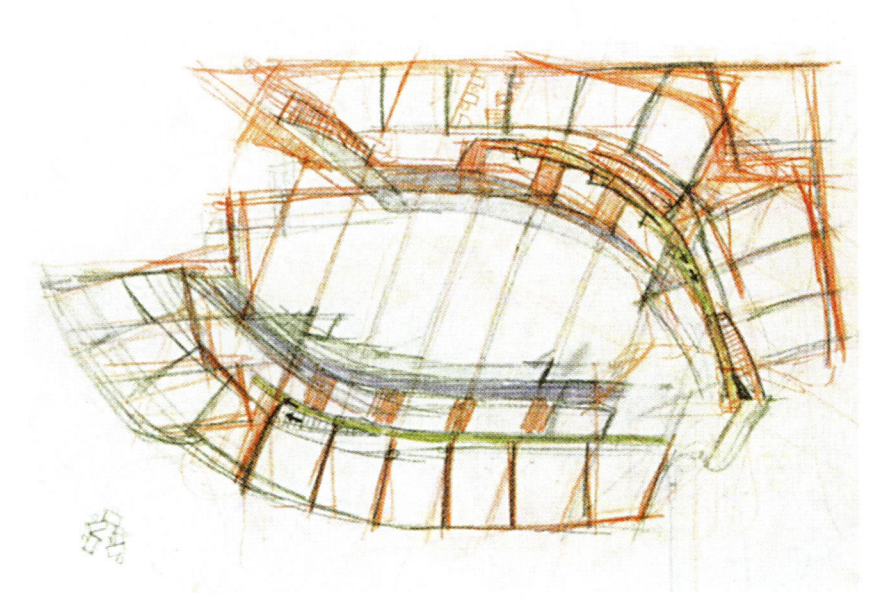

> 90
Studienzentrum der Technischen Universität Graz, Graz, Inffeldgasse 1998–2000, Entwurfsskizze Study centre at Graz Technical University, Graz, Inffeldgasse 1998–2000, design sketch

zuweilen mit Skepsis betrachtet wurde, kommt diesem „Markenzeichen"[45] doch eine bedeutende kulturelle Funktion zu. In dem „vielgliedrigen" Geflecht aus Architektur und den zu Straßen und Plätzen gefaßten Zwischenräumen übernimmt diese Konstruktion einer in ihren Konturen filigranen, im Detail jedoch kraftvollen Großform die Aufgabe des prägnanten, visuellen Zeichens für „einen garantiert erinnerlichen Ort."[46]. Die Lineatur dieses wie eine „Kunst-Installation"[47] wirkenden technischen Objektes macht das weite Oval der zur Mitte hin abfallenden Grundrißfigur des Platzes zum dreidimensionalen Raumerlebnis und aus dem Faktum der Regenwasserregeneration ein atmosphärisches Sinnenereignis. Diese Optik der räumlichen Zuordnung, der Identifikation und des Wiedererkennens hat dem außerordentlich differenzierten Raumgefüge der Siedlungsarchitektur eine Mitte gegeben und damit nicht nur die unterschiedlichen Interessen der sechs verschiedenen Bauträger unter die Dominanz der Gemeinsamkeit gestellt, sondern darüber hinaus dem sozialen Mischungskonzept von kleineren und größeren Familien, von Alleinerziehenden, Ausländern und alten oder behinderten Menschen zugleich einen öffentlichen Raum der Vermittlung gegeben. Um diesen Siedlungskern gruppieren sich die drei sowohl frei finanzierten als auch aus Mitteln des sozialen Wohnungsbaus geförderten, räumlich unterschiedenen Bebauungseinheiten mit den 226 Wohnungen aus Mehrfamilienhäusern, Eigenheimen, Seniorenappartements und dem angelagerten Kindergarten. Zwei Motivationen der Architekten sind als Leitideen des Privathausbaus auch in diesem Siedlungsgefüge prägend: Es ist zum einen die Berücksichtigung des Bedürfnisses nach individueller Distinktion im Kontext des Siedlungsverbandes ebenso wie in den einzelnen Wohnungsgrundrissen und, soweit dies möglich war, in der Erschließung der Wohnungen über separate Eingänge. Und es ist zum anderen deren Einbindung in den umgebenden Landschaftsraum durch die Nutzung der kleinen Gärten, der Dächer und Terrassen oder über die Balkone und minimierten Wintergärten. Auch in diesem Siedlungskomplex schafft ein System aus Pflanzengerüsten immer wieder Zonen der Verschattung, die der Klimaverbesserung ebenso dienen wie der Augenlust. Wiewohl der formale Impuls zur Differenz in den unterschiedlichen Haustypen wirksam gewesen ist, erscheint die Siedlung doch als eine gestaltete Einheit – ein Effekt, der mit Hilfe Karl Gansers gegen die Bauträgergesellschaften durchgesetzt werden konnte. Deren Forderungen nach farblicher Absetzung der einzelnen Planungseinheiten konnte entgegengewirkt werden, so daß der Gesamteindruck der Siedlung vom lichten Graublau der jeweiligen Fassadenoberflächen beherrscht wird.

Mit der *Küppersbuschsiedlung in Gelsenkirchen* ist ein Zwittergebilde entstanden, in dem mit der Reihenhaustypologie und dem frei stehenden Siedlungshaus der traditionellen Ruhrgebietssiedlungen ebenso vertraute Akzente gesetzt worden sind, wie darin Standards anklingen, die das Flair von Urbanität aus der Nähe sozialer Differenzierungen zu übermitteln verstehen. In der Abstufung von öffentlichen, gemeinschaftsorientierten und privaten Raumzonen, im kalkulierten Wechsel von einsehbaren und verschlossenen Raumeinheiten, die von Wegen und Treppen durchzogen auf die Geheimnisse im Inneren der Häuser und Wohnungen verweisen, spricht die Architektur in einer Art *pattern language* vom Charakter des privaten und öffentlichen Lebens. Dies respektiert die kulturelle Resistenz dieser Kategorien im All-

in the centre of the *Gelsenkirchen housing complex* was met with some scepticism, this "trade mark"[45] does have a significant cultural role to play. The structure is set among the "multipartite" tissue of architecture and intermediate spaces turned into streets and squares. It is filigree in its outlines but powerful in its details, a large-scale form, and a concise, visual symbol of a place that is "guaranteed to be memorable".[46] The lines of this technical object, which seems like an "art installation",[47] make the wide oval of the ground plan figure of the square, which slopes down towards the centre, into a three-dimensional spatial experience, and turn rainwater recycling into an atmospheric sensual experience.

This aspect of spatial allocation, identification and recognition gave the extraordinarily sophisticated spatial structure of this housing estate architecture a centre. It thus addressed the different requirements of the various parties funding the building programme, with joint interests dominant. It also provided a public space to convey the social concept of mixing large and small families, single parents, foreigners and old or handicapped people. This is the core of the estate, and around it are grouped the three spatially different development units, both privately financed and funded from social housing resources. They include 226 dwellings in apartment blocks, private houses, accommodation for senior citizens, and a kindergarten. Two of the ideas that drive the architects also helped to shape this estate structure, as guidelines from private house construction. The first is that the need for individuality was considered when planning the housing estate units as well as in the ground plans for the individual apartments and, as far as this was possible, by providing access to the units through separate entrances. The second is that they are tied into the surrounding landscape by the small gardens, roofs and terraces, or by the balconies and mini-conservatories. And this housing estate also has trellises with plants, which create shaded zones that improve the climate as well as being a delight to look at. Even though the formal drive towards different individual house types has been effective, the estate still gives a sense of overall unified design – an effect that Karl Ganser helped to achieve against the wishes of the companies financing the project. It proved possible to resist their demands for colour-coding the individual planning units, so that the overall impression given by the estate is the light greyish blue of the individual façades.

The *Küppersbusch estate in Gelsenkirchen* is a cross between terraced house typology and the free-standing estate houses of the traditional Ruhr housing estate. Familiar emphases have been made, and there is also a sense of creating an atmosphere of urban quality by keeping different social elements together. The architecture makes statements about the character of private and public life in a kind of pattern language, in the gradation of public, community oriented and private spatial zones, in the calculated alternation of spatial units that are closed or can be looked into, criss-crossed by paths and flights of steps, indicating the secrets inside the

⁴⁵ Beatrix Novy, Städtische Inseln.
Die Wohnsiedlungen der IBA Emscher Park,
in: Deutsche Bauzeitung 6/99, S. 92.
Beatrix Novy, Städtische Inseln. Die Wohnsiedlungen der IBA Emscher Park, in:
Deutsche Bauzeitung 6/99, p. 92.
⁴⁶ Manfred Sack, Siebzig Kilometer Hoffnung. Die IBA Emscher-Park-Erneuerung
eines Industriegebiets, Stuttgart 1999,
S. 235. Manfred Sack, Siebzig Kilometer
Hoffnung. Die IBA Emscher-Park-Erneuerung
eines Industriegebiets, Stuttgart 1999,
p.235.
⁴⁷ Op. cit. Op. cit.
⁴⁸ Terence Riley (Hg.), The Un-Private House,
The Museum of Modern Art, New York 1999.
Terence Riley (ed.), The Un-Private House,
The Museum of Modern Art, New York 1999.

tagsleben vieler Menschen, die, aller Diagnosen zum Trotz, nach wie vor den Schutz der Privatheit suchen und die Familie als erstrebenswerte Lebensgemeinschaft favorisieren. Noch artikulieren sich die privaten Wohn(t)räume der meisten Westeuropäer in Raumsprachen von Rückzugsgebieten, die um so deutlicher artikuliert werden, wenn das Wohnen im Kontext der Siedlungsgemeinschaft organisiert werden soll. Dieser Sachverhalt, wie ihn die Architekten im Rahmen des partizipatorischen Bauens in Eisbach-Rein erfahren haben, begründet ihr Anliegen, zwischen den individuellen und gemeinschaftlichen Interessen zu vermitteln. Mit dieser Haltung formulieren sie im derzeitigen Diskurs zum „Un-private House"⁴⁸, das diese Trennungslinien programmatisch negiert, ein Beharrungsvermögen, das nicht der Veröffentlichung des Privaten huldigt, sondern auf einer klaren Unterscheidung, auf der Differenz des Privaten und des Öffentlichen, des Individuellen und des Gemeinschaftlichen pocht.

Ausblick auf eine Architektur

Die Architektur von Karla Kowalski und Michael Szyszkowitz hat das von Giedion angestoßene Programm der Humanisierung nicht an Lebensformen ferner Regionen, den „Tropen" oder den „polaren Gegenden" orientiert, sondern im Klima der jeweiligen vorgefundenen lokalen und individuellen Lebensformen gesucht. Sie haben darin eine ähnliche Haltung entwickelt, welche im Büro von Ralph Erskine für den skandinavischen Raum und dort tatsächlich auch für polare Gegenden umgesetzt wurde. Dessen Credo hatte die Figur des „sozialen Menschen" mit seinen vielfältigen Bedürfnissen nach gemeinschaftsbildenden Erfahrungen umkreist. Für Szyszkowitz+Kowalski manifestieren sich in diesen Erfahrungen darüber hinaus die „Urphänomene des menschlichen Lebens", die der Schweizer Giedion vielleicht in Anlehnung an den großen Psychoanalytiker seines Heimatlandes, C. G. Jung, in die Architekturdebatte zurückgeholt hatte. Dazu

houses and apartments. This respects the fact that many people cling to these categories culturally in their daily lives. Despite all the diagnoses, they want to protect their privacy, and favour the family as the way of life to be aspired to. The private dreams most Western Europeans dream about their living space are expressed in the language of retreat zones, and they are expressed all the more clearly when living is to be organized in the context of a housing estate community. This state of affairs, as experienced by the architects in participatory building projects like Eisbach-Rein, explains their interest in mediating between individual and communal interests. This attitude leads them to persistently cling to their ideas in the context of the current discourse about the "un-private house",⁴⁸ which programmatically negates these dividing lines. This persistence does not pay tribute to making the private public, but insists on a clear distinction, on the difference between the private and the public, the individual and the communal.

Towards a new architecture

Karla Kowalski's and Michael Szyszkowitz's architecture has not directed the humanizing programme adumbrated by Giedion at the life-forms of far-away places, the "tropics" or the "polar regions". It has conducted its search in the climate of the local and individual life-forms that they have found in each project. Here they have developed an attitude similar to the one implemented in Ralph Erskine's practice for Scandinavia, which did actually involve some polar regions. Erskine's credo was built around the figure of "social human beings" with their many and various needs for experiences that go to build a community. For Szyszkowitz+Kowalski the "primal phenomena of human life" are also manifest in these experiences, which Giedion, as a Swiss, was perhaps borrowing from the greatest psychoanalyst in his home country, C. G. Jung, when he reintroduced them to the architecture debate. This includes, despite the dwindling "art of being at home", the individual need for identification patterns that

> 91
Haus in Kumberg, Kumberg 2000–2002, Luftbild der Baustelle House in Kumberg, Kumberg 2000–2002, aerial photograph of the building site

gehört trotz der schwindenden „Kunst zuhause zu sein" das individuelle Bedürfnis nach Identifikationsmustern, dem die Architektur nicht als ein selbstreferentielles Projekt, sondern als ein Raumgefüge symbolischer Ordnungen folgt, die verständlich sind ohne ans Populäre sich zu verschwenden. Auf jeden Fall aber verbietet ihr Konzept der Individualisierung räumlicher Strukturen jegliche Dogmatik. Es erstaunt daher nicht, wenn man in den *Stadtvillen in Graz-Mariagrün* (Abb. S. 196–205) eine am Hang gelegene Erschließung findet, die in Zeilenstruktur erfolgt, deren Wegeführung im Inneren des Siedlungsgefüges wiederum jeweils vier Häuser optisch zusammenbindet und Platzräume schafft, die den Gemeinschaftscharakter dieser Zwischenbereiche betonen. Wenn daher dem *Haus am Ruckerlberg* mit dem *Haus in Kumberg* (Abb. 91, Abb. S. 214–219) bei Graz ein Privathaus folgt, das sich im Grundriß abermals einem Quadrat annähert, wie dies schon im weit gediehenen Konzept eines Fertighauses, dem *Design-*

oder *Traumhaus* (Abb. S. 184–187) der Fall gewesen ist, so offenbart sich darin die ortsbezogene Offenheit dieser Entwurfshaltung. Da die „Bebauungsrichtlinien der Marktgemeinde Kumberg" zudem den Dachausbau nur dann gewähren, „wenn dadurch ein nachteiliger Einfluß auf das Ortsbild ausgeschlossen ist"[49] und im Geiste der Ortsbildpflege daher die Verwendung des traditionellen steilen Giebels gerne gesehen wird, haben Szyszkowitz+Kowalski eine Dachform entwickelt, die das Bogendach aufgreift, dieses aber zur Gartenseite hin durch ein Fensterband aufsprengt, so daß der gesetzlich fixierten Konvention zwar entsprochen, deren uninspiriertem Traditionalismus jedoch zugleich widersprochen wird – und das mit intelligentem, keineswegs reißerischem Kalkül. Außerdem erhält der hohe Raum des Wohnbereichs dadurch die notwendige, zusätzliche Belichtung. Auch in diesem Haus klingt das offene Wohnkonzept an, wenngleich die einzelnen Lebensbereiche durch große

architecture follows not as a self-referential project, but as a spatial structure of symbolic orders that are comprehensible without wasting energy on the popular. But their concept of individualized spatial structures rules out any hints of dogmatism. It is therefore not surprising that access to the *Urban villas in Mariagrün*, Graz (figs. p. 196–205), is on a slope and is structured in rows. Inside the estate its pathways again tie four houses together visually and create squares that emphasize the communal character of these intermediate areas. So when the *House on Ruckerlberg* is followed by the *House in Kumberg* near Graz (2002, fig. 91, figs. p. 214–219), a private house whose ground plan is once more close to being a square, as has been the case in the almost completed concept of a prefabricated house, the *designer* or *dream house* (figs. p. 184–187), this reveals the location-related openness of this design approach. The "Kumberg community building guidelines" only permit a rooftop development "if this has no deleterious effect on the townscape",[49] and so the use of

the traditional steep gable tends to be preferred for the sake of the townscape. For this reason Szyszkowitz+Kowalski developed a roof that takes up the idea of the arched roof but breaks this up on the garden side with ribbon windows. This conforms with the legal requirements, but runs counter to their uninspired traditionalism – and does it calculatedly, intelligently, but by no means sensationally. It also provides the necessary additional lighting for the high living room. The idea of open living is also touched upon in this house, even though the individual living areas are separated from each other by large sliding doors. In this rather smaller house the architects also had to create a sense of distance in a way that was different from the lavish villas. So here we come across the maxims that the architects so appreciated in J. P. Oud's wonderful estate houses in the Weißenhofsiedlung in Stuttgart: "the visible gain from formulated intermediate areas",[50] and the diagonal connections, which make the strictly rectangular paces look large and fluid. The glazed terrace is a fluid

[49] *Die Bebauungsrichtlinien der Marktgemeinde Kumberg, 7.3, § 4 Bauvorschriften im Sinne des STMK Raumordnungsgesetzes ..., Abs.3.1* Die Bebauungsrichtlinien der Marktgemeinde Kumberg, 7.3, § 4 Bauvorschriften im Sinne des STMK Raumordnungsgesetzes ..., para.3.1
[50] *Karla Kowalski, Zwischenräume, unveröffentlichtes Manuskript, 1989/90, S. 25.* Karla Kowalski, Zwischenräume, unpublished manuscript, 1989/90, p. 25.

Schiebetüren wieder von einander separierbar sind. In diesem eher kleinen Wohnhaus müssen die Architekten zudem andere Distanzräume entwickeln, als dies in den großzügigen Villen möglich war. So stößt man hier auf jene Maximen, die das Architektenpaar an den wunderbaren Siedlungshäusern J.P. Ouds in der Stuttgarter Weißenhofsiedlung (1927) so ungemein schätzen: „Der sichtbare Gewinn durch formulierte Zwischenbereiche"[50] und die Diagonalbezüge, wodurch die streng rektangulären Räume groß und fließend erscheinen (Abb. S. 217). Ein derartiger fließender Zwischenbereich ist die glasgedeckte Terrasse, die den Wohnbereich mit dem Garten verbindet und das bekannte Hallenthema in einem verringerten Maßstab mitschwingen läßt. Allemal ist dieses glasgedeckte Volumen ein offener Raum, der die schweifenden Gedanken umhüllt und anregt.

Das Architekturverständnis von Szyszkowitz+Kowalski umfaßt nicht nur den Anspruch, Lebensräume sinnvoll und funktionsfähig zu organisieren, sondern darüber hinaus die „Schatten der Erinnerungen" (Gaston Bachelard) zu stimulieren, um sie als Bestandteil des gelebten Raumes dem Alltag zu integrieren. Dieser Effekt resultiert aus räumlichen Abstufungen, die im Ineinanderfließen unterschiedlich hoher oder aus der Rektangularität ausbrechender intimer Räume eine Nuancierung der Belichtungsvaleurs zwischen hellen, dunkleren oder weitgehend verschatteten Bereichen erhalten, die mit dem Wechsel der Jahres- und Tageszeiten gleichsam atmosphärische Schwingungen erzeugen. Dieses Privathauskonzept versagt sich daher auch eine ästhetische Dominanz, die die Innenraumgestaltung in ein rigides, formalisiertes Gesamtkunstwerk transformiert, in dem die Bewohner als Dekorum placiert erscheinen, gleichsam als Marionetten eines fremdbestimmten Habituskonzeptes. Die „Territorialkunst", die Szyszkowitz+Kowalski pflegen, weiß sehr wohl um die Wünsche der Bewohner nach Zeichen der Erinnerungen zur Markierung von individuellen Lebensräumen. Diese Position vertritt eine im internationalen Architekturgeschehen eigenständige Richtung, deren Programmatik nicht im Repetitiven verharrt, sondern die vielfältigen Möglichkeiten zeigt, die dieser innewohnen. Es tritt darin das leidenschaftliche Bekenntnis zur kulturellen Dimension des Bauens zutage, das im Privathaus seine eindrücklichsten Varianten gezeitigt hat. Als Kulminationspunkt neuer Möglichkeiten der Architektur wird gerade diese Bauaufgabe auch weiterhin einen Ausblick auf die kommende Architektur eröffnen.

(figs. p. 217) intermediate area of this kind. It links the living area with the garden and gives a hint of the familiar hall theme on a reduced scale. In any case, this glazed volume is an open space that envelopes and stimulates wandering thoughts.

Szyszkowitz+Kowalski's architectural understanding does not just involve organizing living spaces meaningfully and so that they can function. They also intend to stimulate the "shades of memory" (Gaston Bachelard), so that they can be integrated in everyday life as a component of the space experienced. This effect is created by spatial graduations that acquire nuances of light between bright, dark or largely shady areas, produced when spaces of different heights flow into each other, or break away from strict right angles. As the time of day and the seasons change, something like an atmospheric oscillation is produced. So this private house concept also denies itself the aesthetic dominance that would transform the interior design into a rigid, formalized universal work of art, in which the occupants seem to be placed as part of the décor, effectively marionettes in a behaviour concept determined by someone else. The "territorial art" cultivated by Szyszkowitz+Kowalski is well aware of the occupants' desire for signs of memories to identify an individual living space. This position represents an independent direction within international architecture. Its programmatic approach is not bogged down in repetition, but shows the many possibilities inherent in it. Here a passionate commitment to the cultural dimension of building is revealed that has produced its most impressive variants in the private house. As a culmination point for new possibilities within architecture it is precisely this type of commission that will open up prospects of the architecture that is to come.

Annäherung an Graz

Die Landeshauptstadt Graz, Europäische Kulturhauptstadt des Jahres 2003, besitzt einen schicken neuen Flughafen. Er liegt im Süden der Stadt, dort, wo die Gegend flach ist, zwischen Gemüsefeldern, Streusiedlungen und einer boomenden Freizeitindustrie überlassenen Baggerseen. Autobahnen führen nahe vorbei, die in alle vier Himmelsrichtungen streben. Am „Knoten Graz" weisen Schilder und Großmarkierungen auf dem Asphalt gen Norden nach „D", gen Süden nach „SLO", gen Westen nach „I" und gen Osten nach „H" und Wien. Ein wahrhaft internationaler Knoten, infrastrukturell ideal gelegen und erschlossen, möchte man meinen. Doch das war nicht immer so, denn die so gerne beschworene Drehscheibe Südostmitteleuropas ist, wie die Drehscheibe auf dem Theater, nur nach einer Seite offen. Die drei anderen Seiten sind, auch hier stimmt die Theatermetapher, amphitheatralisch von den letzten Ausläufern der Alpen bis zu eineinhalbtausend Metern hoch umstellt. Die offene südliche Seite geht nach „SLO", jene Richtung, aus der die Türken ihre Armeen heranführten, um erst an der uneinnehmbaren Festung „Grätz" zu scheitern, aus der später die Studentische Jugend des gesamten, österreichisch besetzten Balkans kam, um die Technische Hochschule und die geisteswissenschaftliche Universität zu besuchen, jene Richtung, in die bis zum Ende des Imperiums die österreichische Marine ihren Nachschub zu den Stützpunkten Venetiens und Dalmatiens verschickte. Ab 1918 war diese Richtung Sackgasse mit ihrem Ende an der jugoslawischen Grenze eine halbe Autostunde entfernt.

Das Zentrum des südlichen Reichsteiles geriet an den Rand und mußte sich in andere, bisher vernachlässigte Richtungen orientieren. Die hufeisenförmig um die im flachen Grazer Becken liegende Stadt gelagerten Höhenzüge wurden mit aufwendigen Verkehrsbauten erschlossen, die bis heute noch nicht zu Ende gebracht worden sind. Am augenscheinlichsten erschließt sich diese komplizierte Situation dem Passagier der vornehmlich aus „D" kommenden internationalen Flugverbindungen. Es sind erhabene Aussichten, die ihm zuteil werden. Die letzten Ausläufer der Alpen, nur im Hochsommer gänzlich schneefrei, durchschneidet in engem Tal die Mur, unvermittelt weitet sich die Enge und gibt den Blick frei auf die Orchestra des Amphitheaters mit der Stadt. Während der Passagier genießt, muß der Pilot arbeiten. Nur im seltenen Fall extrem günstiger Windlage gelingt der Anflug direkt von Norden über den Höhenrand hinweg par terre. Gewöhnlich muß das Flughafengelände südwärts überflogen, dann an der Landmarke eines Kraftwerksschornsteins scharf gewendet werden und der Abstieg nun gen Norden kann beginnen. Man hat was hinter sich, wenn man in Graz gelandet ist, und besonders gilt das für den Autofahrer: Die Alpen mit ihren beklemmenden Tunneldurchfahrten, die berüchtigte „Pack", oder von Wien her die lustig klingende „Bucklige Welt", welche aber zum Beispiel in tiefer Winternacht bei Tanklastzugsunfall bedingt gesperrter Autobahn gar nicht mehr lustig ist. Um so erleichterter ist man, da zu sein. Die Romantiker haben die Stadt und vorzüglich ihre Lage in den höchsten Tönen gelobt, und bei einigen, wie Ernst Moriz Arndt, spürt man in der Begeisterung auch die Erleichterung, hier nach der Beschwerlichkeit, Bedrängnis und Gefahr einer fußmäßigen Alpendurchquerung der Verheißung Italiens in lachender Ebene bereits nahe zu sein.

Heute gibt's in der Ebene nichts mehr zu lachen und den Verlockungen Italiens erliegt man allenfalls in Drive-in-Pizzerien, Fiat-Vetretungen und Agip-Tankstellen. Die Triester Straße, die einst die direkte Verbindung nach Italien bildete, dient allenfalls noch dem Nahverkehr.

Approaching Graz

The Land capital Graz, European city of culture 2003, has a smart new airport. It is south of the town, where the land flattens out, set among fields of vegetables, scattered settlements and flooded gravel pits that are now in the hands of a booming leisure industry. Motorways leading to all point of the compass run close by. At the Graz interchange, signs and large markings on the asphalt point north to "D", south to "SLO", west to "I" and east to "H" and Vienna. So you would think that this really is an international junction, perfectly sited infrastructurally. But this was not always the case. People like to talk about the "Drehscheibe", the hub or revolving stage of south-eastern Central Europe, but like a revolving stage in the theatre it is open on one side only. The other three sides – the theatre metaphor works here as well – are hemmed in like an amphitheatre by the last foothills of the Alps, up to a height of one and a half thousand metres. The open, southern side leads to "SLO"; this is the direction from which the Turks brought their armies, only to be beaten back at the impregnable fortress of "Grätz". Later young students from all the Austrian-occupied Balkans came to the technical college and the arts university. It was also the direction in which the Austrian navy sent supplies to its bases in the Veneto and Dalmatia until the fall of the empire. From 1918 this direction was a cul-de-sac as the Yugoslav border was only half an hour away by car.

The centre of the southern part of the empire shifted to the periphery, and had to face in other directions that it had neglected up to then. Elaborate and expensive transport systems, still incomplete, were designed to open up the horseshoe of mountains surrounding the flat Graz basin. This complicated situation is clearest to passengers on international flights, coming mainly from "D". Their eyes are met with some sublime sights. The narrow Mur valley cuts through last foothills of the Alps, only completely free of snow in high summer. The narrows suddenly open up to reveal the orchestra of the amphitheatre and the city. While the passengers are enjoying this, the pilot has to work. It is only in rare cases of extremely favourable winds that flights are able to land directly beyond the high ground. Usually they have to fly over the airport to the south, turn sharply at a landmark power station chimney and then start the descent in a northerly direction. When you land up in Graz you've been through something, and this applies particularly to car drivers: the Alps with their claustrophobic tunnels, the notorious "Pack", or if you're coming from Vienna the "Bucklige Welt" – "Humpy World" –, which sounds amusing, but there's nothing amusing about it on a winter's night with the motorway down to one lane because a tanker has jack-knifed. So you're all the more relieved to be there. The Romantics praised the city and its position in particular to the skies. In some of their work, Ernst Moriz Arndt's, for example, you can feel relief shining through the enthusiasm: relief at being so close to the promise of Italy's laughing plain after the tribulations, difficulties and dangers of crossing the Alps on foot. Today the plain has nothing to laugh about. You succumb to the pleasures of Italy at best in drive-in pizzerias, Fiat dealerships and Agip petrol stations. The Trieste road, once the direct link with Italy, is used by local traffic only. Like any city, Graz has now girded itself with the typical modern glacis of unregulated commercial development, and you have to suffer your way through this before you cross the river and are welcomed inside the walls of this beautiful old town.

The boundaries of the Graz local authority area roughly describe a square, with an average

Blick in das Grazer Becken nach Osten View of the Graz basin looking east

1 HAUS ÜBER GRAZ HOUSE ABOVE GRAZ
2 GRÜNES HAUS GREEN HOUSE
3 HAUS ZUSERTAL HOUSE IN ZUSERTAL
4 ROTES HAUS RED HOUSE
5 HAUS AM HOHENRAIN HOUSE ON HOHENRAIN
6 GRAUES HAUS GREY HOUSE
7 HAUS HARMISCH HARMISCH HOUSE
8 HÄUSER IN WIEN/HIETZING – OBERES HAUS HOUSES IN HIETZING, VIENNA – LOWER HOUSE
9 HÄUSER IN WIEN/HIETZING – UNTERES HAUS HOUSES IN HIETZING, VIENNA – UPPER HOUSE
10 HAUS IN BAD MERGENTHEIM HOUSE IN BAD MERGENTHEIM
11 HAUS IN MARIA ENZERSDORF HOUSE IN MARIA ENZERSDORF
12 HAUS AM PLATTENWEG HOUSE ON PLATTENWEG
13 TURM FÖLLING TOWER IN FÖLLING
14 DESIGNHAUS DESIGN HOUSE (nicht gebaut, not realized)
15 HAUS IN MOOSBURG HOUSE IN MOOSBURG
16 STADTVILLEN MARIAGRÜN URBAN VILLAS IN MARIAGRÜN
17 HAUS AM RUCKERLBERG HOUSE ON RUCKERLBERG
18 HAUS IN KUMBERG HOUSE IN KUMBERG

Graz mit Gemarkungsgrenze, Flusslauf und Standorten der Häuser, Satellitenaufnahme Graz with boundary line, river course and house sites, satellite photograph

Wie jede Großstadt hat sich auch Graz hier mit jenem neuzeitlichen Glacis aus regelloser Kommerzbebauung umgürtet, das erst einmal durchlitten werden muß, bevor man, den Fluß überquerend, von den Mauern der schönen alten Stadt empfangen wird.

Die Gemeindegrenzen der Kommune Graz umschreiben annähernd ein Quadrat, dessen gemittelte Seitenlänge 11 ¼ km beträgt. Der Fluß Mur zieht eine Teilungsdiagonale von NW nach SO durch dieses Quadrat und schneidet so zwei Siedlungsdreiecke aus, ein privilegiertes: Altstadt, gründerzeitliche Stadterweiterung, Universitäten, Theater und die Zentrale der „schwarzen" Volkspartei, und ein weniger privilegiertes: ehemalige Schiffslände, Nachtjackenviertel, Bahnhof, Friedhof und die Parteizentrale der „roten" Sozialdemokraten. Diese Teilung wird recht anschaulich durch die Siedlungspolitik der zahlreichen in der Stadt der Gegenreformation ansässigen kirchlichen Ordensgemeinschaften repräsentiert. Die Jesuiten gründeten die Universität im Schatten des Domes und auch den nicht mehr ganz so bettelgeordneten Franziskanern gelang es, das „bessere" Murufer zu besetzen. Gleich gegenüber haben sich auf der „schlechten" Flußseite die minderen Brüder der Franziskaner, die Minoriten, angesiedelt, und gleich nebenan gehen die Barmherzigen Brüder ihren karitativen Pflichten nach.

Genau im Zentrum des Stadtquadrates liegt das historistische Rathaus mit dem dazugehörigen straßenbahnverkehrsreichen, mit bunten Marktständen gesprenkelten Hauptplatz. Nähme man jetzt einen riesigen Zirkel mit dem Mittelpunkt im Platzzentrum zu Füßen des taubenbekackten Denkmals des Reichsverwesers Johann von Habsburg und schlüge man einen Halbkreisbogen in die östliche Quadrathälfte des Stadtgebietes, erhielte man eine Linie, die sich in etwa mit der Linie der Höhenzüge auf der „guten" Seite deckt. Hier findet der potentielle Bauherr die begünstigten Süd- und Südwestlagen im sanft aus der Topfebene von Fluß und Altstadt ansteigenden, zuweilen romantisch schöne Stadtblicke gewährenden voralpinen Hügelland. Hierhin hat sich der Besucher der Einfamilienhausbauten des Architekturbüros Szyszkowitz+Kowalski zu wenden.

side length of 11.25 km. The river Mur flows through this square from NW to SE on a dividing diagonal, thus cutting out two triangles of settlement. One is privileged: old town, urban expansion in the early 1870s, universities, theatres and the headquarters of the "black" Volkspartei (populist party), and one that is less privileged: former landing-stage, nightlife quarter, station, cemetery and the party headquarters of the "red" social democrats. This division is pointed up very vividly by the siting policy of the numerous ecclesiastical orders domiciled in the city under the Counter-Reformation. The Jesuits founded the university in the shadow of the cathedral and even the Franciscans, no longer so dependent on begging, managed to occupy the "better" bank of the Mur. The Franciscans' little brothers, the Minorites, settled immediately opposite on the "bad" side of the river, and the Brothers of Mercy discharged their charitable duties just next door.

Right in the centre of the city square is the historic town hall with its main square, full of the usual trams and sprinkled with colourful market stalls. Now if you were to take a gigantic pair of compasses centred on the middle of the square at the feet of the pigeon "be-crapped" monument to the Imperial Regent Johann von Habsburg, and then drew a semicircle in the eastern half of the city, you would have a line that approximately covers the line of the hills on the "good side". Here anyone who is thinking of commissioning a house finds the favoured south- and southwest-facing sites in the pre-alpine hills, rising gently out of the plain of river and old town, sometimes affording romantically beautiful views of the city. This is where visitors to family houses built by the Szyszkowitz+Kowalski architectural practice have to turn.

Das Architekturbüro Szyszkowitz+Kowalski

Man muß nicht unbedingt das neuzeitliche Glacis der von Industrie und Handel ungestaltet geprägten Vorstädte durchqueren, um ins Zentrum der Stadt zu gelangen. Es gibt schönere Wege, dies zu tun. Nur: Diese Wege kennt nicht jeder, dem Fernreisenden aus der Bundeshauptstadt Wien, aus Kärnten oder gar dem Balkan werden sie verschlossen bleiben. Es sind die Wege der Einheimischen und der Bewohner des Umlandes, aus weniger bekannten Ortschaften wie „Faßberg", „Laßnitzhöhe" oder „Kumberg". Während die großen Ausfallstraßen von fernen Zielen sprechen (Kärntner-, Triester, Wiener-Straße), schmücken sich die vertrauten Wege der Ortsansässigen mit Namen von ebenso vertrauten Persönlichkeiten: Heinrich, dem ersten Herzog Österreichs, dem Heiligen Leonhard und der unverzichtbaren Elisabeth. Hier, natürlich befinden wir uns wieder in der „besseren" östlichen Hälfte, geht es nicht flott und langweilig geradeaus. Dafür erreicht man nach kurzer, kurvenreicher Fahrt das vielbesuchte Ausflugslokal „Häuserl im Wald" statt der Bahnhofsgaststätte, nicht den Friedhof, sondern den alten Botanischen Garten mit nahgelegenem Teich zum Bootchenfahren, nicht den Flughafen, sondern die barocke Wallfahrtskirche Maria Trost für anders geartete Kontakte mit dem Himmel.

Ein Eckhaus in der Elisabethstraße beherbergt eine Tanzschule, ein Stockwerk darüber findet man das Architekturbüro Szyszkowitz+Kowalski, Abteilung 37. In der geschlossenen historischen Bebauung mit frisch geputzten Gründerzeitfassaden gehört das Gebäude zu den unrenovierten, in Frieden alternden: Übliche große Portaldurchfahrt mit mächtigem Holztor, alte Remise im Hof, schlanke Gußeisensäulen mit Kapitellen im Treppenhaus, Steinstufen, knarrende Holzdielen, völlig anspruchslose Tür mit Visitenkartenschildchen, scheppernde Klingel. Studentische Wohngemeinschaften könnten angesichts der Weitläufigkeit der großbürgerlichen Zimmerfluchten und der buchstäblichen Katzensprungnähe zu den Universitäten neidisch werden. Szyszkowitz+Kowalski empfangen nicht im prominenten Erkerzimmer des Eckhauses, sondern in ihren Arbeitsräumen an der Straße und zum Innenhof. Die repräsentativen Fluchten bleiben der Arbeit der 20 bis 30 Mitarbeiter vorbehalten. Jeder weiß, daß Büroarbeit bei Architekten mit abendlichen oder gar nächtlichen Überstunden zu rechnen hat. Wenige wissen, daß Zeichenstift und Computermaus des nachts hier von dem Swing der Tango-, Fox-, und Walzermusik aus der Tanzschule geführt werden. Dennoch gehen Rückschlüsse auf die schwungvolle Architektur, die hier produziert wird, in die Irre, denn Abteilung 52 des Büros, ebenfalls an der Elisabethstraße gelegen, jedoch ein paar Blocks weiter stadtauswärts, verfügt über derlei rhythmische Unterstützung nicht. Ebenso in die Irre gehen Vermutungen, die Doppelsitzigkeit des Büros entspräche der Doppeleigentümerschaft. Eine Leitungs-, Funktions- oder Strukturtrennung gibt es nicht, sodaß ein emsiges Hin und Her zwischen den Dependancen die Folge ist und der Eindruck eines einen ganzen Straßenzug beanspruchenden Großraumbüros entsteht. Zur Verständigung über den Aufenthalt an einem Ort jeweils abgängiger Personen oder Dokumente haben sich die genannten Abteilungsnummern eingebürgert, sie bedeuten nichts weiter als die Hausnummern der beiden Gebäude.

In Nr. 52 swingt keine Tanzmusik, dafür weht hier der Atem Grazer Stadtgeschichte. Die geschlossene Blockrandbebauung liegt hinter uns, auf Einzelgrundstücken erkennt man, vergisst man einmal die zwei, drei dazwischen gedrängelten Tankstellen, ländlich herrschaftliche Architektur. Alles ein bißchen zugewachsen, ein wenig angewildert, aber immer noch spürbar das aristokratische Flair der steiermärkischen Adelsgeschlechter, die hier in

Szyszkowitz+Kowalski's practice

You don't absolutely have to traverse the modern glacis of formless suburbs dominated by commerce and industry to get into the city centre. There are more attractive ways of doing this. But not everybody knows them, they will not be found by long-distance travellers from the capital, Vienna, from Carinthia or even from the Balkans. They are ways used by local people and the residents of the surrounding area, from little-known places like "Faßberg", "Laßnitzhöhe" or "Kumberg". The main roads out of town suggest distant destinations (Kärntner- Triester-, Wienerstraße), but the familiar routes used by local residents are graced with the names of equally familiar personalities: Heinrich, Austria's first Duke, St. Leonhard and the inevitable Elisabeth.
Here, of course, we are back in the "better" eastern half, you don't just whiz boringly straight ahead. Instead, after a short, twisty drive you get to the "Häuserl im Wald", a popular excursion destination, rather than the station buffet, to the old Botanical Garden with a nearby boating lake rather than the cemetery, and you don't get to the airport but to the baroque pilgrimage church of Maria Trost, for a rather different kind of contact with the heavens.

A building at the corner of Elisabethstraße houses a dancing school, and on the floor above is Szyszkowitz+Kowalski's architectural practice, section 37. The building is unrenovated and ageing peacefully among its fellows in this uniform historical development with freshly rendered late 19th century façades. There is the usual large carriage entrance with a massive wooden door, an old coach-house in the courtyard, slender cast iron columns with capitals in the stairwell, stone steps, creaking wooden corridors, a very ordinary door with a visiting-card label, a clanging bell. This place would make student flat-sharing communities very envious: the upper middle-class rooms are so spacious and it is literally a stone's throw from the universities. Szyszkowitz+Kowalski do not see you in the prominent bay-windowed room in the corner building, but in their workroom by the road and on the inner courtyard. The prestigious sets of rooms are reserved for the 20 to 30 employees to work in. Everybody knows that architects need to do overtime in their offices in the evening and even at night. But not many people know that at night draughtsman's pen and computer mouse move to the swing of tango, foxtrot or waltz from the dancing school. But any conclusions about the swinging architecture produced here would be wrong: section 52 of the practice, also in Elisabethstraße, but a few blocks farther away from the centre of the town, does not have rhythmic support of this kind. And it is equally erroneous to suppose that the practice's double base relates to its double ownership. There is no separation of management, function or structure. This means that there is a great deal of busy to-ing and fro-ing between the branches, creating an impression of an open-plan office taking up the entire street. The section numbers started to be used to make it clear where documents or people that might have disappeared from one location or the other are to be found, they are simply the house numbers of the two buildings.

So there is no dance music at no. 52, instead we have a hint of Graz's city history. The uniform blocks are behind us, and the individual plots are occupied by grand rural architecture, give or take the two or three petrol stations that have managed to insinuate themselves. It is all a bit overgrown and running wild, but you still have a sense of the aristocratic Styrian

bequemer Entfernung zu ihren innerstädtischen, düsteren Barockpalästen dem Landleben oblagen.
Haus Nr. 52 gehörte dem Grafen Attems, unter den Bedeutenden einer der Ersten, die wahrlich gut daran getan haben, mal kurz vor die Tür zu gehen, denn deren verwaschen dunkelrotbrauner Residenzklotz in der Stadt lässt nur Denkmalschützer strahlen. Erholsam hingegen die Fassade der Attemsschen Villa, deren Hochparterre das Architekturbüro belegt. Das Gartentor quietscht, die Diele knarrt, die Klingel scheppert, ganz wie gewohnt. Das Treppenhaus ist natürlich großzügiger als jenes im bürgerlichen Quartier 300 Meter straßab, dafür taugt es im Winter als prächtiger Urwald frostfliehender Oleanderbüsche. Landleben eben.
Dem unspektakulären, wenn auch mit Sorgfalt gewählten Ambiente der beiden Büros entspricht die private Residenz der Architekten. In das alte trutzig wirkende Haus ist das Ehepaar gezogen, als man einen Stützpunkt für die Überwachung der ersten Bauaufgabe, des *Hauses über Graz* brauchte. Dort haben sie restauriert, renoviert, mit der notwendigen Haustechnik ausgestattet und sind geblieben. Die Notwendigkeit der Errichtung des „Eigenen Hauses" stellte sich nicht. Es fällt im übrigen auch schwer, sich vorzustellen, daß sich Szyszkowitz+Kowalski zu einer solchen Bauaufgabe entschließen könnten, an der man dann „Handschrift", „Stil", „Persönlichkeit" und ähnliches allzu leicht herausinterpretieren könnte. Derartiges entspräche ganz und gar nicht den leicht austernhaften Aussagen der Architekten zu ihrem Werk. Gibt sich das Wohnhaus, ganz dem Wesen der Bewohner entsprechend, verschlossen, gewinnt man doch Einblicke, wenn man eingeladen ist, sich näher umzusehen. Im Garten, der sich hinter der Mauer des Hauses auf dem nicht großen Grundstück erstreckt, bildet sich Seelenlage ab, zeigt sich das „Eigene". Natürlich überrascht es nicht, dass auch hier dem Naturraum große Aufmerksamkeit gewidmet wird, niemand hätte eine langweilige Einheitsgestaltung oder gar eine Wüstenei erwartet. Die Details aber geben Zeugnis von einer engagierten gärtnerischen Arbeit, die man bei den viel beschäftigten, mit Lehr- und Büroverpflichtungen in halb Mitteleuropa mehr als ausgelasteten Architekten nicht vermuten würde. Hochstammrosen, Kamelien und Orchideen, Gardenien und Zitronenbäumchen verraten, dass hier Gestalter am Werke sind, die es sich zur Aufgabe gemacht haben, den Besonderheiten auf den weiten Feldern der Natur wie der Architektur auf die Spur zu kommen. Drinnen, im Haus, steht man verwundert vor der Frage, wie es möglich ist, dass diese in blättrigen Ton gewandeten Tiere nicht zusammenbrechen, und draußen blühen prächtig in bester Gesundheit Pflanzen, die allesamt zur Gattung der den Gärtner zur Verzweiflung treibenden (hier nicht botanisch gemeinten) Mimosen gehören. Die lächelnd gegebene Antwort – man hört geradezu die Auster sich wieder schließen – auf die Frage, wieso man sich das alles zumute und wie das überhaupt funktioniere, kommt aus der Gegend valentinesker Quasi-Antworten und klingt nach: Wenn man's kann, ist es keine Kunst.
Ohne die Gartenkunst am Bau lässt sich die Architektur Szyszkowitz+Kowalskis nicht denken, und es gibt nur wenige Auftraggeber, die das Angebot der Architekten nicht angenommen haben, mitgestaltend bei der Konzeption des Gartens behilflich zu sein. Gartenthemen lassen Kontakte reifen und über Jahre halten, Besuche, die das langsame Einwachsen des Hauses in seine Umgebung miterleben lassen, werden gewünscht und sind erwünscht. Die Zahl der Kunden, die sich mit der grünen Wiese begnügen und zu denen kein Kontakt mehr besteht, sind an einer Hand zu zählen. So findet über die Gärten das an sich endliche Projekt Hausbau seine Fortsetzung, und die These angesichts dieses Phänomens ist zu wagen: Über der swingenden Tanzschule im Bürgerhaus und in dem bescheidenen Landhaus derer von Attems entsteht die Idee eines Traumes von umfassender Architektur.

nobility; they could devote themselves to country life here, a comfortable distance away from their gloomy baroque palaces in the city centre.
No. 52 belonged to Graf Attems, one of the first of the important people who did themselves a good turn by moving out: his town house is a washed-out dark reddish-brown monstrosity that might bring a twinkle to a conservationist's eye, but only just. The façade of the Attems's villa is a pleasure to behold, however. The architectural practice is on the upper ground floor. The garden gate squeaks, the floorboards creak, the bell clangs, all just as usual. The stairwell is of course rather more spacious than the one in the middle-class district 300 metres down the street; in winter it is a haven for a magnificent jungle of oleander bushes sheltering from the frost. Country life, in other words.
The architects' own home has the same unspectacular but carefully chosen ambience as the two offices. The married couple moved into the old, formidable-looking house when they needed a base to supervise their first building project, the *Haus above Graz*. They restored, renovated, installed the necessary domestic services and stayed there. There did not seem to be any necessity to build their "own house". It is also difficult to imagine Szyszkowitz+Kowalski deciding to do that, as it would be all too easy for people to use it to define their "handwriting", "style", "personality" from it. That sort of thing would not fit in at all with the architects' slightly tight-lipped statements about their work. Their home may look reserved, which is completely correct in terms of its occupants' nature, but you do find some revealing things when invited to take a closer look. There is a garden behind the house wall on this not very large plot, and it is here that you get a sense of the architects' souls and what it is their "own". Of course it is not surprising that a great deal of attention has been paid to nature here, no one would have expected a dreary uniform design or a wilderness. But the details are evidence of committed gardening to the extent that you would probably not have expected from these two architects, who have more than enough to do in their busy life of teaching and office commitments in half of Central Europe. Standard roses, camellias and orchids, gardenias and lemon bushes show that designers are at work here who have made it their business to track down distinctive features in the wider fields of both nature and architecture. Inside, in the house, you wonder in some amazement how it is possible that these animals clad in flaky clay do not fall apart; outside, plants are blooming magnificently in the best of health and all of them are tender and hyper-sensitive varieties that usually drive gardeners to distraction. The answer to the question of how they can let themselves in for all this and how does it work comes with a smile – though you do sense the lips might be tightening again. It is at best a witty half-answer, and it goes something like this: there's nothing to it if you can do it. Szyszkowitz+Kowalski's architecture is unthinkable without associated horticulture. There are very few clients who have refused the architects' offer to help them to design their gardens. If a garden is involved, the contacts mature and last for years; the architects are pleased to be asked to come round and share the experience of the house growing into its surroundings, and the clients like it too. The number of customers who are satisfied with a lawn and whom the architects have lost touch with can be counted on the fingers of one hand. So the house building project, which is finite as such, continues via the gardens, and I think we can risk this proposition about the phenomenon: the idea of a dream of all-embracing architecture is born above the swinging school of dancing in the middle-class house and in the von Attems's modest country house.

Wichtigste Realisierungen

1972/74	Haus über Graz, Wohnhaus, A-Graz
1977/78	Aufbahrungshalle, A-Schwarzach/Pongau
1977/79	Grünes Haus, Wohnhaus, A-Graz
1979/81	Schloss Großlobming, Revitalisierung und Erweiterung, Hauswirtschaftsschule mit Internat, A-Großlobming (1. Preis-Wettbewerb 1978)
1979/81	Haus Zusertal, Wohnhaus, A-Graz
1982/84	Schloß Pichl, Revitalisierung und Erweiterung Forstwirtschaftsschule mit Internat, A-Mitterdorf/Mürztal (1. Preis-Wettbewerb 1980)
1982/84	Rotes Haus, Wohnhaus, A-Graz
1982/84	Neues Wohnen – Alte Poststraße, Mitbestimmungsmodell im Geschosswohnbau, 43 Wohneinheiten, A-Graz
1984	Architektur-Vision; Rauminstallation, Ausstellung im Steirischen Herbst, A-Graz
1984/86	Wohnbau Eisbach-Rein, Mitbestimmungsmodell für 24 Wohneinheiten, A-Graz (1. Preis-Wettbewerb 1983)
1983/85	Haus am Hohenrain, Wohnhaus, A-Graz
1984/87	Pfarrzentrum Graz-Ragnitz, Kirche mit Haus der Begegnung, A-Graz (1. Preis-Wettbewerb 1983)
1985	Empfangsloge eines Versicherungsgebäudes, A-Graz
1984/86	Graues Haus, Wohnhaus, A-Graz
1985/91	Biochemie-Biotechnologie, Institut der technischen Universität Graz, A-Graz (1. Preis-Wettbewerb 1983)
1987	Hexen und Zauberer, Ausstellungsgestaltung der Landesausstellung 1987 auf der Riegersburg, A-Riegersburg/Steiermark (1. Preis-Wettbewerb 1986)
1987/88	Haus Harmisch, Wohnhaus, Kohfidisch, A-Burgenland
1986/89	Haus in Wien/Hietzing, Wohnhaus, A-Wien
1987/90	Haus in Wien/Hietzing, Wohnhaus, A-Wien
1989/93	Kaufhaus Kastner & Öhler, Umbau des Haupthauses im Stadtzentrum, A-Graz
1990	Schauspielhaus Graz, Zubau des Depots, A-Graz
1990/91	Wohnbau Sandgasse, 27 Wohneinheiten, A-Graz
1990/92	Wohnbau Knittelfeld, 82 Wohneinheiten (1. Preis Wettbewerb 1987) 1. Bauabschnitt 28 Wohneinheiten, A-Knittelfeld
1991/93	Haus in Bad Mergentheim, Wohnhaus, Bad Mergentheim, D-Würzburg
1991/92	Wohnbau Voitsberg, 51 Wohneinheiten (1. Preis Wettbewerb 1990) 1. Bauabschnitt 17 Wohneinheiten, A-Voitsberg
1992/93	Jugendstilhaus Kastner & Öhler, Umbau des Kaufhauses im Stadtzentrum, A-Graz
1992/93	IGA 93, Experimenteller Wohnbau, Reihenhäuser, D-Stuttgart
1993/94	Haus in Maria Enzersdorf, Wohnhaus, A-Wien
1993/97	Stadtvillen in Mariagrün, A-Graz, 14 Wohneinheiten
1994/95	Sporthaus Kastner & Öhler, Erweiterung des Kaufhauses im Stadtzentrum, A-Graz
1994/96	Integrativer Kindergarten Küppersbuschgelände für die internationale Bauausstellung, IBA-Emscher Park, D-Gelsenkirchen (1. Preis Wettbewerb 1990)
1994/98	Wohnanlage Küppersbuschgelände für die internationale Bauausstellung, IBA-Emscher Park, D-Gelsenkirchen, 250 Wohneinheiten (1. Preis Wettbewerb 1990)
1995	Next Liberty, Umbau Jugendtheater Thalia, A-Graz
1995/96	Wohnbau Knittelfeld, 82 Wohneinheiten, (1. Preis Wettbewerb 1987) 2. Bauabschnitt, 54 Wohneinheiten, A-Knittelfeld
1994/96	Haus am Plattenweg, Wohnhaus, A-Graz
1996/97	Volksschule Schloss Großlobming, A-Großlobming
1994/96	Turm Fölling, Bibliotheksturm, A-Graz
1997/98	UCI-Kinowelt, Multiplex-Kino in der Innenstadt, A-Graz
1997/99	Wohnbau Schießstätte, A-Graz, 34 Wohneinheiten
1995/96	Haus in Moosburg, Wohnhaus, A-Moosburg/Kärnten
1998/99	Wohnbau Voitsberg, 2. Bauabschnitt 34 Wohneinheiten (1. Preis Wettbewerb 1990), A-Voitsberg
1998/00	Studienzentrum der Technischen Universität Graz, Inffeldgasse, A-Graz (1. Preis-Wettbewerb 1990)
1998/00	Wohnbau Kreuzgasse mit Gemeindezentrum, A-Wien, 160 Wohneinheiten (1. Preis Wettbewerb 1994)
1998/00	Kulturhaus St. Ulrich, A-St.Ulrich/Greith
1998/00	Baumit Beratungszentrum, A-Klagenfurt (1. Preis Gutachterverfahren 1998)
1998/02	Haus am Ruckerlberg, Wohnhaus, A-Graz
1999/00	Stadtentwicklung Heidelberg, Städtebauliches Leitprojekt, 520 Wohneinheiten, D-Heidelberg, (1. Preis intern. Gutachtenverfahren 1998)
1997	Designhaus, Fertighaus-Typen
2000/01	Sporthaus Kastner + Öhler, Erweiterung und Umbau des zentralen Bereiches des Gebäudeensembles im Stadtzentrum, A-Graz
1999/02	Biotechnologiezentrum Qiagen, D-Hilden bei Düsseldorf (1. Preis intern. Gutachterverfahren 1998)
2000/02	BHAK & BHAS Pernerstorfergasse, Berufsbildende Höhere Schule, A-Wien 10 (1. Preis Wettbewerb 1999)
2000/02	Haus in Kumberg, Wohnhaus, A-Kumberg

IN PLANUNG / IN BAU

2002/04	BG u. BRG Wiedner Gürtel, Allgemeinbildende Höhere Schule, A-Wien (1. Preis Gutachterverfahren 2000)
2002/04	Bürohaus am Stadtpark, D-Nürnberg (1. Peis intern. Wettbewerb 1992)
2003/04	Regionalmuseum Eisen u. Stahl, Ausstellungsgestaltung, A-Leoben (2. Preis u. Nachrücker Gutachterverfahren 1999)
2002/03	Bürohaus w&p, Erweiterung und Umbau, A-Klagenfurt
2002/03	Kastner + Öhler Tiefgarage, Neubau einer Tiefgarage (500 Pl.) unter dem historischen Gebäudeensemble der Innenstadt, A-Graz
2002/03	Wohnbau Flurgasse, 25 Wohneinheiten mit Kinderhort, A-Graz
2002/03	Platzgestaltung Piazza d'Italia, D-Wolfsburg
2002/04	Bürohaus in Mariagrün, A-Graz
2003–	HBLV für Gartenbau, Schönbrunn, Berufsbildende Höhere Schule, A-Wien (1. Preis Wettbewerb 2002)

Most important realizations

1972/74	House above Graz, private house, A-Graz
1977/78	Funeral parlour, A-Schwarzach/Pongau
1977/79	Green House, private house, A-Graz
1979/81	Schloss Großlobming, renovation and new construction, School of Home Economics (also Boarding School) A-Großlobming (1st prize in competition 1978)
1979/81	House in Zusertal, private house, A-Graz
1982/84	Schloß Pichl, renovation and new construction, School of Forestry (also Boarding School), A-Mitterdorf/Mürztal (1st prize in competition 1980)
1982/84	Red House, private house, A-Graz
1982/84	Housing Complex Alte Poststraße, codetermination model for multi-storey residential buildings, 43 accommodation units, A-Graz
1984	Visionary architecture, installation, exhibition for 'steirischer herbst', A-Graz
1984/86	Housing Complex Eisbach-Rein, codetermination model for multi-storey residential buildings, 24 accommodation units, A-Graz (1st prize in competition 1983)
1983/85	House on Hohenrain, private house, A-Graz
1984/87	Catholic Parish Centre Graz-Ragnitz, A-Graz (1st prize in competition 1983)
1985	Lobby in the building of an insurance company, A-Graz
1984/86	Grey Haus, private house, A-Graz
1985/91	Institutes for Biochemistry and Biotechnology, Graz Technical University, A-Graz (1st prize in competition 1983)
1987	'Witches and Wizards', exhibition design for the 1987 regional exhibition in Riegersburg castle, A-Riegersburg/Steiermark (1st prize in competition 1986)
1987/88	Harmisch House, private house, Kohfidisch, A-Burgenland
1987/89	House in Hietzing, Vienna, private house, A-Vienna
1988/90	House in Hietzing, Vienna, private house, A-Vienna
1989/93	Haupthaus Kastner & Öhler, department store conversion in central Graz, A-Graz
1990	Schauspielhaus Graz, extension (depot), A-Graz
1990/91	Housing Complex Sandgasse, 27 accommodation units, A-Graz
1990/92	Housing Complex Knittelfeld, 82 accommodation units (1st prize in competition 1987) 1st stage of construction, 28 accommodation units, A-Knittelfeld
1991/92	Housing Complex Voitsberg, 51 accommodation units (1st prize in competition 1990) 1st stage of construction, 17 accommodation units, A-Voitsberg
1991/93	House in Bad Mergentheim, private house, Bad Mergentheim, D-Würzburg
1992/93	Jugendstilhaus Kastner & Öhler, department store conversion in central Graz, A-Graz
1992/93	IGA 93, experimental residential buildings, terraced houses, D-Stuttgart
1991/94	House in Maria Enzersdorf, private house, A-Vienna
1993/97	Urban Villas in Mariagrün, A-Graz, 14 accommodation units
1994/95	Sporthaus Kastner & Öhler, department store conversion in Graz city centre, A-Graz
1994/96	Integrated kindergarten Küppersbuschgelände for the International Building Exhibition Emscher Park, D-Gelsenkirchen (1st prize in competition 1990)
1995	Next Liberty, conversion of the Thalia youth theatre, A-Graz
1994/96	House at Plattenweg, private house, A-Graz
1995/96	Housing Complex Knittelfeld, 82 accommodation units, (1st prize in competition 1987) 2nd stage of construction, 54 accommodation units, A-Knittelfeld
1996/97	Primary School Schloss Großlobming, A-Großlobming
1994/96	Tower Fölling, library tower, A-Graz
1994/98	Housing Complex Küppersbuschgelände für die internationale Bauausstellung, IBA-Emscher Park, D-Gelsenkirchen, 250 accommodation units (1st prize in competition 1990)
1997/98	UCI-Cinema World, multiplex-cinema in central Graz, A-Graz
1997/99	Housing Complex Schießstätte, A-Graz, 34 accommodation units
1995/96	House in Moosburg, private house, A-Moosburg/Kärnten
1998/99	Housing Complex Voitsberg, 2nd stage of construction, 34 accommodation units (1st prize in competition 1990), A-Voitsberg
1998/00	Study Centre – Inffeldgründe Graz, University of Technology, A-Graz, (1st prize in competition 1990)
1998/00	Cultural Centre St. Ulrich, A-St.Ulrich/Greith
1998/00	Baumit – Advice Centre, A-Klagenfurt (1st prize experts' report proceedings 1998)
1998/00	Housing Complex Kreuzgasse with community centre, A-Vienna, 160 accommodation units (1st prize in competition 1994)
1998/02	House on Ruckerlberg, private house, A-Graz
1999/00	Urban Development Heidelberg, urban guidelines project, 520 units, D-Heidelberg, (1st prize intern. experts' report proceedings 1998)
1997	Design House, types of prefabricated houses – construction of the prototype
2000/01	Sporthaus Kastner + Öhler, department store extension in Graz city centre, A-Graz
1999/02	Biotechnology Centre Qiagen, D-Hilden near Düsseldorf (1st prize intern. experts' report proceedings 1998)
2000/02	BHAK & BHAS Pernerstorfergasse, education building, A-Vienna X (1st prize in competition 1999)
2000/02	House in Kumberg, private house, A-Kumberg

IN DESIGN AND DEVELOPMENT STAGE

2002/04	BG u. BRG Wiedner Gürtel, education building, A-Vienna (1st prize intern. experts' report proceedings 2000)
2002/04	Office Building in the municipal park, D-Nuremberg (1st prize intern. competition 1992)
2003/04	Regional Museum Iron and Steel, A-Leoben (follow experts' report proceedings 1999)
2002/03	Office Building w&p, extension and conversion, A-Klagenfurt
2002/03	Kastner + Öhler underground-parking, underground-parking (500 pl.) below the historical ensemble of the inner city, A-Graz
2002/03	Housing Complex Flurgasse, 25 accommodation units with day-nursery, A-Graz
2002/03	Piazza d'Italia, D-Wolfsburg
2002/04	Office Building in Mariagrün, A-Graz
2003–	HBLV for horticulture Schönbrunn, education building, A-Vienna (1st prize competition 2002)

Büro 37 im oberen Geschoß
Office 37 in upper storey

Büro 52 im Erdgeschoß
Office 52 on the ground floor

o. Univ. Prof. Arch. DI
KARLA KOWALSKI

1941 geboren in Beuthen, Oberschlesien

Schulbesuch in Sachsen, Thüringen und Hessen
1962–1968 Architekturstudium, TU Darmstadt
Aufnahme in die Studienstiftung des Deutschen Volkes

1966–1967 Zwischenpraktikum bei Candilis, Josic, und Woods, Paris
1968–1969 Postgraduate Studium an der Architectural Association School, London
1969–1971 Mitarbeit bei Behnisch & Partner, Olympiabauten München

Seit **1973** Zusammenarbeit mit Michael Szyszkowitz in Frankfurt, München, Graz und Stuttgart
und
seit **1978** gemeinsames Architekturbüro in Graz

1971–1972 Lehrauftrag an der Gesamthochschule Kassel zum Thema „Topographie und Entwurf"

Seit **1988** o. Univ. Prof. an der Technischen Universität Stuttgart, Direktorin des Institutes für Öffentliche Bauten und Entwerfen

Seit **1993** Mitglied der Akademie der Künste Berlin, Abteilung Baukunst

Seit **1998** Mitglied der Academie Internationale d'Architecture, Sofia

o. Univ. Prof. Arch. DI
KARLA KOWALSKI

Born **1941** in Beuthen, Upper Silesia

Attended school in Sachsen, Thüringen and Hessen
1962–1968 Studies of architecture at DarmstadtTechnical University
Admission to the "Studienstiftung des Deutschen Volkes"

1966–1967 intermediate training with Candilis, Josic and Woods, Paris
1968–1969 postgraduate study at the Architectural Association School, London
1969–1971 collaboration in the planning for the Olympia buildings at Behnisch & Partner

Since **1973** collaboration with Michael Szyszkowitz in Frankfurt, München, Graz und Stuttgart
and
since **1978** own architects' office in Graz

1971–1972 lectureship at Kassel Gesamthochschule on the subject of topography and design

Since **1988** o. Univ. Prof. at Stuttgart Technical University, head of the Institute for Public Buildings and Design

Since **1993** member of the Academy of Fine Arts Berlin, department for architecture

Since **1998** member of the Academie Internationale d'Architecture, Sofia

o. Univ. Prof. Arch. DI
MICHAEL SZYSZKOWITZ

1944 geboren in Graz, Steiermark

Besuch des Akademischen Gymnasiums in Graz
1962–1970 Architekturstudium, TU Graz
Teilnahme an Städtebau-Seminaren der Internationalen
Sommerakademie Salzburg bei Bakema, Rotterdam
und Candilis, Paris

1970–1971 Mitarbeit bei Domenig und Huth für die Projekte
innerhalb der Olympiabauen von Behnisch & Partner in München

Seit **1973** Zusammenarbeit mit Karla Kowalski in Frankfurt,
München, Graz und Stuttgart
und
seit **1978** gemeinsames Architekturbüro in Graz

1984–1991 Vizepräsident der Zentralvereinigung der Architekten
Österreichs, Landesverband Steiermark

Seit **1989** Mitglied und ab **1998** stellvertretender Vorsitzender
der Altstadt-Sachverständigen-Kommission ASVK, Graz

1987–1993 Mitbegründer und Vizevorsitzender und
1994–1999 Präsident des Hauses der Architektur, Graz

1989–1998 Prüfungskommissär an der TU Graz bzw. TU Stuttgart

Seit **1998** o. Univ. Prof. an der Technischen Universität
Braunschweig,
Vorstand des Institutes für Gebäudelehre und Entwerfen

o. Univ. Prof. Arch. DI
MICHAEL SZYSZKOWITZ

Born **1944** in Graz, Styria

Attended grammar school in Graz (classical education)
1962–1970 Studies of architecture at Graz Technical University
Participation in urban design seminars at the international
summer academy in Salzburg with Bakema, Rotterdam
and Candilis, Paris

1970–1971 collaboration with Domenig and Huth for the
Olympic projects by Behnisch & Partner in Munich

Since **1973** collaboration with Karla Kowalski in Frankfurt,
Munich, Graz and Stuttgart
and
since **1978** own architects' office in Graz

1984–1991 Vicepresident of the "Zentralvereinigung der
Architekten Österreichs", Landesverband Styria

Since **1989** member and since **1998** deputy chairman
of the „Altstadt-Sachverständigen-Kommission" ASVK, Graz

1987–1993 co-founder and vicechairman and
1994–1999 president of "Haus der Architektur" in Graz

1989–1998 examination commissioner at the Graz Technical
University and Stuttgart University

Since **1998** o. Univ. Prof. at Braunschweig Technical University,
head of the Institute for Building Construction and Design

www.szy-kow.at

Ein Hausbesuch

Die Tontiere, die Karla Kowalski auf den Traggestellen von Michael Szyszkowitz errichtet, werden der interessierten Öffentlichkeit als „Monster" präsentiert. Einen „vorzüglichen" Titel nannte Walter Jens diese Zuschreibung, indem er auf die weiterreichende Bedeutung der lateinischen Vokabel als z.B. „Wunderwesen"-haft verwies und alle „Scheusal"-Konnotationen verbannte. Dem ist uneingeschränkt zu folgen, ähnelt doch der „Stehende Bär" beispielsweise eher dem rührenden Exemplar aus der F.K. Waechter-Karikatur „Nur Dritter im Brummen" als einem monströs grimmigen Raubzeug. Mehr Pu als Grizzly, mehr Honig als blutiges Fleisch. Wieder einmal haben uns Szyszkowitz+Kowalski aufs Glatteis geführt, und die Architekturpublizistik ist auch prompt darauf ausgerutscht. Dem Sinnsuchenden scheinen sich diese Tiere vorzüglich als Vehikel für weitergehende Aussagen zum architektonischen Material zu eignen, und so finden wir Entzifferungen aus dem Architekturtext als „Monster", „Käfertiere", „Reptilien" aus „urzeitlicher" Ferne. Der unbedingte Wille zum romantischen Gestus, das durch nichts zu erschütternde Bekenntnis zur Kreation von Paradiesen in unserer Welt der pardises lost wird so übersetzt, als führe uns die Architektur Szyszkowitz+Kowalskis in die „Lost World" des „Jurassic Parc" voller Panzerechsen, Krabbelwesen und Flugbiestern. Natürlich kann man die Zeichnungen als durchs geologische Geschiebe verdrehte Skelettformationen lesen, die Kuppeldächer als Panzerschalen, Balkone als im Gebrüll erstarrte Mäuler, doch erweist sich dieser Befund schnell als durch Fixierung auf das graphische, zweidimensionale Material verführt. Dieser Architekturtext entziffert sich nicht allein durchs Lesen, er will geschaut und erlebt werden. Seine Bedeutung erschließt sich im Gebrauch. Wo sinnsuchende Hermeneutiker nichts als einen Zoo zu finden glauben, erlebt der Nutzer der Architektur Szyszkowitz+Kowalskis und seine Gäste die Gesamtheit der Natur.

Bad Mergentheim, an der Grenze zwischen Baden und Württemberg gelegen und seit der Vertreibung aus den preußischen Stammlanden jahrhundertelang Sitz der Deutschmeister des Deutschen Ordens, eignet sich prächtig als Ruhesitz für kampfesmüde Ritter. Wein wächst an den Hängen des Taubertals, und die Heilquelle des „Karlsbades" labt die Anhänger von alkoholfreien Flüssigkeiten. Vom leicht westernhaft anmutenden Bahnhof kommend, der nichts mehr zu erzählen weiß von seiner ehemals stolzen Funktion als Verbindungsknoten der Badischen und Württembergischen Staatsbahnen, geht es sogleich, wie könnte es anders sein, bergan. Hinter dem Kurviertel nach einigen Serpentinen bietet die Straße, in den zunehmend steiler werdenden Hang gekratzt, bald nur noch Raum für eine Fahrzeugbreite. Den Weinbau haben die praktischen Württemberger hier aufgegeben und sich ihrer mindestens ebenso hingebungsvoll betriebenen Passion gewidmet. Häusle schweben jetzt rechter Hand am Steilhang, erschlossen mit mehr oder weniger phantasievollen Zufahrten und Treppenanlagen. Das Haus des Psychotherapeutenpaares ist eines der am höchsten schwebenden und gleich verbietet sich jeder Eindruck, trotz des deutlich erkennbaren Dachbogens, von irgendwelchem schildkrötigen, hingekauerten Urgetier. In der extremen Untersicht wächst es ragend aus den alten Weinterrassen heraus, und das Dach ist nichts weiter als die Verlängerung des Hauses in den Himmel. Das Nachbargrundstück ist mit einer gewaltigen Mauer aus Findlingen abgefangen, und man fragt sich, welcher geologischen Kapriole diese Formation hier in den Mergelterrassen wohl zu verdanken sei. Der Hausherr, ein verschmitzter Württemberger, wie er im Buche steht, grinst sich eins und bittet, näher hinzuschauen. Man

A home visit

The clay animals that Karla Kowalski builds on Michael Szyszkowitz's bases are presented to the interested public as "Monsters". Walter Jens called this an "excellent" title, pointing out that the Latin word also suggested "miraculous creatures" and ruling out any sense of "monstrousness". This is entirely acceptable, as the "Standing Bear", for example, is more like the touching specimen in the F.K. Waechter caricature "Only Third in Growling" than a monstrously grim predator. More Pooh than grizzly, more honey than bloody meat. Once again Szyszkowitz+Kowalski have taken us out on to thin ice, and the architectural journalists promptly slipped on it. People hunting around to find a meaning seem to take these creatures mainly as vehicles for additional statements about the architecture, and so we find them decoded from the architecture text as "monsters", "beetles", "reptiles" from "primeval" times. Absolute determination to make a romantic gesture, an utterly unshakeable commitment to creating paradises in our world of paradise lost is translated like this: Szyszkowitz+Kowalski's architecture is taking us into the "Lost World" of "Jurassic Park", full of crocodilia, creepy-crawlies and flying beasties. Of course the drawings can be read as skeletal formations distorted by geological debris, the domed roofs as armoured shells, balconies as mouths paralysed in roaring, but thus discovery quickly turns out to have been tempted by undue fixation on the graphic, two-dimensional material. This architectural text cannot be deciphered by reading alone, it has to be looked at and experienced. Its significance is revealed by use. Where would-be interpreters think they have found nothing but a zoo, users and guests of Szyszkowitz+Kowalski's architecture experience nature in its totality.

Bad Mergentheim is on the border between Baden and Württemberg. It was the seat of the German Masters of the Knights of the Teutonic Order for centuries, after they had been driven out of their Prussian homeland. It is ideal as a place for battle-weary knights to rest. Vines grow on the slopes of the Tauber valley, and the "Karlsbad" sacred spring refreshes devotees of non-alcoholic liquids. The station has a slightly Western feel to it, and certainly bears no traces of its formerly proud function as a junction for the Baden and Württemberg State Railways. On leaving it you head for the hills, where else. Beyond the spa area, after a few hairpin bends, the road, scratched into the increasingly steep slope, is only one vehicle wide. The practical Württembergers have stopped planting vines here, and have devoted themselves to their other passion, which they cultivate equally vigorously. Little houses now sit high on the right-hand slope, reached by more or less imaginative drives and flights of steps. The psychotherapist couple's house is one of the highest, and there is absolutely no sense of any sort of tortoise-like, crouching primeval creature, despite the clearly visible curve of the roof. Seen from way below, it towers out of the old vineyard terraces, and the roof is no more than an extension of the house into the sky. The neighbouring plot is shored up by a massive wall of erratics, and you wonder what trick of geology brought this formation to these marl terraces. The owner, a typical mischievous Württemberger, grins to himself and asks us to look more closely. We do so – and we're going to have to do a lot of that, as the owner is not just a witty Württemberger, but a wily psychologist as well. He does not explain the secrets of his house to visitors through demonstrative gestures ("Here is the fireplace and the

Haus in Bad Mergentheim, Bad Mergentheim 1991–1993, Blick aus dem Obstgarten auf die Rückfront des Hauses House in Bad Mergentheim, Bad Mergentheim 1991–1993, view from the orchard of the rear façade of the house

gehorcht – das wird man im Folgenden noch häufiger tun, denn der Hausherr ist nicht nur gewitzter Württemberger, sondern zugleich ausgefuchster Psychologe, der dem Besucher die Geheimnisse seines Hauses nicht durch demonstrative Gesten („Hier ist der Kamin und dahinten das WC") erklärt, sondern durch herauskitzelnde Fragestellerei („Warum, glauben Sie, ist hier kein Fenster in der Wand?") – man gehorcht also, schaut genauer hin, und der liebe Gott entpuppt sich als ein profaner Schöpfer des Namens Dykerhoff: Die ganze Felswand ist nichts als auf den Hanggrund gespritzter Zement, ungestrichen, geradeso, wie er aus dem Pumpenrüssel herausgequollen ist. Treppen, Podeste, Treppen, Terrassen, Treppen. Was müssen die Traubenkiepenträger früher hier geschnauft haben!

Endlich oben angekommen, sind wir unten, auf dem Niveau des Kellergeschosses. Die Eingänge zu den Praxisräumen sind durch ovale Hohlkörper voneinander geschieden. Der Empfang beim Herrn oder der Frau Doktor ist intim und individuell. Gleichzeitig präsentieren sich die Hohlkörper, die auch noch das weit vorspringende Dach stützen, als riesige Blumentöpfe. Platz genug für ausladende Büsche hoch über unseren Köpfen. Drei Meter ist gleich sieben Jahre Wachstumswartezeit gespart! Weiter geht's, und da wir schon dabei sind, geht es gleich ganz hinauf über die Hauptterrasse mit dem parallel zum geschwungenen Dach gespannten, eleganten Sonnensegel, noch eine Treppe, bis hinter das Haus. Die Mühe hat sich gelohnt. Selten ist man hinter einem Wohnhaus weniger „hinten" als hier. Auf seinem dritten Geschoßniveau läuft der Hauskörper in zwei Flügeln V-förmig aus – rechts der elterliche, links der der Kinder – und umfaßt einen idyllischen Obstgarten, welcher, gottlob, eben ist. Wohltat für Blick und Bein. Das Dach ist derart stark gebogen, daß die Kinder noch im dritten Geschoß in himmelhohen gewölbten Zimmern wohnen. Platz genug für Hochbetten, als gäbe es in diesem Haus nicht genug zu klettern. Aber was macht das Kindern schon aus. Von nun an geht's bergab. Das Obergeschoß schwingt über der Erdgeschoßhalle in einer Brückengalerie aus, von der afrikanische Masken ernst herabblicken, Sammelpassion der Psychologen. Unten am Wohnzimmertisch ein weiter Blick ins Taubertal und endlich ein Stuhl. Der Tauberwein ist köstlich gewesen.

WC is through there"), but by asking leading questions ("Can you think why there isn't a window in this wall?") – so you do as you're told, look more closely and God turns out to be a mundane creator called Dykerhoff: the whole rock wall is nothing more than cement sprayed on to the slope, unpainted, exactly as it came out of the pump hose. Steps, landings, steps, terraces, steps. The grape basket carriers must have got completely out of breath. Once we get up to the top we're at the bottom. At cellar level. The entrances to the consulting rooms are distinguished from each other by oval hollow bodies; reception by the male or the female doctor is intimate and individual. At the same time, the hollow bodies support the greatly protruding roof, and also function as gigantic flowerpots. Plenty of room for large bushes high above our heads. Three metres means seven years of growing time saved. On we go, and as we're already climbing we go right up over the main terrace with the elegant sun awning hung parallel with the curved roof, up another flight of steps, to the back of the house. It has been worth the effort. It's rare to feel so little sense of being behind a house as at the back of this one. On the third floor level the body of the building runs out into to V-shaped wings – for the parents on the right and the children on the left – framing an idyllic orchard which, thank God, is flat. A blissful relief for eyes and legs. The roof curves so much that the children still live in sky-high vaulted rooms on the third floor. Plenty of room for high bunk beds, as if there weren't already enough climbing to do in this house. But what does that matter to children. It's downhill from now on. The top floor curves out over the ground floor hall in a bridging gallery with African masks, which the psychologists have a passion for collecting, looking sternly down from it. Downstairs at the living room table there is an open view into the Tauber valley, and a chair at last. The Tauber wine was delicious.

Häuser Houses

HAUS ÜBER GRAZ HOUSE ABOVE GRAZ

ORT LOCATION: Rosenberg, A-8010 Graz   BAUHERRSCHAFT CLIENT: Dr. phil I.W. und Dr. jur. K.W.   PLANUNGS- UND BAUZEIT DESIGN AND REALIZATION: 1972–1974   STATIK STATICS: Christo Grigorow   WOHNNUTZFLÄCHE USABLE LIVING SPACE: 390 m²   UMBAUTER RAUM BUILDING VOLUME: 1.200 m³   KONSTRUKTION UND MATERIALIEN: Holzriegelwand-Konstruktion, 2-schalig in Fertigteilbauweise, Geschoßdecken und einige Wände massiv CONSTRUCTION AND MATERIALS: double timber-rail wall structure, prefabricated, floors and some walls solid   DACH UND WAND-EINDECKUNG: verzinkte Blechbahnen, PVDF-beschichtet ROOF AND WALL CLADDING: galvanized metal strips, PVDF-coated   TÜREN- UND FENSTERELEMENTE: Douglas-Kiefer DOORS AND WINDOWS: Douglas fir   <<< S. ABB. SEE FIGS. 1, 8–11

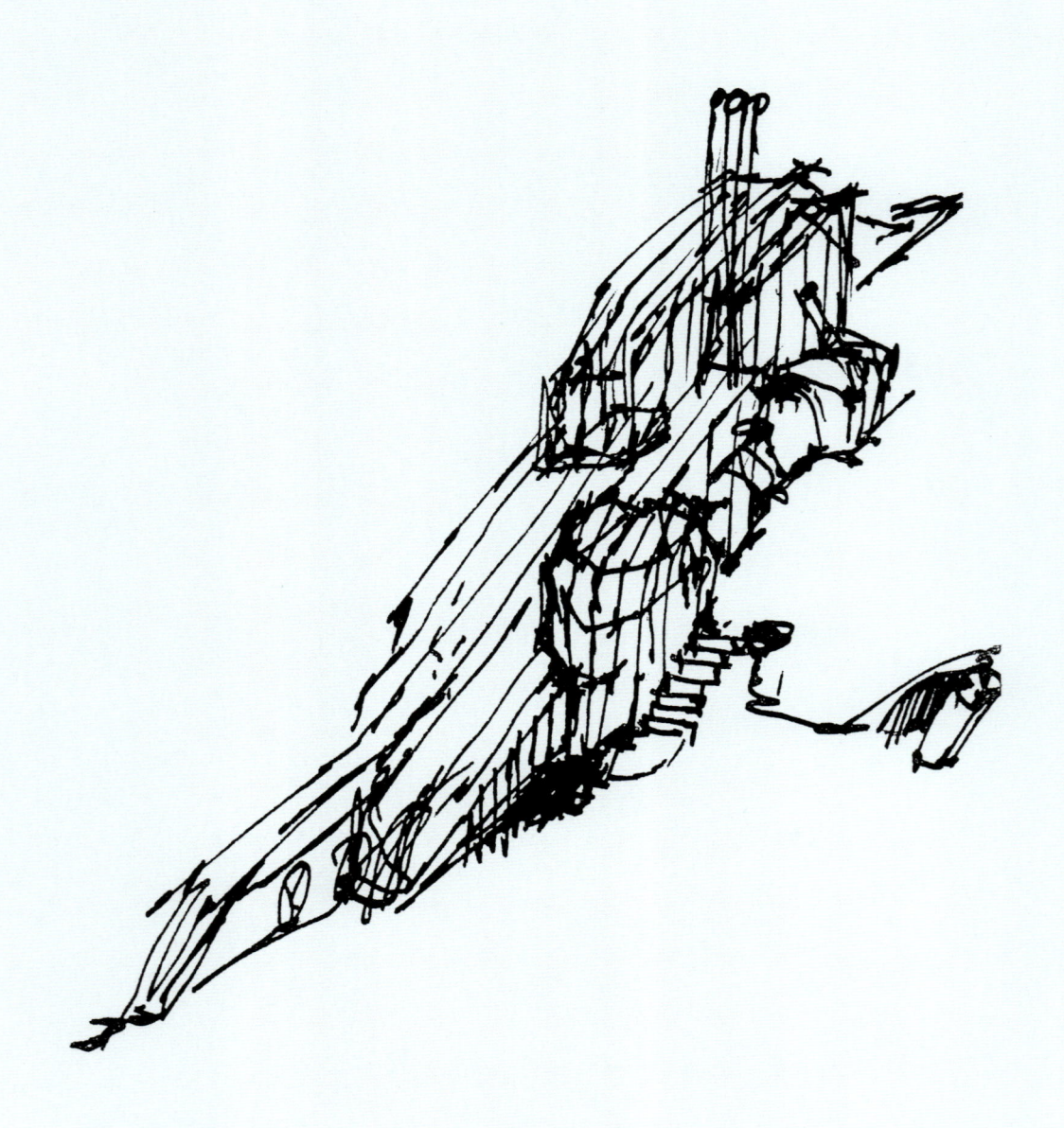

Skizze Sketch
Ansicht von Südwesten View from the south-west

HOUSE ABOVE GRAZ HAUS ÜBER GRAZ

Ansicht von Osten View from the east
Westfassade, Kücheneingang West façade, kitchen entrance
Detail Westfassade Detail of the west façade

Ansicht von Süden View from the south
Ansicht von Osten View from the east
Südfassade mit Pergola South façade with pergola

HOUSE ABOVE GRAZ   HAUS ÜBER GRAZ   106 | 107

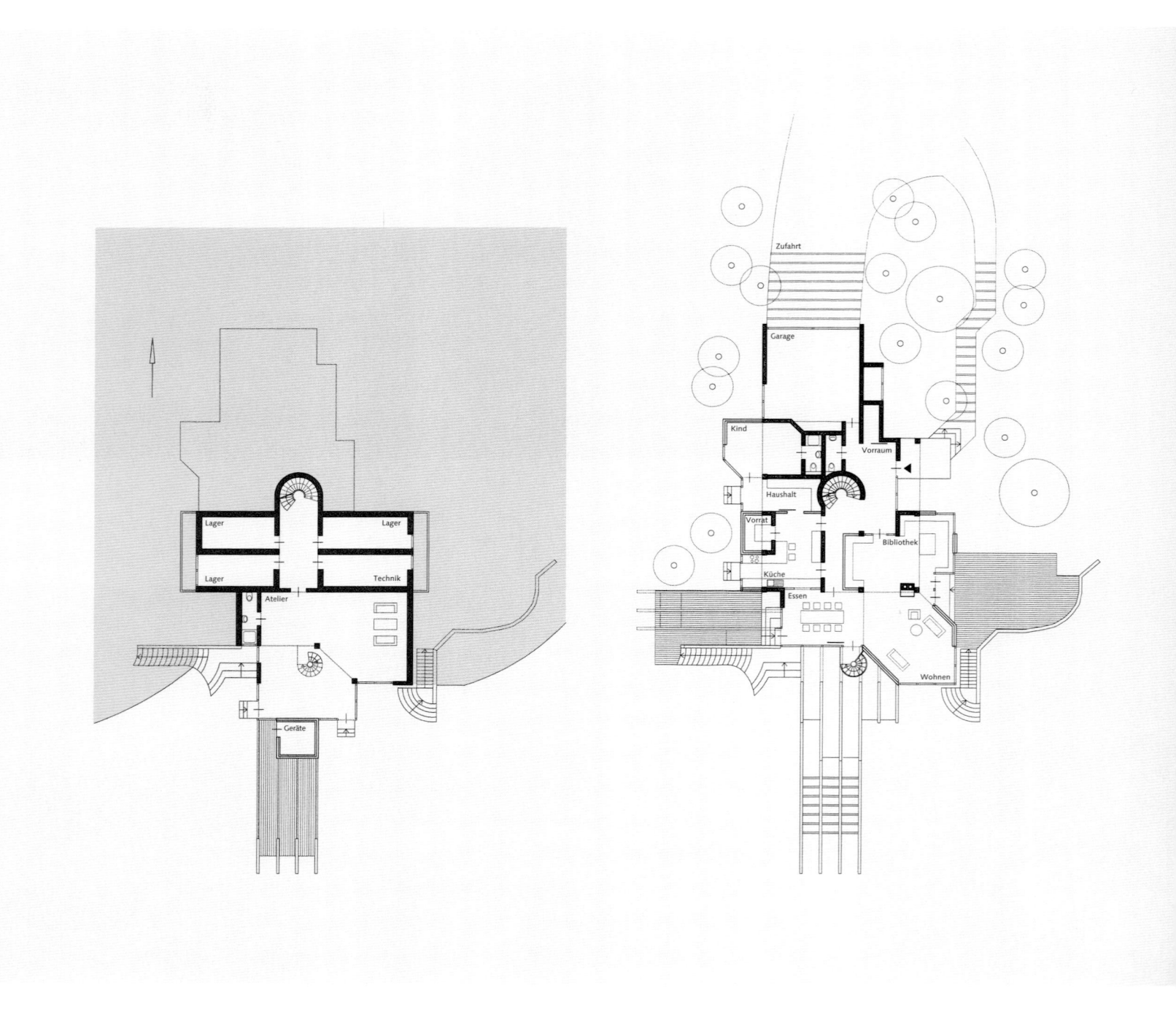

Die Bezeichnung *Haus über Graz* kann als Motto für nahezu alle folgenden Einfamilienhausbauten gelten. Umfaßt sie doch: Hanglage am Stadtrand und eine prominente Aussicht auf die Stadt Graz und die umgebende Landschaft. Das Haus ist durch einen dichten alten Baumbewuchs gegen die umgebende Villenbebauung und den sie erschließenden Verkehr geschützt. „Das Haus ist in Farbe, Form und Funktion auf diese Situation entworfen. Die Elemente Haus-Hügel-Bäume bedingen sich gegenseitig. Die Farbe des Hauses ist rosa-violett, mit ockerrötlichen Holzteilen, die im Inneren durch gelb, weiß und graugrün ergänzt wird. Die drei Geschosse des Hauses umfassen im Untergeschoß neben Kellerräumen die Spielräume, im Hauptgeschoß den Wohnbereich mit Küche und kleiner Bibliothek sowie die Schlafräume im oberen Geschoß. Sie können dem Wunsche der Bauherren gemäß ohne größeren baulichen Aufwand in getrennte Wohnungen mit eigenen Eingängen umgebaut werden." (Szyszkowitz+Kowalski)

Auf Wunsch der Familie, die längere Zeit in den Vereinigten Staaten von Amerika gelebt hatte, sollte das Gebäude ein Holzhaus sein, um derart die Erinnerung an jene Jahre architektonisch wachzuhalten. In diesem Haus finden sich bereits alle räumlichen Erschließungen und architektonischen Landschaftsbezüge, die die Häuser von Szyszkowitz+Kowalski seither auszeichnen. Dieses sind: ein der Topographie folgender fließender, freier Grundriß und die Betonung der familiären Kommunikationsbereiche auf der Erdgeschoßebene, die Anordnung der Schlafräume und größeren Bäder in den oberen Geschossen sowie die Möglichkeit, die Wohnräume für die Kinder und das Kindermädchen separat zugänglich und bei Bedarf im Inneren auch erweitern zu können. Das Haus schafft von innen heraus durch eine akzentuierte Durchfensterung Blickpunkte zum Außenraum, von dem aus das Licht derart von allen Seiten in die Innenbereiche einfließen kann. Die in den Garten ausgreifenden Pergolen schaffen kleinere Landschaftsräume als Bestandteile des Hauses, das in der Außenraumerschließung durch Niveaustufungen und Terrassierungen nicht nur auf verschiedenen Ebenen selbständig zu betreten ist, sondern als eine künstlich gestaltete Landschaft in der Natur erlebbar wird.

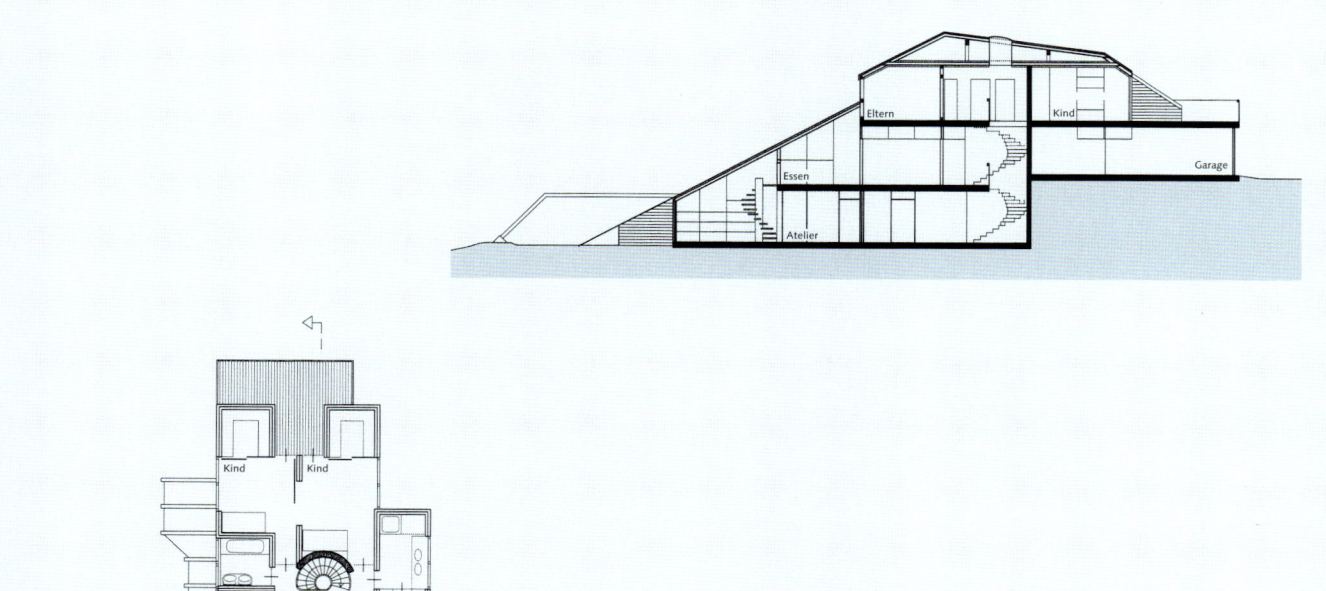

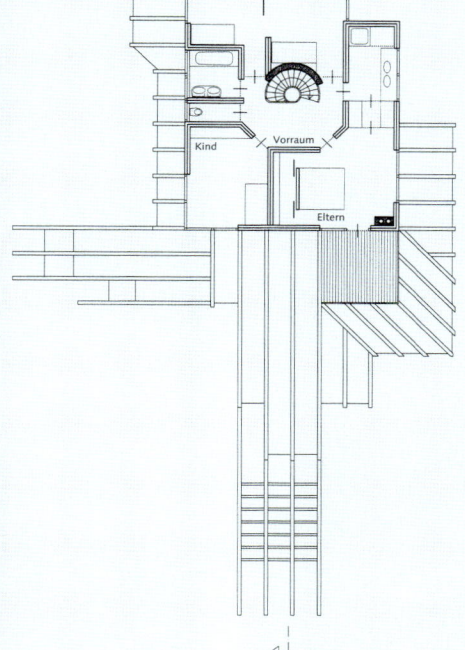

Grundrisse Floor plans:
Untergeschoß Basement
Erdgeschoß Ground floor
Obergeschoß First floor

Schnitt Section

The name of this house can stand as a motto for almost all the subsequent family houses. It implies: a sloping site on the outskirts of the town and a extensive view of Graz and the surrounding countryside. The house is sheltered from the surrounding villa development and the traffic accessing it by a dense screen of old trees. "The house is designed for this site in terms of colour, form and function. The elements house-hill-trees are mutually inclusive. The house is pink-purple in colour, with ochre-reddish timber parts, complemented in the interior by yellow, white and grey-green. The three storeys of the house contain playrooms and cellars in the basement, the living area with kitchen and a small library on the main floor and the bedrooms on the top floor. According to the clients' request, they can be converted into separate flats with their own entrances without a great deal of building work." (Szyszkowitz+Kowalski).

At the request of the family, who had spent an extended period in the United States, the building was to be in wood, to keep their memories of those years awake in architectural form. This house contains all the spatial access modes and architectural links with the landscape that have characterized Szyszkowitz+Kowalski's buildings ever since. These are: a fluid, open ground plan following the topography and emphasis on communal family areas on the ground floor level, bedrooms and large bathrooms placed on the upper floors and the possibility of making the children's and nannies' living space accessible separately, and if necessary able to be extended internally. From the inside, the accentuated sequence of windows provides views of the outside world and natural light from all sides to the interior. The pergolas thrust out into the garden to create small landscapes as part of the house, which can be entered from the outside on several levels independently, by means of level gradations and terraces, and can also be perceived as an artificially designed landscape in natural surroundings.

GRÜNES HAUS GREEN HOUSE

ORT LOCATION: **Weinitzen, A-8045 Graz** BAUHERRSCHAFT CLIENT: **Dr. med. L. D. und Univ. Prof. Dr. med. H. D.** PLANUNGS- UND BAUZEIT DESIGN AND REALISATION: **1977–1979** PROJEKTLEITER PROJECT LEADER: **Hermann Eisenköck** STATIK STATICS: **Christo Grigorow** WOHNNUTZFLÄCHE USABLE LIVING SPACE: **180 m²** UMBAUTER RAUM BUILDING VOLUME: **680 m³** KONSTRUKTION UND MATERIALIEN: **Stahlbetonskelettbau mit Holzriegelwandausfachungen** CONSTRUCTION AND MATERIALS: **reinforced concrete frame building with timber-rail infill** EINDECKUNG ROOF CLADDING: **Eternit**

<<< S. ABB. SEE FIGS. 24–26, 29, 30

Ansicht von Süden View from the south

Isometrische Entwurfsskizzen Isometric design sketches
Detail Südfassade Detail of the south façade

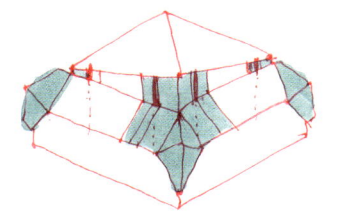

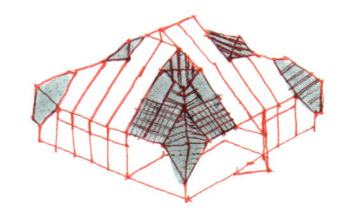

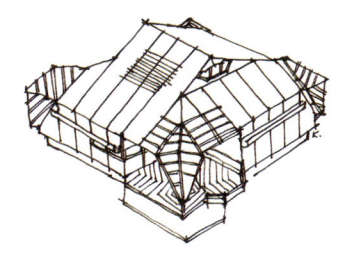

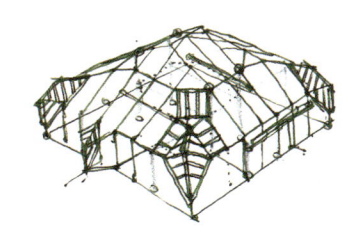

GREEN HOUSE   GRÜNES HAUS | 110 | 111

Grundrisse Floor plans:
Obergeschoß First floor
Erdgeschoß Ground floor

Ansicht von Süden Elevation from the south
Schnitt Section

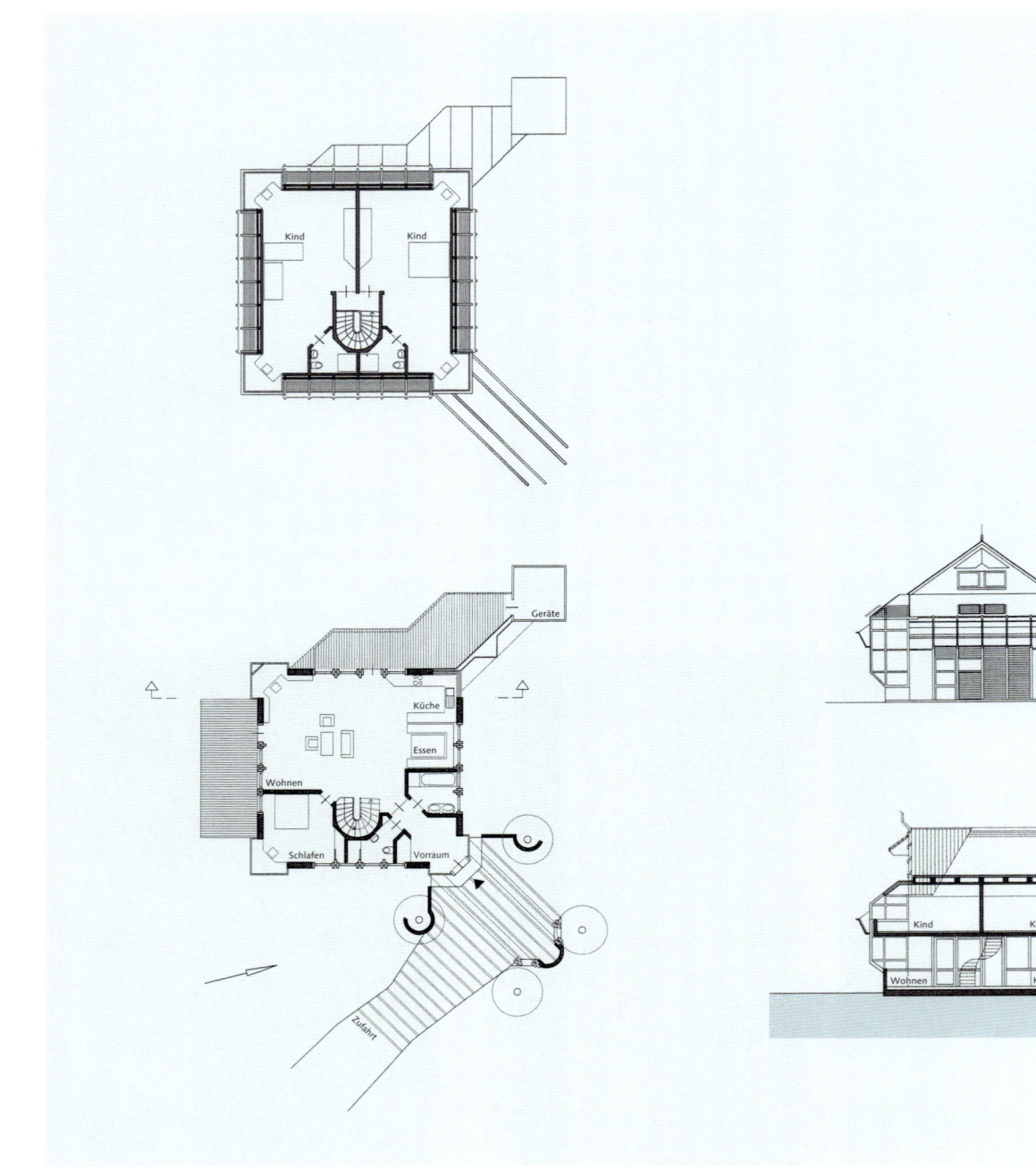

Das Haus ist ursprünglich als Sommerhaus geplant worden, weshalb die Nutzungsansprüche nicht groß und schon gar nicht auf Repräsentation ausgelegt waren. Dieses kleine Gebäude erhebt sich auf einer nahe der nordöstlichen Stadtgrenze von Graz gelegenen Hochfläche, die den Blick auf die voralpine Landschaft mit dem 1446 m hohen Schöckel freigibt. Die dominante Grundfigur ist das Quadrat, dessen Diagonalen durch kleine vorgelagerte Erker in den jeweiligen Ecken geschoßübergreifend betont sind und jeweils kleine intime Räume schaffen, die den Blick auf die umgebende Natur lenken.
Im Erdgeschoß liegt in einem dieser Diagonalerker der Eingang. Bis auf ein Arbeitszimmer dient dieses Geschoß dem Wohnen. Das OG ist für zwei große Schlafräume vorgesehen, kann aber auch für vier Räume adaptiert werden. Die von einem gerichteten Giebel zu einem Quadrat entwickelte Dachform hat zwischen den vier Erkern sehr groß dimensionierte Regenrinnen. Die auf acht breiten Betonstützen basierende Konstruktion ist im Rastermaß mit Holzelementen ausgefacht, deren Verdachung in rötlich orangenem Ton gehalten ist und mit den verschiedenartigen Grüntönen der Erker und Rinnen kontrastiert.

This was originally designed as a holiday home, which means that few demands were made on it in terms of either use or prestige. This little building is set on an eminence near the north-eastern boundary of Graz, giving a view of the pre-alpine landscape with the 1446 m high Schöckel. The dominant primary figure is the square. Its diagonals are emphasized by small bays placed in front of the corners, rising through both floors, each creating a small, intimate space that draws the eye to the natural surroundings.
The entrance is on the ground floor through one of these diagonal bays. This floor is used for living purposes, with the exception of a study. The upper floor is intended for two large bedrooms, but it can also be adapted for four. The shape of the roof comes out as a square because of an angled gable; there are very large gutters between the four oriels. The structure rests on eight broad concrete supports, and the grid thus formed is filled in with timber elements. These are reddish-orange at the top, and contrast with the various primary shades of the oriels and gutters.

Südost-Erker South-east bay

HAUS ZUSERTAL HOUSE IN ZUSERTAL

ORT LOCATION: **Rosenberg, A-8010 Graz**   BAUHERRSCHAFT CLIENT: **Dr. rer. nat. T. S. und Univ. Prof. Dr. med. R. S.**   PLANUNGS- UND BAUZEIT DESIGN AND REALISATION: **1979–1981**   PROJEKTLEITER PROJECT LEADER: **Ernst Giselbrecht**   STATIK STATICS: **Christo Grigorow**   WOHNNUTZFLÄCHE USABLE LIVING SPACE: **230 m²**   UMBAUTER RAUM BUILDING VOLUME: **950 m³**   KONSTRUKTION UND MATERIALIEN: **Stahlbetonskelettbau, Außenwände Massivbauweise** CONSTRUCTION AND MATERIALS: **reinforced concrete frame building, solid exterior walls**   EINDECKUNG: **Bitumen-Dachplatten** ROOF CLADDING: **bitumen roofing slabs**   <<< S. ABB. SEE FIGS. 45–50

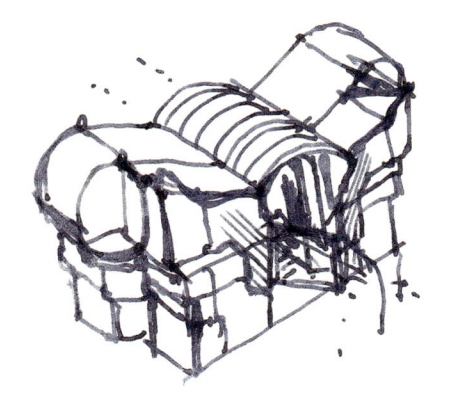

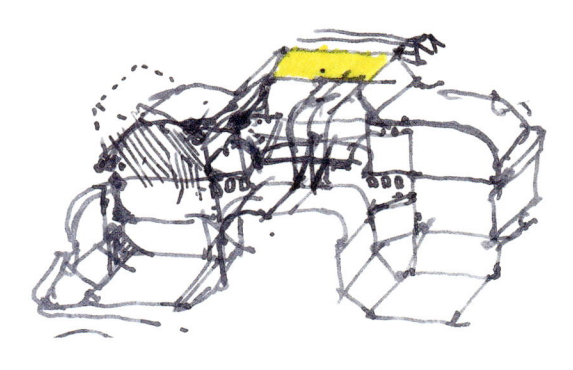

Ansicht von Nordosten View from the north-east

Entwurfsskizzen Design sketches
Ost-Ecke East corner
Blick in die Oberlichtkonstruktion der Halle View of the hall skylight structure

HOUSE IN ZUSERTAL HAUS ZUSERTAL

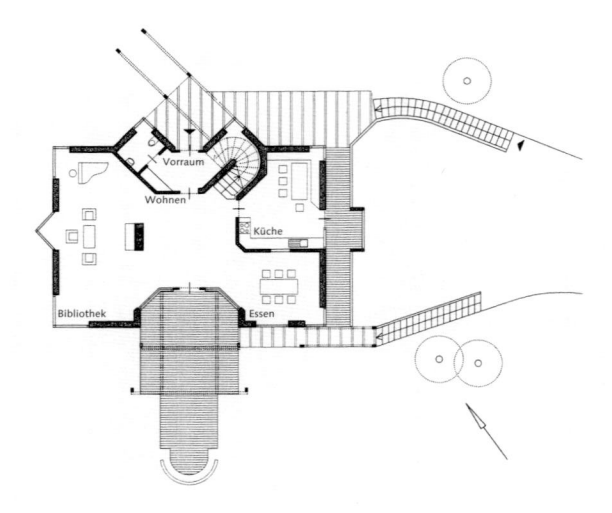

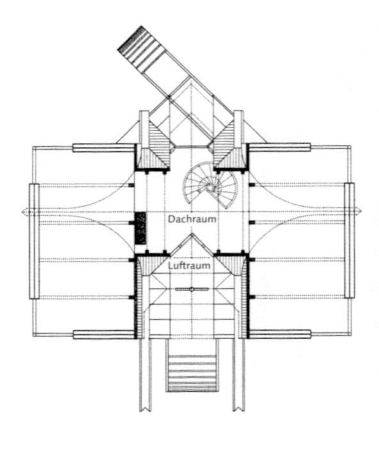

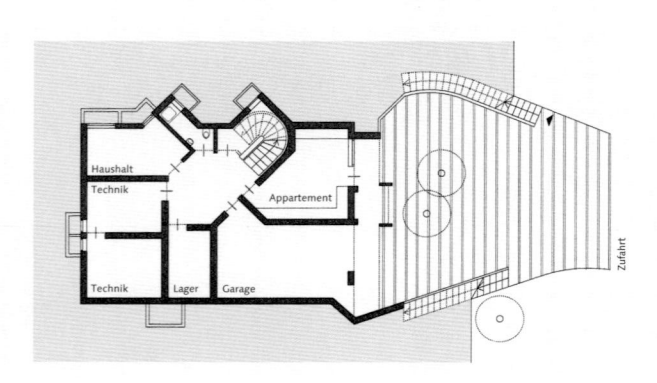

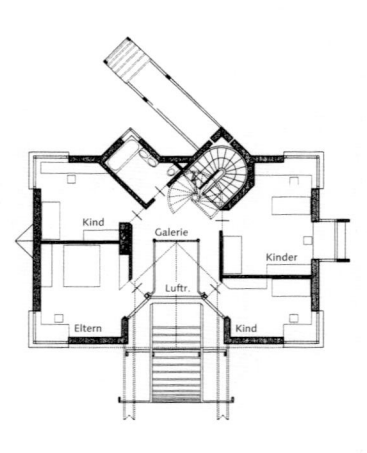

Das Haus liegt, im Gegensatz zu den meisten anderen, in einem Tal an ein leicht abfallendes Gelände geschmiegt und ist von einem alten Baumbestand eingefaßt, der Teil eines Landschaftsschutzgebietes ist. Das dreigeschossige Haus für ein Ehepaar mit vier Kindern basiert auf einem rechteckigen Grundriß, dessen Schmalseite zur Auffahrt ausgerichtet ist. Die Eingangsfront und damit der Empfangsteil des Hauses ist in die zunächst unsichtbar bleibende Längsseite des rechteckigen Hauskörpers integriert und durch einen kleinen Glasgiebel akzentuiert. Eine strenge Achsensymmetrie betont diese Längsseite der Hauptfassade und leitet zur signifikanten Dachform mit den auseinander strebenden Vierteltonnen über.

Oberhalb des Untergeschoßes mit der Garage und den Kellerräumen und einem Gästezimmer erhebt sich im Erdgeschoß eine galeriegesäumte, 7,50 m hohe Wohnhalle, ein Motiv, das in diesem Haus erstmals realisiert wurde und fortan in den repräsentativen Häusern immer wiederkehrt. „Den in jeder Beziehung Gestalt bestimmenden Mittelpunkt des Bauwerkes bildet die großzügig dimensionierte zentrale Halle. Der Raum reicht über zwei Geschosse, im Erdgeschoß umfassen ihn neben der Küche, Eßplatz, Sitzecke, und Musikzimmer in offener, fließender Anordnung. Der ganze Raum öffnet sich optisch nach Süden und seine konvex eingeschnittene Fassade und die Glaseindeckung als oberer Abschluß lassen die Sonne bis in die Tiefe des Hauses dringen. Im Obergeschoß reihen sich entlang der U-förmigen Galerie die klein gehaltenen fünf Schlafzimmer der Familie. Das Haus greift über die Pflanzengerüste und die Terrasse in die natürliche Landschaft ein und bildet im Zusammenwirken mit der Bepflanzung einen vegetativen Mantel um das Haus." (Szyszkowitz+Kowalski)

Die dominierende Farbe ist der graugrüne Anstrich der Holzverschalungen, der sich farblich auf den umgebenden Grünraum bezieht, zu dem ein gedecktes Rot der Putzteile und ein kräftiges Rot der Türlaibungen kontrastiert. Diese Farbpalette kehrt im Inneren der Halle vor allem im Rot der Oberlichtkonstruktion wieder.

Grundrisse Floor plans:
Erdgeschoß Ground floor
Untergeschoß Basement

Dachgeschoß Attic floor
Obergeschoß First floor

Axonometrie Axonometric elevation

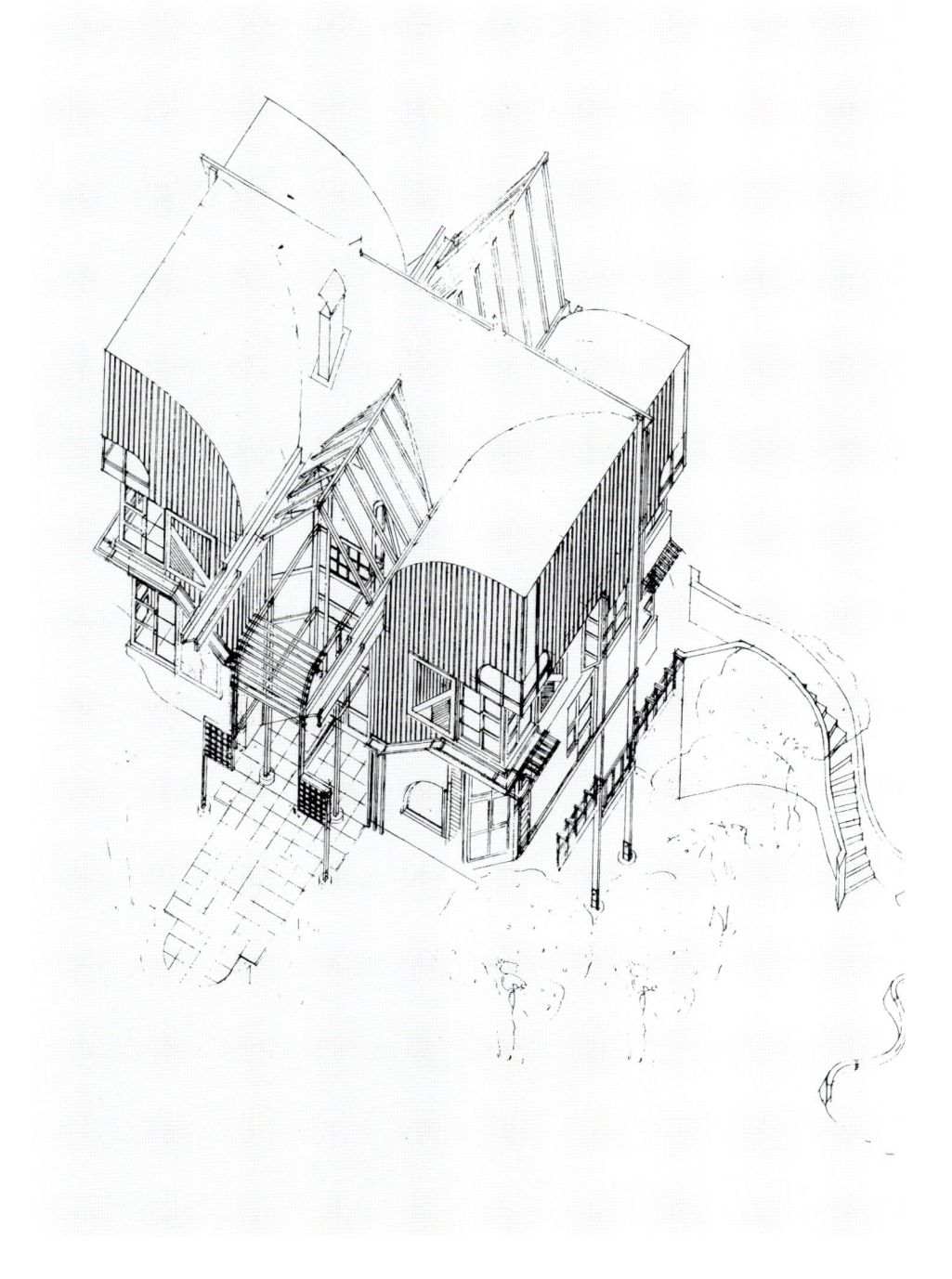

This house, unlike most of the others, is in a valley, snuggling up to a slightly sloping site and framed by old trees in a landscape conservation area. The three-storey house for a couple with four children is built on a rectangular ground plan with the narrow side facing the drive. The entrance façade, accentuated by a small glass gable, and thus the reception area of the house is built into the long side of the rectangular building, which remains invisible at first. Strong axial symmetry emphasizes this long side of the main façade and leads on to the striking roof with its quarter barrels thrusting out from each other. Above the basement with garage, cellars and a guestroom is a living hall on the ground floor, surrounded by a gallery and 7.5 metres high, a motif that was first realized in this house and that recurs constantly in the more prestigious designs. "The generously dimensioned central hall is the centre of the building, defining its form in every respect. The space rises through two storeys containing on the ground floor in an open, fluent arrangement the kitchen, dining area, sitting corner and the music room. The space as a whole opens up to the south visually, and its convex incised façade and the glass covering at the top allow the sun to penetrate deep into the house. On the upper level, the family's five small bedrooms are arranged along the U-shaped gallery. The house reaches out into the natural landscape with its trellises and the terrace and interacts with the planting to give the house a vegetative mantle." (Szyszkowitz+Kowalski).

The dominant colour is the grey-green paint on the timber cladding, which relates to the surrounding green space, with contrasting muted red for the rendered areas and strong red for the door reveals. This colour scheme then returns inside the hall, above all in the red of the skylight structure.

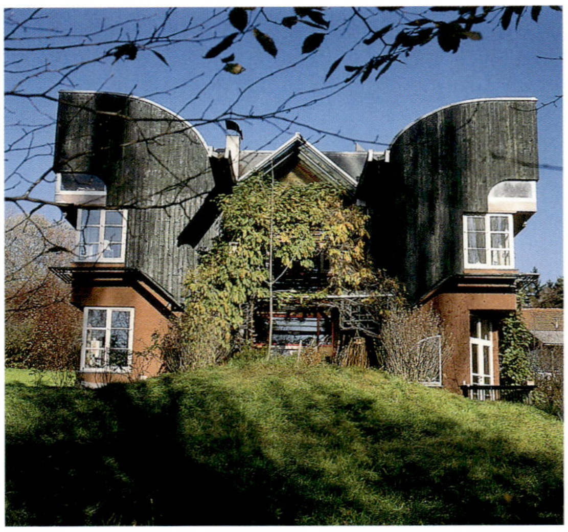
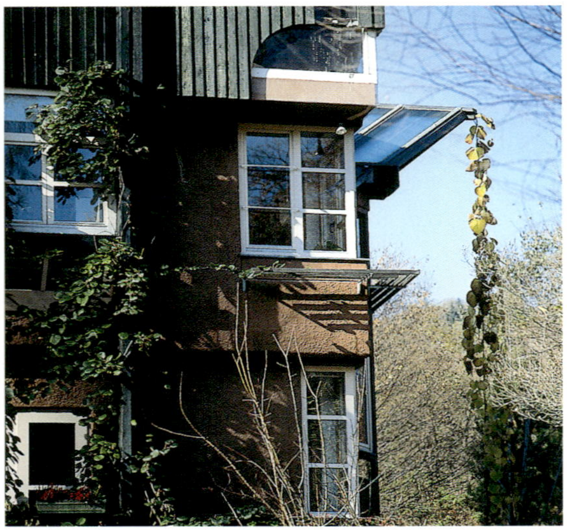
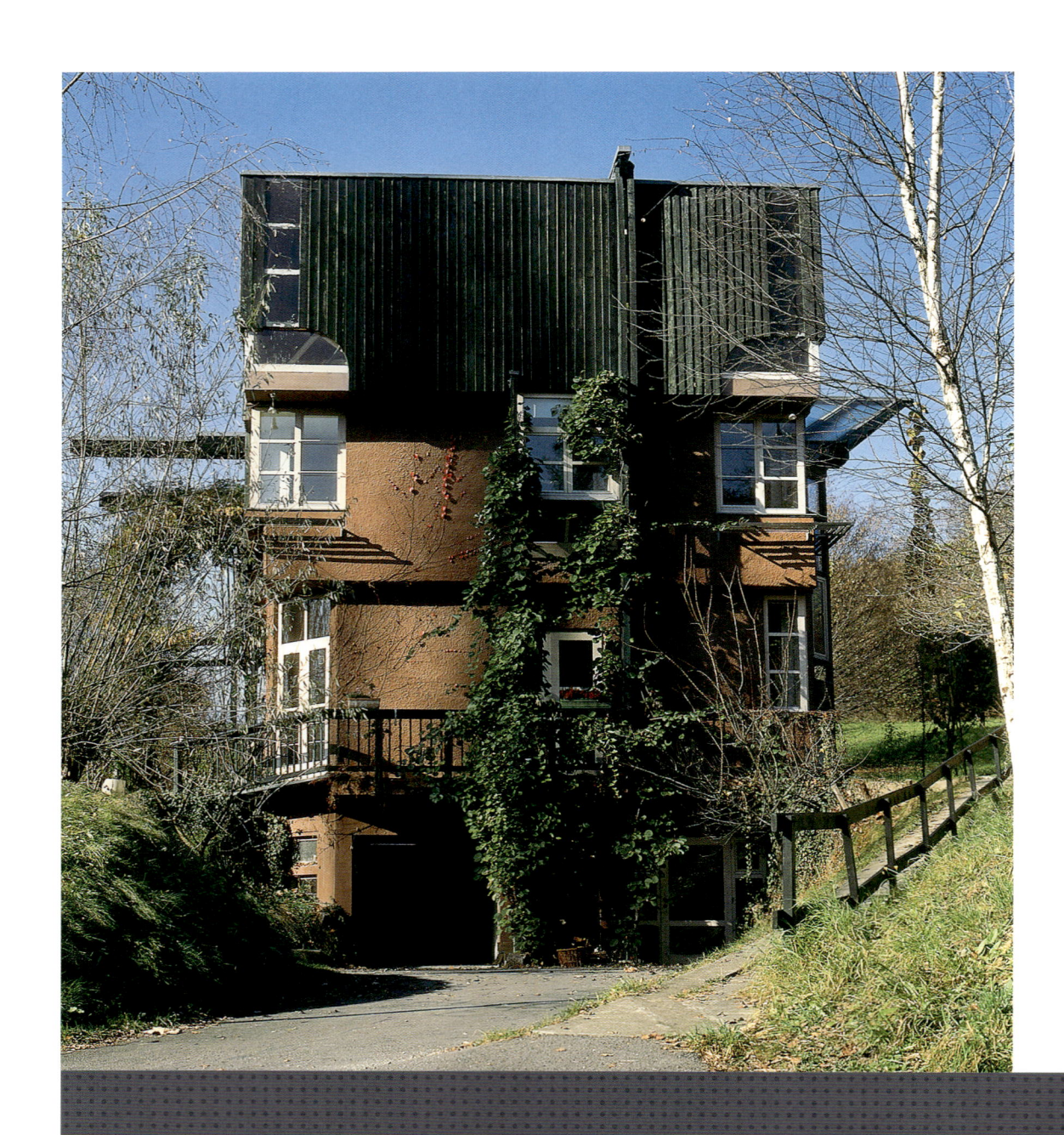

Ansicht von Südwesten View from the south-west
Ost-Ecke East corner
Ansicht von Südosten View from the south-east

Südwesteingang von Innen South-west entrance from inside
Ansicht von Westen View from the west

HOUSE IN ZUSERTAL   HAUS ZUSERTAL

ROTES HAUS RED HOUSE

ORT LOCATION: **Stiftingtal, A-8044 Graz** BAUHERRSCHAFT CLIENT: **B. S. und DI J. S.** PLANUNGS- UND BAUZEIT DESIGN AND REALISATION: **1982–1984** PROJEKTLEITER PROJECT LEADER: **Florian Riegler** STATIK STATICS: **Christo Grigorow** WOHNNUTZFLÄCHE USABLE LIVING SPACE: **220 m²** UMBAUTER RAUM BUILDING VOLUME: **890 m³** KONSTRUKTION UND MATERIALIEN: **Massivbauweise und Holzskelettbauweise** CONSTRUCTION AND MATERIALS: **solid construction and timber frame** EINDECKUNG: **Bitumen-Dachplatten** ROOF CLADDING: **bitumen roofing slabs**

<<< S. ABB. SEE FIG. 15

Ansicht von Nordosten View from the north-east

Rankgerüst an der Ostfassade Trellis on the east façade
Ansicht von Osten View from the east
Detail an der Ostfassade Detail on the east façade

RED HOUSE ROTES HAUS | 120 | 121

Grundrisse Floor plans:
Untergeschoß Basement

Obergeschoß First floor
Erdgeschoß Ground floor

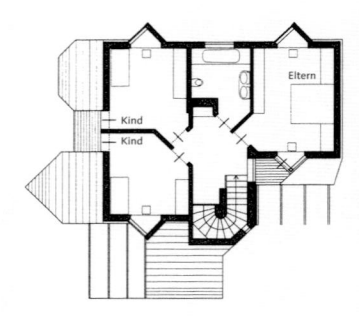

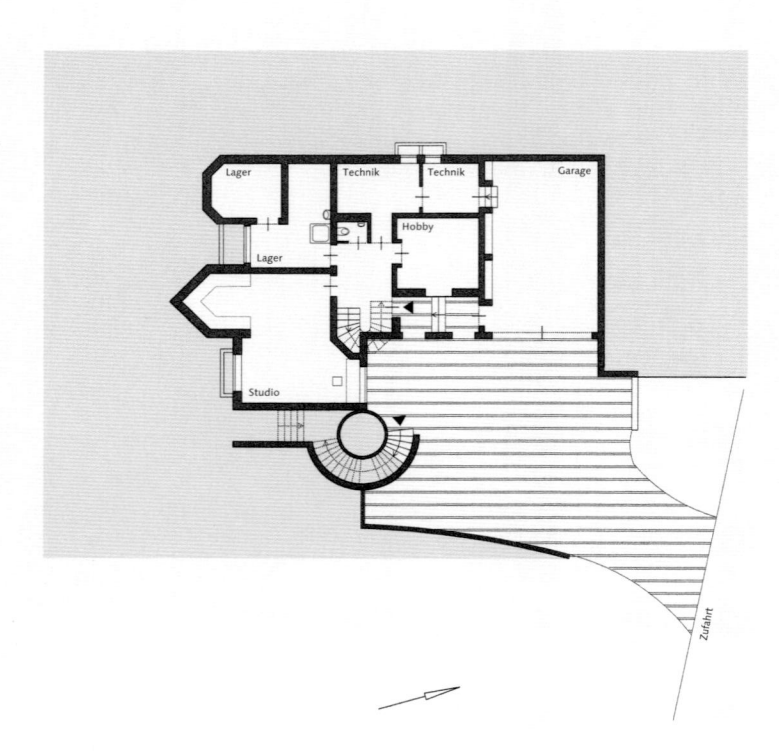

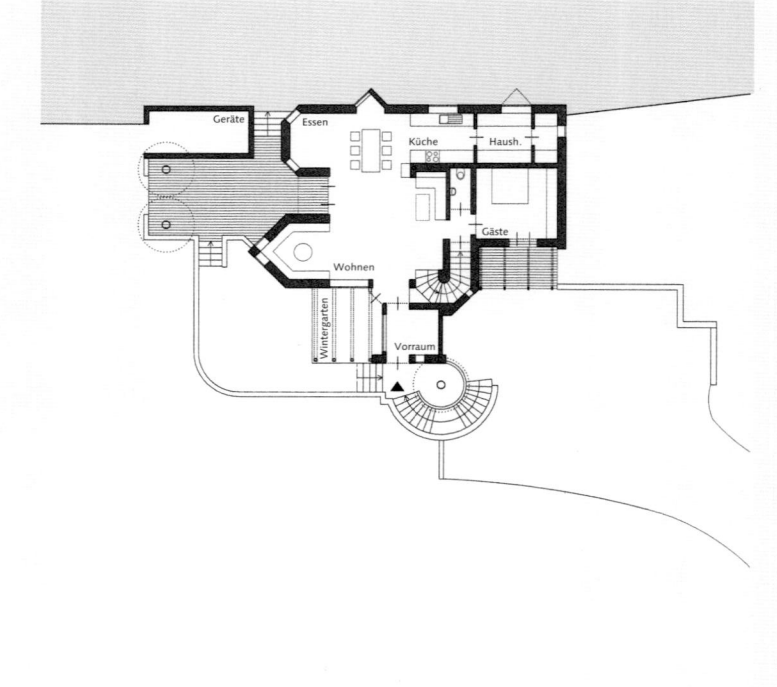

Das Haus entstand für ein junges Ehepaar mit drei Kindern an einem außerordentlich schwer zu bebauenden, steilen Nordhang im Weichbild von Graz. Die der Anthroposophie verbundene Bauherrschaft hatte dezidierte Vorstellungen über das biologische Bauen und eine Farbpalette, die im wesentlichen Rot- und Ockertöne aufweisen sollte. Das mit einem geringeren finanziellen Budget zu errichtende Haus ist im Schatten eines Buchenwaldes an den Steilhang gesetzt und macht diese Dramatik der Topographie zum Thema der Erschließung. Zu dem dreigeschossigen Haus, das eine herrliche Aussicht auf die umgebende Landschaft eröffnet, gelangt man über eine gewendete äußere Treppenanlage und betritt es durch ein kleines Entree. Dahinter befindet sich der Wohnbereich, der Eßplatz und die angelagerte Küche. Auf dieser Ebene sind kleinere, erkerförmige intime Räumen situiert, die den Blick in den Garten freigeben. Eine offene Innentreppe führt in das obere Geschoß mit den Schlaf- und Kinderzimmern, die unterhalb der geknickten Halbtonnen liegen, die dem Haus in der Außenwirkung die prägende Konturierung geben.

Die teilweise verwendete Holzskelettbauweise kehrt in der Verwendung des Materials in der Fassade wieder und prägt in der Diagonalschichtung der Holzschalung die beiden Gibelfronten. Kleinere Balkons im oberen Geschoß und um das Haus geführte Terrassen vermitteln zum Außenraum, wobei punktuell gesetzte Pflanzgerüste als klimatische und räumliche Zwischenbereiche wirken.

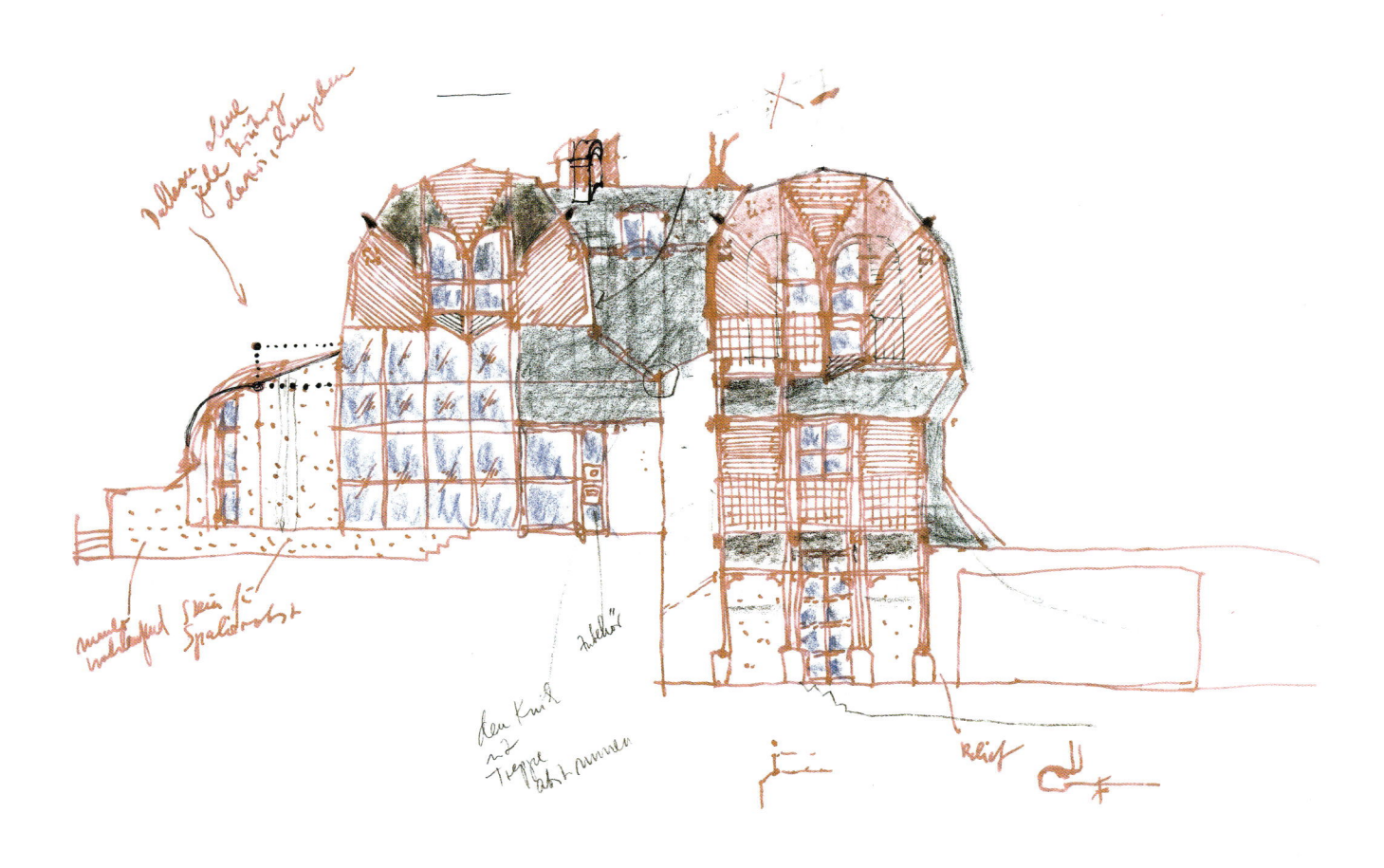

Skizze Sketch

This house was built for a young married couple with three children on a steep north-facing slope in the outskirts of Graz that was extraordinarily difficult to build on. The clients were interested in anthroposophy, and had definite ideas about organic building and a colour scheme that was to consist mainly of red and ochre shades. The house was to be built on a low budget. It is set on the steep slope in the shade of a beech wood, and makes this dramatic topography into its access theme. The three-storey house, which affords a splendid view over the surrounding landscape, is reached by a curved external staircase and a small entrance hall. Behind this is the living area, the dining area and the adjacent kitchen. Small, oriel-shaped, intimate rooms are situated on this plane, opening up views into the garden. An open internal staircase leads on to the top floor with the bedrooms and children's rooms, which are accommodated under the folded half-barrels that give the house its striking external outline.

The timber skeleton structure that is used in part recurs in the materials used for the façade, giving a characteristic look to the gable façades in the diagonal layering of the timber cladding. Small balconies on the top floor and terraces running round the house mediate with the outside space, with trellises placed at key points to create climatic and spatial intermediate areas.

HAUS AM HOHENRAIN HOUSE ON HOHENRAIN

ORT LOCATION: Hart, A-8075 Graz   BAUHERRSCHAFT CLIENT: H. P. und Univ. Doz. Dr. med. A. P.   PLANUNGS-UND BAUZEIT DESIGN AND REALISATION: 1983–1985
PROJEKTLEITER PROJECT LEADER: Gerald Wratschko   STATIK STATICS: Ortwin Vatter   WOHNNUTZFLÄCHE USABLE LIVING SPACE: 150 m²   UMBAUTER RAUM BUILDING VOLUME: 620 m³   KONSTRUKTION UND MATERIALIEN: Sockel: Massivbauweise, Holzleimbinderkonstruktion mit Holzausfachung CONSTRUCTION AND MATERIALS: base: solid construction, glulam beam construction with timber infill   EINDECKUNG: Titanzink ROOF CLADDING: zinc roofing   <<< S. ABB. SEE FIGS. 19, 37

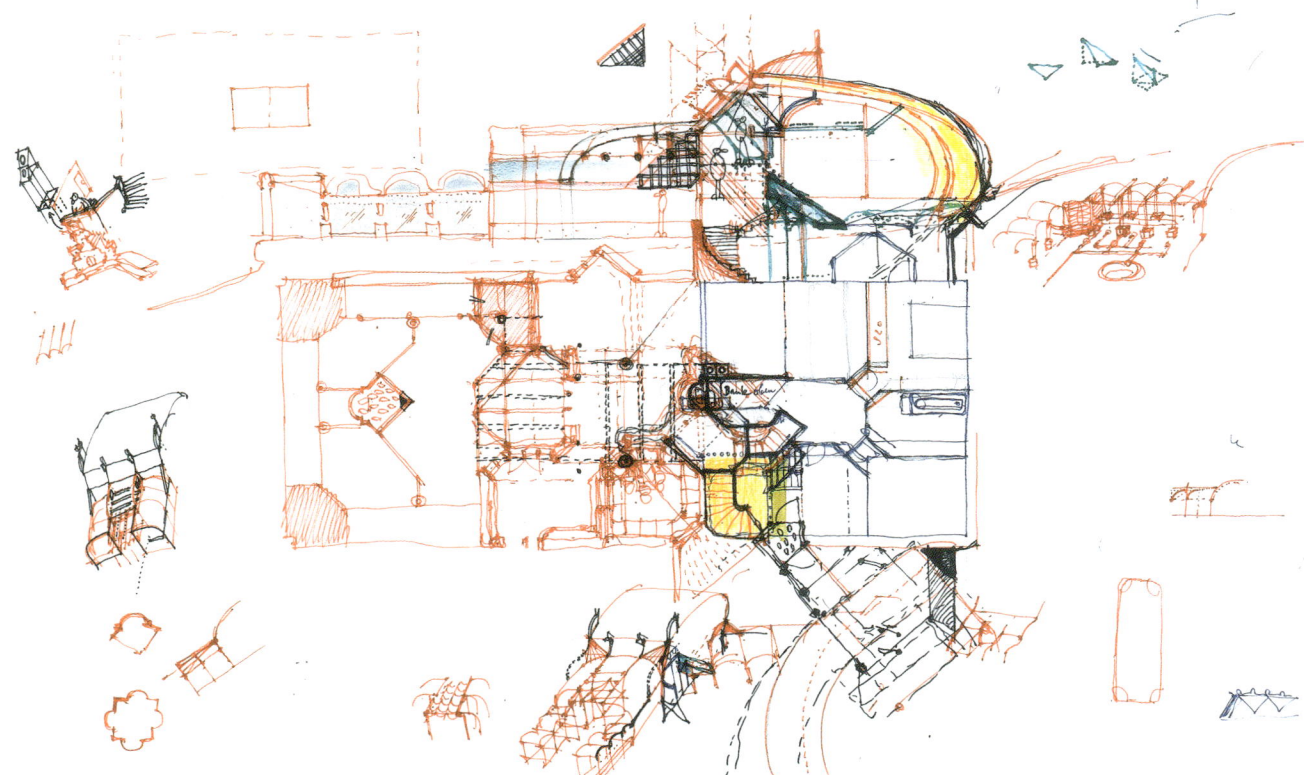

Ansicht von Westen View from the west

Südwestfassade South-west façade
Nordostfassade North-east façade
Skizze Sketch

HOUSE ON HOHENRAIN   HAUS AM HOHENRAIN   124 | 125

Grundrisse Floor plans:
Obergeschoß First floor
Erdgeschoß Ground floor

Schnitt Section

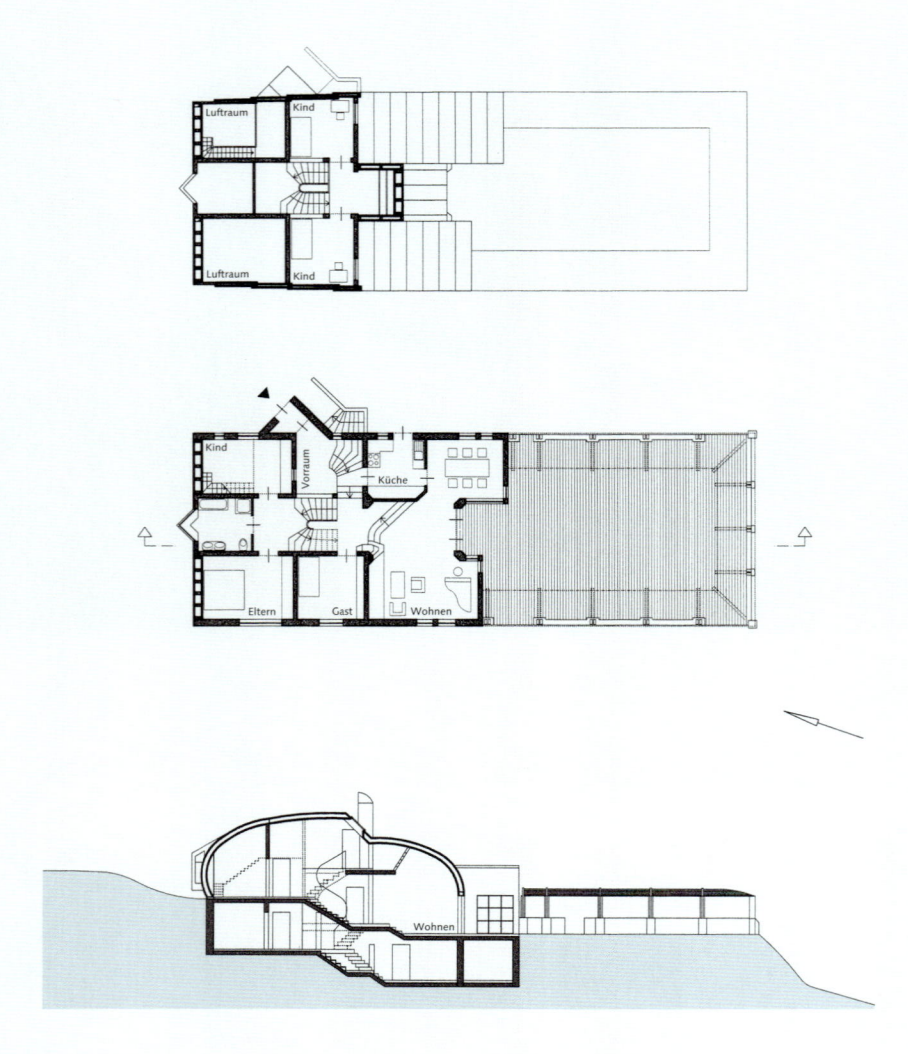

Das Haus, das in der älteren Literatur auch „Haus am Lustbühel" genannt wird, liegt auf einer den voralpinen Fallwinden ausgesetzten Hochfläche östlich von Graz. Dieser Lage entspricht der zur Wetterseite hin abgerundete kompakte Baukörper, der nach Süden hin geöffnet ist. Der Gesamtgrundriß mit einem Atrium stellt ein Rechteck dar. Im Inneren sind die Eß- und Wohnbereiche mit der Küche um ein großzügiges, zentrales Treppenhaus gruppiert, das zugleich als Kommunikationsraum für die fünfköpfige Familie dient.

Im Erdgeschoß befindet sich neben dem tiefer liegenden Wohnraum ein Eßplatz, dem die Küche zugeordnet ist, sowie eine Musizierecke und ein großer Kamin. Ein wenig erhöht sind von der zentralen Treppenanlage aus die Schlafzimmer und ein Bad zu erreichen. Im oberen Geschoß sind weitere, kleine Räume für die Kinder untergebracht, die um einen Luftraum mit einer Lattenkonstruktion, von der aus in den Wohnraum hinunter geschaut werden kann, gruppiert sind. Die oberen Niveaus und die südlichen Teile des split level-Hauses wurden als konstruktiver Holzbau ausgeführt, der in seiner Zangenkonstruktion und der Schalung zwischen blauviolett und türkis wechselnden Lasierungen mit dem grautürkisen Fassadenanstrich eine polyvalente Wandschichtung erzeugt. „Wir haben das Haus mit zum Norden hin geschlossenen Rücken und im Inneren mit Niveausprüngen so entworfen, daß es mit halbgeschossigen Versetzungen an die Eigenschaften des Hanges angepaßt ist. Das Atrium und der Wintergarten sind nicht ausgeführt worden, auch sie sollten den sanften Übergang zwischen gebauter und natürlicher Umwelt betonen." (Szyszkowitz+Kowalski)

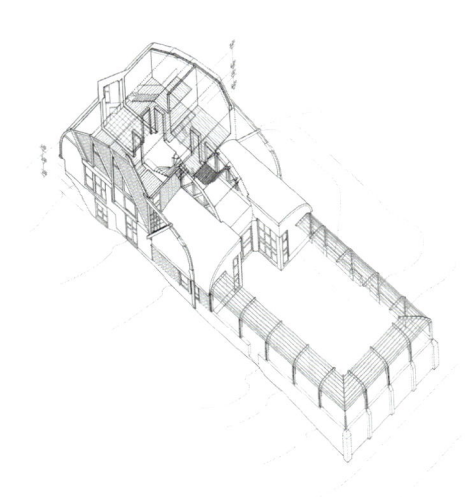

Ansicht von Süden Elevation from the south

Ansicht von Nordwesten Elevation from the north-west

Axonometrie Axonometric view

This house, which is also known as the "Haus am Lustbühel" in older literature, is on an eminence to the east of Graz exposed to the katabatic pre-alpine winds. The compact building, rounded off on the weather side and open to the south, is appropriate for the site. The overall ground plan with atrium is a rectangle. Inside are the dining and living areas with the kitchen, grouped around a generous, central stairwell that also serves as a communication area for the five-member family.

On the ground floor are the dining area with kitchen off it, the living area, which is set lower, and also a music corner and a large fireplace. The bedrooms and bathroom are accessed at a slightly higher level from the central staircase. The upper floor accommodates additional small rooms for the children, grouped around an air-space with a lath structure making it possible to look down into the living space. The upper levels and the southern sections of this split level house were built as a timber structure, which creates polyvalent wall strata with its tie beam structure, a wall covering alternating between blue-purple and turquoise glazing, and the grey-turquoise façade paint. "We designed the house with its back closed to the north and internal changes in level so that it adapts to the qualities of the slope by shifts of half a storey. The atrium and the conservatory were not built, but they too were intended to emphasize a gentle transition between the built and the natural environment." (Szyszkowitz+Kowalski).

GRAUES HAUS GREY HOUSE

ORT LOCATION: Ruckerlberg, A-8010 Graz   BAUHERRSCHAFT CLIENT: I. L. und DI F. L.   PLANUNGS- UND BAUZEIT DESIGN AND REALISATION: 1984–1986   PROJEKTLEITER PROJECT LEADER: Gerald Wratschko   STATIK STATICS: Ernst Tappauf   WOHNNUTZFLÄCHE USABLE LIVING SPACE: 210 m²   UMBAUTER RAUM BUILDING VOLUME: 790 m³   KONSTRUKTION UND MATERIALIEN: Massivbauweise, Dachgeschoß Holzkonstruktion   CONSTRUCTION AND MATERIALS: solid construction, attic storey timber   EINDECKUNG: Titanzink   ROOF CLADDING: zinc roofing

<<< S. ABB. SEE FIGS. 18, 19, 28

Ansicht von Süden View from the south

Ansicht von Südwesten View from the south-west
Dachaufsicht von Osten Roof view from the east
Ansicht von Südosten View from the south-east

GREY HOUSE   GRAUES HAUS   128 | 129

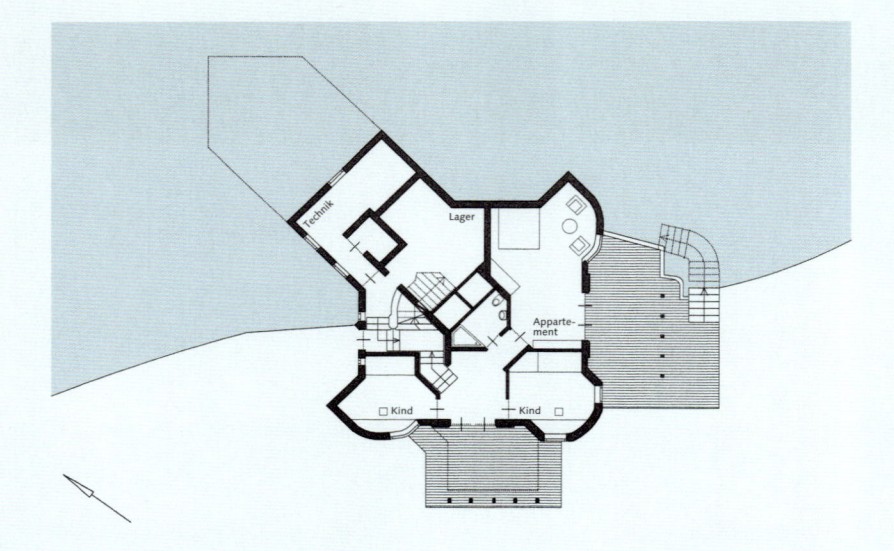

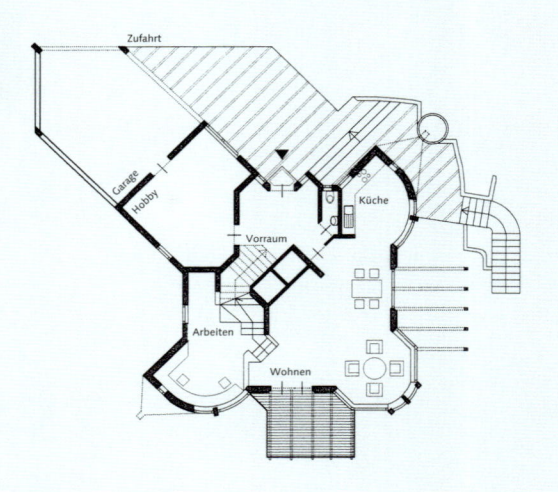

Mit diesem Auftrag wurde erstmals ein Privathaus im innerstädtischen Bereich von Graz errichtet. Es entstand auf einem leicht gewellten Baugrund in dichter Einfamilienhaus-Besiedelung. Der Grundriß ist aus dem Quadrat entwickelt mit einer Betonung der sich kreuzenden Diagonalen, ähnlich wie im *Grünen Haus*. „Die Diagonalstellung im Grundriß erlaubt, durch den flügelartigen Gestus, verschiedene Außenbereiche." (Szyzkowitz+Kowalski)

Den Mittelpunkt des Hauses und damit die entwurfsleitende Idee der Grundrißentwicklung bilden die beiden Heißluftschächte für ein verwirbelungsfreies Heizsystem – ein Wunsch der Auftraggeber. Die Treppenanlage windet sich als eine landschaftlich aufgefaßte Stufenfolge mit Absätzen im Inneren um diesen zentralen Versorgungskern herum und ist als ein Teil des Lebensraumes aufgefaßt.

Das dreigeschossige Wohnhaus für ein Ehepaar mit drei Kindern hat im unteren Bereich neben den Versorgungsräumen ein kleines Appartement und zwei Kinderzimmer, die vom Garten aus separat zugänglich sind. Das Haus ist auf der Nordseite über einen Vorraum erschlossen, von dem aus der Wohnbereich mit der Küche, die in der nordöstlich ausgreifenden Ecke situiert ist, betreten wird. Im oberen Stockwerk ist der lange Schlafraum mit dem Bad auf eine der Diagonalen des Grundrisses gelegt und ragt daher als eigenständiger Körper über die seitlichen Dachschrägen auf. Der nach Süden orientierte kleine Balkon wird im äußeren Erscheinungsbild des Gebäudes zum dominanten Zeichen und weist in der Fassadengestaltung ähnliche Elemente wie im Roten Haus auf. Die polygonale Fenstertür ist im aufragenden Giebelvorbau mit einer voroxydierten Holzbrettschalung gefaßt, so daß sich aus dem Zusammenspiel der gebogenen, spitz zulaufenden Balkongeländer und den gezackten Holzstreben mit ihren Überlagerungen eine gleichsam ornamentale Oberflächenwirkung ergibt. Diesen Reichtum im Detail zeigen auch die unterschiedlichen Fensterformen, die im Kontext mit den eingeschnittenen Pultdächern den Baukörper zu einem fragmentierten Volumen aus differierenden Fassadenelementen werden läßt. Vorgeschobene Glasdächer schützen den seitlichen Balkon und die Terrassen, die durch Rankgerüste räumlich definiert sind. Eine äußere Treppenführung umgreift das Haus auf den verschiedenen Niveaus des Gartens.

Grundrisse Floor plans:
Untergeschoß Basement
Erdgeschoß Ground floor
Obergeschoß First floor

Dachaufsicht Roof-top view

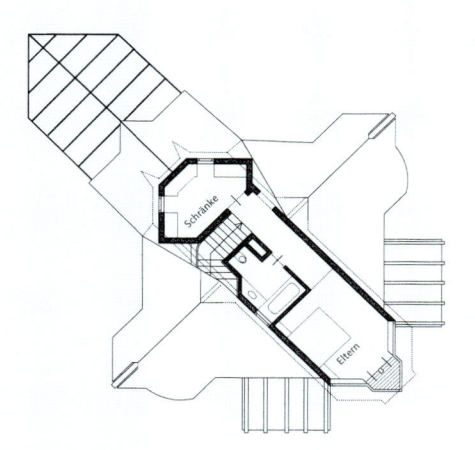

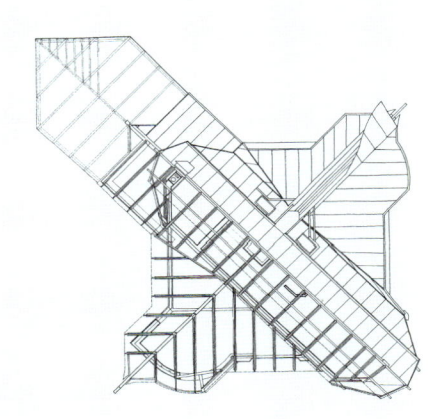

This commission was the first private house to be built in central Graz. It is set on a slightly undulating site among tightly-packed family houses. The ground plan is developed from a square, and the intersecting diagonals are emphasized, similarly to the *Green House*. "The diagonal lines in the ground plan make it possible to create various outside areas because of the wing-like gesture." (Szyszkowitz+Kowalski)

The central point in the house, and thus the idea that drives the ground plan design is made up of the two hot air shafts for the turbulence-free heating system – a request from the client. The stairs twist around this central service core as a landscaped sequence of steps with internal landings, and are seen as part of the living room.

This three-storey house for a married couple with three children has in the lower storey a small apartment and two children's bedrooms, separately accessible from the garden, and also the service rooms. Access to the house is on the north side via an anteroom leading to the living area and kitchen, which is situated in the corner thrusting out to the north-east. On the upper floor is the long bedroom with bathroom, placed on one of the ground plan diagonals, thus rising above the lateral roof slopes as an independent volume. The small south-facing balcony becomes the dominant sign in the exterior appearance of the building, showing elements similar to the *Red House* in the façade design. The polygonal french window in the rising gable structure is framed with pre-oxidized timber, thus producing a quasi-ornamental surface effect in the interplay of the curved balcony balustrade, pointed at the top, and the overlapping serrated timber braces. The various window shapes are similarly lavish in their detail. In the context of the incised penthouse roofs they make the building into a fragmented volume made up of different façade elements. Protruding glass roofs protect the side balconies and terraces, which are defined spatially by trellises. Outside steps surround the house on the various levels of the garden.

HAUS HARMISCH HARMISCH HOUSE

ORT LOCATION: **Harmisch, A-7512 Kohfidisch** BAUHERRSCHAFT CLIENT: **B. A. und DI A. K.-E.** PLANUNGS- UND BAUZEIT DESIGN AND REALISATION: **1986–1988**
PROJEKTLEITER PROJECT LEADER: **Roger Riewe** STATIK STATICS: **Rüdiger Koberg** WOHNNUTZFLÄCHE USABLE LIVING SPACE: **310 m²** UMBAUTER RAUM BUILDING
VOLUME: **1.240 m³** KONSTRUKTION UND MATERIALIEN: **Massivbauweise** CONSTRUCTION AND MATERIALS: **solid construction** EINDECKUNG: **glasierte Tonziegel**
ROOF CLADDING: **glazed clay tiles** <<< S. ABB. SEE FIGS. **51–53**

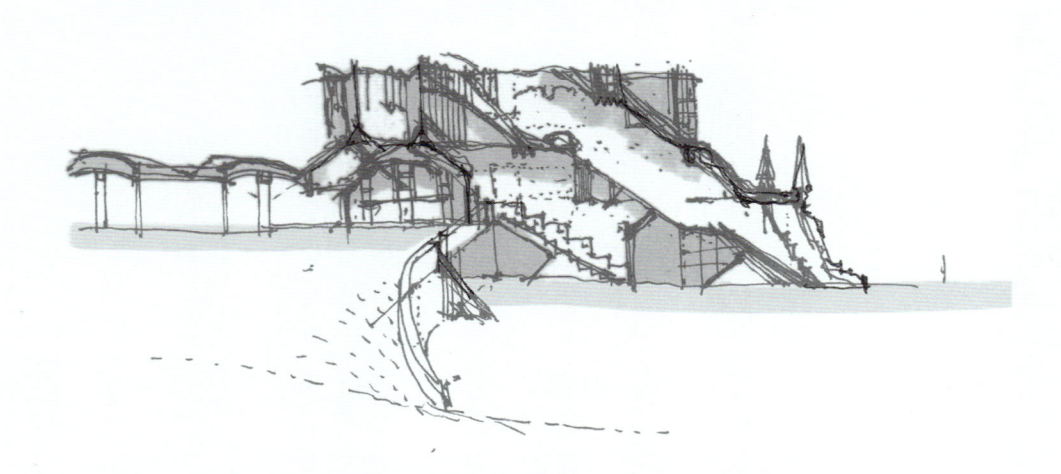

Skizze Sketch
Ansicht von Norden View from the north

Gesamtansicht von Nordwesten General view from the north-west

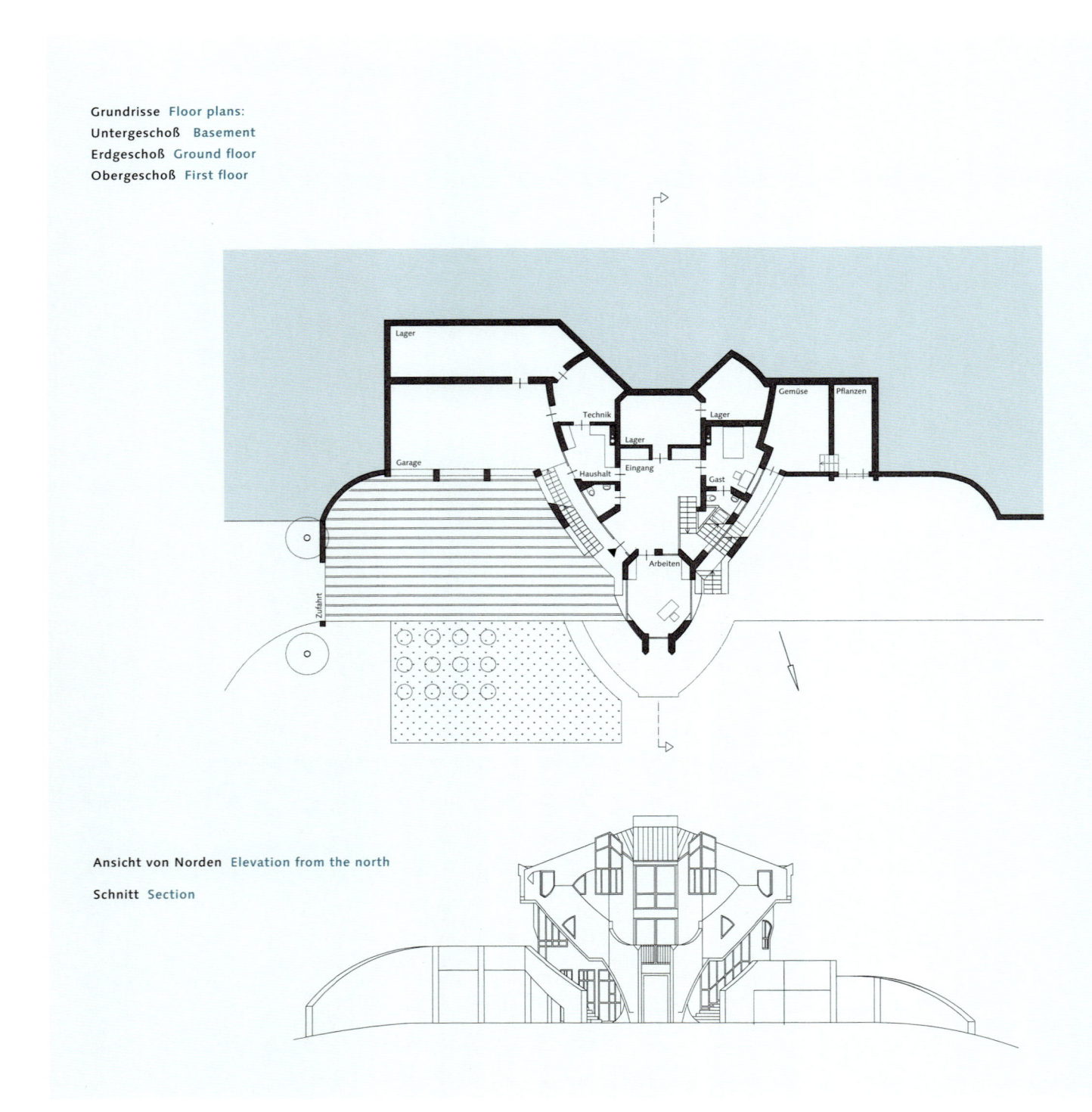

Grundrisse Floor plans:
Untergeschoß Basement
Erdgeschoß Ground floor
Obergeschoß First floor

Ansicht von Norden Elevation from the north

Schnitt Section

Diese dreigeschossige Villa ist der erste Privathausbau außerhalb der Steiermark. In der Nähe eines kleinen Dorfes im Burgenland ist es auf einem weiten, zur Bauzeit noch unbewachsenen, wenngleich von Wald begrenzten, weitläufigen Hanggrundstück entstanden. Die Bauherrschaft suchte Ersatz für das nahe gelegene Schloß, so daß sich mit dem Haus zwar nicht die traditionellen Repräsentationsansprüche verbanden, aber doch Anforderungen formuliert wurden, die dem Lebensstil einer alten österreichischen Adelsfamilie zueigen sind. So wurde auf den ausdrücklichen Wunsch des Bauherrn eine hohe Halle in einem kompakten Steinhaus errichtet, das mit seinen geschwungenen Konturen von Ferne betrachtet wie ein Monolith in der Landschaft erscheint. Eine längere Auffahrt führt zu einem weitläufigen Vorplatz mit den Garagen, und seitliche Treppenführungen umschließen den äußeren Baukörper mit den konvexen Wänden. Das Türkisgrau des Putzes ist auf das Betongrau der Konstruktion abgestimmt.

Das Gebäude ist achsialsymmetrisch aufgefaßt und verdeutlicht derart die Ausrichtung nach zwei Seiten. Die Durchfensterung schafft den Durchblick durch das gesamte Haus von Norden nach Süden, wo dem Haus im Mittelgeschoß ein ummauerter Hof angelagert ist. Im unteren Geschoß befinden sich neben den Keller- und Vorratsräumen ein großzügiges Vestibül, das von der Seite des Hauses aus betreten wird, ein Arbeitsraum für den Hausherrn sowie ein Gästezimmer. Das eigentliche Zentrum des Hauses für die ursprünglich sechsköpfige Familie, die bel étage, ist die über zwei Geschosse geführte, 9 m hohe Halle mit einem zum Tal hin ausgerichteten Balkon und der seitlich angelagerten, großen Küche. Diese Halle ist mit einer großen Oberlichtkonstruktion geschlossen und birgt die differenzierte Folge der einzelnen Wohnbereiche. Im oberen Stockwerk wird die Wohnhalle von einer Bibliotheksgalerie umfaßt. Von hier aus gelangt man in die vier Schlafzimmer mit den Bädern.

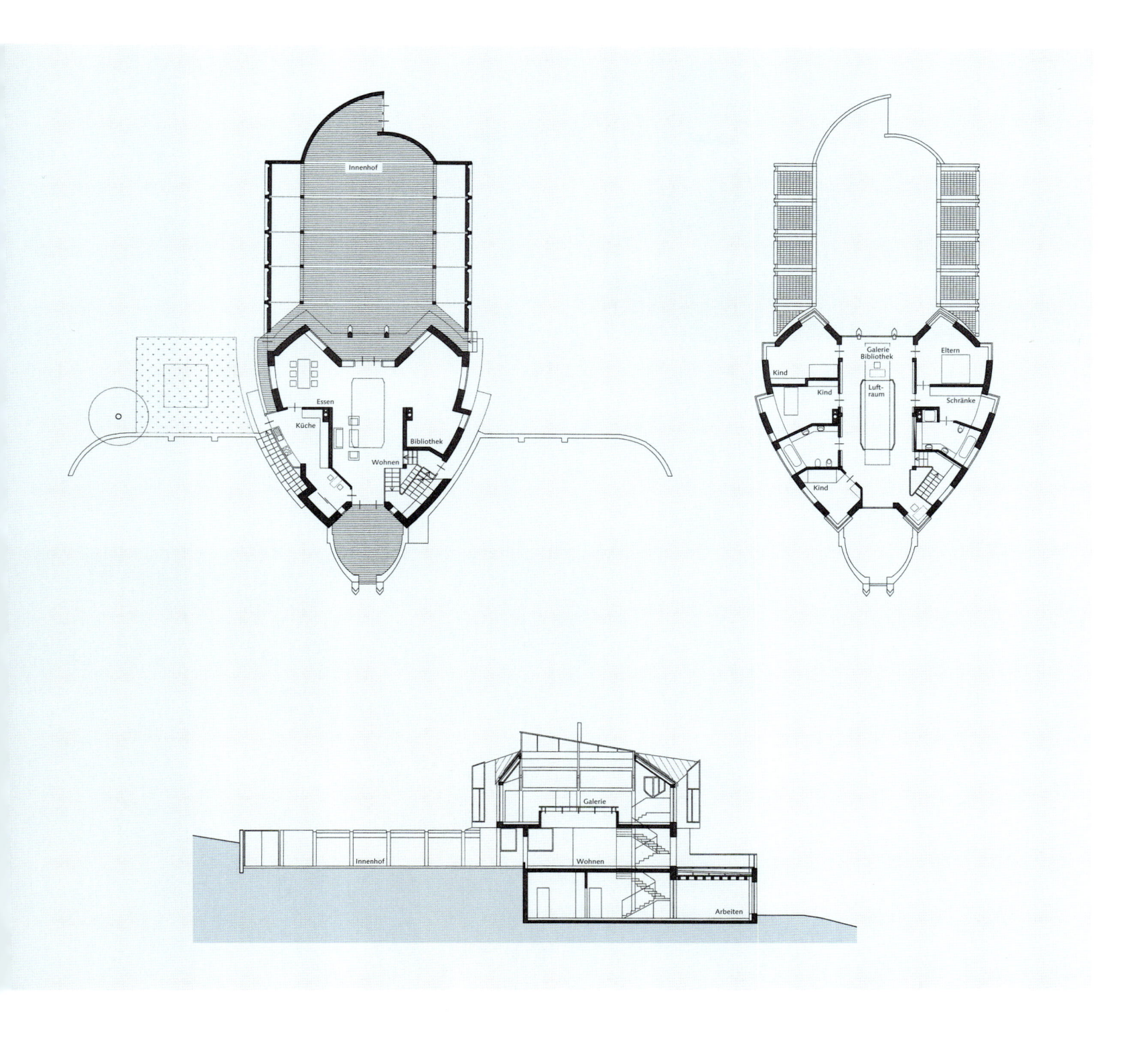

This three-storey villa is the first private house to be constructed outside Styria. It is set on an extensive, sloping plot, without vegetation at the time of building but bordered by woodland, near a little village in Burgenland. The client was looking to replace the nearby "Schloss" (castle); the new house did not have to meet the traditional prestige requirements, but had to be appropriate to the life-style of a family from the old Austrian nobility. So it was the client's express wish that a high hall should be built in a compact stone house. Seen from a distance, its curving lines make it seem like a monolith in the landscape. A long drive leads to an extensive forecourt containing the garages, and side steps enclose the outer section of the building with its convex walls. The turquoise-grey of the rendering matches the concrete-grey of the structure.

The building is axially symmetrical, which makes it clear that it is oriented to two sides. The open arrangement of the windows makes it possible to see through the whole house from north to south, where there is a walled courtyard opening at the middle floor. The basement storey contains cellars and storerooms and also a generous vestibule entered from the side of the house, a study for the man householder and a guest room. The actual centre of the house for the family, which originally had six members, is the first floor, which accommodates the 9 metre high hall, rising through two storeys, with a balcony facing the valley and a large kitchen at the side. This hall is topped by a large skylight system, and contains the sophisticated sequence of individual living areas. A library gallery runs round the living-hall on the top floor, giving access to the four bedrooms and bathrooms.

Ansicht von Süden View from the south
Detail an der Westfassade Detail on the west façade

Ansicht von Osten View from the east
Treppenaufgang an der Ostfassade Stairs on the east façade
Treppenaufgang an der Westfassade Stairs on the west façade

HARMISCH HOUSE · HAUS HARMISCH

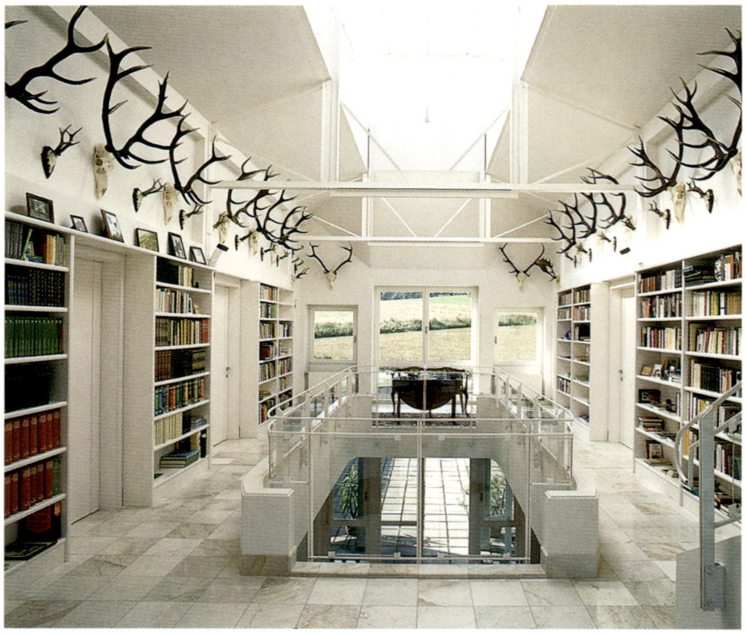

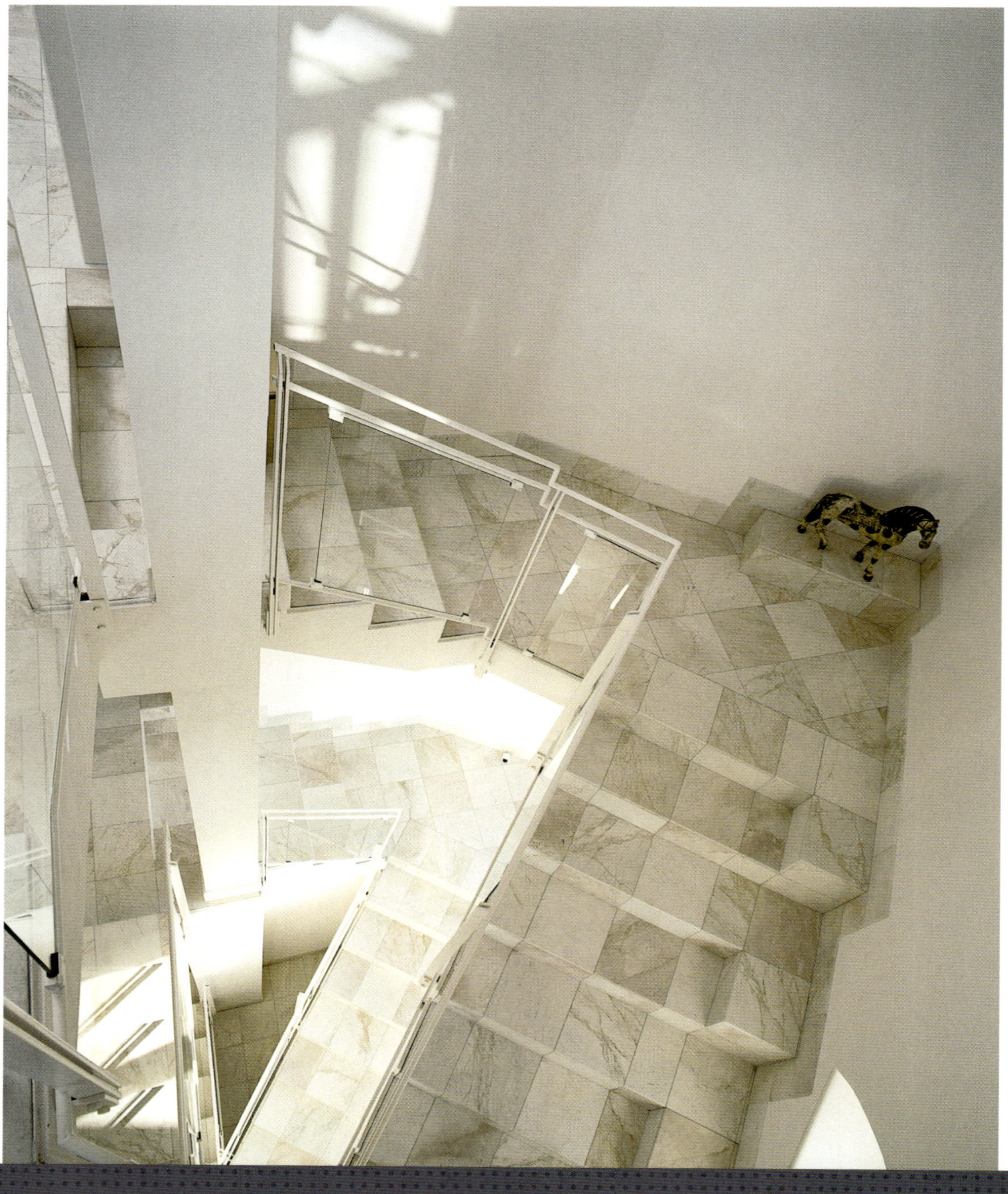

Halle im Obergeschoß, Bibliothek, Blick nach Süden Hall on the first floor, library, view to the south
Treppenanlage vom Obergeschoß aus Staircase seen from the first floor

Treppenanlage von der Halle aus Staircase seen from the hall

WIEN/HIETZING – UNTERES HAUS
HIETZING, VIENNA – LOWER HOUSE

ORT LOCATION: **Hietzing, A-1130 Wien** BAUHERRSCHAFT CLIENT: **S.W. und Dr. W.W.** PLANUNGS- UND BAUZEIT DESIGN AND REALISATION: **1986–1989** PROJEKTLEITER PROJECT LEADER: **Gerald Wratschko** STATIK STATICS: **Manfred Petschnigg** WOHNNUTZFLÄCHE USABLE LIVING SPACE: **410 m²** UMBAUTER RAUM BUILDING VOLUME: **1.790 m³** KONSTRUKTION UND MATERIALIEN: **Massivbauweise** CONSTRUCTION AND MATERIALS: **solid construction** EINDECKUNG: **glasierte Tonziegel** ROOF CLADDING: **glazed clay tiles**

<<< S. ABB. SEE FIGS. **72, 75, 80**

Ansicht von Süden View from the south

Ansicht Südwestfassade View of the south-west façade
Dachaufsicht Roof-top view

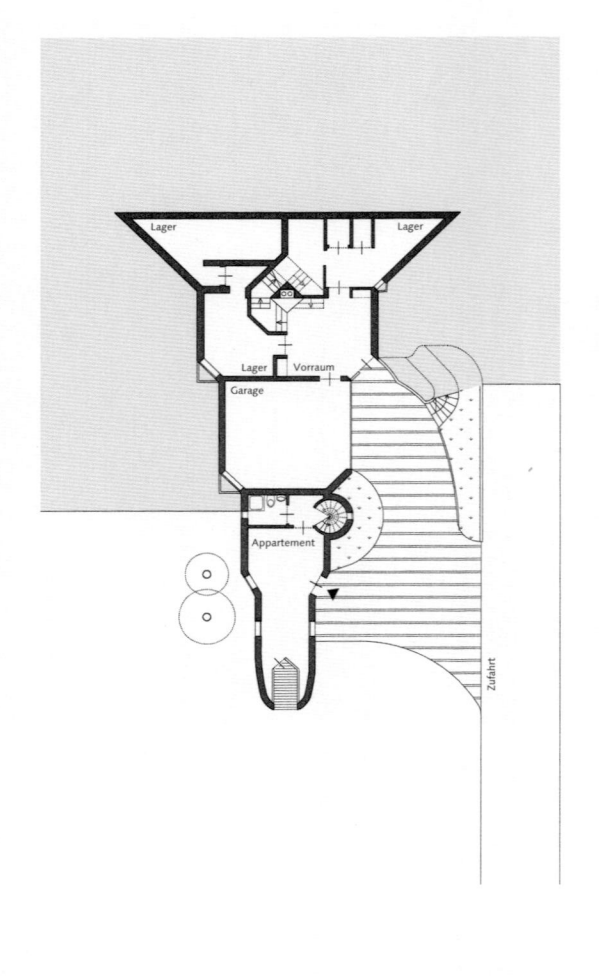

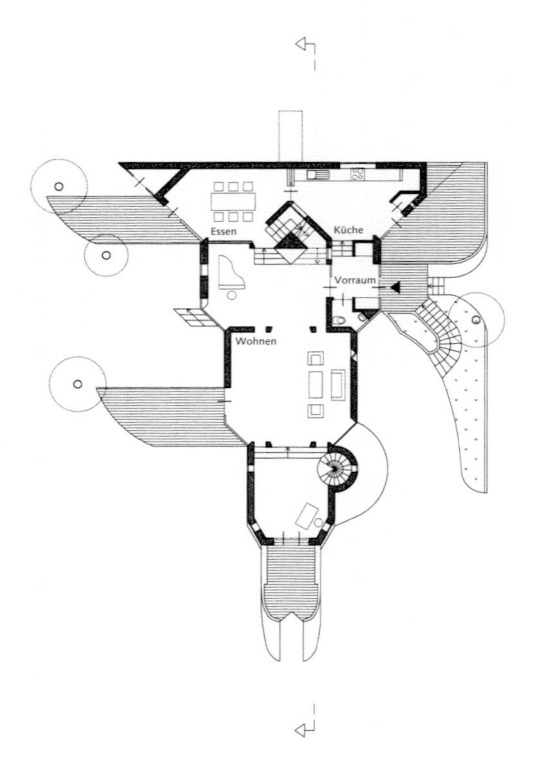

Dieses Ensemble in einem Wiener Vorort gehört zu den bekanntesten Privathäusern der Architekten. Auf einem langen, schmalen Hanggrundstück gelegen sind die beiden Häuser für zwei Familien achsial auf einander bezogen.

Das obere Haus ist quer zum Hang an die obere Grundstückskante gesetzt, das untere nimmt die Höhenlinien des Geländes längsgerichtet auf und verjüngt sich im unteren Abschluß. Die Farbgestaltung berücksichtigt den Wunsch nach Differenzierung der beiden Familien im vorherrschenden fahlen Violett des oberen und im zurückhaltenden Grautürkis des unteren Hauses. „Das schmale, nach Süden orientierte Grundstück führte zu der Entscheidung, die Baukörper in achsialer Anordnung hintereinander aufzureihen. Durch die sich von Süden nach Norden auffächernden Baumassen konnte die gewünschte Öffnung einer Vielzahl von Räumen nach Süden und zu den Seiten hin erreicht werden. Zwischen den beiden Häusern und vor ihren jeweiligen Zugängen entstand ein von einem Laubengang eingefaßter innenhofartiger Bereich. Zusammen mit der formalen Abstimmung der Baukörper faßt dieser die beiden Häuser äußerlich zu einer gemeinsamen Bausubstanz zusammen. „Im Inneren der Häuser indessen und in den Einzelheiten ihrer Fassadengestaltung entfaltet sich jeweils ein räumlich-architektonisches Eigenleben, das in enger Beziehung zu den Wünschen ihrer Bewohner steht." (Szyszkowitz+Kowalski)

Grundrisse Floor plans:
Untergeschoß Basement
Erdgeschoß Ground floor
Obergeschoß First floor

Schnitt unteres und oberes Haus
Section upper and lower house

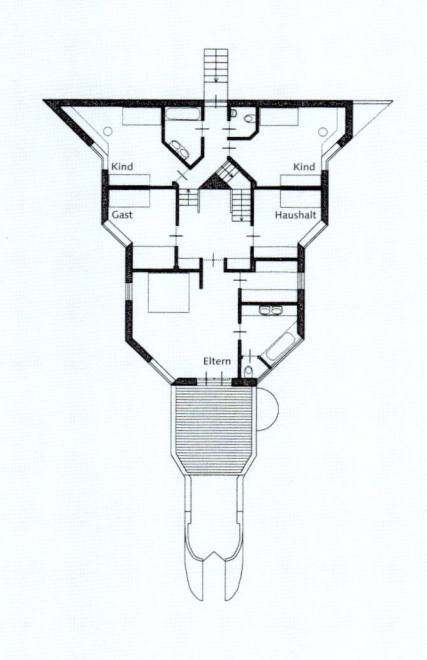

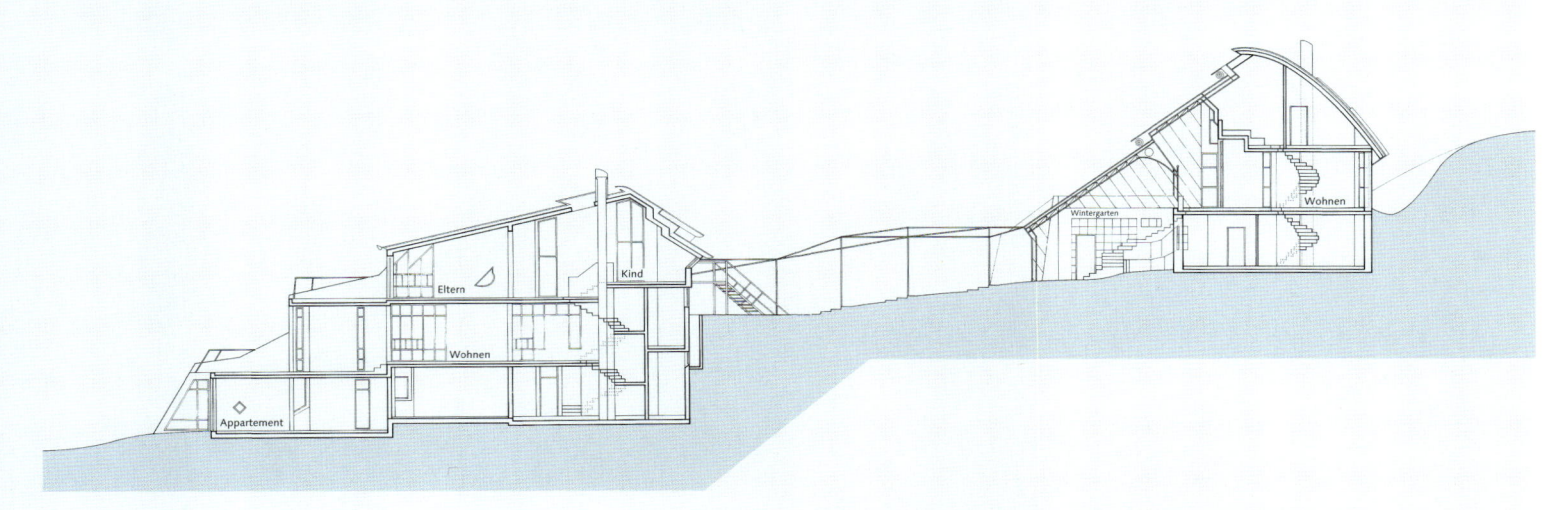

This ensemble in a Viennese suburb is one of the architects' best-known private buildings. The two houses for two families placed on a long, narrow plot relate to each other axially. The upper house is placed sideways to the slope on the upper edge of the site. The lower one takes up the site contours longitudinally and tapers at its lower end. The colour scheme acknowledges the two families' request that the houses should look different with the dominant pale purple of the upper one and the reticent grey-turquoise of the lower one. "The narrow, south-facing plot led to the decision to place the buildings almost axially one behind the other. As the building masses open up from south to north, it was possible to meet the request that a large number of rooms should face south and to the sides. An area like an inner courtyard, framed by an open passage, emerged between the two houses and outside the entrance to each of them. This and the fact that the forms of the two houses match gives the two houses the sense of being a single building when seen from the outside. But the interior of the houses and the details of the façade design in each case show that they lead independent lives in terms of space and architecture, which corresponds closely with what their occupants wanted." (Szyszkowitz+Kowalski).

Skizze Sketch
Ansicht von Osten View from the east

Ansicht von Südosten View from the south-east
Gesamtanlage Complete complex
Gesamtanlage Complete complex

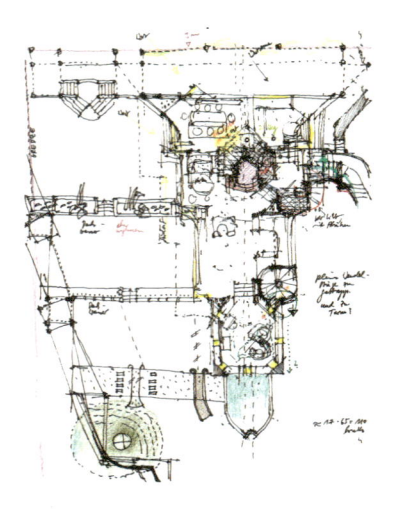

HOUSE IN HIETZING, VIENNA HAUS IN WIEN/HIETZING

WIEN/HIETZING – OBERES HAUS
HIETZING, VIENNA – UPPER HOUSE

ORT LOCATION: **Hietzing, A-1130 Wien** BAUHERRSCHAFT CLIENT: **D. St. und F. St.** PLANUNGS- UND BAUZEIT DESIGN AND REALISATION: **1987–1990** PROJEKTLEITER PROJECT LEADER: **Andreas Lichtblau, Gerald Wratschko** STATIK STATICS: **Manfred Petschnigg** WOHNNUTZFLÄCHE USABLE LIVING SPACE: **430 m²** UMBAUTER RAUM BUILDING VOLUME: **1.820 m³** KONSTRUKTION UND MATERIALIEN: **Massivbauweise, Wintergarten in Stahlkonstruktion** CONSTRUCTION AND MATERIALS: **solid construction, conservatory in steel** EINDECKUNG: **glasierte Tonziegel** ROOF CLADDING: **glazed clay tiles** <<< S. ABB. SEE FIGS. **72–77**

Dachaufsicht Roof-top view

Eingangsbereich und Wintergarten bei Nacht Lobby and conservatory at night

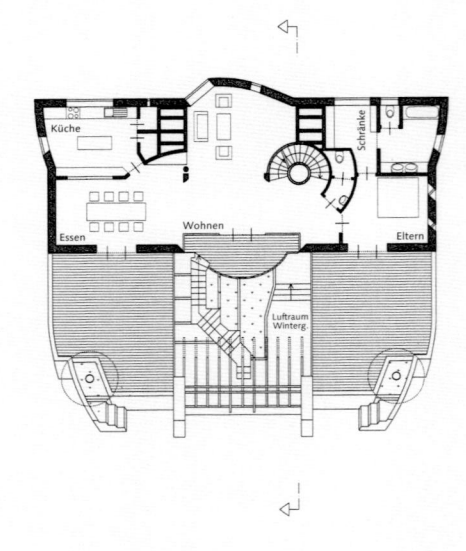

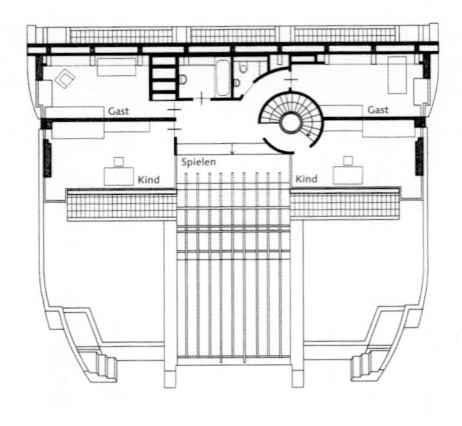

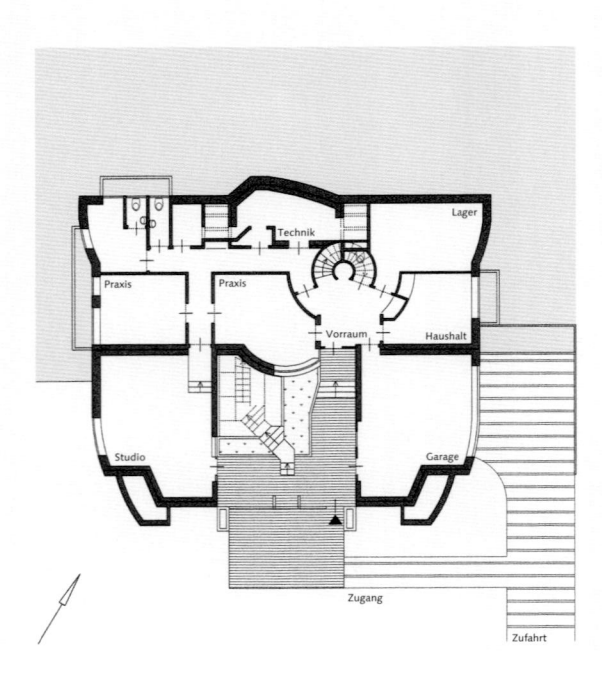

Grundrisse Floor plans:
Erdgeschoß Ground floor
Untergeschoß Basement
Obergeschoß First floor

Das äußere Erscheinungsbild des oberen dreigeschossigen Hauses wird durch den auf die Symmetrieachse gesetzten, großen Wintergarten bestimmt, der zugleich den Eingang zum Haus in sich birgt. Das untere Geschoß nimmt neben den Garagen auch die Büro- und Praxisräume auf, das Erdgeschoß, welches zusätzlich über eine Wendeltreppe erreicht werden kann, den Wohnbereich mit der großzügig ausgelegten Küche und den beiden Terrassen sowie das Schlafzimmer des Ehepaares. Das obere Stockwerk hat neben den beiden Kinderzimmern zwei weitere Räume für die Gäste. Die exponierte Lage am Hang ist in Hinsicht auf den gebuckelten Baukörper ähnlich wie im *Haus am Hohenrain* interpretiert, wenngleich im Hietzinger Haus das gewölbte Dach im hinteren Bereich abgestuft ist.

Gegenüber dem breit gelagerten, verschwiegen erscheinenden oberen Haus folgt das untere dreigeschossige Haus dem Fluß des leicht abfallenden Geländes als ein ineinander greifendes Raumkontinuum. Die Familie mit zwei Kindern hat ihren Wohnbereich im Erdgeschoß, der von dem leicht erhöhten Plateau der abgeschlossenen Küche über zwei Niveausprünge in der Tiefe erschlossen ist. Das obere Geschoß mit den Schlafräumen für die Eltern und Kinder ist über eine zentrale Treppe zu erreichen.

Dieser differenziert abfallende Raumfluß ist auch im äußeren Gebäudekörper ablesbar, denn das Haus erscheint in den Geschossen von oben nach unten abgestuft und verjüngt sich gleichsam wie ein Flaschenhals. Dem winzigen von zwei Wangen umschlossenen Höfchen entspricht im mittleren Geschoßbereich eine kleine, durch Brüstungsmauern umfaßte, Terrasse, und eine großflächige, variantenreiche Durchfensterung in den Wänden gibt den Innenbereichen eine umfassende Helligkeit aus allen Himmelsrichtungen. Wie im *Haus Harmisch* und im *Bad Mergentheimer Haus* wird auch hier der Zugang zu den Wohnhäusern durch eine großzügige Linienführung der Treppenanlage zum Erlebnis.

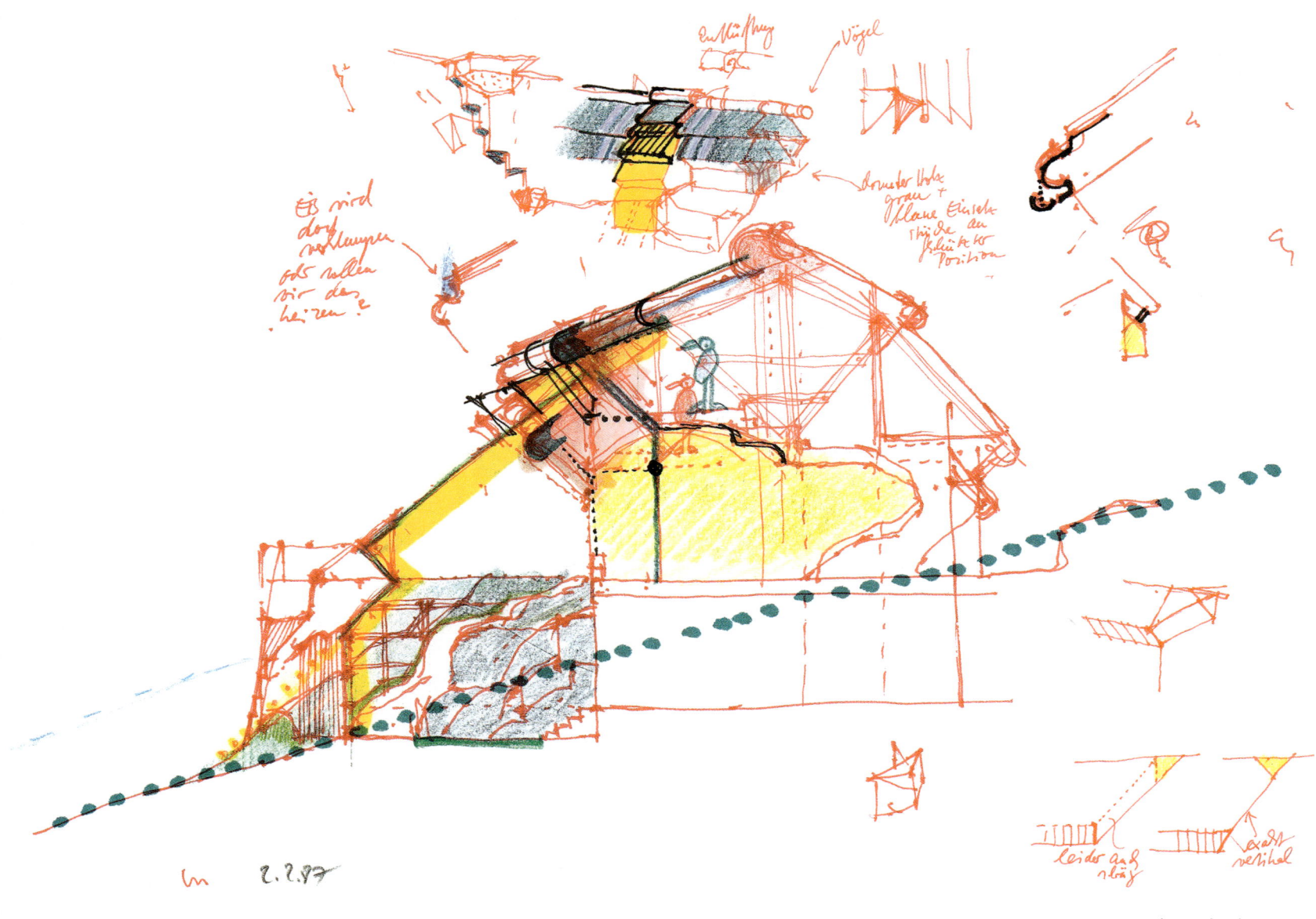

Skizze Sketch

The external appearance of the upper three-storey house is determined by the large conservatory, set on the axis of symmetry, which also contains the entrance to the house. The bottom storey accommodates the office and consulting rooms as well as the garages. The ground floor, which can also be reached via a spiral staircase, features the living area with the lavishly designed kitchen and the two terraces, and also the master bedroom, and the top floor has two other rooms for guests as well as the two children's rooms. The exposed site on the slop is interpreted similarly to the *Haus am Hohenrain* as far as the humped building is concerned, though in the case of the *House in Hietzing* the vaulted roof is terraced at the back.

In contrast with the broad, secluded-looking upper house, the lower three-storey house follows the flow of the slightly sloping terrain as an interlocking spatial continuum. The family with two children have their living area on the ground floor, which is accessed from the slightly raised plateau of the closed kitchen by two changes of level down below. The top floor contains the parents' and the children's bedrooms and can be reached by a central staircase.

This subtly dropping spatial flow is also intelligible in the outer body of the building: the floors of the house seem to be terraced from top to bottom, and it tapers rather like the neck of a bottle. A small terrace framed with balustraded walls on the middle level corresponds with the tiny little courtyard enclosed by two side walls and large areas of differently designed windows in the walls provided light from all sides. Like *Harmisch House* and the *House in Bad Mergentheim*, here too entering the houses becomes an experience because of the generous lines of the staircase.

Ansicht von Südosten View from the south-east

HOUSE IN HIETZING, VIENNA | HAUS IN WIEN/HIETZING

Südwestfassade South-west façade

Obere Terrasse neben Wintergarten Upper terrace by the conservatory
Nordostfassade North-east façade
Nordostfassade North-east façade

HOUSE IN HIETZING, VIENNA   HAUS IN WIEN/HIETZING   152 | 153

Treppenaufgang vom Wohnraum aus Stairs seen from the living-room
Wintergarten im Wohngeschoss Conservatory on the living floor

Obergeschoß, Blicke zu den Schlafräumen nach Südwesten und Nordosten
First floor, views of the bedrooms to the south-west and north-east
Obergeschoß, Aufenthaltsraum, Blick nach Nordosten First floor, leisure room,
view to the north-east

HOUSE IN HIETZING, VIENNA   HAUS IN WIEN/HIETZING

HAUS IN BAD MERGENTHEIM
HOUSE IN BAD MERGENTHEIM

ORT LOCATION: **D-97980 Bad Mergentheim** BAUHERRSCHAFT CLIENT: **Dr. R. H. und H. H.** PLANUNGS- UND BAUZEIT DESIGN AND REALISATION: **1991–1993** STATIK STATICS: **Johann Birner** WOHNNUTZFLÄCHE USABLE LIVING SPACE: **360 m²** UMBAUTER RAUM BUILDING VOLUME: **1.220 m³** KONSTRUKTION UND MATERIALIEN: **Sockel in Massivbauweise, Stahlstützen mit gekrümmten Holzleimbindern** CONSTRUCTION AND MATERIALS: **base solid construction, steel columns with curved glulam beams** EINDECKUNG: **Titanzink** ROOF CLADDING: **zinc roofing**

<<< S. ABB. SEE FIGS. **32, 35, 43, 44, 66, 82**

Ansicht vom unteren Garten View from the lower garden
Ostfassade East façade

HOUSE IN BAD MERGENTHEIM HAUS IN BAD MERGENTHEIM

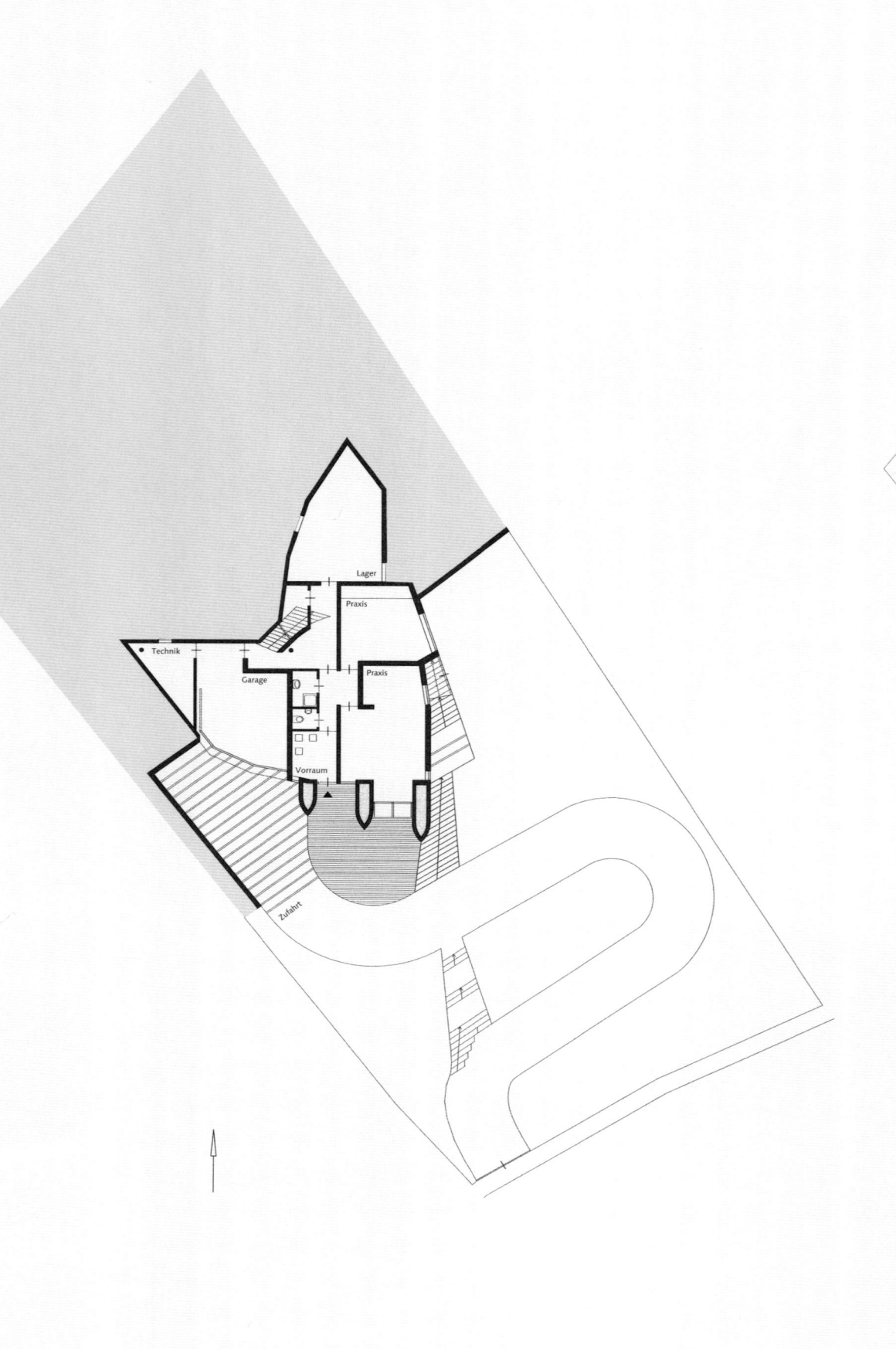

Lager
Praxis
Praxis
Technik
Garage
Vorraum
Zufahrt

Grundrisse Floor plans:
Untergeschoß Basement
Erdgeschoß Ground floor
Obergeschoß First floor

Schnitt Section

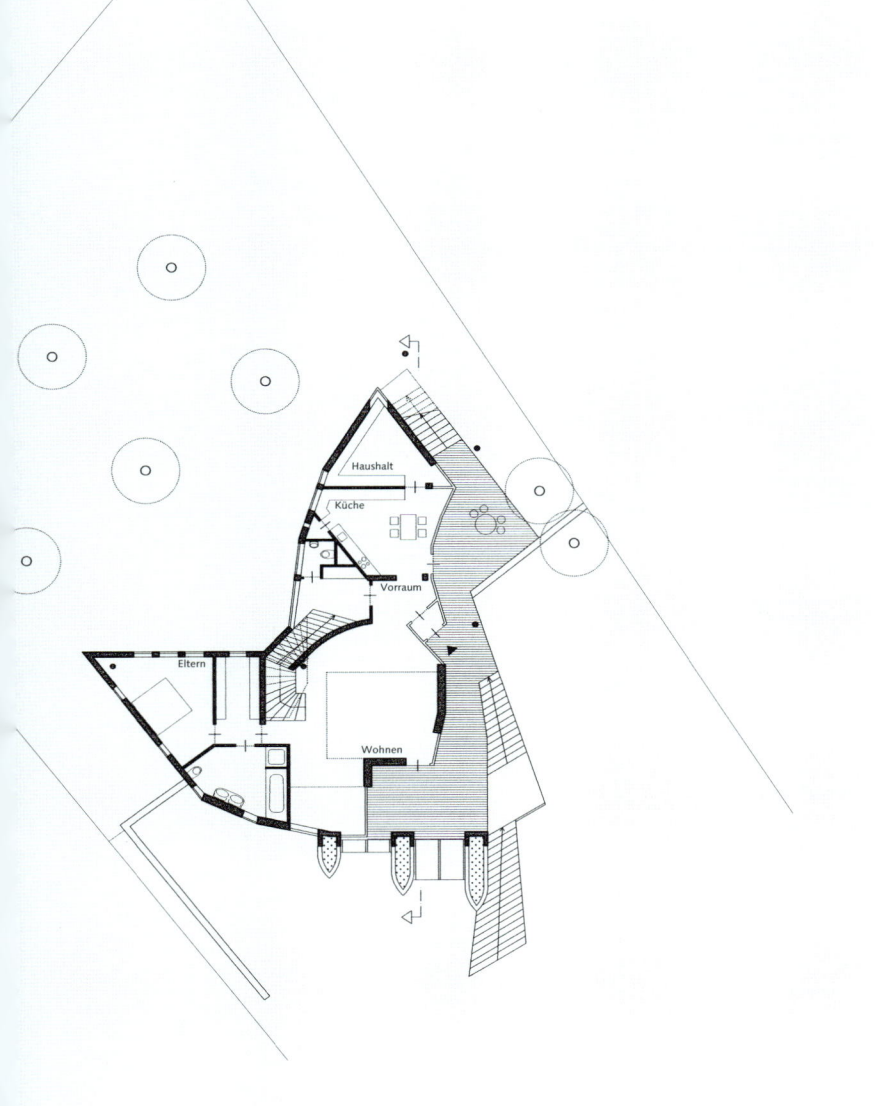

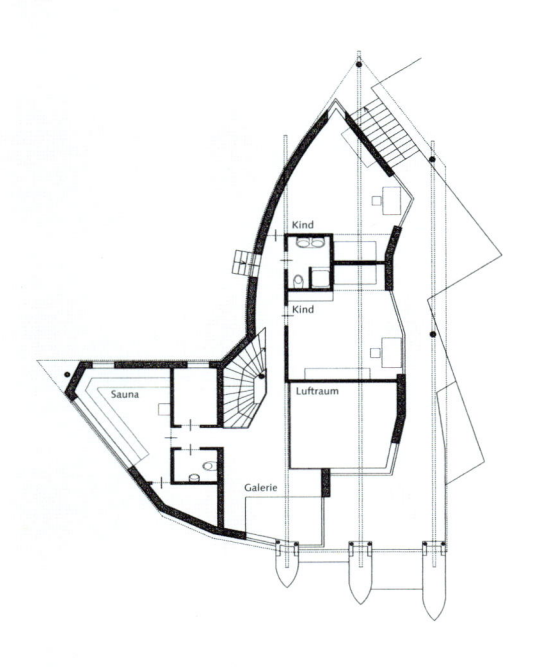

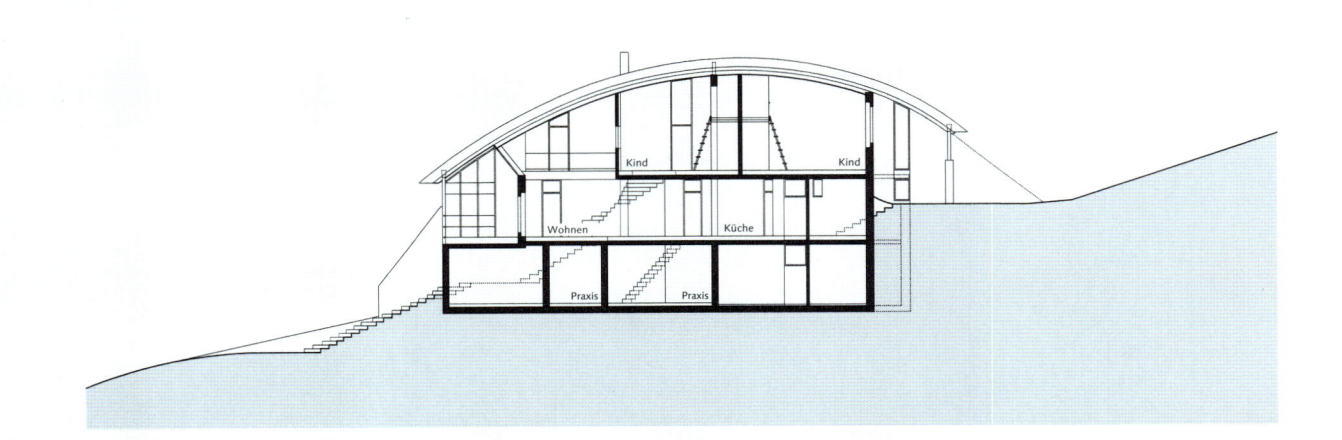

HOUSE IN BAD MERGENTHEIM   HAUS IN BAD MERGENTHEIM   158 | 159

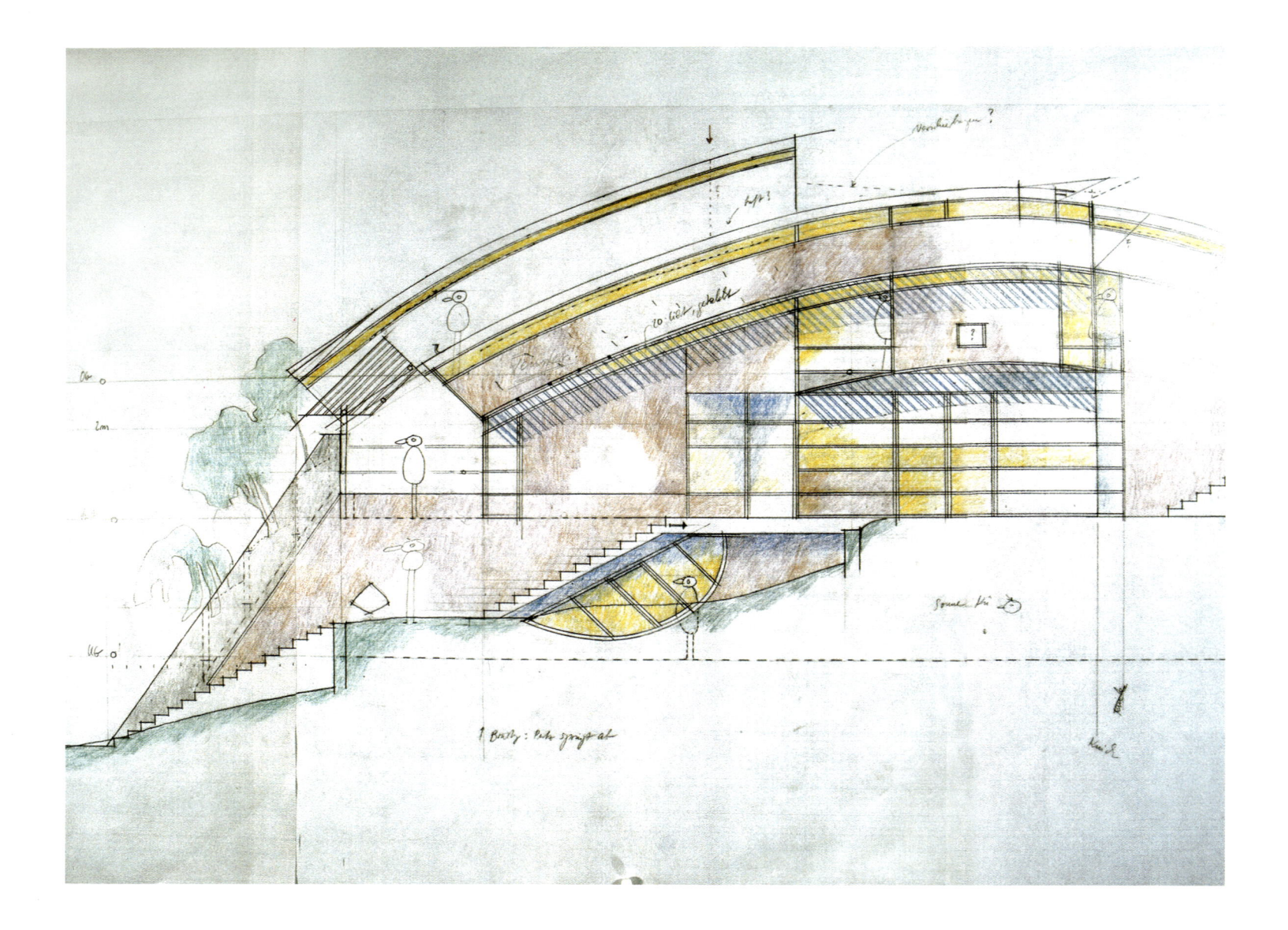

Dieses Einfamilienhaus mit Praxisräumen für die Auftraggeber entstand in Bad Mergentheim, einem kleinen, idyllisch gelegenen Kurort an der Tauber zwischen Stuttgart und Würzburg. Die Bauherren besaßen ein von ehemaligen Weinbergen geprägtes steiles Hanggrundstück in Süd-Westlage. Das dreigeschossige Haus nimmt auf der unteren Ebene die Garage, den Keller und die Ordinationsräume des Psychotherapeutenehepaares auf. Das mittlere Geschoß umfaßt die über zwei Geschosse gezogene, hohe Wohnhalle mit einer Galerie, die vom weiten Bogen des Daches abgeschlossen wird. Es nimmt außerdem den Eßplatz, die Sitzecke, die angelagerte, abtrennbare, große Küche sowie das Elternschlafzimmer auf.
Im oberen Geschoß sind die Zimmer für die beiden Kinder untergebracht, die bei Bedarf zu separieren und von der hinteren Gartenseite aus zu betreten sind. Von der Straße führt im vorderen Teil eine Treppenkaskade zum Niveau der Terrasse mit einem eingehängten Sonnenflügel. Das Haus erstrahlt in einem abgetönten Siena-Rot. „Das eigentlich Unkonventionelle in der Planung dieses Hauses ist dessen Schiefstellung. Durch die Geländekonturen bot sich ein zum Hang parallel, bzw. senkrecht laufendes Gebäude an, wie es bei derartigen Standorten üblich ist. Statt dessen wurde das Haus gedreht, um eine längere südseitige Fassade und Queraussichten in mehrere Richtungen zu schaffen. Das Haus liegt unter einer Reihe paralleler, bogenförmiger Träger des Daches, die jeweils an verschiedene, selbsttragende Wände anknüpfen. Der Grundriß ist annähernd V-förmig angelegt, wobei hinten zwischen den beiden Flügeln ein intimer, von einer alten Baumgruppe bestandener Obstgarten eingebunden ist." (Szyszkowitz+ Kowalski)

This family house with consulting rooms for the clients was built in Bad Mergentheim, a small, idyllic resort on the Tauber between Stuttgart and Würzburg. The clients owned a steep, south-west facing plot surrounded by former vineyards. The three-storey house accommodates the garage, the cellar and the psychotherapist couple's consulting rooms on the bottom floor. The middle floor contains the high living hall, rising through two storeys, with a gallery topped by the broad arch of the roof. It also accommodates the dining area, the sitting corner, the adjacent large kitchen, which can be separated off, and the master bedroom. The rooms for the two children are on the top floor; if necessary they can be separated and accessed from the back garden. A cascade of steps on the street side at the front leads to the terrace level with a suspended sun awning. The house is resplendent in shades of red sienna. "The actual unconventional feature in the planning of this house is its angled position. The contours of the site suggested a building that ran parallel to the slope, or vertically, as is customary in such locations. Instead the house was turned to create a longer south façade and diagonal outside views in various directions. The house is under a series of parallel, arch-shaped roof supports, each linked to different, self-supporting walls. The ground plan is almost V-shaped, including an intimate orchard with a group of old trees between the two wings." (Szyszkowitz+ Kowalski).

Zeichnung Ostfassade Drawing of the east façade

Rückwärtiger Garteneingang zum Obergeschoß Rear garden entrance to the upper floor
Ostfassade East façade
Ostfassade East façade
Ostfassade mit Haupteingang East façade with main entrance

HOUSE IN BAD MERGENTHEIM HAUS IN BAD MERGENTHEIM 160 | 161

Skizze Sketch

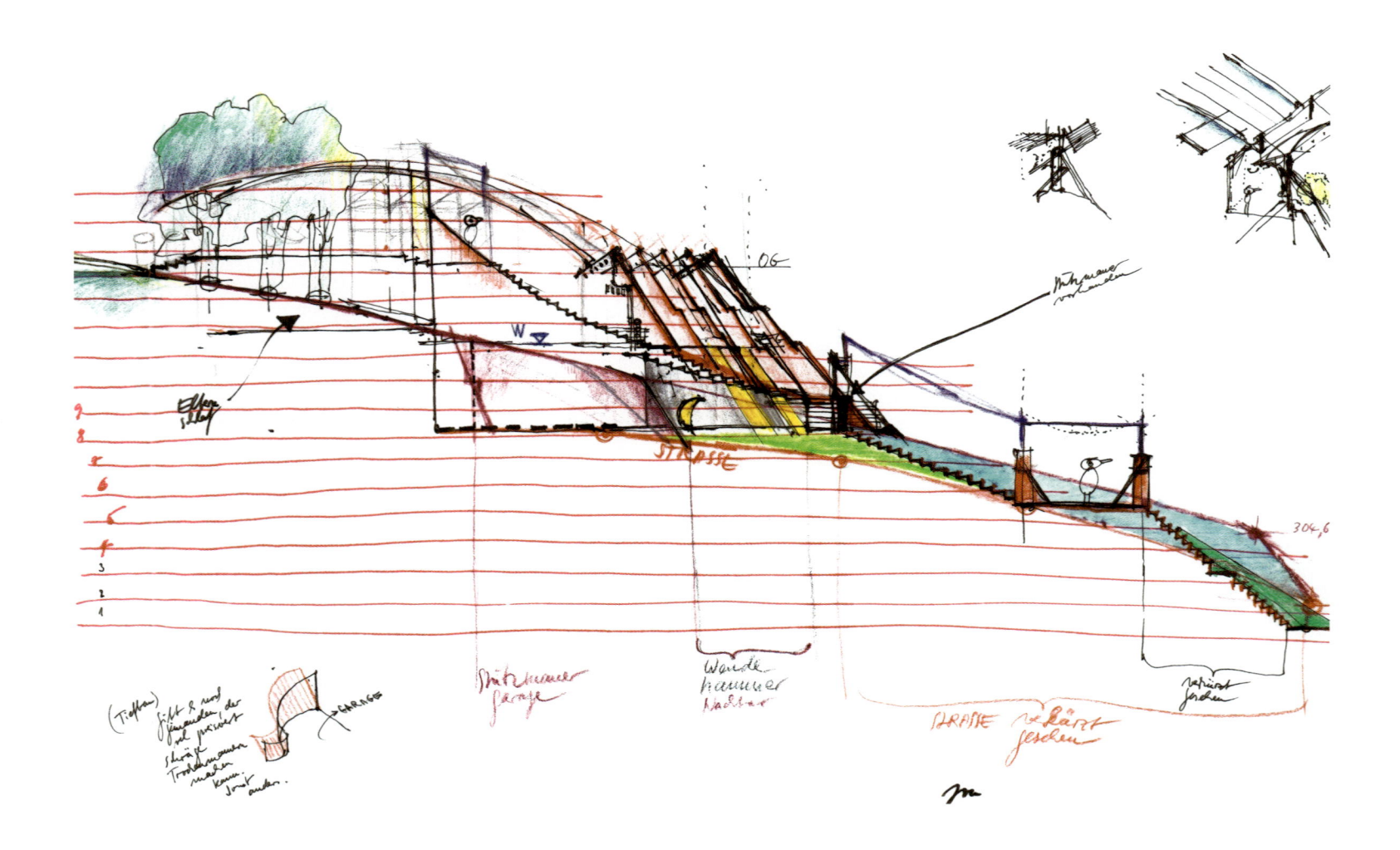

Treppe von der Halle ins Obergeschoß Stairs from the hall to the first floor
Erdgeschoß, Blick ins Tal nach Süden Ground floor, view into the valley to the south

HOUSE IN BAD MERGENTHEIM   HAUS IN BAD MERGENTHEIM | 162 | 163

HAUS IN MARIA ENZERSDORF
HOUSE IN MARIA ENZERSDORF

ORT LOCATION: A-2344 Maria Enzersdorf am Gebirge   BAUHERRSCHAFT CLIENT: Dr. jur. G. H. und Dr. jur. W. H.   PLANUNGS- UND BAUZEIT DESIGN AND REALISATION: 1991–1994   PROJEKTLEITER PROJECT LEADER: Michael Lyssy   STATIK STATICS: Johann Birner   WOHNNUTZFLÄCHE USABLE LIVING SPACE: 170 m²   UMBAUTER RAUM BUILDING VOLUME: 670 m³   KONSTRUKTION UND MATERIALIEN: Stahlbetonstützen, Stahlfachwerkträger, Außenmauern: Massivbauweise CONSTRUCTION AND MATERIALS: reinforced concrete columns, steel trusses, exterior walls: solid construction   EINDECKUNG: Titanzink ROOF CLADDING: zinc roofing

<<< S. ABB. SEE FIGS. 34, 36

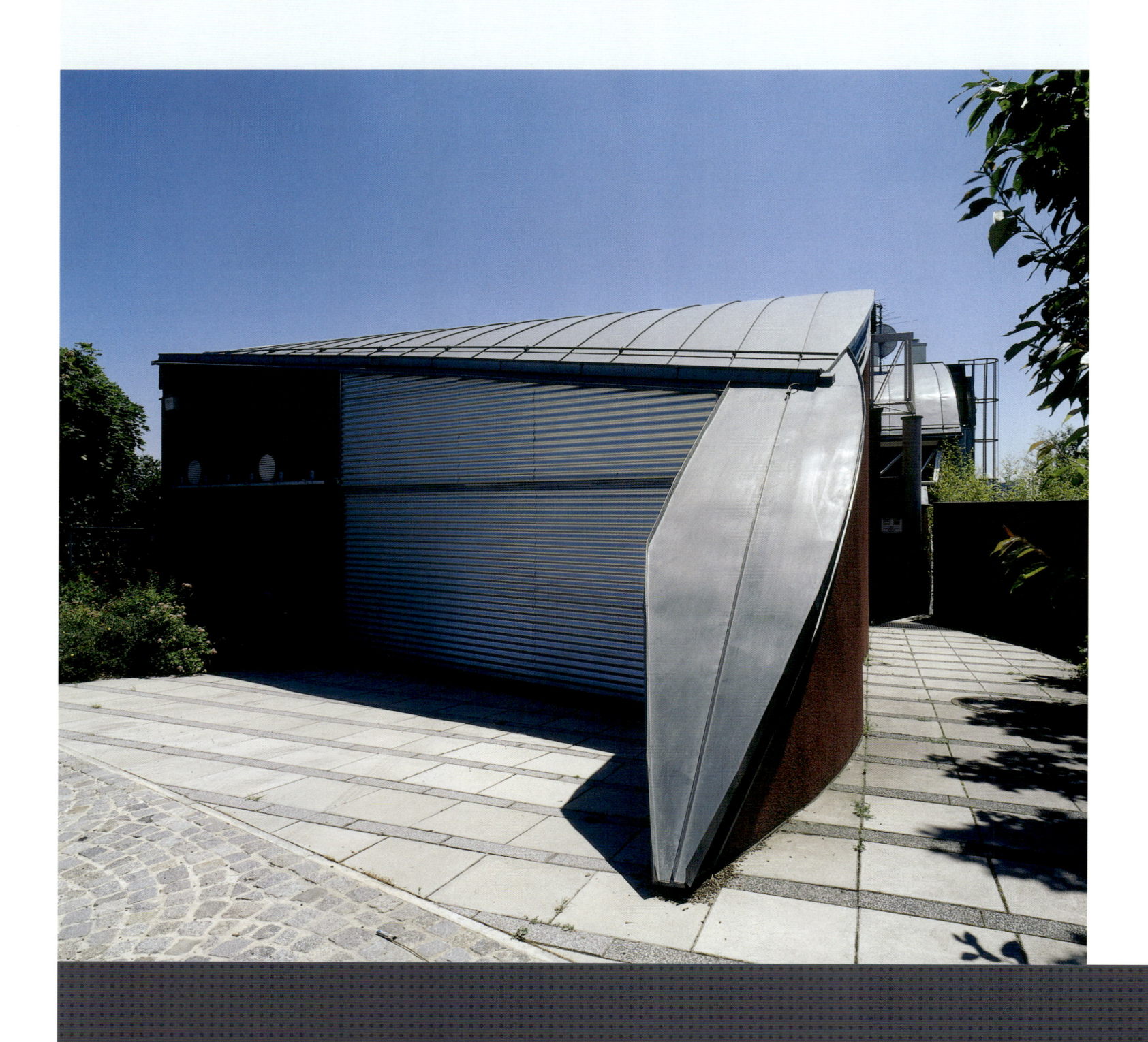

Ansicht von Norden View from the north

Ansicht von Süden View from the south
Treppe mit Bibliothek Stairs with library

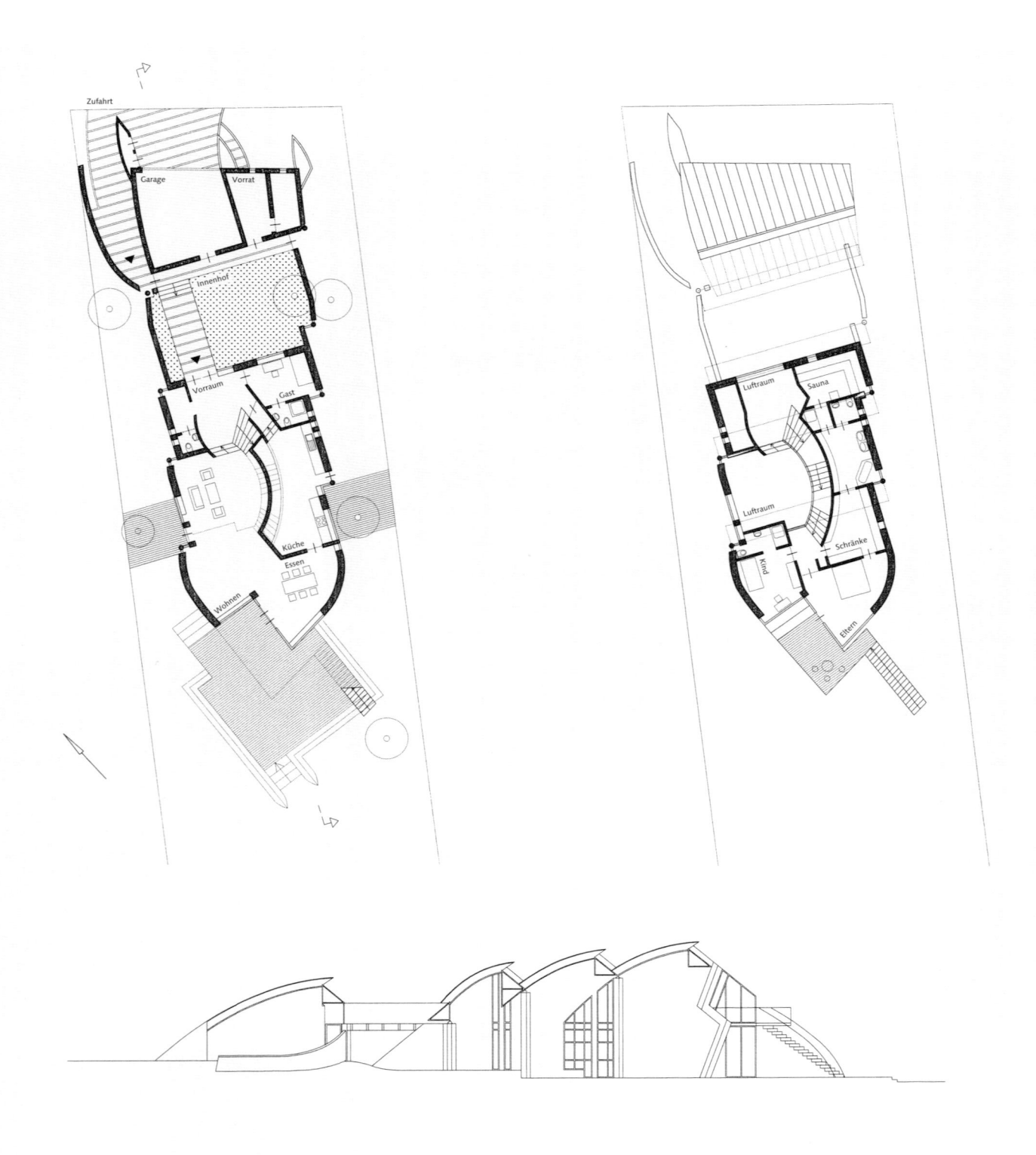

Das schmale, lange Grundstück liegt in einem zersiedelten Einfamilienhausgebiet in Maria Enzersdorf bei Wien. Entsprechend ist das Haus aus einzelnen Kompartimenten in Querrichtung entwickelt und von der Straße durch die Garage abgeschirmt. Ein großer Innenhof bildet den Auftakt zum dahinterliegenden zweigeschossigen Raumkontinuum des Hauses. Über einen Eingangsbereich betritt man neben einem Gästezimmer die hohe, über zwei Geschosse auf nahezu 8 m aufragende Wohnhalle mit der parallel hinter dem Wohnbereich positionierten Küche. Die Schlafzimmer der dreiköpfigen Familie liegen mit den Bädern und der Sauna im oberen Geschoß, die über eine leicht geschwungene Bibliothekstreppe vom Entree aus zu erreichen sind. Die Wirkung zwischen den Geschossen wird von dem hohen, freien Luftraum dominiert.

Die Außenansichten der Gebäudekompartimente erhalten durch die geschwungen gestellten Wände eine dynamisierte Kontur, und das Haus erscheint mit den variierten Fassaden als Addition verschiedener Funktionseinheiten. Bestimmend ist die Wiederholung von Dreigurtbindern, die die einzelnen Dachschalen tragen. Die gebogenen Dachelemente spannen von Binder zu Binder, decken die einzelnen Gebäudekompartimente ab und schaffen über schräg, im Längsverlauf der Binder gestellte Oberlichter (sheds) für die darunter liegenden Räume eine zusätzliche Belichtung. Der Gebäudekörper zeigt außen ein tiefes dunkles Rot und ist im Inneren weiß gehalten.

Grundrisse Floor plans:
Erdgeschoß Ground floor
Obergeschoß First floor

Dachaufsicht Roof-top view

Ansicht von Nordwesten
Elevation from the north-west

Schnitt Section

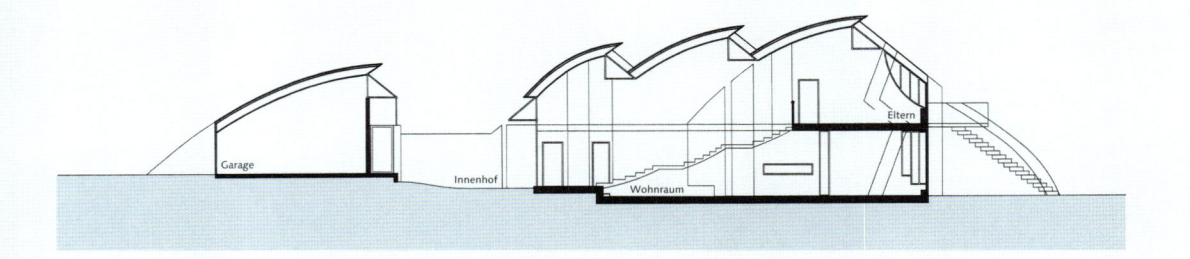

The narrow, long plot is in an overdeveloped area of detached houses in Maria Enzersdorf near Vienna. So the house is designed in individual transversely arranged compartments and protected from the street by a garage. A large inner courtyard is the first stage of the two-storey spatial continuum of the house behind. An entrance area leads to a guest room and also to the high living hall, rising through two storeys to a height of almost 8 metres, with the kitchen placed parallel behind the living area. The bedrooms for the three-member family are on the upper floor with the bathrooms and sauna, and can be reached from the entrance via a slightly curved library staircase. The effect between the floors is of a high, open air-space.

The outside appearance of the building compartments is dynamized by the curved positioning of the walls, and the house with its finely varied façades seems like an accumulation of various functional units. A defining feature is the repetition of triangular trusses supporting the individual roof shells. The curved roof elements span across from truss to truss, cover the individual building compartments and provide additional light for the rooms underneath via diagonal skylights (sheds) placed on the longitudinal line of the trusses. The outside of the building is a deep, dark red, and the interior is white.

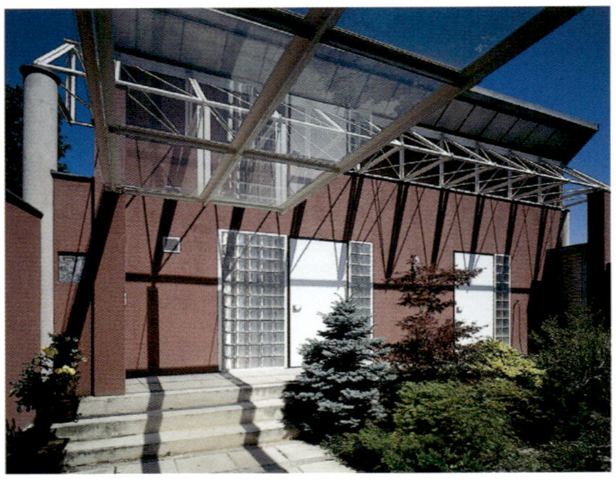

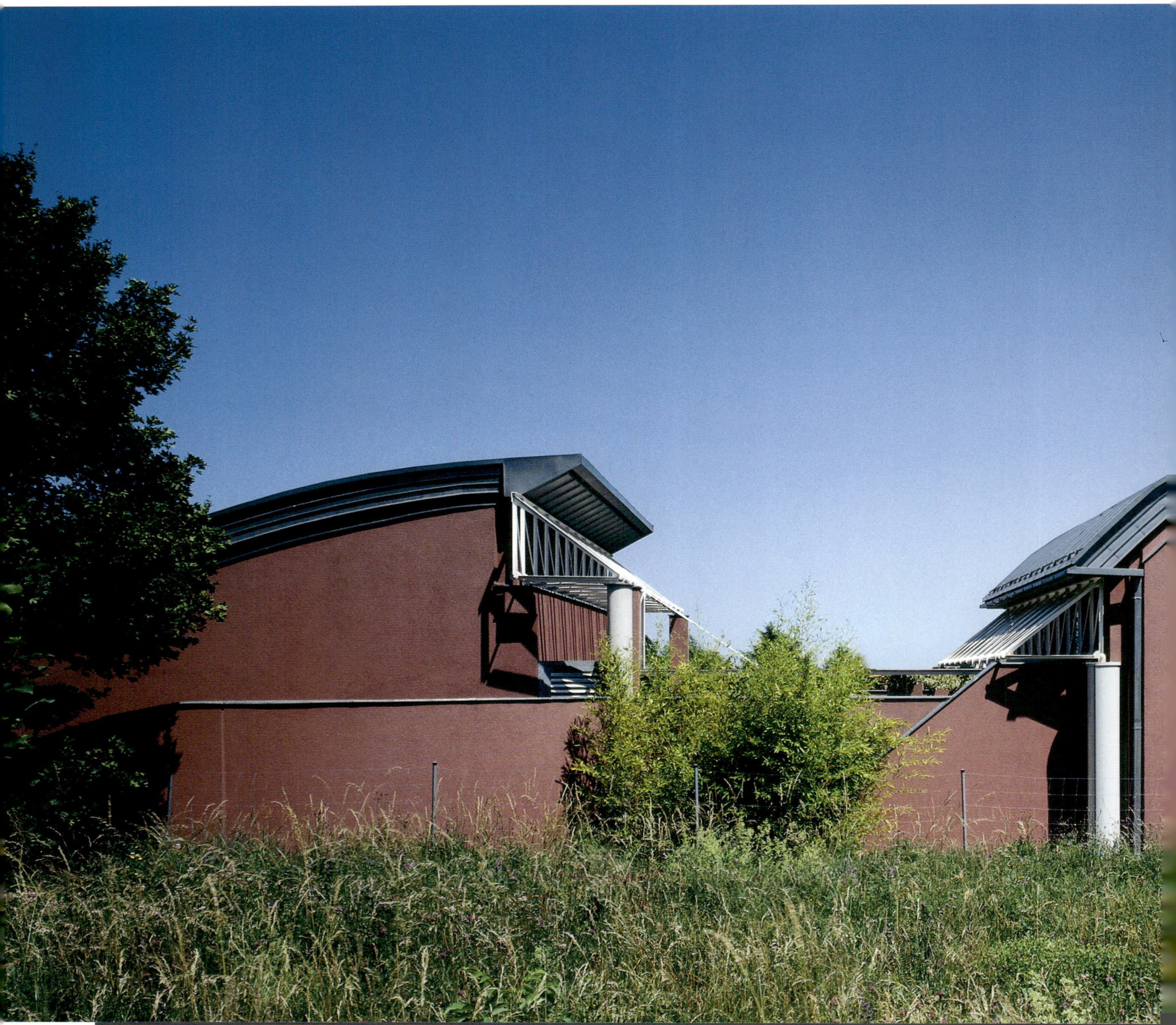

Innenhofeingang zur Garage Courtyard entrance to the garage
Nordwestfassade North-west façade

Südostfassade South-east façade

HOUSE IN MARIA ENZERSDORF   HAUS IN MARIA ENZERSDORF   168 | 169

HAUS AM PLATTENWEG HOUSE ON PLATTENWEG

ORT LOCATION: **A-8043 Graz**   BAUHERRSCHAFT CLIENT: **Mag. Ch. K. und Univ. Doz. Dr. med. P. K.**   PLANUNGS- UND BAUZEIT DESIGN AND REALISATION: **1994–1996**
PROJEKTLEITER PROJECT LEADER: **Paul M. Pilz**   STATIK STATICS: **Johann Birner**   WOHNNUTZFLÄCHE USABLE LIVING SPACE: **430 m²**   UMBAUTER RAUM BUILDING
VOLUME: **1.740 m³**   KONSTRUKTION UND MATERIALIEN: **Massivbauweise mit Klinkervormauerungen**   CONSTRUCTION AND MATERIALS: **solid construction with clinker facing**   EINDECKUNG: **glasierte Tonziegel** ROOF CLADDING: **glazed clay tiles**   <<< S. ABB. SEE FIGS. **4, 55, 62, 67–70**

Zeichnung Drawing

Ansicht von Nordosten View from the north-east

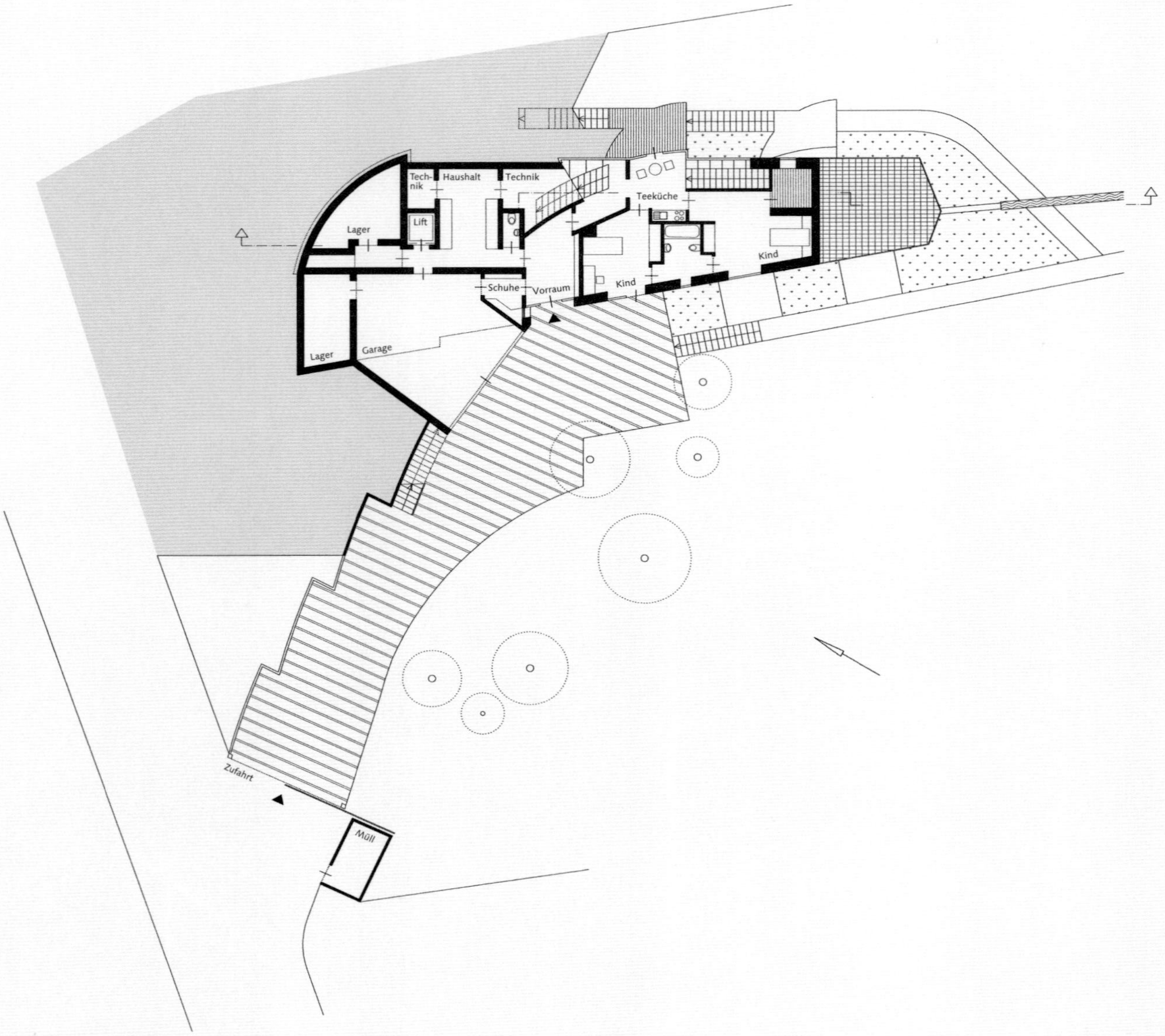
Tech-nik
Haushalt
Technik
Teeküche
Lager
Lift
Kind
Kind
Schuhe
Vorraum
Lager
Garage
Zufahrt
Müll

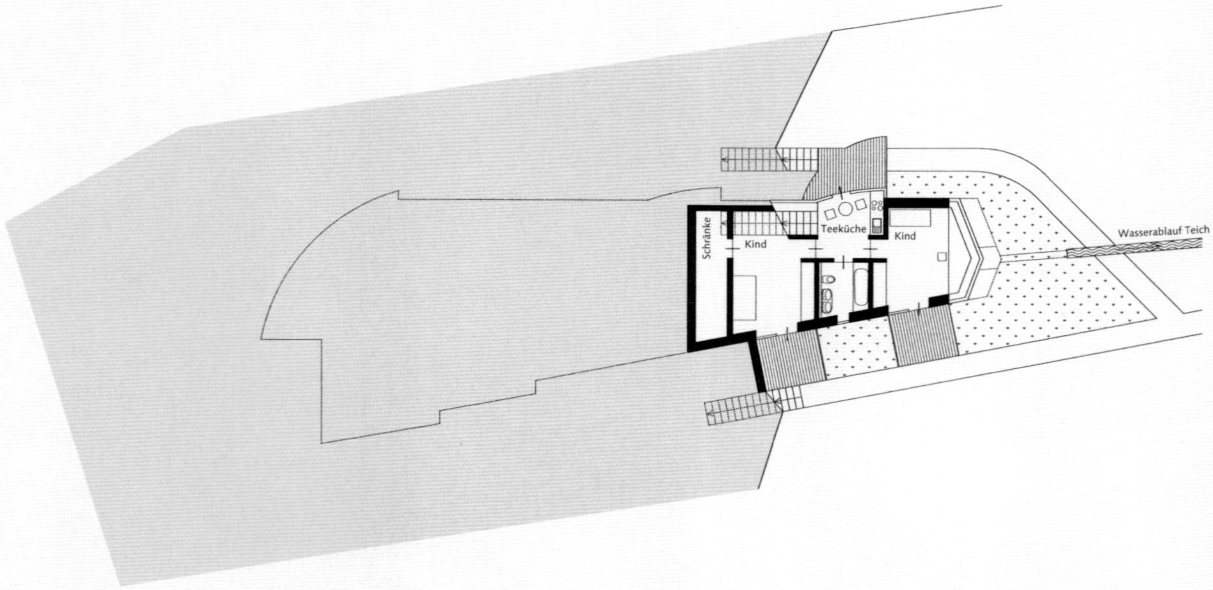
Schränke
Kind
Teeküche
Kind
Wasserablauf Teich

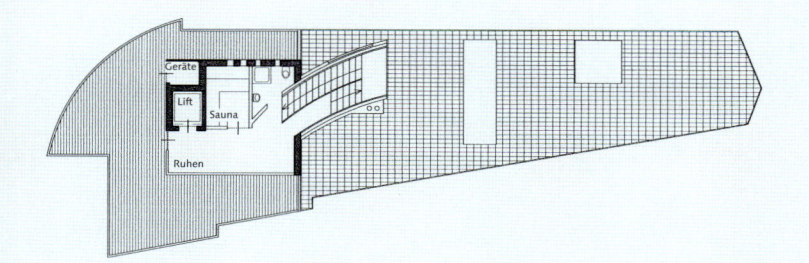

Grundrisse Floor plans:
Untergeschoß Basement
Zweites Untergeschoß Second basement

Zweites Obergeschoß Second floor
Erstes Obergeschoß First floor
Erdgeschoß Ground floor

Schnitt Section

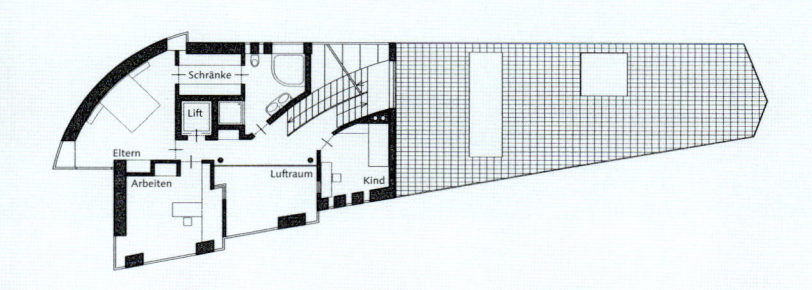

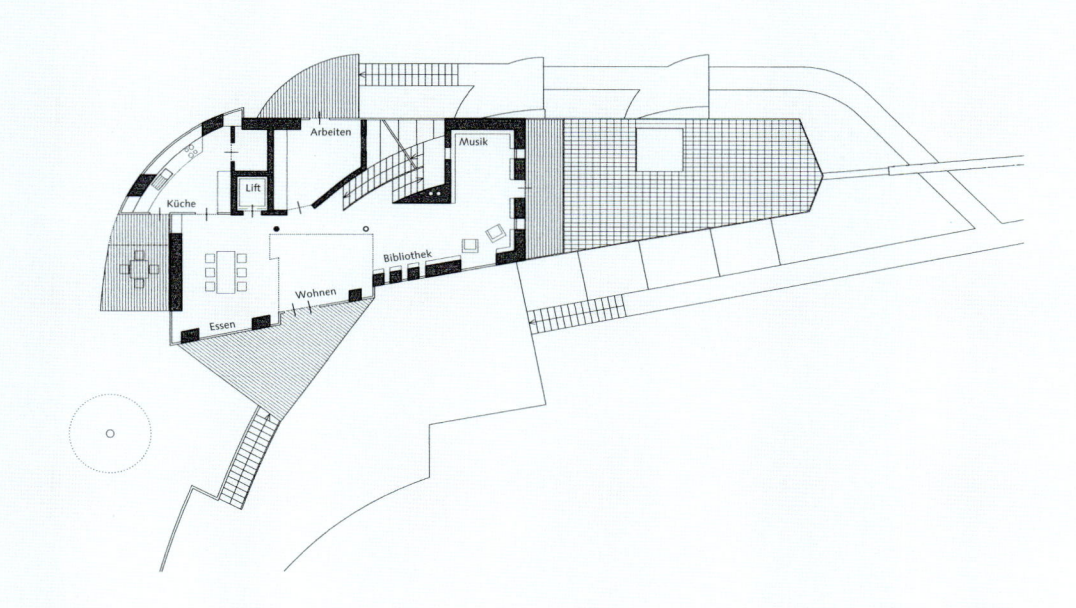

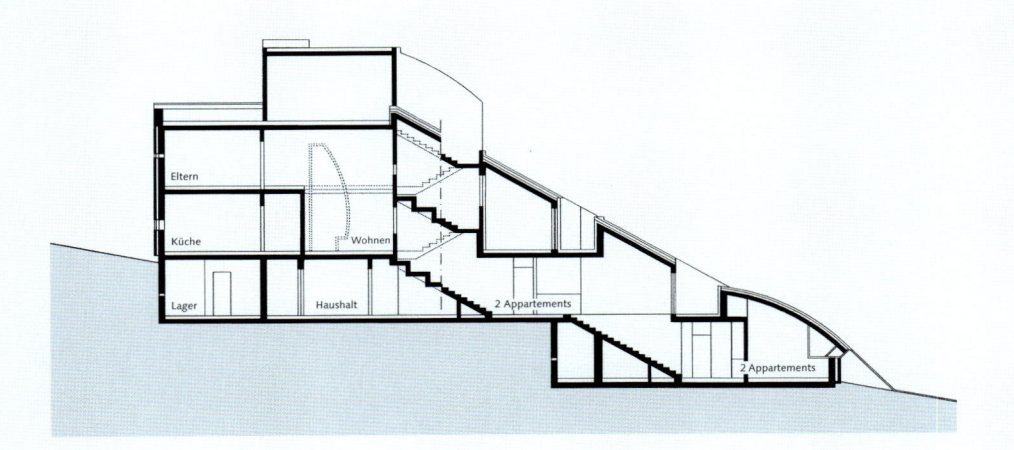

HOUSE ON PLATTENWEG   HAUS AM PLATTENWEG   172 | 173

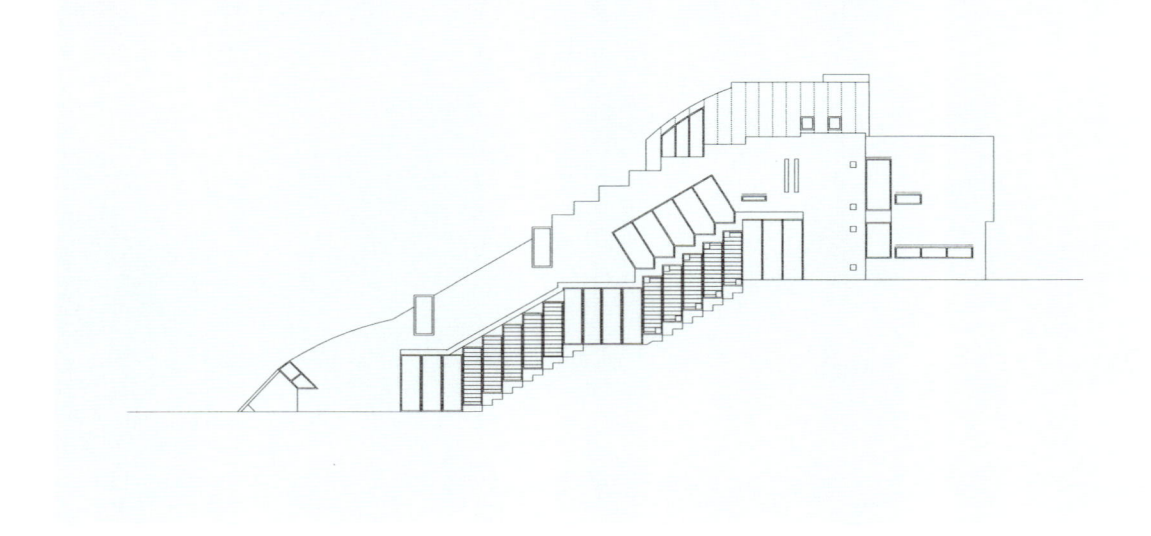

Blick von Nordosten View from the north-east
Ansicht von Nordosten North-east elevation

Auf einem wunderschönen Grundstück, im Grazer Stadtteil Mariagrün gelegen, hatte die Planung den alten Baumbestand und den Wunsch der Bauherren zu berücksichtigen, das Gebäude aus Backstein zu errichten. Daraus ergab sich die Position des Hauses am abfallenden Hang an einer seitlichen Grundstücksgrenze. Das über fünf Geschosse abgetreppte Haus folgt der Fallinie des Baugeländes und wirkt wie ein Bestandteil des umgebenden Naturraumes mit einem tiefer gelegenen großen Schwimmteich im unteren Grundstücksabschluß des Parks. Das größtenteils einheitliche Schrägdach, dessen Wasser den Teich speist, ist von zwei kleinen Terrassen zerschnitten und mit schwarz glasierten Ziegeln eingedeckt. Im Inneren bildet eine über zwei Geschosse geführte, nahezu 6 Meter hohe Halle mit Galerie den zentralen Raum für die sechsköpfige Familie. Diesem Wohnbereich ist talwärts ein eigener Musikraum eingegliedert.

Im unteren Teil des längsgerichteten Hauses befinden sich zwei Appartements für die Kinder mit je einer Miniküche und einem Tisch auf den Absätzen der Stufen. Diese Räume können mit separaten Eingängen unabhängig bewirtschaftet werden.

Der Wohnbereich ist durch ein großes geschwungenes Fenster belichtet. Schwarze Aluminiumprofile der Fenster und schwarze Stahlunterzüge über den Maueröffnungen stehen neben dem schwach gesandeten Rot der Klinker.

In den oberen Geschossen befinden sich Schlaf- und Badezimmer, und den oberen Hausabschluß bildet eine weiträumige Terrasse mit dem Aufbau für die Sauna. Das gesamte Haus ist durch eine in Längsrichtung leicht geschwungene Treppe und einen internen Aufzug erschlossen.

Blick von Südwesten View from the south-west
Ansicht von Südwesten South-west elevation

Planning for this beautiful plot in the Graz district of Mariagrün had to take account of the old trees and the clients' wish that the building should be in brick. This led to the position of the house on the downward slope at one side of the plot. The house is terraced over five storeys. It follows the fall line of the plot and seems like part of the natural space it occupies, with a swimming-pond below in the bottom end section of the parkland plot. The sloping roof is largely uniform. Water from it supplies the pond, and two little terraces covered in with black glazed tiles cut into it. Inside is a hall, rising through two storeys, almost 6 metres high with a gallery, the central space for this family of six. On the valley side a music room is integrated into this hall.

The lower part of the longitudinally organized house contains two apartments for the children, each with a mini-kitchen and a table on the stair landing. These spaces can be run independently, with separate entrances. The living area is lit by a large, curved window. The black aluminium window bars and black steel joists above the wall apertures are placed next to the pale sandy red of the brick.

Bed- and bathrooms are to be found on the top floor, and the house is topped by an extensive terrace with the sauna built in it. The whole house is linked by a slightly curved longitudinal staircase and an internal lift.

HOUSE ON PLATTENWEG HAUS AM PLATTENWEG

Nordostfassade North-east façade
Schlitzfenster an der Südwestfassade Slit window on the south-west façade
Dachaufsicht, Detail Roof-top view, detail

Ansicht von Westen View from the west

HOUSE ON PLATTENWEG   HAUS AM PLATTENWEG

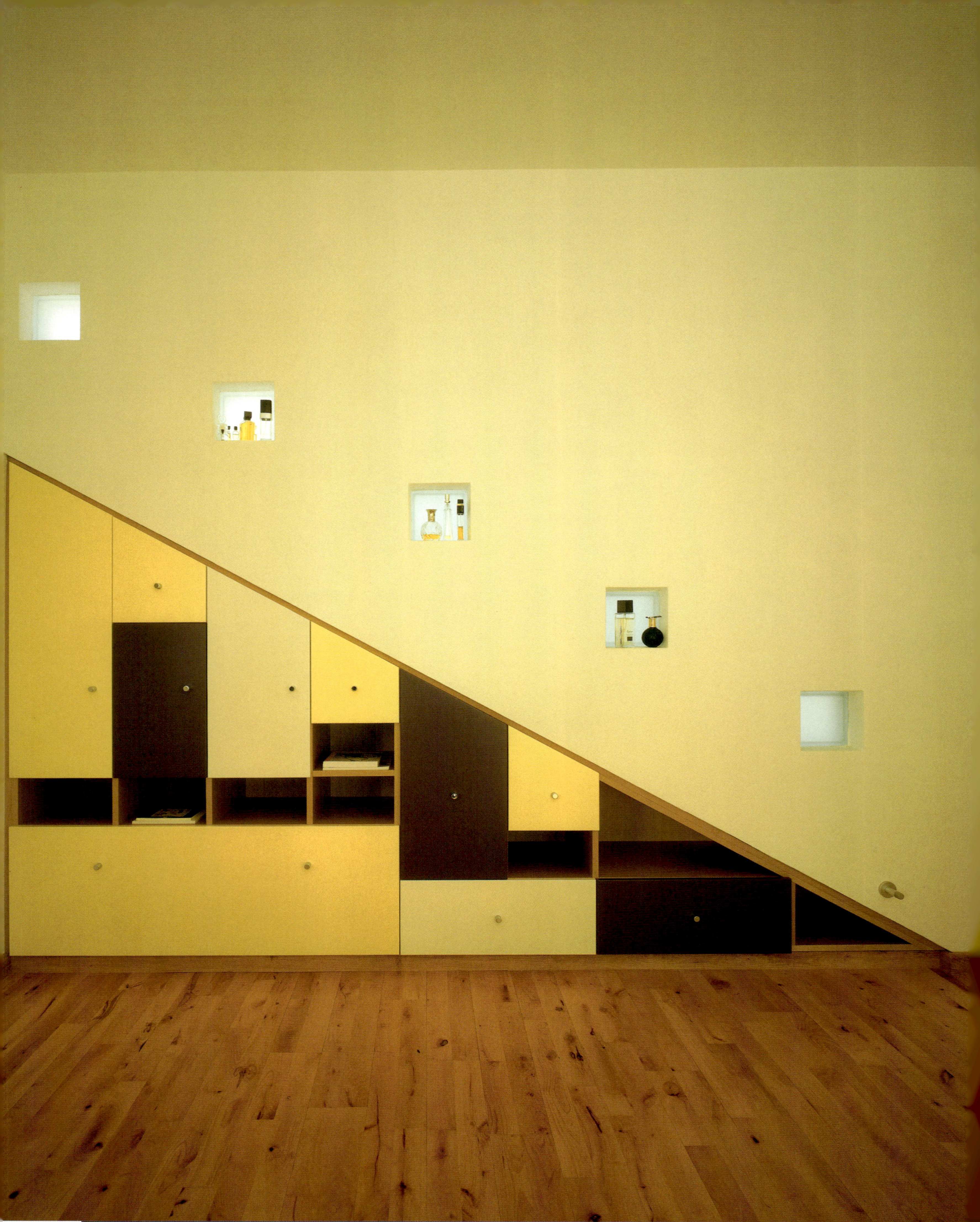

Treppenunterbauung in einem Kinderzimmer
Children's bedroom furniture fitted under the stairs

Lange Treppe Long stairs
Erstes Obergeschoß, Wohnhalle First floor, living hall
Zweites Obergeschoß, Bad Second floor, bathroom

HOUSE ON PLATTENWEG HAUS AM PLATTENWEG

TURM FÖLLING TOWER IN FÖLLING

ORT LOCATION: **Mariatrost, A-8044 Graz**   BAUHERRSCHAFT CLIENT: **Univ. Prof. Dr. phil. K. W. und J. S.**   PLANUNGS- UND BAUZEIT DESIGN AND REALISATION: **1994–1996**
PROJEKTLEITER PROJECT LEADER: **Horst Schwarzl**   STATIK STATICS: **Johann Birner**   WOHNNUTZFLÄCHE USABLE LIVING SPACE: **190 m²**   UMBAUTER RAUM BUILDING VOLUME: **620 m³**   KONSTRUKTION UND MATERIALIEN: **Massivbauweise** CONSTRUCTION AND MATERIALS: **solid construction**   EINDECKUNG: **Titanzinkbahnen** ROOF CLADDING: **zinc roofing strips**

<<< S. ABB. SEE FIGS. 56–60

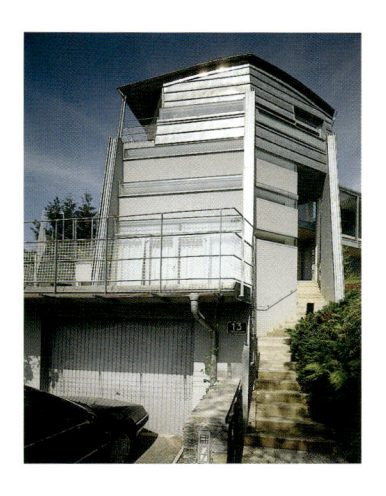

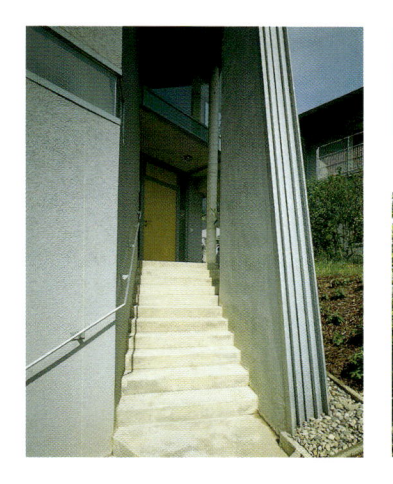

Treppe ins Obergeschoß mit Bibliothek Steps to the first floor with library

Ansicht von Osten View from the east
Ansicht von Süden View from the south
Treppe zum Eingang in der Ostfassade Stairs to the entrance in the east façade
Eingang mit Verbindungsbrücke zum Altbau Entrance with linking bridge to the existing building

TOWER IN FÖLLING TURM FÖLLING 180 | 181

Grundrisse Floor plans:
Untergeschoß Basement
Erdgeschoß Ground floor
Obergeschoß First floor

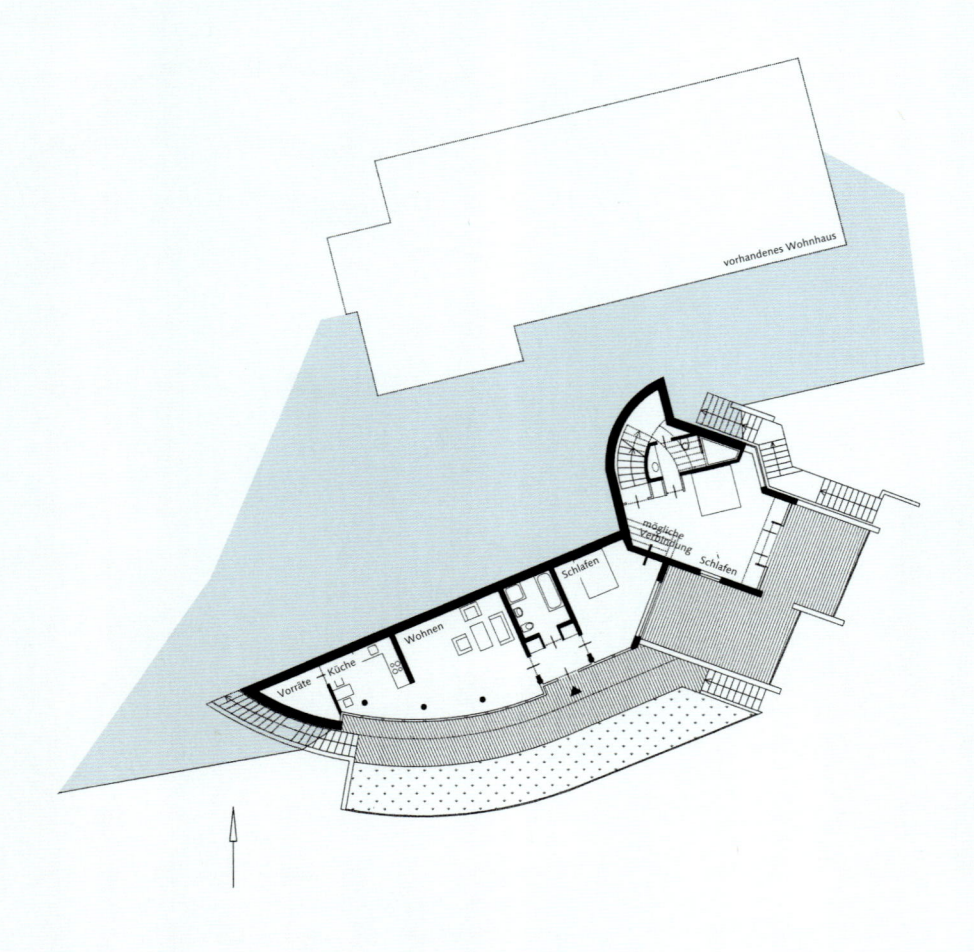

Ansicht von Osten mit Altbau
Elevation from the east with existing building

Schnitt Section

Dieser Bibliotheksturm mit einer in den Hang hineingeschobenen Einliegerwohnung ist als Anbau an ein freundliches, aber unscheinbares Wohnhaus aus den sechziger Jahren in Graz-Mariatrost errichtet worden. Der Turm erhebt sich über einer bereits vorhandenen Garage über drei Geschosse, das untere Stockwerk dient wie der zentrale Bibliotheksraum zugleich als Arbeitszimmer der beiden Auftraggeber. Der hohe, über zwei Geschosse aufragende Zentralraum ist zum Garten orientiert und zur umgebenden Kleinhaussiedlung nahezu uneinsehbar. „Der Turm ist durch einen gläsernen Übergang mit dem alten Wohnhaus verbunden. Die Wände des Zentralraumes sind teilweise mit horizontalen schlitzähnlichen Fenstern versehen, die sich mit den Reihen der an den Wänden befestigten Bücherregalen abwechseln. So erhält der Bibliotheksturm eine mit gleichmäßigem Licht durchflutete, besondere Atmosphäre. Im oberen Teil des Turmes ist ein kleines Bad neben einem Schlafplatz, von dessen Bett man in direkter Linie eine ferne Wallfahrtskirche sehen kann, untergebracht." (Szyszkowitz+Kowalski)

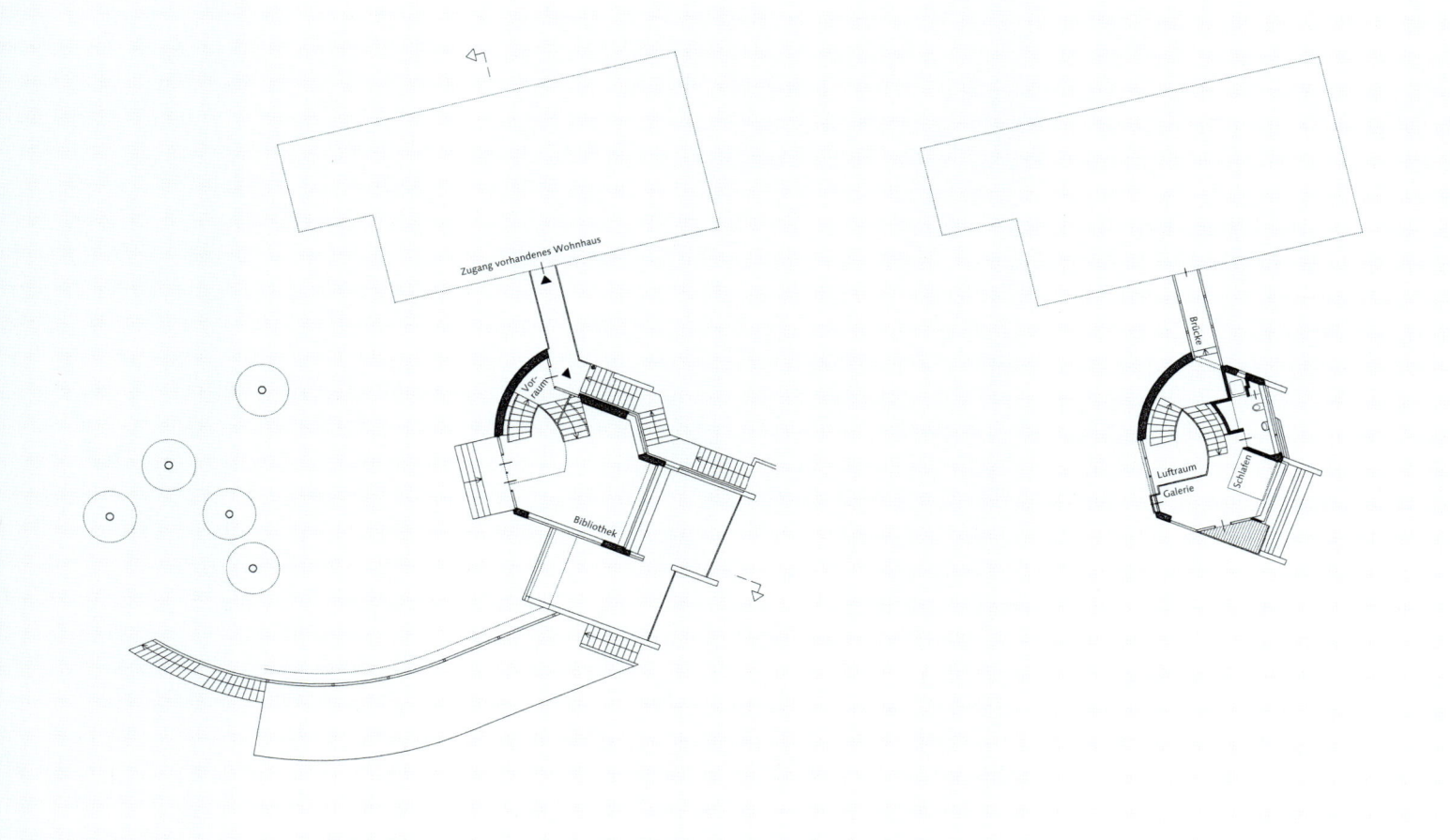

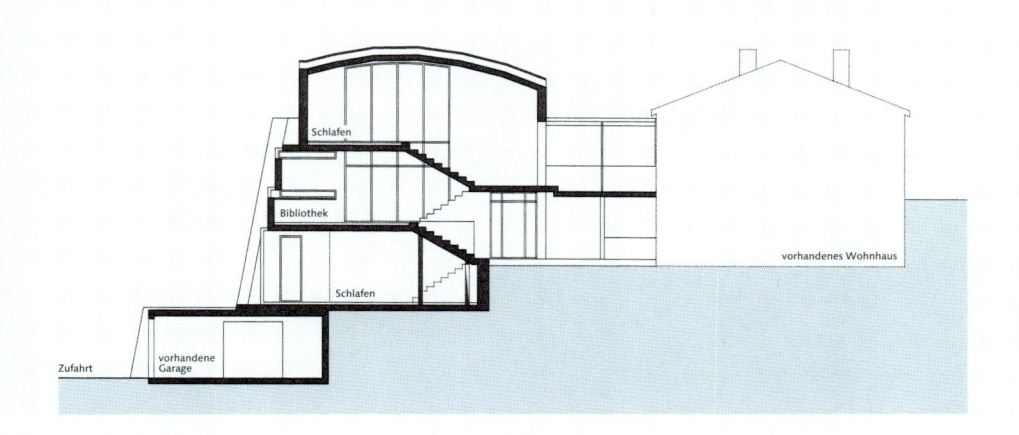

This *library tower* including a granny-flat that worms its way into the slope was built as an extension to a pleasing but unassuming sixties house in Mariatrost, Graz. The three-storey tower is above an existing garage. Both the bottom floor and the central library space serve as study accommodation for the two clients. The high central space, rising through two storeys, faces the garden; it is almost impossible to see into it from the surrounding estate of small houses. "The tower is linked to the old house by a glazed transitional space. Some of the walls in the central room have horizontal, slit-like windows, alternating with the rows of bookshelves fixed to the walls. This gives the library tower an atmosphere all its own, flooded with even light. The top part of the tower accommodates a small bathroom and a sleeping niche; a distant pilgrimage church is visible in a direct line from the bed." (Szyszkowitz+Kowalski)

DESIGNHAUS DESIGN HOUSE

Prototyp, noch nicht realisiert Prototype, not realised as yet   BAUHERRSCHAFT CLIENT: Designhouse E. und G. GmbH   PLANUNGSZEIT DESIGN: 1997   PROJEKTLEITER PROJECT LEADER: Paul M. Pilz   STATIK STATICS: Johann Birner   WOHNNUTZFLÄCHE USABLE LIVING SPACE: 180 m²   UMBAUTER RAUM BUILDING VOLUME: 700 m³   KONSTRUKTION UND MATERIALIEN: Holzskelettbau in Fertigteilbauweise, Erker in Stahlbau   CONSTRUCTION AND MATERIALS: prefabricated timber frame, bay window in steel   EINDECKUNG: Titanzinkbahnen oder Paradachschalen ROOF CLADDING: zinc roofing strips or Para roof shells   <<< S. ABB. SEE FIGS. 27, 81

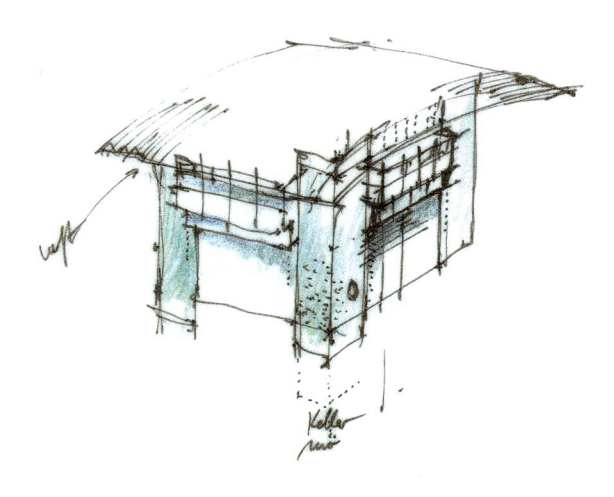

Ansicht, Computermodell View, computer model

Skizzen Sketches

DESIGN HOUSE DESIGNHAUS

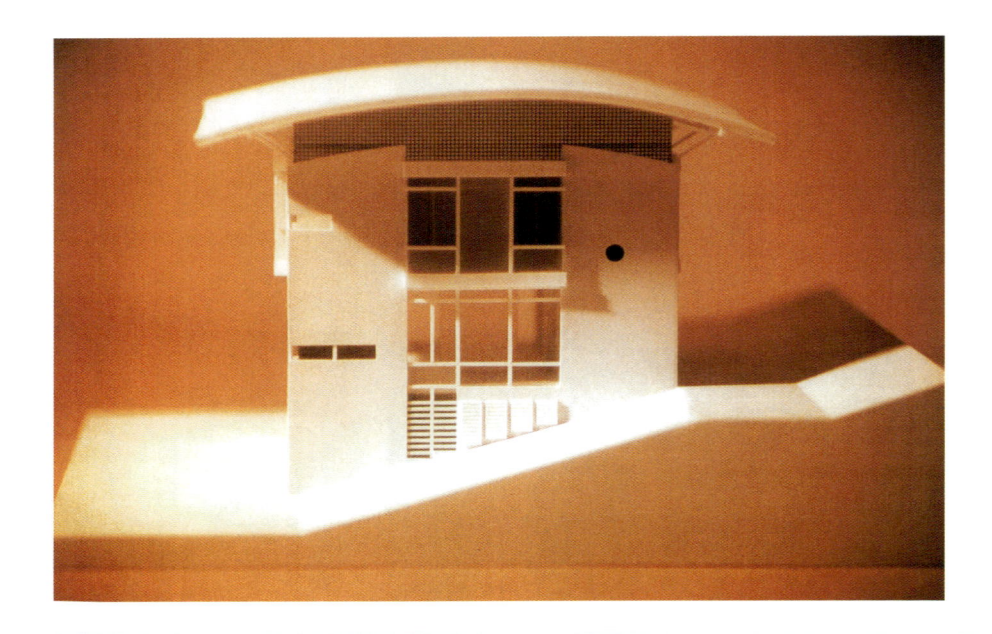

Grundrisse Floor plans:
Erdgeschoß Ground floor
Obergeschoß First floor
Dachgeschoß Attic storey

Schnitte Sections

Ansicht Elevation

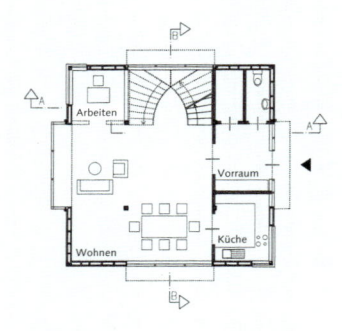

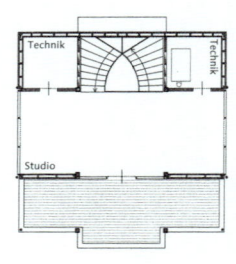

Dieses nicht zur Ausführung gelangte Projekt basiert auf einem geladenen Wettbewerb durch eine junge Münchner Unternehmergruppe. Gefordert war der Entwurf für ein Fertighaus, das die Standardbedingungen dieser Aufgabe (preisgünstig, schnell zu errichten und viel Raum auf kalkuliert rentablen Grundrissen) erfüllen und dennoch architektonisch attraktiv sein sollte. Über einem quadratischen Grundriß ist die 185 qm umfassende Nutzfläche über drei Geschosse verteilt. Im Erdgeschoß befindet sich der zentrale Wohnraum, der aus allen vier Himmelsrichtungen Licht erhält, das über die auf der Symmetrieachse liegenden gläsernen Flügeltüren oder über vor die Fassade gesetzte Veranden in den Innenraum fließt, die auf die andere Symmetrieachse gesetzt sind. Von diesem Zentralraum sind wahlweise die kleineren Seitenkabinette für die Küche oder die Arbeitsecke abtrennbar. Aus dem Erdgeschoß führt eine leicht geschwungene Treppe in das darüber liegende Geschoß mit den drei Schlaf- und dazugehörigen Nebenräumen, die um einen kleinen, mittig auf die Treppenachse gesetzten Raum gruppierbar sind. Die Belichtung dieser Räume erfolgt auch hier über transluzide, aus dem Baukörper heraustretende Erker. Beide Geschosse erhalten zudem über schmale, über Eck gestellte Fensterbänder in den vier in sich geschlossenen Gebäudekanten zusätzliches Tageslicht. Im Obergeschoß ist ein Studio untergebracht, das an einer Seite von einer Terrasse gesäumt wird. Darüber bildet die Stahlunterkonstruktion mit selbsttragenden Kunststoffprofilschalen die sanfte Wölbung des auskragenden Tonnendaches.

Der Hauskörper besteht aus einer Holzkonstruktion in Verbindung mit den Stahl-Glas-Elementen für die vier Erker, wobei „vier innenliegende Stützen mit kreuzweise davon ausgehenden Tragelementen und in die Ecken integrierte Stützfunktionen" (Szyszkowitz+Kowalski) die tragende Struktur bilden. Im Inneren des Hauses können Holzzwischenwände gesetzt werden, die auch als Schrankwände konzipierbar sind. Für die Farben der Häuser waren unterschiedlich variable Nuancen ausgearbeitet.

Obwohl die Produktion dieses Fertighauses mit einer Kärntner Holzbaufirma bis in einzelne Details hinein ausgearbeitet war, scheiterte das Projekt letztlich an den Finanzierungsmodalitäten. Das Projekt ist bis heute insofern bemerkenswert, als es aus dem Kanon der architektonischen Traditionalismen, die im Fertighausbau noch immer vorherrschend sind, ausbricht und demgegenüber eine hohe identifikatorische Qualität in der räumlichen Konzeption, wie sie in den aufwendigeren Privathäusern vorherrscht, aufweist.

Modell Model

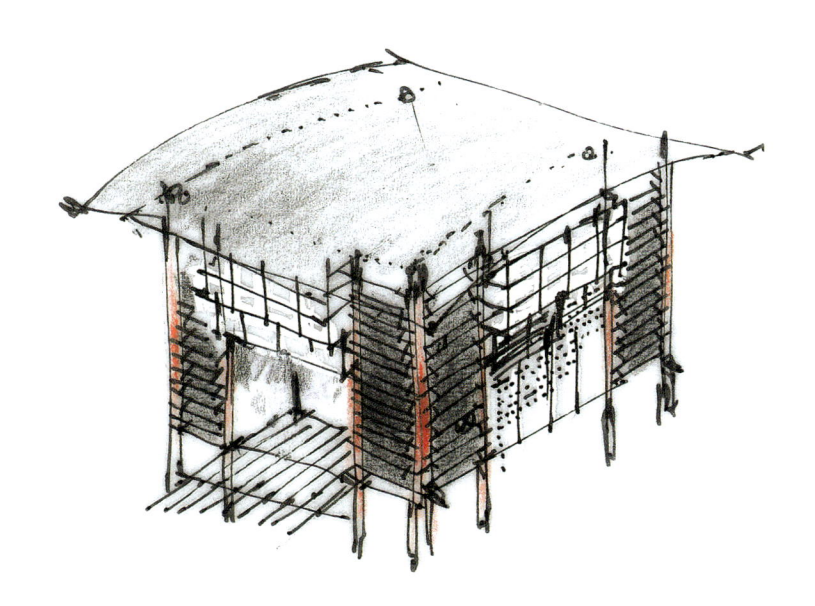

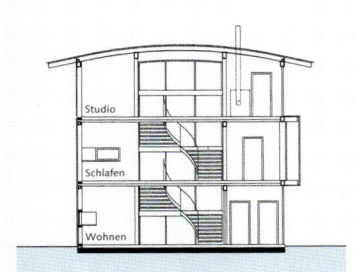

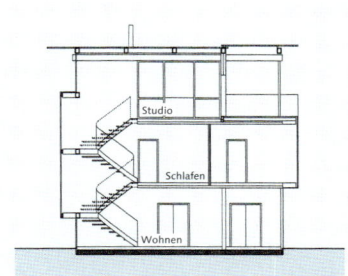

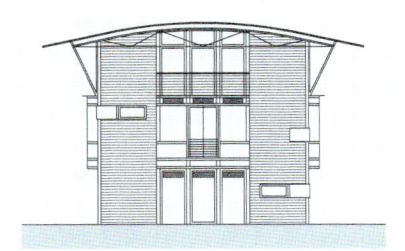

Skizze Sketch

This unbuilt project is based on a competition by invitation run by a group of young Munich entrepreneurs. They wanted a design for a prefabricated house that would meet the standard requirements for such a building (reasonably priced, quick to build and a lot of space on profitable ground plans) and yet be architecturally attractive. The usable space of 185 sq m is distributed over three floors on a square ground plan. The central living room is on the ground floor. It is lit from all sides via glazed doors set on the symmetrical axis or via verandas placed in front of the façade on the other symmetrical axis. Small side cabinets for the kitchen or work-corner can be separated from this central space if wished. A slightly curved staircase on the ground floor leads up to the floor above with the three bedrooms and additional facilities, which can be grouped around a small space set centrally on the staircase axis. Here too the rooms are lit by translucent bay windows protruding from the body of the building. Both floors also receive addition daylight from narrow, diagonally placed ribbon windows in the four closed edges of the building. The top floor accommodates a studio with a terrace on one side. Above this the steel substructure with self-supporting plastic profile shells forms the gentle curve of the protruding barrel roof.

The body of the house is made up of a timber structure combined with the steel and glass elements for the four bay windows, with "four internal supports with load-bearing elements going out from them crosswise and support functions integrated in the corners" (Szyszkowitz+Kowalski) providing the load-bearing structure. Wooden screens can be placed inside the house, and they can also be designed as cupboard walls. Various colour schemes were devised for the houses. Although the production of this prefabricated house was worked out in detail with a Carinthian timber construction firm, the project finally failed because of the financial conditions. The project remains remarkable, however, in that it breaks away from the canon of traditional architectural features that are still predominant in prefabricated building construction. Instead it offers a high level of individual identity in the spatial conception, of the kind more usually found in more expensive private houses.

HAUS IN MOOSBURG HOUSE IN MOOSBURG

ORT LOCATION: **Moosburg, A-9062 Klagenfurt**   BAUHERRSCHAFT CLIENT: **H. R. und Dr. mont. P. R.**   PLANUNGS- UND BAUZEIT DESIGN AND REALISATION: **1995–1996**   PROJEKTLEITER PROJECT LEADER: **Paul M. Pilz**   STATIK STATICS: **Johann Birner**   WOHNNUTZFLÄCHE USABLE LIVING SPACE: **230 m²**   UMBAUTER RAUM BUILDING VOLUME: **920 m³**   KONSTRUKTION UND MATERIALIEN: **Massivbauweise, gekrümmte Leimbinderkonstruktion** CONSTRUCTION AND MATERIALS: **solid construction, curved glulam beam construction**   EINDECKUNG: **glasierte Tonziegel**   ROOF CLADDING: **glazed clay tiles**   <<< S. ABB. SEE FIGS. **3, 7, 33, 65, 79**

Ansicht von Süden View from the south

Ansicht von Westen View from the west
Detail der Dachkonstruktion mit Stahlmanschetten
Detail of the roof structure with steel jackets
Unterspannte Regenrinnen Braced guttering

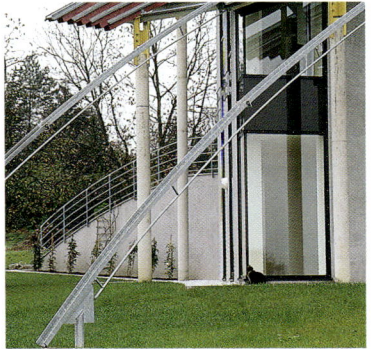

HOUSE IN MOOSBURG   HAUS IN MOOSBURG   188 | 189

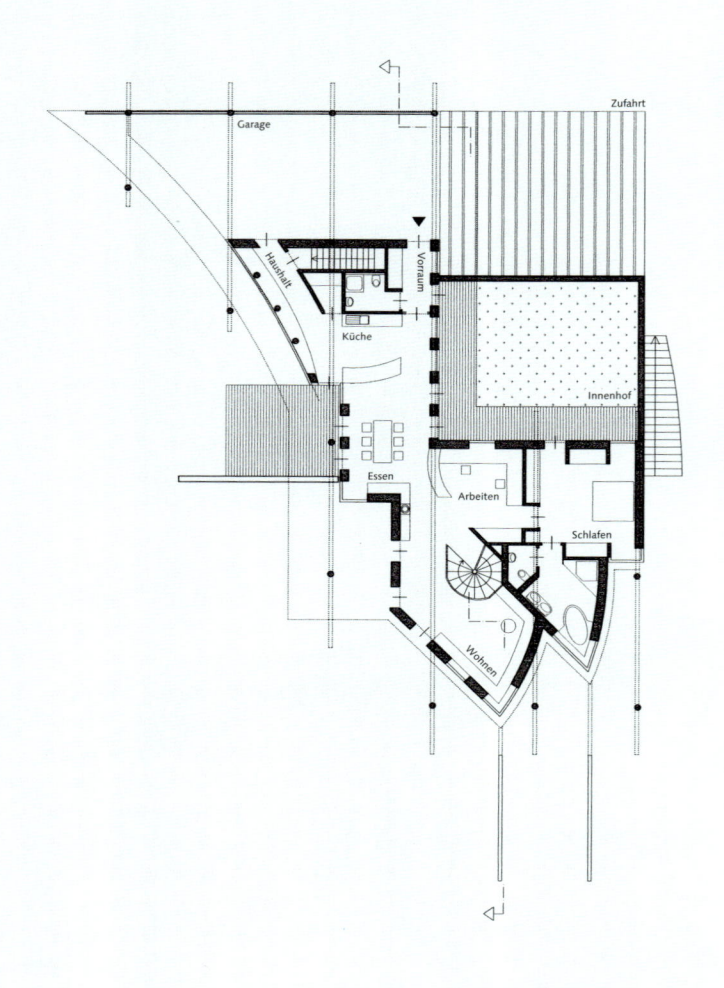

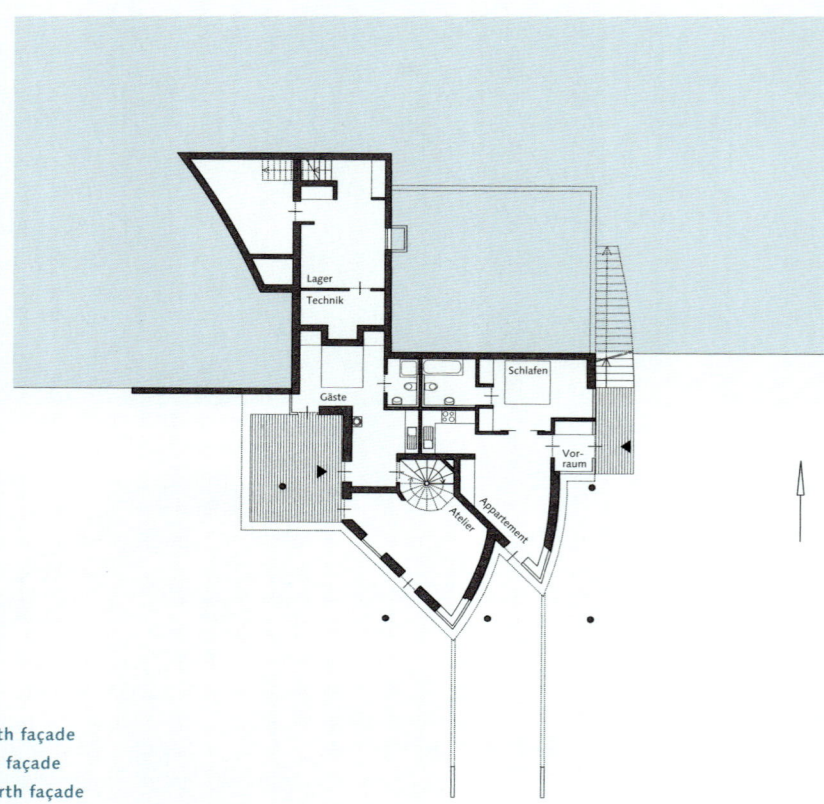

Grundrisse Floor plans:
Untergeschoß Basement
Erdgeschoß Ground floor

Schnitt Section
Ansicht Südfassade Elevation of the south façade
Ansicht Ostfassade Elevation of the east façade
Ansicht Nordfassade Elevation of the north façade

HOUSE IN MOOSBURG　HAUS IN MOOSBURG

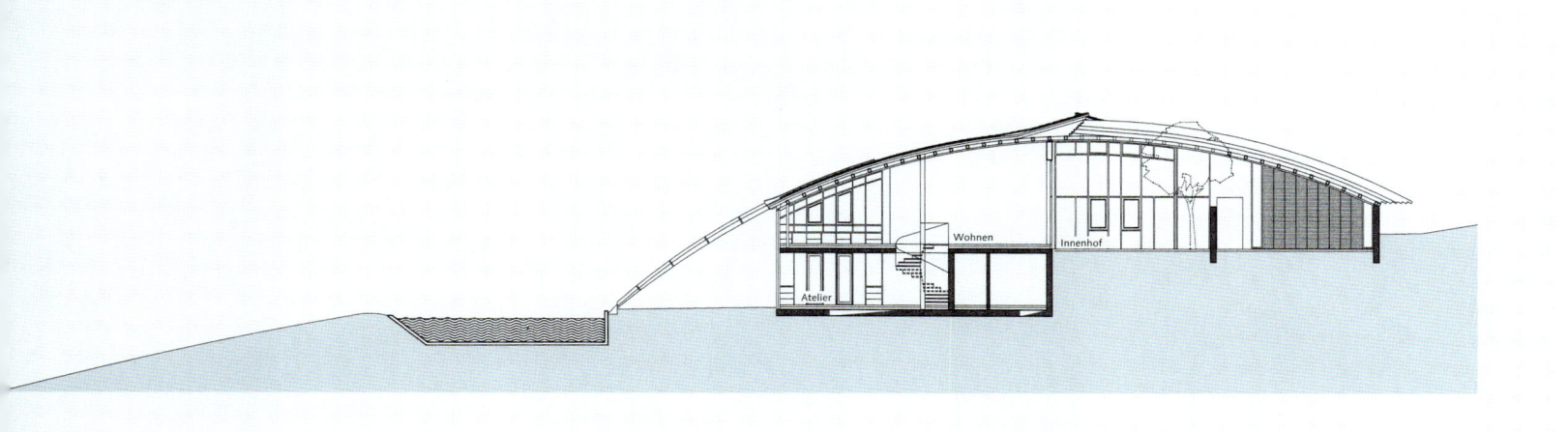

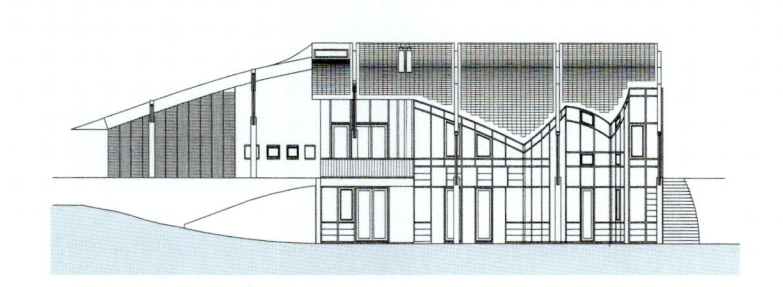

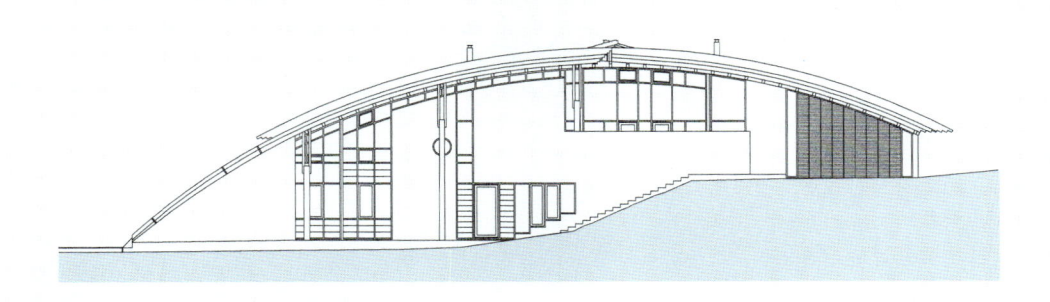

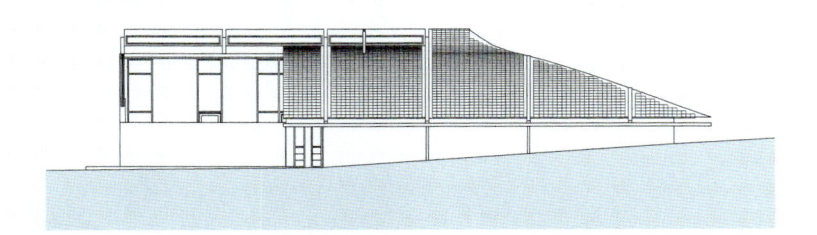

Skizze Sketch

Dieses Zweithaus für eine Familie mit zwei erwachsenen Kindern entstand in Kärnten in der Nähe von Klagenfurt. Eingebettet in eine leicht hügelige Umgebung liegt es in einem landschaftlich reizvollen Gebiet, das allerdings ein hohes Maß an Zersiedelung mit Einfamilienhäusern aufweist, die im „Fertighausstil" Traditionspflege zu betreiben bestrebt sind. Der Wunsch der Bauherren war es daher, mit der Architektur des Hauses einen ästhetisch reizvollen Gegenpol zu schaffen. „Das eigentliche Zentrum des Hauses ist ein Hohlraum – ein Hof zwischen Wohnräumen und Mauern. Entlang dieses Hofes entwickeln sich locker aneinandergefügt dem Wohnen zugeordnete Räume in Längsrichtung zum Tal hin, versehen mit einer Reihe von kantigen Glaserkern als Ausblicksposten zu den zwei entfernt liegenden Burgen auf den gegenüberliegenden Hügeln. Auf der Talseite ist das Haus zweigeschossig mit einer Einliegerwohnung und Räumen für die Gäste. Ein großes gebogenes Dach, das aus dem oberen Hang heraussteigt, überwölbt den hohen Wohnbereich und ist in Längsrichtung derart auf Stützen aufgelagert, daß es frei die Räume und ein Teil des Außenraumes überspannt. Die strukturgebenden Holzträgerbögen halten zwischen sich die Dachflächen als Schattenelemente. Das ganze Haus, bis auf kleine Elemente in starker Farbe, ist in unterschiedlichen Grautönen gehalten." (Szyszkowitz+Kowalski)

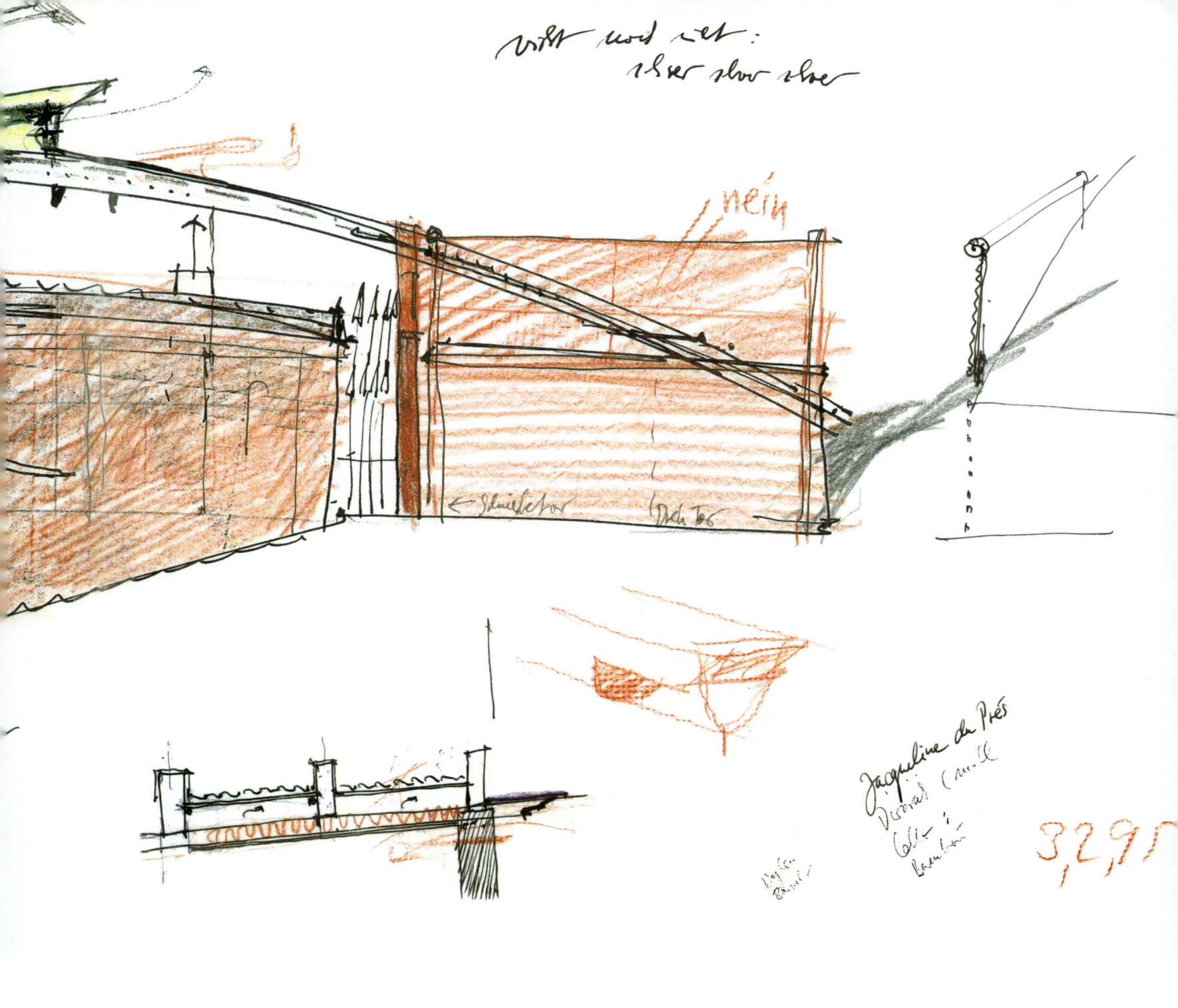

This second house for a family with two grown-up children was built in Carinthia, near Klagenfurt. It is set in gently rolling surroundings in a very attractive landscape, though there is a great deal of overdevelopment trying to maintain tradition in the "prefabricated style". The clients therefore wanted to create an aesthetically attractive opposite pole with the architecture of their house. "The actual centre of the house is a cavity – a courtyard between living spaces and walls. The spaces intended for living are placed in loose sequence along this courtyard longitudinally to the valley, and provided with a series of angular glazed bays as observation posts for the two distant castles on the hills opposite. On the valley side the house has two storeys, with a granny flat and guest rooms. A large, curved roof, rising from the upper slope, arches over the high living area and is supported longitudinally in such a way that it covers the rooms and part of the external space as an open span. The structuring timber girders support the roof areas as shading elements. The whole house, with the exception of small elements in strong colours, is in various shades of grey." (Szyszkowitz+Kowalski).

Wohnbereich nach Süden Living area looking south
Wohnbereich nach Westen Living area looking west
Oberlicht nach Norden Skylight looking north

HOUSE IN MOOSBURG   HAUS IN MOOSBURG | 194 | 195

STADTVILLEN MARIAGRÜN
URBAN VILLAS IN MARIAGRÜN

ORT LOCATION: **Mariagrün, A-8010 Graz**   BAUHERRSCHAFT CLIENT: **INWOG-Wohnbaugesellschaft**   PLANUNGS- UND BAUZEIT DESIGN AND REALISATION: **1993–1997**
PROJEKTLEITER PROJECT LEADER: **Rolf Seifert**   STATIK STATICS: **Herbert Eisner**   WOHNNUTZFLÄCHE USABLE LIVING SPACE: **total 1.260 m²**   UMBAUTER RAUM BUILDING VOLUME: **total 3.780 m³**   KONSTRUKTION UND MATERIALIEN: **Massivbauweise** CONSTRUCTION AND MATERIALS: **solid construction**   EINDECKUNG: **glasierte Tonziegel** ROOF CLADDING: **glazed clay tiles**

<<< S. ABB. SEE FIGS. **64, 83**

Ansicht der unteren Häuser von Nordwesten View of the lower houses from the north-west

Blick auf den Corso View of the avenue

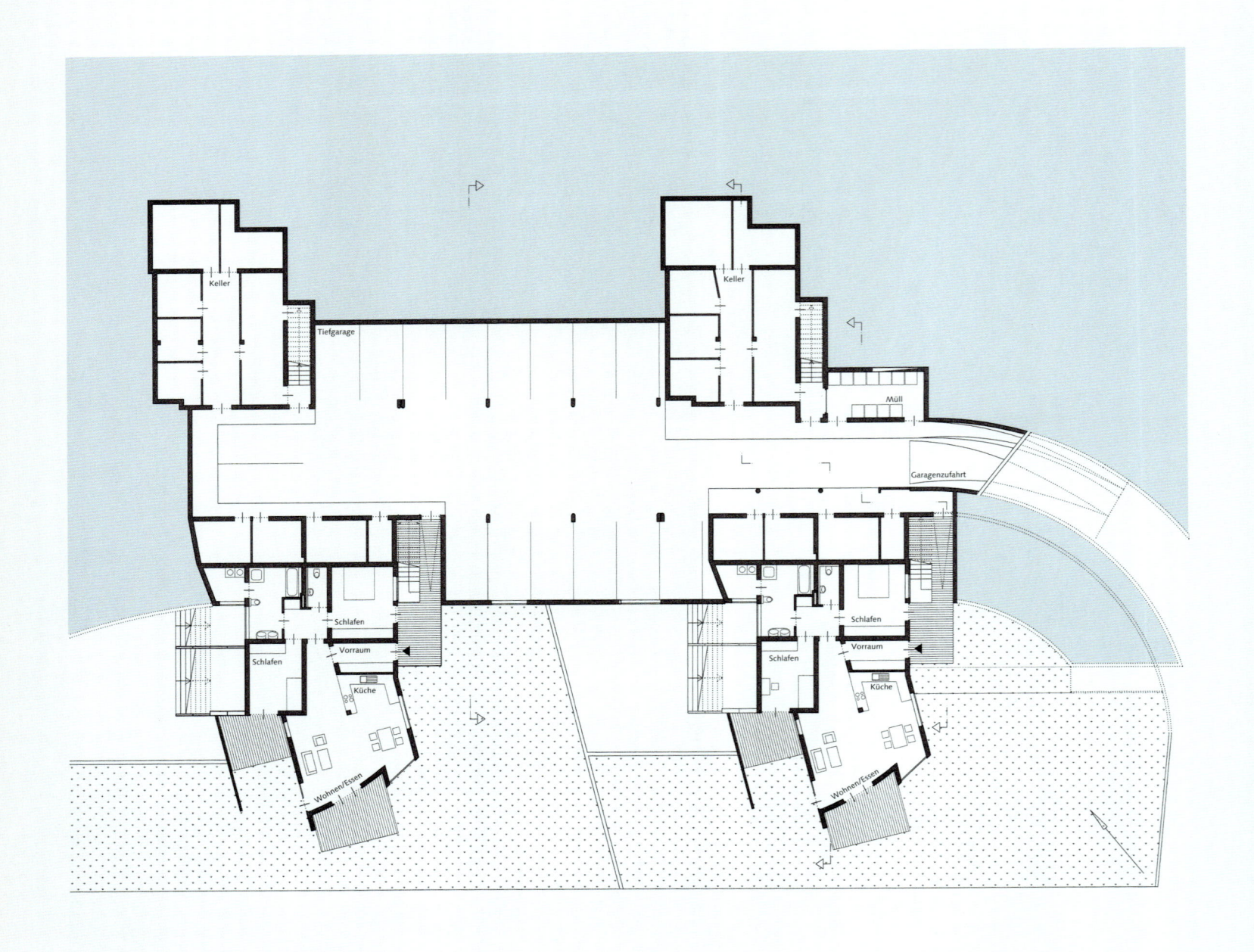

Auf einem stadtnahen Hanggrundstück in Mariagrün sind vier Stadtvillen mit insgesamt 14 Wohnungen gehobeneren Standards entstanden. Die vier Hauseinheiten sind um einen kleinen, länglichen Corso angeordnet, der fußläufig über eine geschwungene Wegeführung erreicht wird, die der Erschließung der *Hietzinger Häuser* in Wien ähnlich ist. Von diesem zentralen Ort sind die einzelnen Wohneinheiten separat erreichbar. Eine Tiefgarage unter den Häusern schafft die notwendigen Abstellplätze für die Autos der Bewohner. Die Silhouette der Häuser nimmt die Schräglage des Hanges auf, deren Wandscheiben teilweise aus dem Baukörper heraustreten und derart die Stützelemente des *Bibliotheksturmes in Graz Fölling* paraphrasieren. Kleine privat zugeordnete Gärten und öffentliche Grünzonen umfassen die Gebäude auf unterschiedlichen Niveaus im Erdgeschoßbereich, die oberen Etagen, die über den gemeinschaftlichen Corso hinweg durch Pflanzgerüste miteinander verbunden sind, verfügen über große Dachterrassen. Diese Mauerwerksbauten sind in einem hellen Grautürkis verputzt, das im Farbton der verschieden großen Holzfenster und in den glasierten Tonziegeln der Dacheindeckung wiederkehrt. Dieses Bauensemble erhält derart einen harmonischen Gleichklang, der mit der individuell konzipierten Architektur in einem wechselvollen Spannungsverhältnis steht.

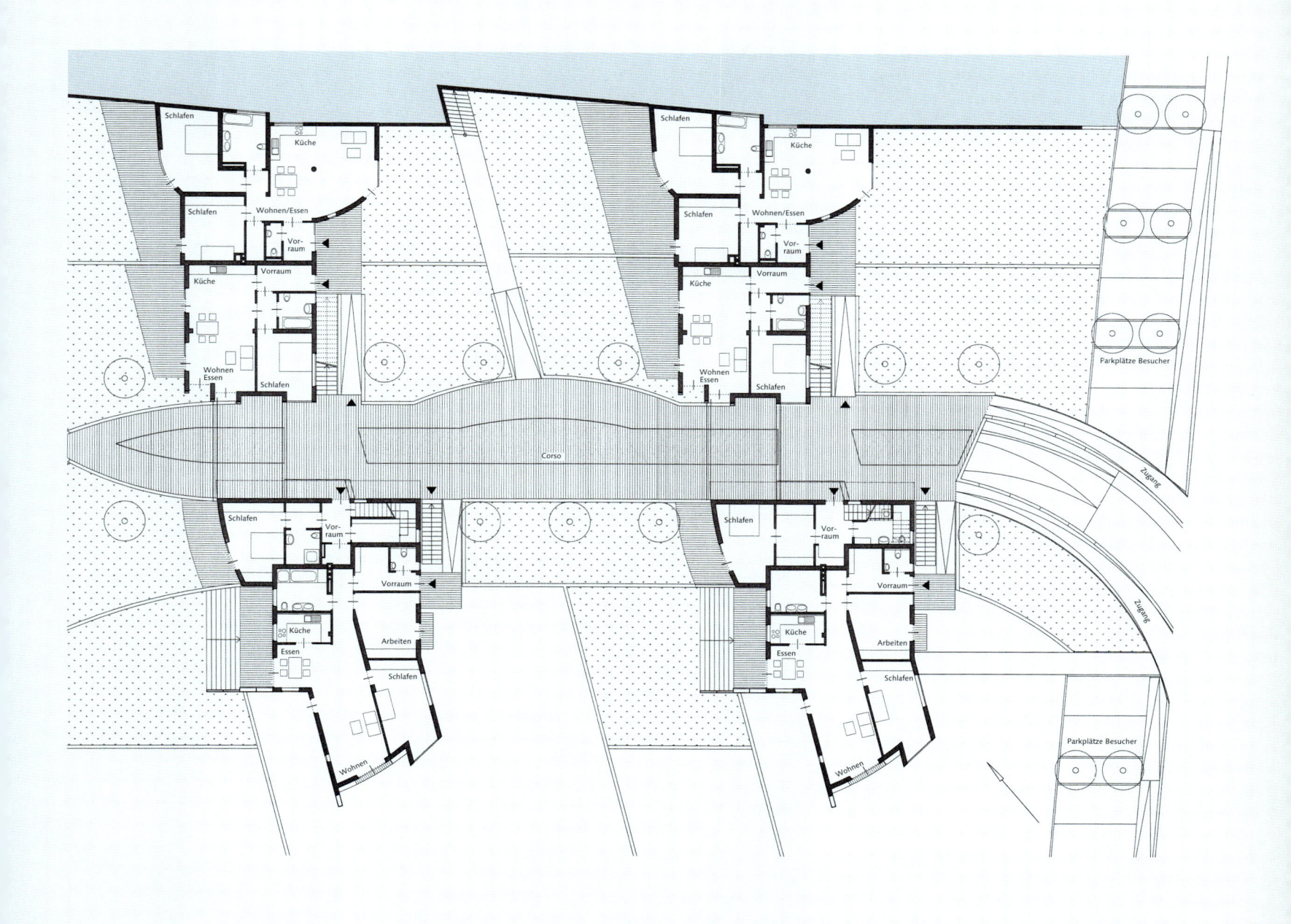

Grundrisse Floor plans:
Ebene 0.0 m Level 0.0 m
Ebene 3.0 m Level 3.0 m

Four town houses containing a total of 14 high-quality homes have been built on a sloping site near the town in Mariagrün. The four buildings are arranged around a long, contained corso reached on foot via a curved path, similar to the access arrangements for the *House in Hietzing*, Vienna. The individual residential units are accessed separately from this central place. A garage under the buildings provides the necessary parking-spaces for the residents' cars. The silhouette of the buildings picks up the diagonal of the slope; some of their walls protrude from the main body, thus paraphrasing the support elements of the *library tower in Fölling, Graz*. The buildings are enclosed at ground floor level by small private gardens and public green areas at various levels. The upper storeys, linked with each other by plant trellises above the communal avenue, have large roof terraces. These masonry buildings are rendered in a light turquoise-grey, recurring in the colour shades of the various large wooden windows and the glazed clay roofing tiles. This gives the ensemble a sense of harmony together and also a fine contrast with the highly individual architecture.

URBAN VILLAS IN MARIAGRÜN STADTVILLEN MARIAGRÜN 198 | 199

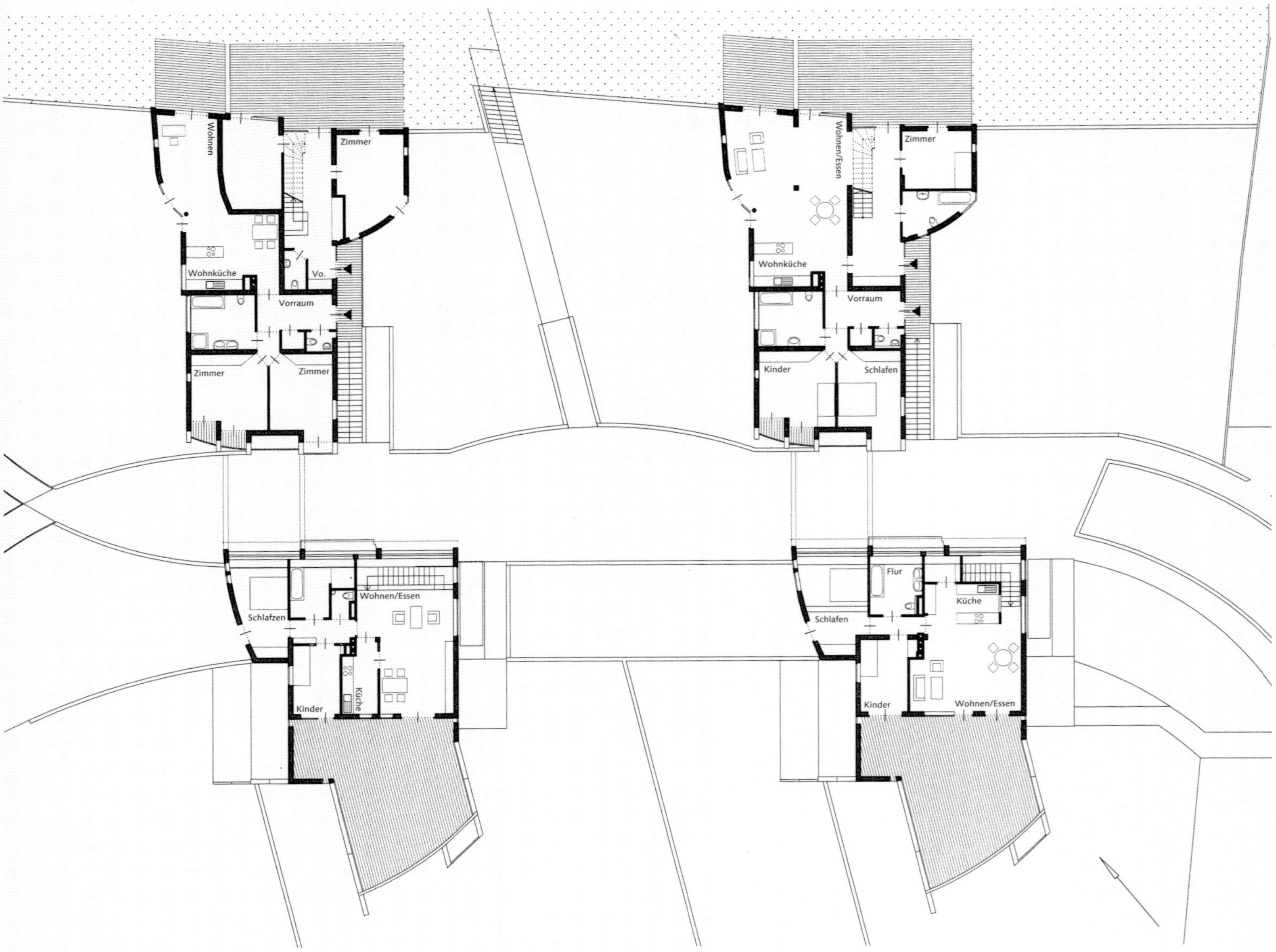
Wohnen
Zimmer
Wohnküche
Vo.
Vorraum
Zimmer
Zimmer
Wohnen/Essen
Zimmer
Wohnküche
Vorraum
Kinder
Schlafen
Schlafzen
Wohnen/Essen
Kinder
Küche
Flur
Küche
Schlafen
Kinder
Wohnen/Essen

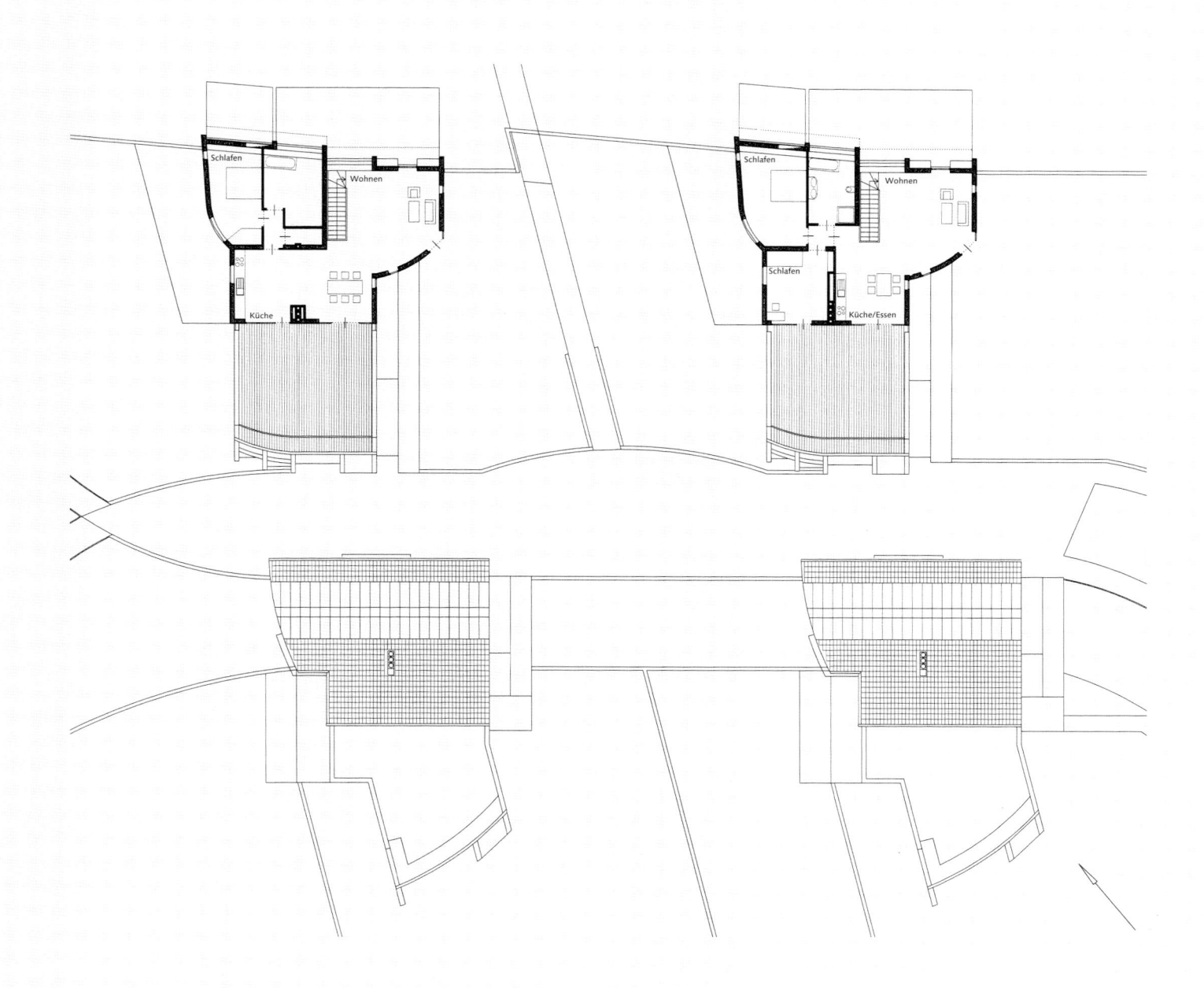

Grundrisse Floor plans:
Ebene 6.0 m Level 6.0 m
Ebene 9.0 m Level 9.0 m

URBAN VILLAS IN MARIAGRÜN   STADTVILLEN MARIAGRÜN   200 | 201

Schnittansicht Nordwestfassaden
Section elevation of the north-west façades
Schnittansicht Südostfassaden
Section elevation of the north-east façades

Schnitt Section

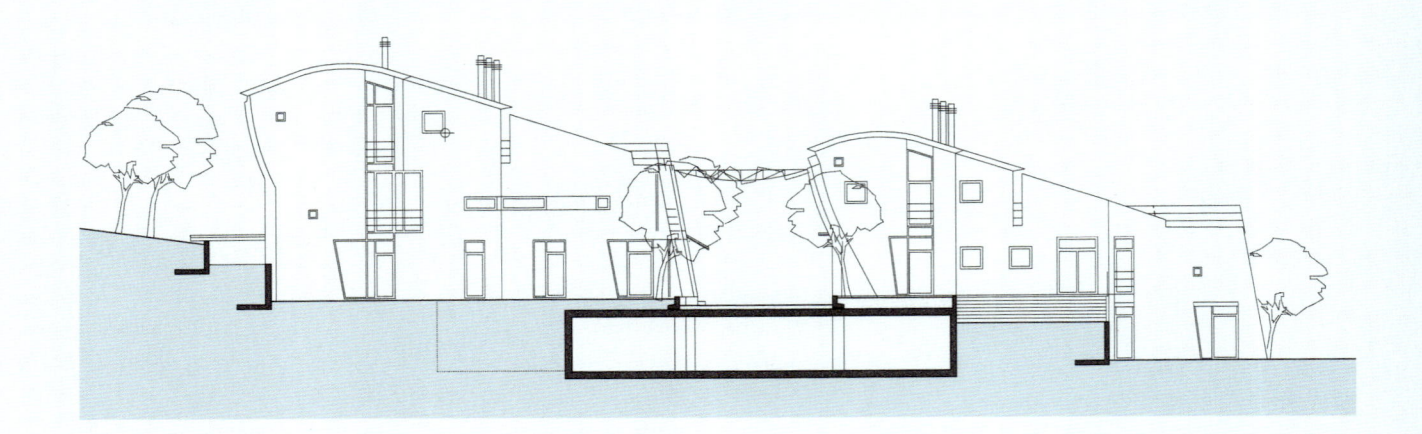

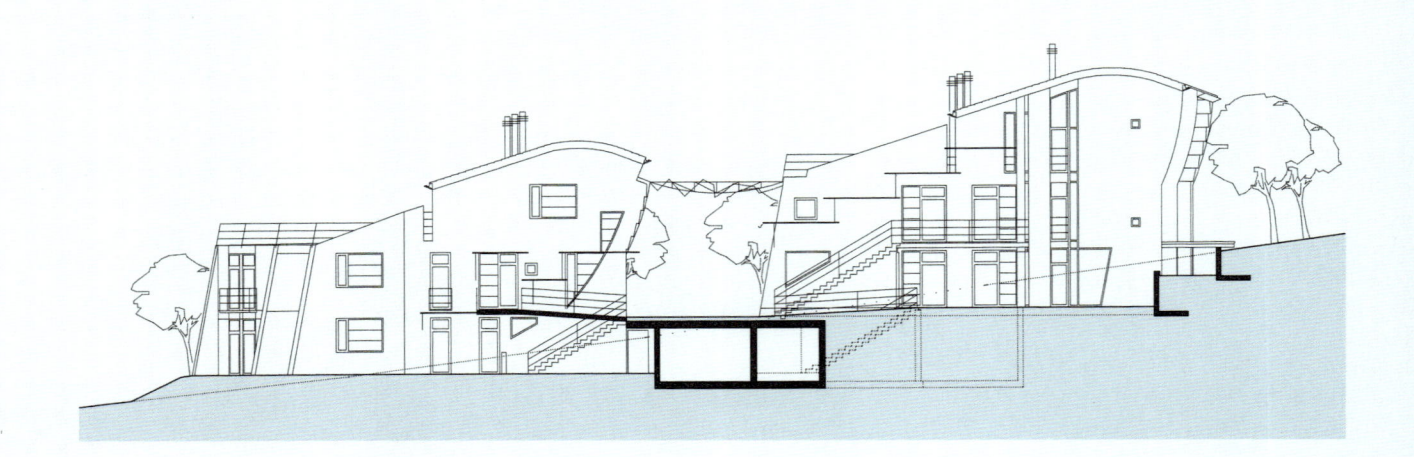

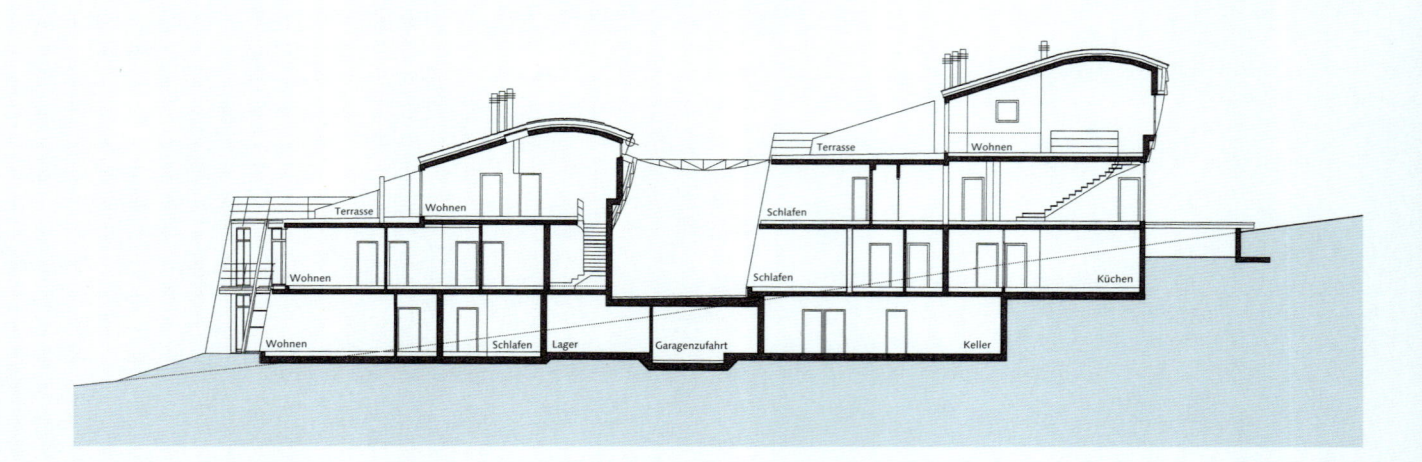

Skizzen Sketches

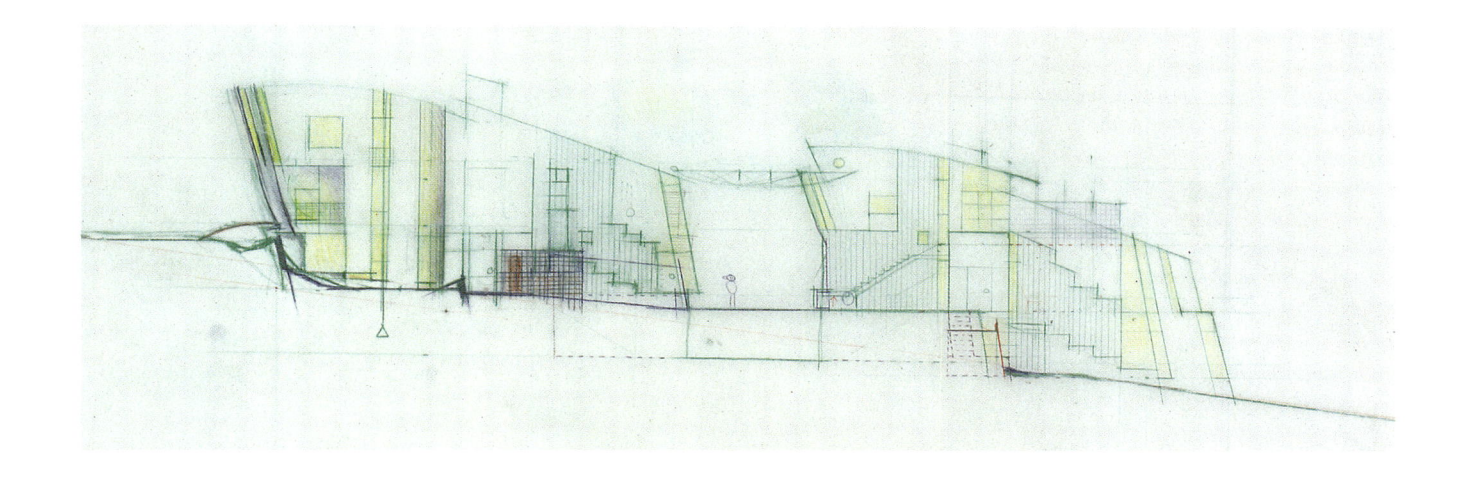

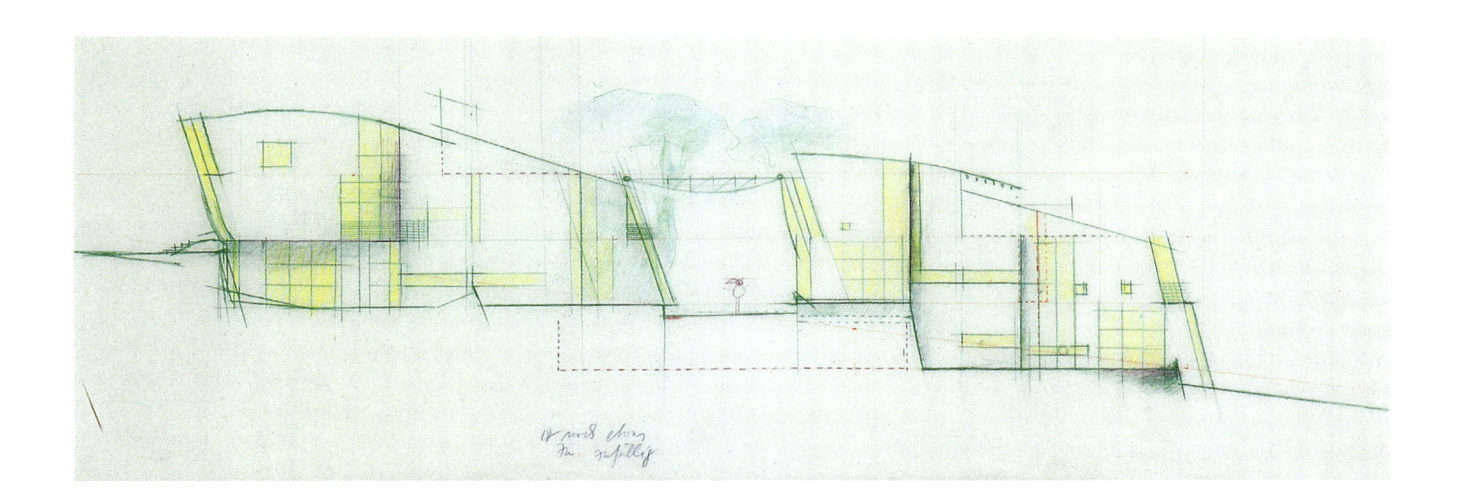

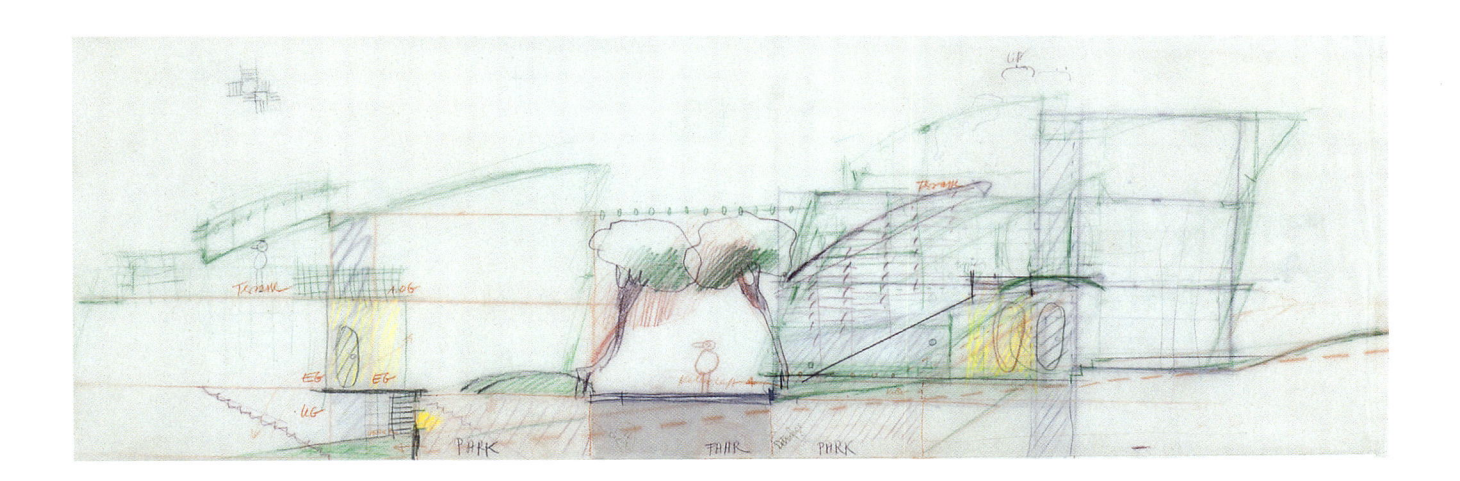

URBAN VILLAS IN MARIAGRÜN STADTVILLEN MARIAGRÜN | 202 | 203

Blick auf den Corso von Südosten View of the avenue from the south-east
Pflanzenpergola über Corso Planted pergola above the avenue

Aufgang zur Ebene 6.0 m Steps to level 6.0 m
Glasdächer über Aufgang Glass roofs over steps
Detail Aufgang Detail of the steps

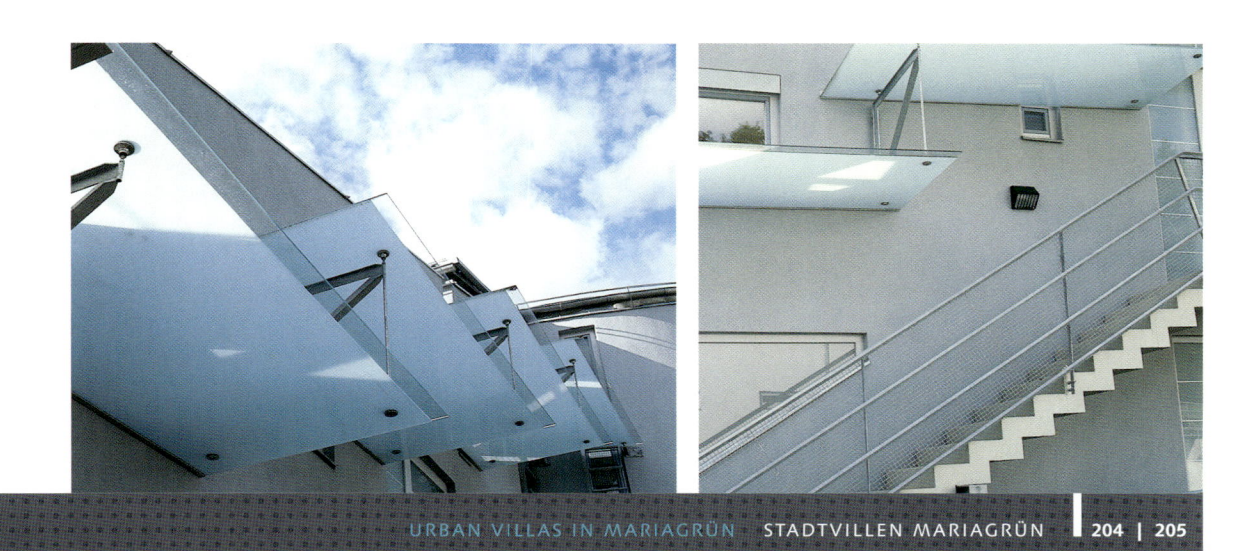

URBAN VILLAS IN MARIAGRÜN   STADTVILLEN MARIAGRÜN

HAUS AM RUCKERLBERG
HOUSE ON RUCKERLBERG

ORT LOCATION: A-8010 Graz   PLANUNGS- UND BAUZEIT DESIGN AND REALISATION: 1998–2002   BAUHERRSCHAFT CLIENT: J. B. und DI J. B.   PROJEKTLEITER PROJECT LEADER: Andreas Gratl   STATIK STATICS: Johann Birner   WOHNNUTZFLÄCHE USABLE LIVING SPACE: 280 m²   UMBAUTER RAUM BUILDING VOLUME: 1.120 m³   KONSTRUKTION UND MATERIALIEN: Massivbauweise, Wintergarten Stahlbau CONSTRUCTION AND MATERIALS: solid construction, conservatory in steel   EINDECKUNG: Flachdach mit Steinplatten, Dachgarten ROOF CLADDING: flat roof with stone slabs, roof garden   <<< S. ABB. SEE FIGS. 2, 31, 54, 63

Ansicht von Westen View from the west

Ansicht von Süden View from the south

Ansicht von Südosten View from the south-east

HOUSE ON RUCKERLBERG   HAUS AM RUCKERLBERG   206 | 207

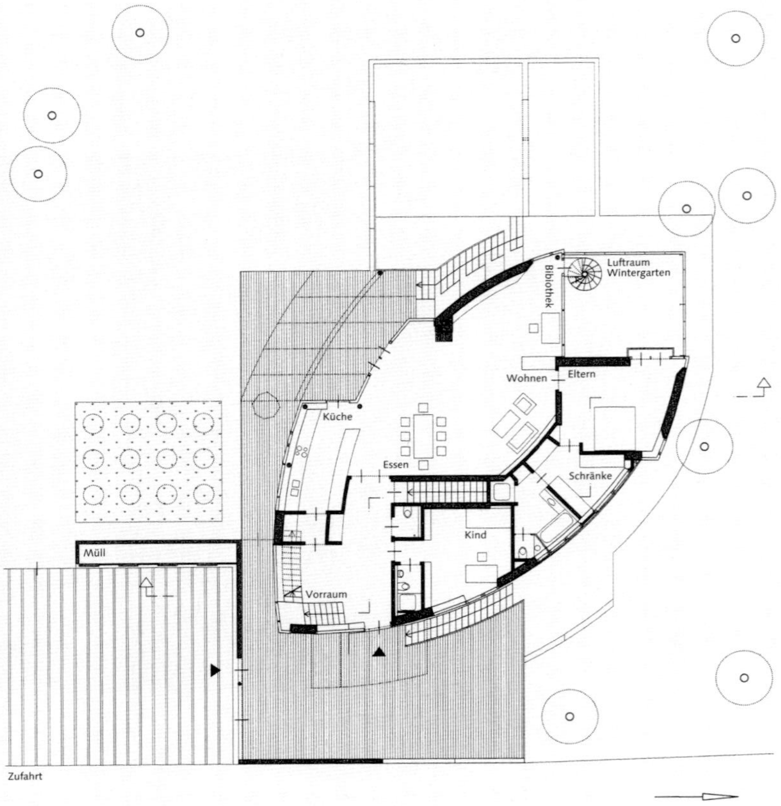
Luftraum Wintergarten
Bibliothek
Wohnen
Eltern
Küche
Essen
Schränke
Kind
Vorraum
Müll
Zufahrt

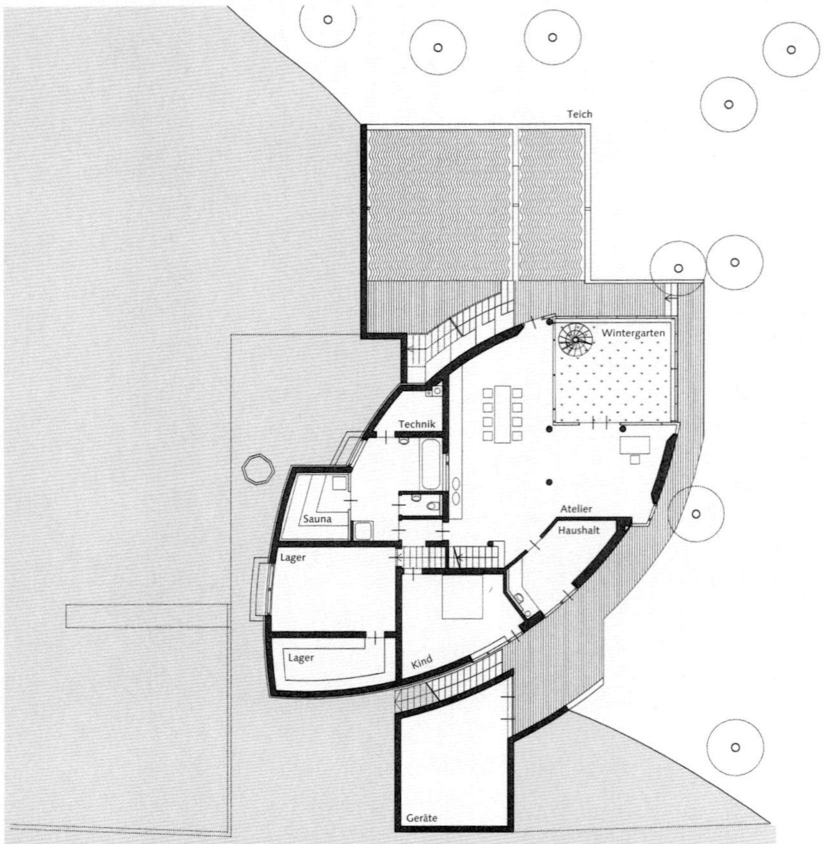
Teich
Wintergarten
Technik
Sauna
Atelier
Haushalt
Lager
Lager
Kind
Geräte

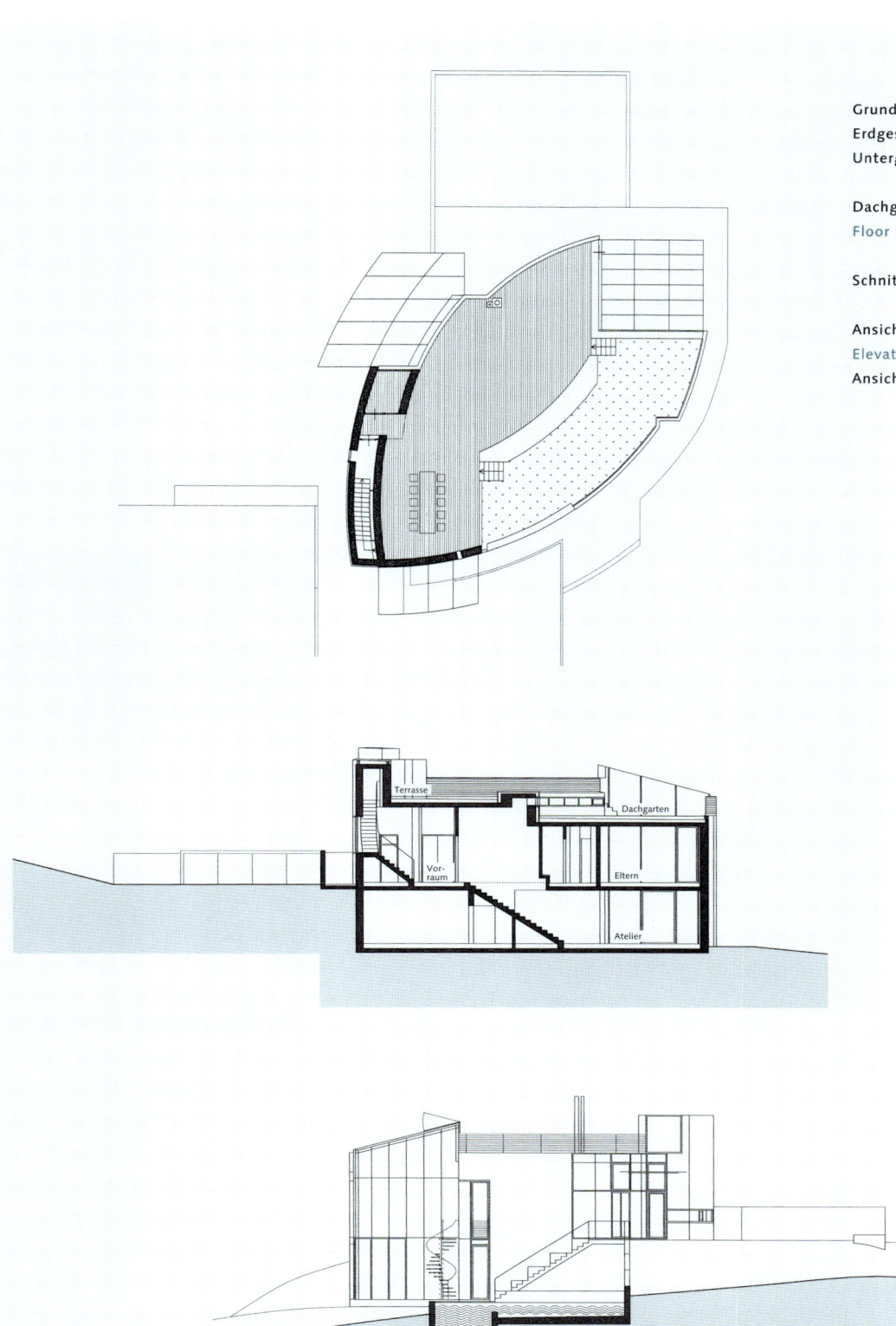

Grundrisse Floor plans:
Erdgeschoß Ground floor
Untergeschoß Basement

Dachgeschoß mit Dachgarten und Terrasse
Floor plan attic floor with roof garden and terrace

Schnitt Section

Ansicht von Westen
Elevation from the west
Ansicht von Norden Elevation from the north

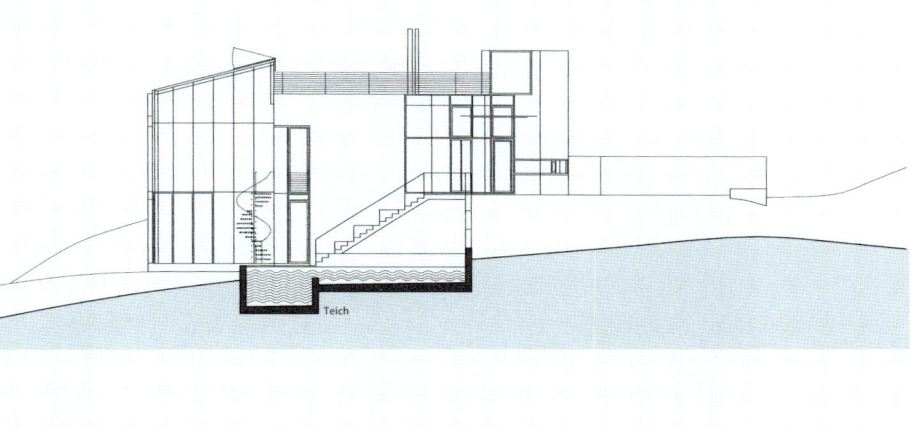

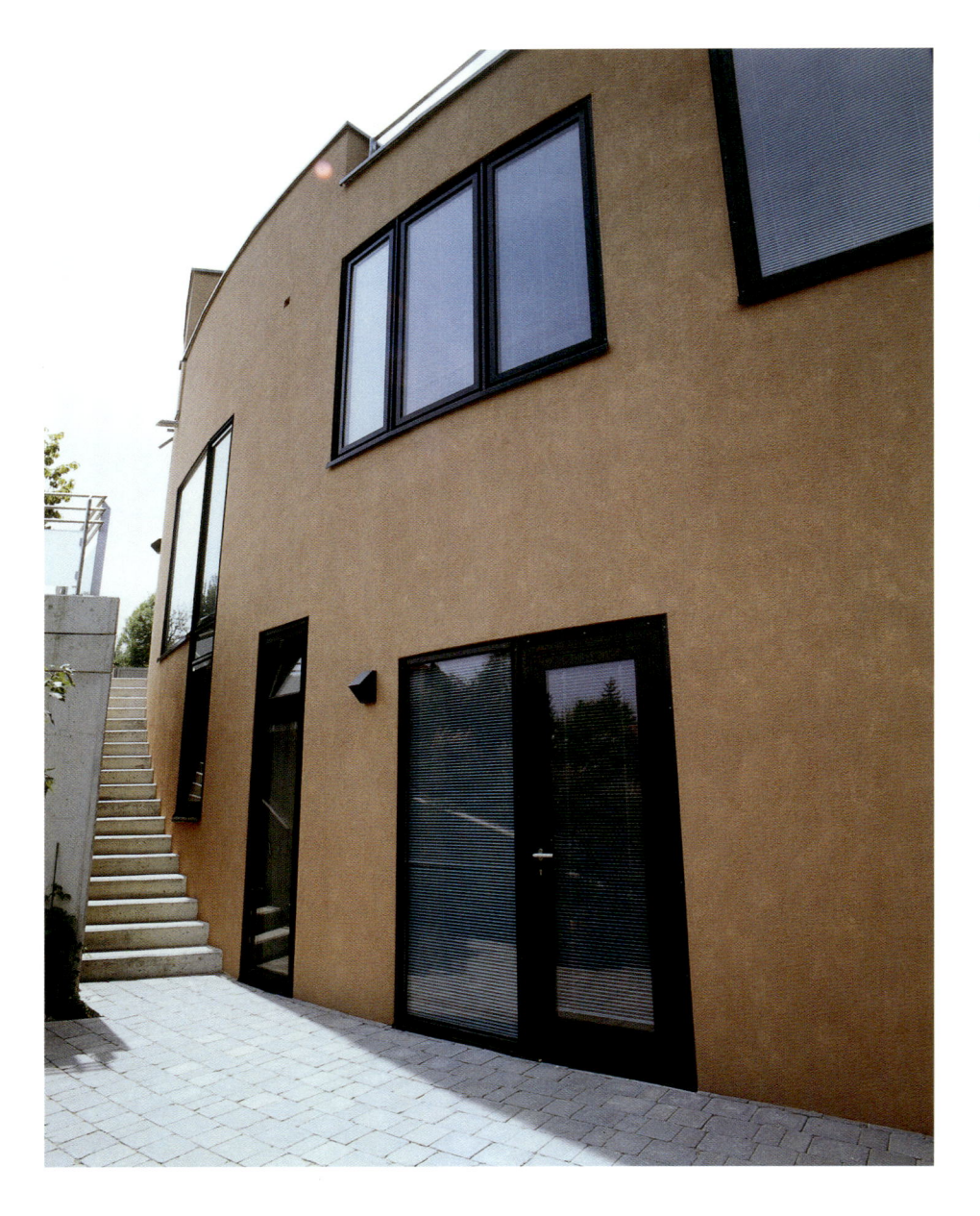

Nordostfassade North-east façade
Treppe zum Schwimmteich Stairs to the swimming pond
Glasdach über Terrasse, Südfassade Glass roof over terrace, south façade

Blick von der Dachterrasse auf den Schwimmteich
View of the swimming pond from the roof terrace

Diese zweigeschossige Villa, in einer bevorzugten Wohngegend der Stadt Graz gelegen, war der Auftrag einer Bauherrschaft, die den Architekten seit längerem auch beruflich verbunden ist. Gleichfalls an einem Hanggrundstück, das nach Norden hin abfällt, errichtet, liegt der Eingang an der Straßenseite in einer Kante des linsenförmigen Hausgrundrisses, eine Form, die die Architekten auch im öffentlichen Raum als ein Gemeinschaftsmotiv nutzen. Hinter Milchglasscheiben verborgen ist das Vestibül angeordnet, von dem aus eine Treppe auf das Dach, eine weitere ins Untergeschoß führt. Im Erdgeschoß bildet ein 4.40 Meter hoher Wohnraum das Zentrum des Hauses, in dem die offene Küche integriert ist. Ihr gegenüber ist eine kleine Bibliothek und ein Kamin situiert, so daß das Familienleben in einem fließenden, luftigen Raumkontinuum zwischen Küche, einem Eßplatz und einem Sitzbereich stattfindet. Um diesen zentralen Raum sind das Schlafzimmer der Eltern mit einem Balkon und der (noch nicht fertiggestellte) über zweieinhalb Geschosse in die Höhe geführte Wintergarten, der die dem Eingang gegenüberliegende Kante der Linse bildet, sowie ein weiteres kleines Zimmer für ein Kind angeordnet. Der Wintergarten ist von der Bibliothek aus zugänglich. Vom Mittelpunkt des Hauses wird der Blick durch eine wohltemperierte Variation unterschiedlicher Fensterformen aus Schlitzen und großflächigen Fenstereinheiten in den geschwungenen Wänden zum Garten oder über ein kleines Tal zu der gegenüberliegenden Hügelkette geführt.

Im Untergeschoß befindet sich ein großes Atelier, das dem Wintergarten angelagert ist und neben den notwendigen Wirtschafts- und Hobbyräumen ein weiteres Kinderzimmer aufnimmt. Sowohl aus dem Erdgeschoß- wie dem Untergeschoßbereich kann der dem Hanggefälle angeglichene Garten betreten werden. Hier dominiert ein großes, rechteckiges Wasserbecken die Atmosphäre des Naturraumes. Mit einem kleinen Bereich zum Schwimmen wird der Teich durch einen Brunnen gespeist und erhält zusätzlich Regenerationswasser.

Der Dachbereich ist als eine große Terrassenfläche begehbar und hat zudem eine etwas tiefer liegende, mit dem Erdaushub des Gartens ausgefüllte Pflanzzone. Wie im Haus am Plattenweg, so hat man auch von hier aus einen weit in die umgebende Landschaft reichenden Panoramablick.

Der Baukörper ist eine Mischung aus Mauerwerks-, Stahlbeton- und Glasbau, der in seinen geschlossenen Wandelementen in einem gedeckten Sienarot verputzt ist, mit dem die schwarzen Metallprofile der Fensterrahmungen eine kontrastreiche Fassadenoberfläche ergeben.

This two-storey villa in a privileged Graz neighbourhood was commissioned by clients who have long been professionally associated with the architects. Built on a plot that slopes down to the north, its entrance is on the street side, on one edge of the lenticular ground plan, a shape that the architects also use as a community motif in public places. The vestibule is concealed behind panes of frosted glass, with one flight of stairs leading out from it to the roof and another into the basement. A 4.4 metre high living room on the ground floor forms the centre of the house, with the open kitchen built into it. Opposite the kitchen are a little library and a fireplace, so that family life can unfold in a fluent, airy spatial continuum between the kitchen, a dining area and a sitting area. Arranged around this central space are the master bedroom with a balcony and the (as yet incomplete) conservatory, which rises through two and a half storeys, forming the edge of the lentil-shape opposite the entrance, and also another small room for a child. The conservatory is accessible from the library. From the central point in the house, the eye is led through well-tempered variations on different window shapes, ranging from slits to large window units in the curved walls overlooking the garden, or via a little valley to the chain of hills opposite.

The basement contains a large studio attached to the conservatory, and also another child's bedroom, as well as the necessary utility and hobby rooms. There is access to the garden, which is adapted to the slope, from both the ground floor and the basement. Here a large, rectangular pool of water dominates the natural space. The pool is fed from a well, and also benefits from a regenerated water supply. There is a small area for swimming.

The roof is accessible as a large terrace, and also has a planted zone set a little lower, using soil removed from the garden. As in the *House on Plattenweg*, here too there is a panoramic view extending far into the surrounding countryside.

The building is constructed in a mixture of masonry, reinforced concrete and glass. The closed areas of the walls are rendered in a muted red sienna, creating a high-contrast façade surface along with the black metal profiles.

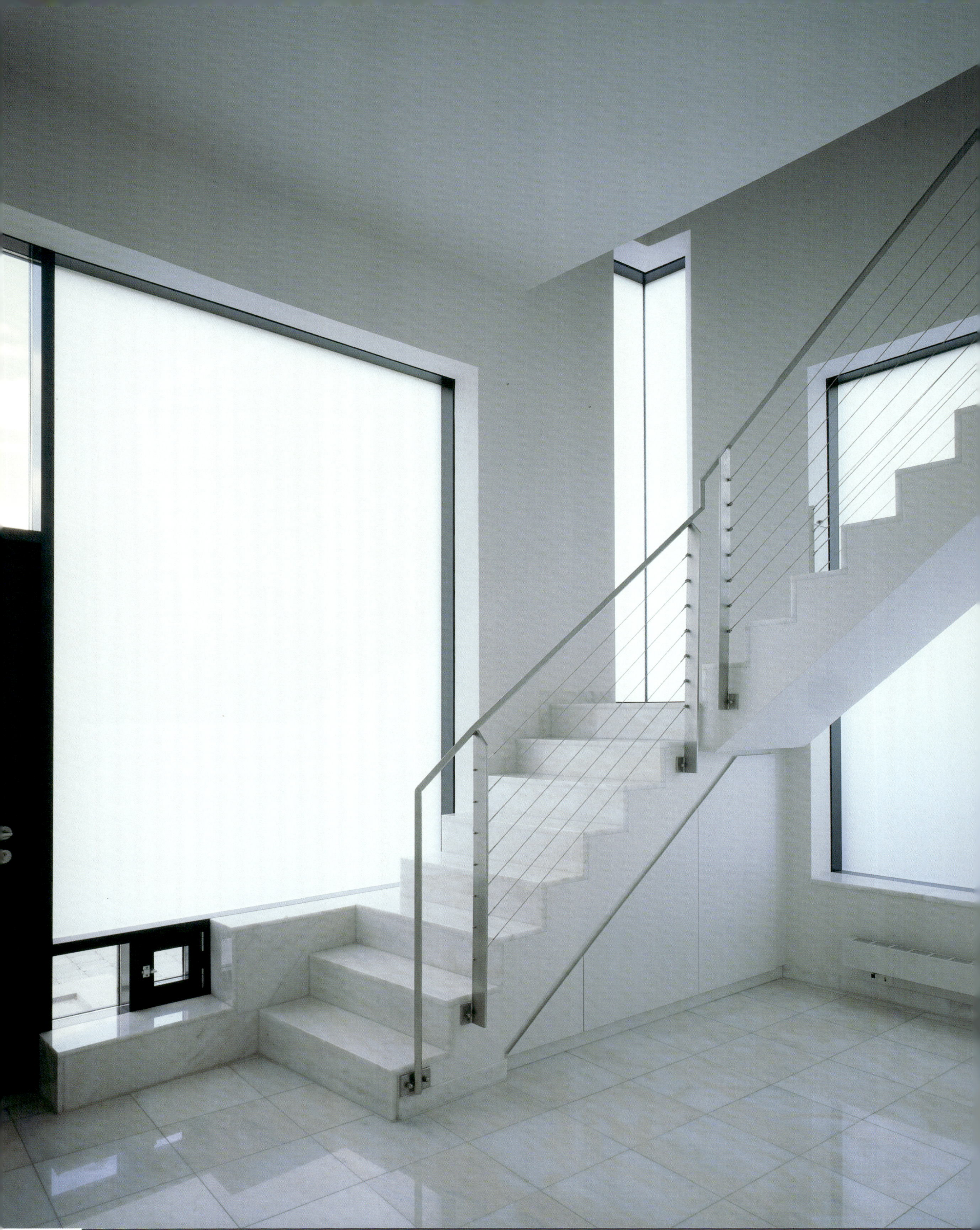

Vorraum Treppe zur Dachterrasse Anteroom steps to the roof terrace

Skizze Sketch
Katzeneingang Catflap
Erdgeschoß, Wohnbereich nach Westen Ground floor, living area looking west

HOUSE ON RUCKERLBERG   HAUS AM RUCKERLBERG   212 | 213

HAUS IN KUMBERG HOUSE IN KUMBERG

ORT LOCATION: **A-8062 Kumberg**   BAUHERRSCHAFT CLIENT: **C. St.-M. und Dr. med. A. St.**   PLANUNGS- UND BAUZEIT DESIGN AND REALISATION: **2000–2002**   PROJEKTLEITER PROJECT LEADER: **Gerald Flock**   STATIK STATICS: **Adolf Graber – Tassilo Szyszkowitz**   WOHNNUTZFLÄCHE USABLE LIVING SPACE: **210 m²**   UMBAUTER RAUM BUILDING VOLUME: **1.100 m³**   KONSTRUKTION UND MATERIALIEN: **Massivbauweise** CONSTRUCTION AND MATERIALS: **solid construction**   EINDECKUNG: **glasierte Tonziegel** ROOF CLADDING: **glazed clay tiles**

<<< S. ABB. SEE FIG. **91**

Ansicht von Südwesten, in Bau – nachbearbeitet
View from the south-west, under construction, revised

Ansicht von Nordosten, in Bau – nachbearbeitet
View from the north-east, under construction, revised

Ansicht Südwestfassade View of the south-west façade
Ansicht Südostfassade View of the south-east façade
Ansicht Nordwestfassade View of the north-west façade
Ansicht Nordostfassade View of the north-east façade

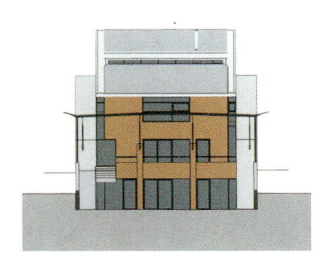

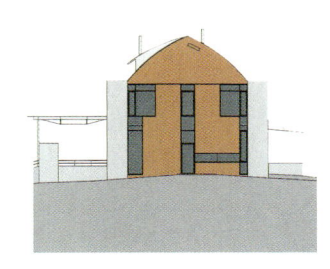

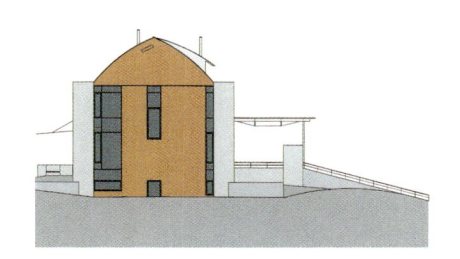

HOUSE IN KUMBERG   HAUS IN KUMBERG   214 | 215

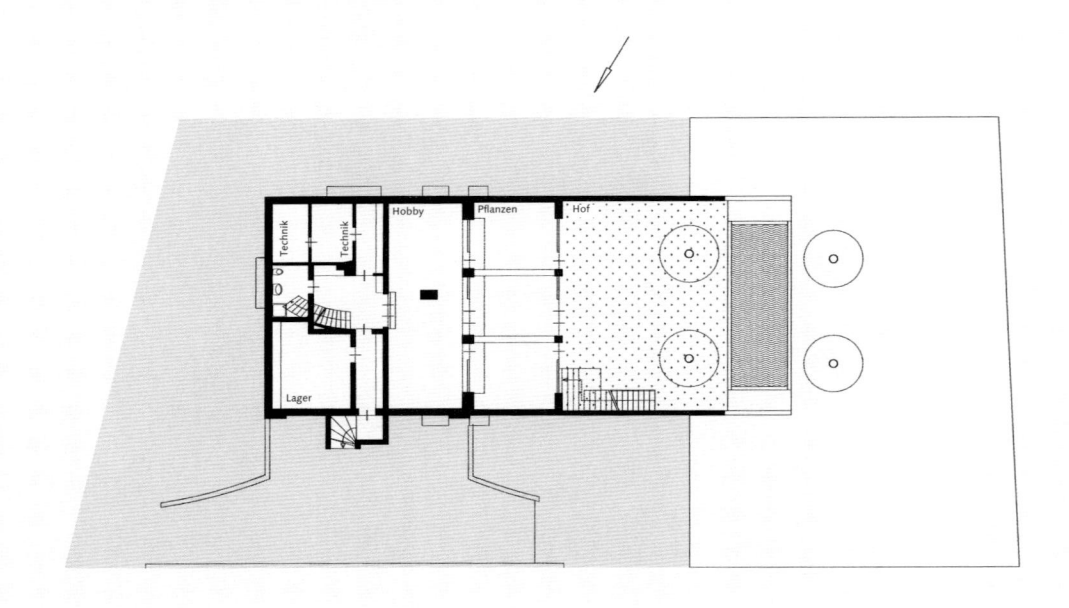

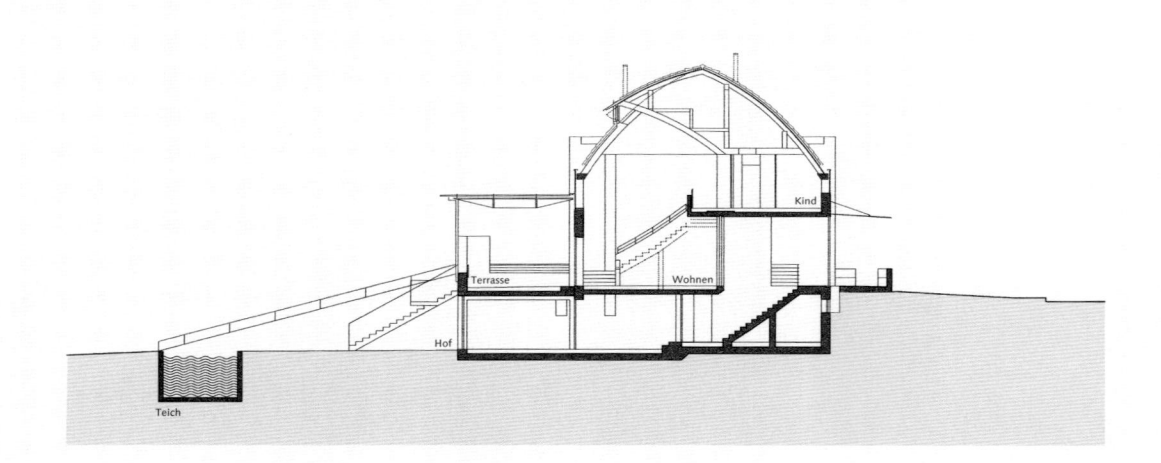

In der östlichen Steiermark, unweit der Landeshauptstadt Graz, liegt der kleine Ort Kumberg. Hier entsteht das derzeit letzte Einfamilienhaus der Architekten auf einem schmalen, leicht abfallenden Hanggrundstück am Ortsrand umgeben von der typischen Einfamilienhausbebauung dieser Region. Das seit längerem durchgespielte Repertoire der Längsentwicklung für Wohnhäuser in derartigen Hanglagen, wie man es etwa aus dem *Haus in Maria Enzersdorf* kennt, dominiert auch dieses Haus, wenngleich die seit dem *Grünen Haus* bekannte geometrische Primärform des Quadrats in dieser konzeptionellen Eindeutigkeit des rechten Winkels bisher noch nicht durchgeführt wurde. Eine Begründung dafür mag in der vorhandenen, restriktiven Bauordnung zu finden sein, die in diesem Projekt jedoch außerordentlich intelligent interpretiert wird. Entscheidend aber mag sein, daß die Definition des Baukörpers und seiner Elemente, die Wand, die Stütze, das Dach und der Bezug zum Außenraum neuerlich durchdacht worden ist.

Das dreigeschossige Einfamilienhaus ist ein auf fast quadratischem Grundriß definierter Kubus mit herausgestellten Eckpfeilern, zwischen die die Wandelemente und die Fenster eingepaßt sind. Im Erdgeschoß führt eine geschwungene Treppe vom zentralen Eingangsbereich in das darunterliegende Untergeschoß, das die Keller- und Hobbyräume aufnimmt. Hinter dem Haupteingangsbereich des Erdgeschosses befindet sich auch in diesem Haus ein hoher, über zwei Geschosse reichender Wohnraum, der den Blick in die gewölbte, glatte Oberfläche der dahinter verborgenen gebogenen Holzbinderkonstruktion des Daches freigibt und im Obergeschoß eine Galerie aufweist. Im Erdgeschoß befinden sich außerdem die Küche, ein kleines Wohnzimmer mit Kamin und ein Atelierraum. Aus diesen durch Schiebetüren voneinander abtrennbaren Funktionseinheiten wird der Weg über eine vorgelagerte, überdachte Terrasse in den Garten hinein achsial dominiert. Eine untere Kiesfläche ist durch klappenartige Einschnitte dem Hang vorgelagert, die zu dem abschließenden Wasserbecken überleitet.

Im Obergeschoß befinden sich unter dem Giebel des Spitztonnendaches ein Elternschlafraum sowie die beiden Kinderzimmer in den Ecken mit den kleineren Badezimmern. Für die Eindeckung des in Massivbauweise errichteten Hauses werden abermals glasierte Tonziegel verwendet. Die Farbigkeit des Gebäudes ist durch ein lichtes Grau und ein kräftiges Sienarot für die Fenstergliederungen, deren Konstruktionsteile schwarz abgesetzt sind, bestimmt.

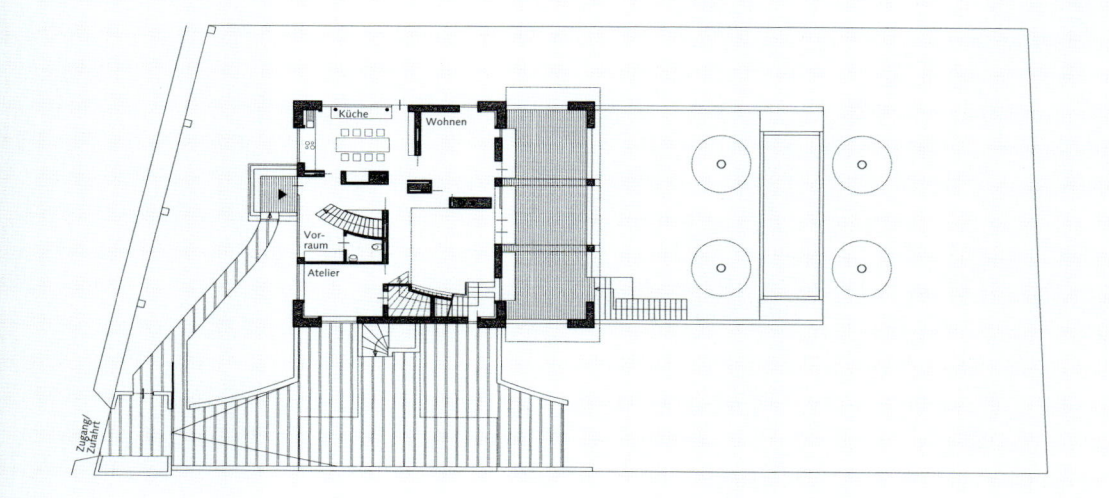

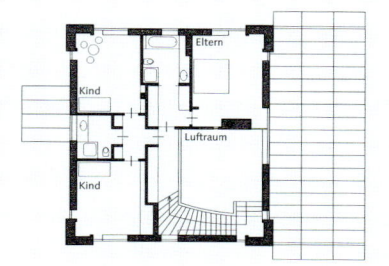

Grundrisse Floor plans:
Untergeschoß Basement
Erdgeschoß Ground floor
Obergeschoß First floor

Schnitt Section

In eastern Styria, not far from the capital, Graz, is the little town of Kumberg. What is so far the architects' last house is being built here on a narrow site sloping slightly downwards on the edge of the town, surrounded by the region's typical detached houses. This house also draws on the long-used repertoire of longitudinal development for such houses on sloping sites, as familiar from the *House in Maria Enzersdorf* – though the primary geometrical shape of the square, known since the *Green House*, has never previously been deployed with the right angle showing such a high degree of conceptual clarity. One justification for this may lie in the restrictive building regulations that prevail here, though they have been interpreted extraordinarily intelligently for this project. But the crucial factor may be that the definition of the building and its elements – the wall, the supports, the roof and the relationship with the exterior space – has been thought through again. The three-storey detached house is a cube defined on an almost square ground plan, with protruding corner piers, between which the wall elements and the windows are fitted. On the ground floor a curved staircase leads from the central entrance area into the basement below, which accommodates the cellars and hobby rooms. Behind the main entrance area on the ground floor, this house too has a high living room rising through two floors, opening up a view into the vaulted, smooth surface of the timber-frame roof structure concealed behind it; there is a gallery on the top floor. The ground floor also houses the kitchen, a small living room with a fireplace and a studio space. Emerging from these functional units, separated by sliding doors, the route into the garden via a roofed terrace placed in front is dominated axially. A lower gravelled area has vent-like incisions into the slope in front of it; the gravelled area itself leads to the pool at the end of the site. On the top floor, under the gable of the roof with its pointed tunnel vault, are the master bedroom and the two children's rooms in the corners, with smaller bathrooms. Glazed clay tiles are again being used to cover the masonry-built house. The colour scheme of the building is determined by a light grey and a powerful red sienna for the window articulations, with structural parts picked out in black.

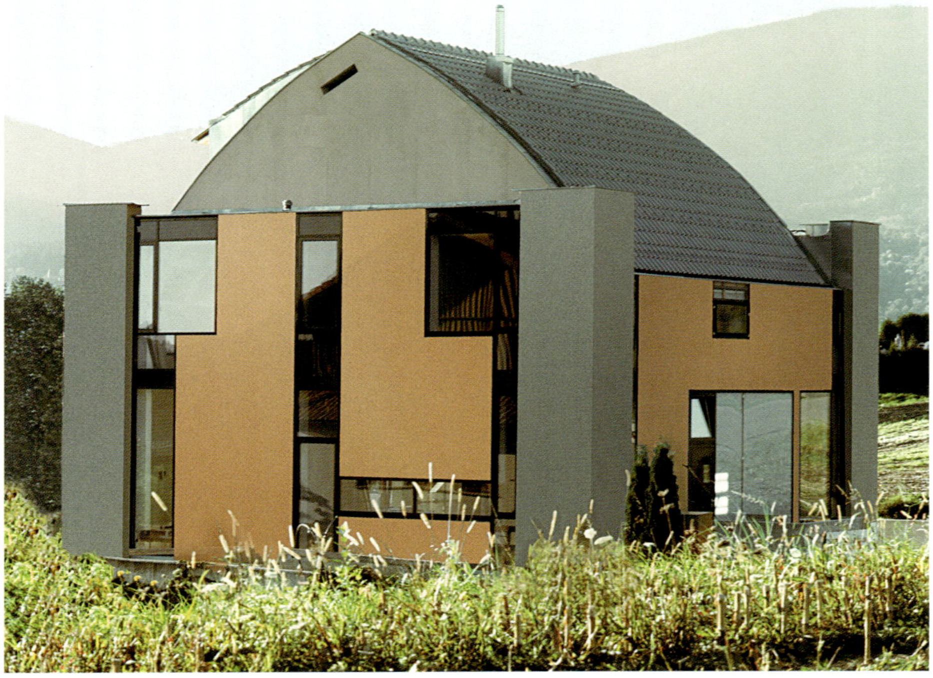

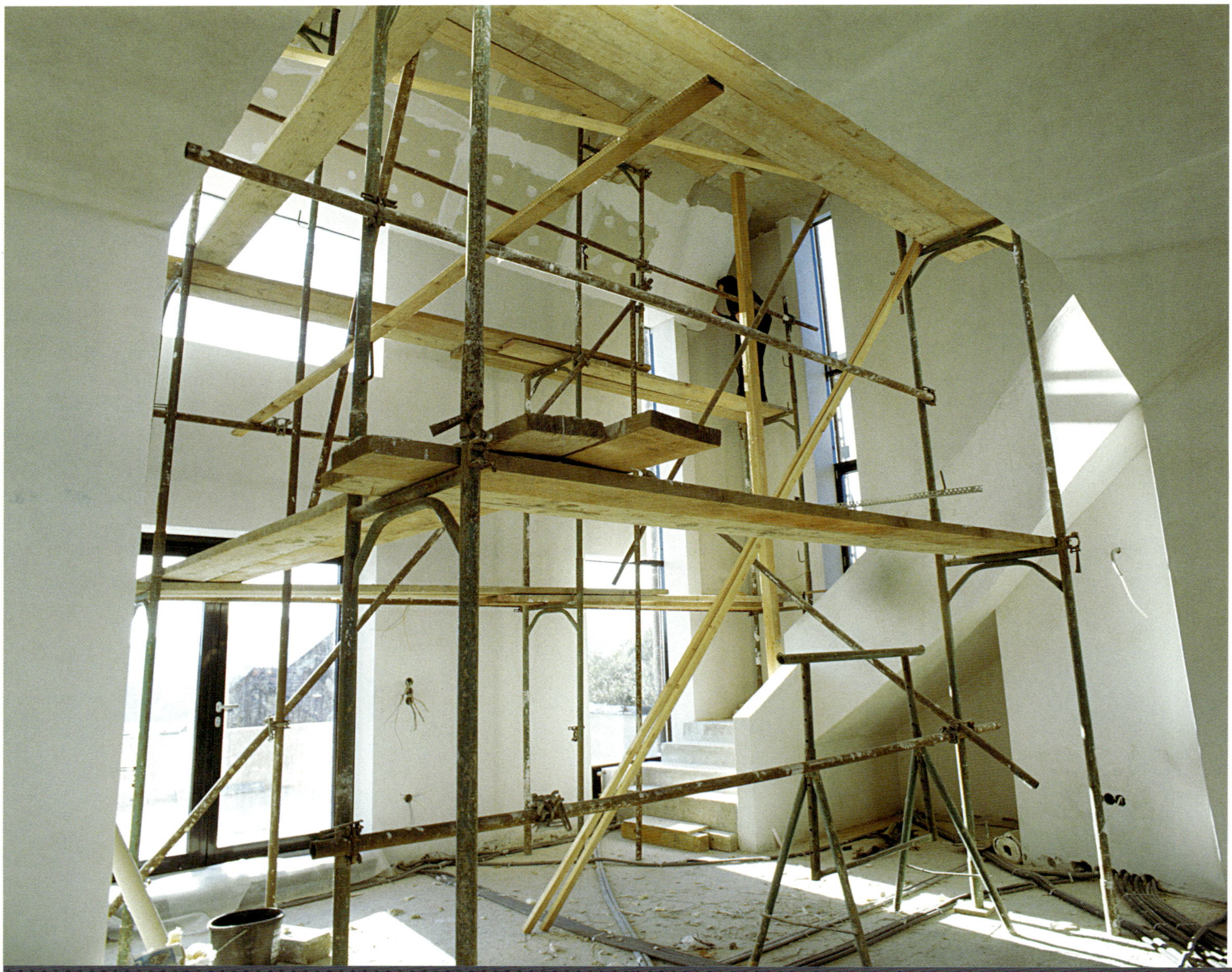

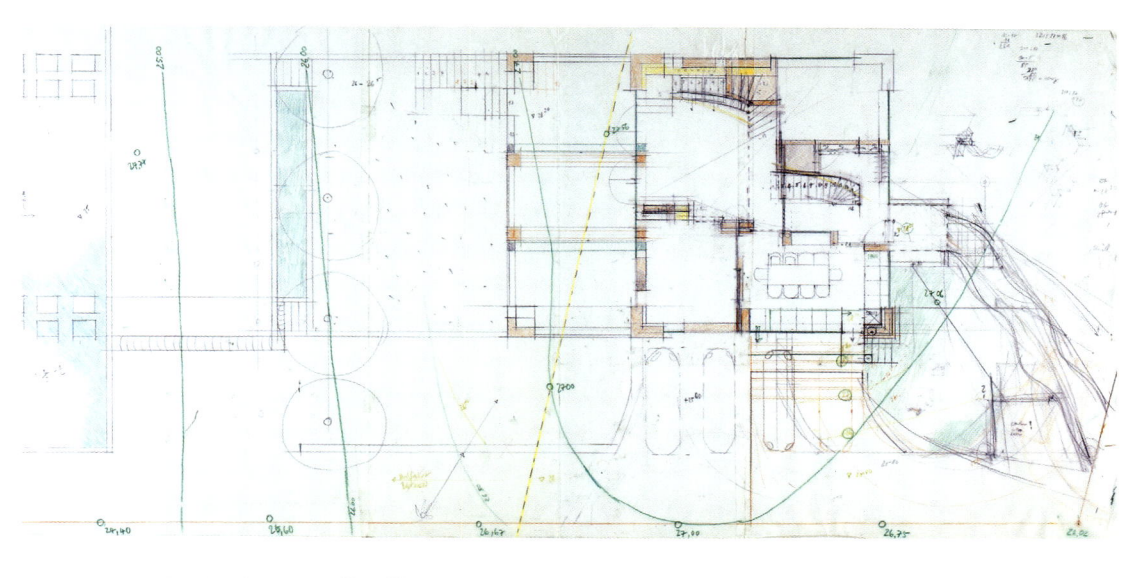

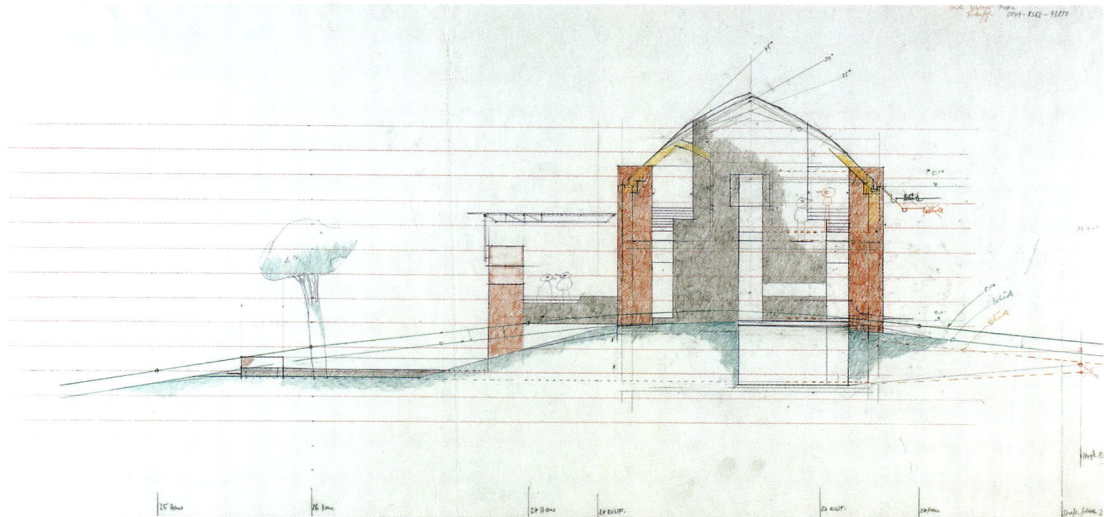

Ansicht von Nordosten, in Bau – nachbearbeitet
View from the north-east, under construction – revised
Wohnbereich nach Südosten, in Bau
Living area looking south-east, under construction

Skizzen Sketches

Preise und Auszeichnungen Prizes and awards

GEMEINSAME AUSZEICHNUNGEN UND PREISE

Würdigungspreis für Bildende Kunst 1990 des Bundesministeriums für Unterricht und Kunst

Dreimaliger Preis der Zentralvereinigung der Architekten Österreichs 1982 (Schloss Großlobming), 1988 (Pfarrzentrum Graz-Ragnitz) und 2001 (Kulturhaus St. Ulrich)

Auszeichnung zum Deutschen Architekturpreis 1999 (IBA Emscherpark Wohnanlage Gelsenkirchen)

5malige Auszeichnung mit der Gerambmedaille des Landes Steiermark 1981 (Haus über Graz), 1982 (Schloss Großlobming), 1985 (Schloss Pichl), 1992 (Kastner + Öhler Haupthaus) und 1997 (Volksschule Schloss Großlobming)

Sonderpreis des großen österreichischen Wohnbaupreises 1987 (Wohnanlage Eisbach-Rein)

Preis des Landes Steiermark für Architektur 1983 (Schloss Großlobming)

Erster österreichischer Holzbaupreis 1979 (Aufbahrungshalle Schwarzach)

Weiters seit 1978 dreiundzwanzig 1. Preise bei nationalen und internationalen Wettbewerben

EINZELAUSSTELLUNGEN

In Graz, Wien, Oslo, Edinburgh, Aberdeen, London, Liège, Nantes, Breslau, St. Moritz, Darmstadt, Gelsenkirchen, Stuttgart, Millstatt, Weimar, Berlin, Vancouver, Bologna, Klagenfurt, Mürzzuschlag

AUSSTELLUNGSBETEILIGUNGEN

Unter anderem in Berlin, Köln, Hamburg, New York, Los Angeles, Rom, Paris, Kairo, Moskau, Budapest, Prag, Lyon, Kopenhagen, Brüssel, Belgrad, Sevilla, Buenos Aires, Kassel, Karlsruhe, Krakau, Turin, Cambridge (USA), Montreal etc.

JOINT PRIZES AND AWARDS

Merit Award from the Ministry for Education and the Arts in 1990

Winners of the Award of the Zentralvereinigung der Architekten Österreichs (Central Association of Austrian Architects) in 1982 (Schloss Großlobming), 1988 (Catholic Parish Centre Graz-Ragnitz) and 2001 (Cultural Center-St.Ulrich/Greith)

Distinguished with the German Architecture Prize 1999 (Housing Complex for the International Building Exhibition Emscher Park, Gelsenkirchen)

Winners of Styrian Geramb Award in 1981, (House above Graz) 1982 (Schloss Großlobming), 1985 (Schloss Pichl), 1992 (Kastner + Öhler Haupthaus) and 1997 (Primary School, Schloss Großlobming)

Special Austrian Residential Building Award 1987 (Housing Complex in Eisbach-Rein)

Styrian Prize for Architecture 1983 (Schloss Großlobming)

First Austrian Timber Construction Award 1979 (Funeral parlour, Schwarzach)

Since 1978 winner of twenty-three national and international competitions

INDIVIDUAL EXHIBITIONS

In Graz, Vienna, Oslo, Edinburgh, Aberdeen, London, Liège, Nantes, Wroclaw, St. Moritz, Darmstadt, Gelsenkirchen, Stuttgart, Millstatt, Weimar, Berlin, Vancouver, Bologna, Klagenfurt, Mürzzuschlag

JOINT EXHIBITIONS

In Berlin, Cologne, Hamburg, New York, Los Angeles, Rome, Paris, Cairo, Moscow, Budapest, Prague, Lyon, Copenhagen, Brussels, Belgrade, Seville, Buenos Aires, Kassel, Karlsruhe, Cracow, Turin, Cambridge (USA), Montreal etc.

Publikationen Publications

HAUS ÜBER GRAZ, 1973/74, *Wohnhaus in Graz*

Haus über Graz, Broschüre, Eigenverlag

Österreichische Architektur im 20. Jahrhundert Band II, Friedrich Achleitner, Residenz Verlag

Baumeister, Deutschland, 6, 1975

L'Architecture d'Aujourd'hui, Frankreich, 5/6, 1976

Domus Nr. 550, Italien, 1976

Architecture, Frankreich, 4, 1977

Toshi Jutaku, Architekturmagazin, Japan, 11, 1977

Architektur & Wohnen, 1, 1980

Transparent, Manuskripte für Arch., Theorie, Umraum, Kunst, Red.: G. Feuerstein, 7/8, 1981

Architektur aus Graz, Ausstellungskatalog, 1981, Herausgeber: Zentralvereinigung der Architekten

Architektur-Investitionen. „Grazer Schule", 13 Standpunkte, 1986, Herausgeber: Dietmar Steiner, ISBN 3-201-01307-2

Architektur aus Graz. Öffentliche Bauten und Projekte von 1980 bis heute, Katalog zur Ausstellung „Architektur aus Graz", 1987

db, Deutsche Bauzeitung, 2, 1992

FAZ, Magazin, Heft 751, 1994

AUFBAHRUNGSHALLE SCHWARZACH, 1977/78

Bauen + Wohnen, 11, 1979

Domus Nr. 613, Italien, 1981

Architektur aus Graz, Ausstellungskatalog, 1981, Herausgeber: Zentralvereinigung der Architekten

Kunst und Kirche, Ökumenische Zeitschrift für Architektur u. Kunst, 2, 1981, Herausgegeben vom Arbeitsausschuß des Evangelischen Kirchenbautages und vom Diözesan-Kunstverein Linz

Transparent, Manuskript für Arch., Theorie, Umraum, Kunst, Red.: G. Feuerstein, 7/8, 1981

L'Architecture d'Aujourd'hui, Frankreich, 12, 1982

Friends of Kebyar, Portland, Oregan, USA, 2/3, 1986

Parametro, Internat. Magazin für Architektur, Italien, 151/152, 1986

SD, Space Design, Japan, 1, 1987

GRÜNES HAUS, 1978/79, *Wohnhaus in Graz*

Bauen + Wohnen, 11, 1979

Architektur Aktuell, Österreich, 8, 1980

Toshi Jutaku, Architekturmagazin, Japan, 12, 1980

Architektur aus Graz, Ausstellungskatalog, 1981, Herausgeber: Zentralvereinigung der Architekten

Domus Nr. 613, Italien, 1981

Transparent, Manuskripte für Arch., Theorie, Umraum, Kunst, Red.: G. Feuerstein, 7/8, 1981

a+u, Architectur+Urbanism, Tokyo, Nr. 151, 4, 1983

Architektur & Wohnen, 2/3, 1991

SCHLOSS GROSSLOBMING, 1979/81, *Revitalisierung und Erweiterung, Hauwirtschaftsschule mit Internat, 1979–1981, 1. Preis – Wettbewerb 1978, Neubau der Volksschule, 1994 – 1996*

Wettbewerbe Österreich 3. Jahrgang, Heft 8, 1979

Bauen + Wohnen, 11, 1979

Transparent, Manuskript für Arch., Theorie, Umraum, Kunst, Red.: G. Feuerstein, 7/8, 1981

L'Architecture d'Aujourd'hui, Frankreich, 12, 1982

Wettbewerbe, Österreich 6. Jahrgang Heft 23, 2, 1982

Bauwelt, Deutschland, 4, 1982

Bauen in Österreich, 1983, Edition Christian Brandstätter, ISBN 3-085447-070-3

Architektur aus Graz, Ausstellungskatalog, 1981, Herausgeber: Zentralvereinigung der Architekten

a+u, Architectur + Urbanism, Tokyo, Nr. 148

Junge Architekten in Europa, 1983, von Helge und Margret Botnigen Verlag: Kohlhammer, ISBN 3-17-007713-0

Frauen in der Architektur der Gegenwart, 1984, Katalog zur Ausstellung UIFA Berlin '84

Bauwelt, Deutschland, 3, 1985

Klassizismen und Klassiker, 1985, Herausgeber: Frank Werner, Stuttgart

db, Deutsche Bauzeitung, 4, 1986

Architektinnen, Ideen-Projekte-Bauten, 1986, Verlag W. Kohlhammer GmbH, Stuttgart, ISBN 3-17-009336-3

Architektur-Investitionen, „Grazer Schule", 13 Standpunke, 1986, Herausgeber: Dietmar Steiner, ISBN 3-201-01307-2

Arkitektnytt, Norwegen, 1, 1986

Parametro, Magazin für Architektur, Italien, 151/152, 1986

db, Deutsche Bauzeitung, 4, 1986

Architektur aus Graz, Öffentliche Bauten und Projekte von 1980 bis heute, 1987, Katalog zur Ausstellung „Architektur aus Graz"

Archithese, Deutschland, 5, 1988

Archithese, Deutschland, 8, 1988

Architektur Wettbewerbe, 1989

Architektur Aktuell Sonderheft, Architektur+Ästhetik, Österreich, 4, 1982

Architektur & Wohnen, 2/3, 1991

Baujahre, 1992, Österreichische Architektur 1967–1991, Herausgeber: Zentralvereinigung der Architekten Österreichs, ISBN 3-205-98072-7

db, Deutsche Bauzeitung, 2, 1992

Architecture and Prestige, Ukraine, 1995

Architektur & Bau Forum, Österreich, 6/7, 1996

Architektur & Bau Forum, Österreich, 9/10, 1996

Metamorphosen eines Schlosses, 1996, Herausgeber: Haus der Architektur, Graz, ISBN 3-901174-22-2

Glas, Architektur und Technik, 4/5, 1997

Leonardo, Deutschland, 2, 1997

a+u, Architectur + Urbanism, Tokyo, Nr. 325, 10, 1997

Architetture di confine, Triennale di Milano, Ausstellungskatalog, 1997

Glas Architektur und Technik, 4/5, 1997

Dialogues in time, 1998, Herausgeber: Haus der Architektur, ISBN 3-901174-36-2

KA Nr. 169, Korean Architects, Seoul, 9, 1998

The Contemporary Architecture Guide Vol2, Europe, 1999, von Masayuki Fuchigami Herausgeber: TOTO Shuppan, Tokyo; ISBN4-88706-184-6

WEISSES HAUS, 1980, *Wohnhaus in Graz*

Parametro, Internat. Magazin für Architektur, Italien, 151/152, 1986

HAUS ZUSERTAL, 1980/81, *Wohnhaus in Graz*

Transparent, Manuskript für Arch., Theorie, Umraum, Kunst, Red.: G. Feuerstein, 7/8, 1981

Architektur aus Graz, Ausstellungskatalog, 1981, Herausgeber: Zentralvereinigung der Architekten

L'Architecture d'Aujourd'hui, Frankreich, 12, 1982

Bauen in Österreich, 1983, Edition Christian Brandstätter, ISBN 3-85447-070-3

a+u, Architectur + Urbanism, Tokyo, 4, 1983

L'Architecture d'Aujourd'hui, Frankreich, 4, 1984

L'Architecture d'Aujourd'hui, Frankreich, 7/8, 1984

Interni, Nr. 342, Italien

Architektinnen, Ideen-Projekte-Bauten, 1986, Verlag W. Kohlhammer GmbH, Stuttgart, ISBN 3-17-009336-3

Arkitektnytt, Norwegen, 1, 1986

SD, Space Design, Japan, 1, 1987

Dialogues in time, 1998, Herausgeber: Haus der Architektur, ISBN 3-901174-36-2

SCHLOSS PICHL, 1982/84, *Revitalisierung und Erweiterung, Forstwirtschaftsschule mit Internat in Mitterdorf/Mürztal, 1. Preis – Wettbewerb 1980*

Transparent, Manuskripte für Arch., Theorie, Umraum, Kunst, Red.: G. Feuerstein, 7/8, 1981

Architektur aus Graz, Ausstellungskatalog, 1981, Herausgeber: Zentralvereinigung der Architekten

L'Architecture d'Aujourd'hui, Frankreich, 12, 1982

Bauwelt, Deutschland, 3, 1985

Wettbewerbe, Österreich 6. Jahrgang Heft 24, 4, 1982

Bauwelt, Deutschland, 8, 1985

Klassizismen und Klassiker, 1985, Herausgeber: Frank Werner, Stuttgart

Architektur-Investitionen. Grazer „Schule", 13 Standpunkte, 1986, Herausgeber: Dietmar Steiner, ISBN 3-201-01307-2

Arkitektnytt, Norwegen, 1, 1986

Parametro, Magazin für Architektur, Italien, 151/152, 1986

a+u, Architectur + Urbanism, Tokyo, Nr. 187, 4, 1986

Architektinnen, Ideen-Projekte-Bauten, 1986, Verlag W. Kohlhammer GmbH, Stuttgart, ISBN 3-17-009336-3

Architektur aus Graz. Öffentliche Bauten und Projekte von 1980 bis heute, 1987, Katalog zur Ausstellung „Architektur aus Graz"

SD, Space Design, Japan, 1, 1987

Österreich Moderne Architektur, 1988, Herausgeber: Bundeskanzleramt, Bundespressedienst, Wien

Der Architekt, 9, 1988

Archithese, Deutschland, 5, 1988

Archithese, Deutschland, 8, 1988

db, Deutsche Bauzeitung, 3, 1989

Dialogues in time, 1998, Herausgeber: Haus der Architektur, ISBN 3-901174-36-2

NEUES WOHNEN – ALTE POSTSTRASSE
1982/84, Mitbestimmungsmodell im Geschosswohnbau, 43 Wohneinheiten in Graz

Dialogues in time, 1998, Herausgeber: Haus der Architektur, ISBN 3-901174-36-2

Wohnbau in der Steiermark 1986-92, 1993, Herausgeber: Ziviltechniker Forum, ZV der Architekten Österr., ISBN 3-9500237-0-4

db, Deutsche Bauzeitung, 2, 1992

SD, Space Design, Japan, 3, 1990

AJ, The Architects Journal, United Kingdom 11, 1988

The Architectural Review, United Kingdom 12, 1988

Architektur aus Graz. Öffentliche Bauten und Projekte von1980 bis heute, 1987, Katalog zur Ausstellung „Architektur aus Graz"

Mitbestimmung im Wohnbau, 1987, Picus Verlag, ISBN 3-85452-104-9

Wohnbau in Graz 1980–86, 1986, Ausstellungskatalog „Wohnbau in der Steiermark 1980–86", Zentralvereinigung der Architekten Österreichs

AJ, The Architect's Journal United Kingdom, 49, 1986

Architektur + Wettbewerbe, 6, 1986

a+u, Architectur + Urbanism, Tokyo Nr. 187, 4, 1986

db, Deutsche Bauzeitung, 9, 1986

Parametro, Magazin für Architektur, Italien, 151/152, 1986

Arkitektnytt, Norwegen, 1, 1986

L'Architecture d'Aujourd'hui, Frankreich, 10, 1985

Bauwelt, Deutschland, 3, 1985

Architektur Aktuell, Österreich, 4, 1985

Wettbewerbe Österreich, 9. Jahrgang Heft 45/46, 4, 1985

Transparent, Manuskript f. Arch., Theorie, Umraum, Kunst, Red.: G. Feuerstein, 11/12, 1983

HAUS AM HOHENRAIN, 1984/85, *Wohnhaus bei Graz*

Der Architekt, 9, 1988, „Das Lächeln in der Architektur- Souveränität der Haltung"

Architektur & Bau Forum, Österreich, 139, 1990

Schöner Wohnen, 6, 1991

WOHNBAU – EISBACH REIN, 1984/86, *Mitbestimmungsmodell für 24 Wohneinheiten in Graz, 1. Preis – Wettbewerb 1983*

Wettbewerbe, Österreich, 10. Jahrgang Heft 53/54, 4/5, 1986

Transparent, Manuskript für Arch., Theorie, Umraum, Kunst. Red. G. Feuerstein, 5/6/7, 1986

Parametro, Internat. Magazin für Architektur, Italien, 151/152, 1986

Architektur Aktuell, Österreich, 10, 1987

Mitbestimmung im Wohnbau, 1987, Picus Verlag Wien, ISBN 3-85452-104-9

Architektur aus Graz. Öffentliche Bauten und Projekte von 1980 bis heute, 1987, Katalog zur Ausstellung „Architektur aus Graz"

Transparent, Manuskript f. Architektur, Theorie, Umraum, Kunst, Red.: G. Feuerstein, 3/4/5, 1988

The Architectural Review, United Kingdom, 12, 1988

AJ, The Architects' Journal, United Kingdom, 11, 1988

Transparent, Manuskript für Arch., Theorie, Umraum, Kunst, Red. G. Feuerstein, 3/4/5, 1988

L'Architecture d'Aujourd'hui, Frankreich, 9, 1989

Leonardo, Deutschland, 1, 1989

Wohnbau in der Steiermark 1986–92, 1993, Herausgeber: Ziviltechniker Forum, ZV der Architekten Österr., ISBN 3-9500237-0-4

ARCHITEKTUR Beispiele, 1994, Dietmar Steiner; Löcker Verlag, Wien

Dialogues in time, 1998, Herausgeber: Haus der Architektur, ISBN 3-901174-36-2

PFARRZENTRUM GRAZ – RAGNITZ, 1984/87, *Kirche mit Haus der Begegnung, 1. Preis – Wettbewerb 1983*

Wettbewerbe, Österreich 6.Jahrgang Heft 25, 7, 1982

Transparent, Manuskript f. Arch., Theorie, Umraum, Kunst, Red.: G. Feuerstein, 3/4, 1982

Klassizismen und Klassiker, 1985, Herausgeber: Frank Werner, Stuttgart

Bauwelt, Deutschland, 3, 1985

Architektur-Investitionen. Grazer „Schule, 13 Standpunkte, 1986, Herausgeber: Dietmar Steiner, ISBN 3-201-01307-2

Architektinnen, Ideen-Projekte-Bauten, 1986, Verlag W. Kohlhammer GmbH, Stuttgart, ISBN 3-17-009336-3

Parametro, Internat. Magazin für Architektur, Italien, 151/152, 1986

a+u, Architectur + Urbanism, Tokyo Nr. 187, 4, 1986

Arch. & Life, Belgien, 9/10, 1987

Architektur Aktuell, Österreich, 10, 1987

Architektur aus Graz, Öffentliche Bauten und Projekte von 1980 bis heute, 1987, Katalog zur Ausstellung „Architektur aus Graz"

Archithese, Deutschland, 5, 1988

Architektur & Wettbewerbe, Die Kirche als Bauherr, 3, 1988

Transparent, Manuskript für Arch., Theorie, Umraum, Kunst, Red. G. Feuerstein, 3/4/5, 1988

Bauwelt, Deutschland, 6, 1988

The Architectural Review, United Kingdom, 2, 1988

DBZ, Deutsche Bauzeitschrift, 8, 1989

Bauen für die Kirche – Beispiele aus den 80er Jahren, 1989, Galerieinformationen der Deutschen Gesellschaft für christliche Kunst e.V. München

a+u, Architectur + Urbanism, Tokyo, Nr. 238, 7, 1990

Architektur & Bau Forum, Österreich, 39, 1990

SD, Space Design, Japan, 3, 1990

A + Architecture, 1, 1990

Architektur & Wohnen, 2/3, 1991

Im Gespräch zwischen Baum und Architektur, 1991, Herausgeber: Mario Terzic, ISBN 3-05-05436-9

Baujahre, Österreichische Architektur 1967–1991, Herausgeber: Zentralvereinigung der Architekten Österreichs, ISBN 3-205-98072-7

Funktion und Zeichen, Kirchenbau in der Stmk. seit dem II. Vatikanum, 1992, Herausgeber: Wolfgang Bergthaler, ISBN 3-900993-14-9

db, Deutsche Bauzeitung, 2, 1992

Jahrbuch für Licht und Architektur 1993, Herausgeberin Ingeborg Flagge; Ernst & Sohn, Verlag für Architektur und technische Wissenschaften GmbH, Berlin; ISBN 1-85490-900-2

Kunst als Ort der Selbstfindung, Krakow 93, 1993

DBZ, Deutsche Bauzeitschrift, 7, 1994

Dialogues in time 1998, Herausgeber: Haus der Architektur, ISBN 3-901174-36-2

GRAUES HAUS, 1985/86, *Wohnhaus in Graz*

Architektur-Investitionen. 13 Standpunkte „Grazer Schule", 1986, herausgegeben von Dietmar Steiner, ISBN 3-201-01307-2

Transparent, Manuskript für Arch., Theorie, Umraum, Kunst, Red.: G. Feuerstein, 5/6/7, 1986

Architektur aus Graz. Öffentliche Bauten und Projekte, von 1980 bis heute, 1987, Katalog zur Ausstellung „Architektur aus Graz"

Transparent, Manuskript für Arch., Theorie, Umraum, Kunst, Red.: G. Feuerstein, 3/4/5, 1988

archithese, Deutschland, 5, 1988

archithese, Deutschland, 8, 1988

Der Architekt, 9, 1988

Architektur & Bau Forum, Österreich, 139, 1990

SD, Space Design, Japan, 3, 1990

Architektur & Wohnen, 2/3, 1991

FAZ, Magazin, Heft 751, 1994

Architektur and Prestige, Kiev, Ukraine, 1/2, 1999

„BIOCHEMIE – BIOTECHNOLOGIE GRAZ"
für die TU Graz, 1985/91, Institutsgebäude für die Technische Universität Graz, 1. Preis – Wettbewerb 1983

Transparent, Manuskript für Arch.; Theorie, Umraum, Kunst, Red. G. Feuerstein, 3/4/5, 1988

archithese, Deutschland, 5, 1988

archithese, Deutschland, 8, 1988

Der Architekt, 9, 1988, „Das Lächeln in der Architektur- Souveränität der Haltung"

Szyszkowitz und Kowalski; 5 Bauten 1985–1990, 5 Projekte

Architektur & Bau Forum, Sonderdruck Österreich, >Arche-Tonik pur<, 139, 1990

a+u, Architectur + Urbanism, Tokyo, Nr. 238, 7, 1990

Wettbewerbe, Österreich, 8. Jahrgang Heft 37, 4, 1984

Transparent, Manuskript für Arch., Theorie, Umraum, Kunst, Red.: G. Feuerstein, 7/8, 1984

Wettbewerbe, Österreich, 101/102

Transparent, Manuskript für Arch., Theorie, Umraum, Kunst. Red. G. Feuerstein, 5/6/7, 1986

Architektur aus Graz. Öffentliche Bauten und Projekte von 1980 bis heute, 1987, Ausstellungskatalog „Architektur aus Graz"

Transparent, Manuskript für Arch., Theorie, Umraum, Kunst, Red. G. Feuerstein, 3/4/5, 1988

Techniques & Architecture, Frankreich, 386, 1989

Bauwelt, Deutschland, 8, 1989

The Architect, 1, 1990

SD, Space Design, Japan, 3, 1990

Architektur & Bau Forum, Österreich, 139, 1990

Szyszkowitz & Kowalski, zwei Projekte für die Forschung, 1991, Aedes, Galerie und Architekturforum, Berlin

Baumeister, Deutschland, 9, 1991

Biochemie und Biotechnologie, 1991, Herausgeber: Haus der Architektur, ISBN 3-901174-01-X

Universitès écoles supérieures, 1992 Éditions du Moniteur, Paris; ISBN 2-281-19069-2

Glasforum, Deutschland, 1, 1992

db, Deutsche Bauzeitung, 2, 1992

Architektur als Engagement, 50/51, 1993, Herausgeber: Haus der Architektur, Graz, ISBN 3-901174-09-5

Jahrbuch für Licht und Architektur, 1993, Herausgeberin Ingeborg Flagge; Ernst & Sohn Verlag für Architektur und technische Wissenschaften GmbH, Berlin; ISBN 1-85490-900-2

db, Deutsche Bauzeitung, 12, 1993

a+u, Architectur + Urbanism, Tokyo, 6, 1993

Standpunkte 94, 1994, Herausgeber: Forum Stadtpark Graz, Referat für Architektur, ISBN 3-201-01615-2

DBZ, Deutsche Bauzeitschrift, 7, 1994

FAZ, Magazin, Heft 751, 1994

Die neue Österreichische Architektur, 1995, von Frank Dimster, ISBN 3-17-012539-7

Dialogues in time, 1998, Herausgeber: Haus der Architektur, ISBN 3-901174-36-2

Architekturtheorie des 20. Jahrhunderts – Zeit Raum, 1999, von Prof. Jürgen Pahl; Prestel-Verlag ISBN 3-7913-2019-x

The Contemporary Architecture Guide Vol2, Europe, 1999, von Masayuki Fuchigami, Herausgeber: TOTO Shuppan, Tokyo; ISBN 4-88706-184-6,

HAUS HARMISCH, 1987/88, *Wohnhaus im Burgenland*

SD, Space Design, Japan, 3, 1990

Häuser, Magazin für internationales Wohnen, 1, 1991

db, Deutsche Bauzeitung, 2, 1992

FAZ, Magazin, Heft 751, 1994

Die neue Österreichische Architektur, 1995, von Frank Dimster, ISBN 3-17-012539-7

Dialogues in time, 1998, Haus der Architektur, ISBN 3-901174-36-2

KASTNER + ÖHLER
1989/93, Umbau eines Kaufhauses in der Grazer Altstadt
1992/93, Umbau Jugendstilhaus, Kaufhaus in der Grazer Altstadt
1994/95, Neubau Sporthaus
2001, Umbau des Sporthaus-Altbaus

Glasforum, Deutschland, 2, 1992

Architektur als Engagement, 126, 1993, Herausgeber: Haus der Architektur, Graz, ISBN 3-901174-09-5

The Architectural Review, United Kingdom, 6, 1995

Innovationen eines Kaufhauses in Graz, 1995, Herausgeber: Haus der Architektur-Graz-Österreich, ISBN 3-901174-05-2

Leonardo, Deutschland, 6, 1995

Wettbewerbe Österreich, 129/130

The Architectural Review, United Kingdom, 6, 1995

Architektur und Wettbewerbe, 6, 1996

Dialogues in time, 1998, Herausgeber: Haus der Architektur, ISBN 3-901174-36-2

Architekturtheorie des 20. Jahrhunderts – Zeit Raum, 1999, von Prof. Jürgen Pahl; Prestel-Verlag ISBN 3-7913-2019-x

Architektur and Prestige, Kiev, Ukraine, 1/2, 1999

The Contemporary Architecture Guide Vol2, Europe, 1999, von Masayuki Fuchigami, Herausgeber: TOTO Shuppan, Tokyo; ISBN 4-88706-184-6

GELSENKIRCHEN; IBA EMSCHERPARK WOHNBEBAUUNG KÜPPERSBUSCH
1990/96, Wohnanlage für die internationale Bauausstellung, 250 Wohneinheiten, Kindergarten 1. Preis – Wettbewerb 1990

Bauwelt, Deutschland, 6, 1991

Deutsches Architektenblatt, 2, 1991

Centrum, Jahrbuch Architektur und Stadt 1992, Herausgeber: Peter Neitzke und Carl Steckeweh, ISBN 3-528-08801-X

Architektur als Engagement, 99, 1993, Herausgeber: Haus der Architektur, Graz, ISBN 3-901174-09-5

Wohnbau in der Steiermark 1986–92, 1993, Herausgeber: Ziviltechniker Forum, ZV der Architekten Österr., ISBN 3-9500237-0-4

IBA Emscher Park, Katalog zum Stand der Projekte, 1993

DBZ, Deutsche Bauzeitschrift, 7, 1994

Standpunkte 94, 1994, Forum Stadtpark Graz, Referat für Architektur, ISBN 3-201-01615-2

Architektur Aktuell, Österreich, 9, 1995

Future housing projects in germany, INTER NATIONS 1996, Herausgeber: Jörg Blume

IBA Emscher Park Projekte im Rahmen der Internationalen Bauausstellung, Emscher Park, Herausgeber: IBA Emscher Park GmbH, 1997

Architektur Aktuell, Österreich, 10, 1997

Wettbewerbe Aktuell, 10, 1998

KA, Nr. 169, Korea, 9, 1998

Architektur Aktuell, Österreich, 10, 1998

Baumeister, Deutschland, 5, 1998

Leonardo, Deutschland, 3, 1998

The Architectural Review, United Kingdom, 4, 1998

Der Architekt, Deutschland, 12, 1998

Bauen in Europa, Österreichische Architekten in Europa des 20. Jahrhunderts, 12, 1998

Dialogues in time, 1998, Herausgeber: Haus der Architektur, ISBN 3-901174-36-2

Wohnsiedlungen, 1998, Verlag Birkhäuser, ISBN 3-7643-5631-6

Topos European Landscape Magazine, Deutschland, 1999, Internationale Bauausstellung Emscher Park, IBA – a renewal concept for a region

Architekturtheorie des 20. Jahrhunderts – Zeit Raum, 1999, von Prof. Jürgen Pahl; Prestel-Verlag ISBN 3-7913-2019-x

db, Deutsche Bauzeitung, Stadt-Landschaften, 6, 1999

Siebzig Kilometer Hoffnung Die IBA Emscher Park (Titelbild), 1999, von Manfred Sack, DVA, Stuttgart ISBN 3-421-03190-8

Siedlungskultur, Neue und alte Gartenstädte im Ruhrgebiet, 1999, Herausgegeben von H. Beierlorzer, J. Boll, K. Ganser, Verlag Vieweg ISBN 3-528-02425-9

Räume und Freiräume, 1999, von Frank R. Werner, Baudokumentation 16, Verlag HdA, Graz, ISBN 3-901174-38-9

Architektur and Prestige, Kiev, Ukraine, 1/2, 1999

Abitare, Nr. 386, Italien, 7, 1999

Byggekunst, Oslo Norwegen, Nr. 8/99, 12, 1999

Architektur in Deutschland '99, Wohnbebauung Küppersbuschgelände, In Gelsenkirchen – Feldmark, Krämer Verlag Stuttgart + Zürich, 2000

Siedlungskultur Neue und alte Gartenstädte im Ruhrgebiet, IBA Emscher Park, 2000

Ambiente, Argentinien, Comunidad experimental, 3/4/5, 2000

Exhibition: Contemporary European Landscape Design; Havard Graduate School of Design, 03, 2001

Bauen in Europa, Österreichische Architekten in Europa des 20. Jahrhunderts, Ausstellung in Krakau, Polen, 5, 2002

HAUS IN BAD MERGENTHEIM, 1992/93,
Wohnhaus in Bad Mergentheim, Deutschland

DBZ, Deutsche Bauzeitschrift, 7, 1994

GA Houses Nr. 41 Japan, Tokyo, 1994

The Architectural Review, United Kingdom, 10, 1996

Glas, Architektur und Technik, 6, 1998

KA, Nr. 169 Korean Architects; Seoul, 9, 1998

Bauen in Europa, Österreichische Architekten in Europa im 20. Jahrhundert, 12, 1998

Dialogues in time, 1998, Haus der Architektur, ISBN 3-901174-36-2

The Home Office, architectural showcase, von Arian Mostaedi, 1999, Herausgeber: Carlos Broto & Joseph Minguet; Barcelona ISBN 84-89861-10-2

HÄUSER IN WIEN-HIETZING, 1988/90,
Wohnhäuser in Wien-Hietzing

Architektur & Bau Forum, Sonderdruck Österreich, >Arche-Tektonik pur<, 139, 1990

Szyszkowitz und Kowalski; 5 Bauten 1985–1990, 5 Projekte

Costruire, Italien, 111, 1992, Il momento di Graz; Die Grazer Architekturszene

Architektur als Engagement, 1993, Herausgeber: Haus der Architektur, Graz, ISBN 3-901174-09-5

Häuser, Magazin für internationales Wohnen, 3, 1993

Architektur Aktuell, Österreich, 4, 1993

A+U, Architectur + Urbanism, Tokyo, 6, 1993

DBZ, Deutsche Bauzeitschrift, 7, 1994, Romatischer Konstruktivismus; Die Architekten Szyszkowitz und Kowalski im Gespräch

FAZ, Magazin, Heft 751, 1994

Standpunkte 94, 1994, Forum Stadtpark Graz, Verlag für Architektur, ISBN 3-201-01615-2

Architektur and Prestige, Kiev, Ukraine, 1/2, 1999

HAUS IN MARIA ENZERSDORF, 1993/94,
Wohnhaus in Wien

GA Houses, Nr. 41 Japan, Tokyo, 1994

HAUS AM PLATTENWEG, 1996/97, *Wohnhaus in Graz*

GA Houses Nr. 41 projects Japan, Japan, Tokyo, 1994

Architektur Aktuell, Österreich, 6/7, 1996

Häuser, Magazin für internat. Wohnen, 2, 1997

Schöner Wohnen, 10, 1998

Schöner Wohnen, Österreich Sonderheft, 1999

Architektur and Prestige, Kiev, Ukraine, 1/2, 1999

HAUS IN MOOSBURG, 1996/97, *Wohnhaus in Moosburg, Kärnten*

GA houses 48, Project 1996, Japan, Tokyo, 1996

4 STADTVILLEN IN MARIAGRÜN, 1998/99,
14 Wohneinheiten in Graz

GA Houses Nr 41, Japan, Tokyo, 1994

Studienzentrum Inffeldgasse, *1999/00, Institutsgebäude für die Technische Universität Graz, 1. Preis – Wettbewerb 1990*

DBZ, Deutsche Bauzeitschrift, 7, 1994

Wettbewerbe, Österreich, 98/99

l'ARCA, Organicismo manipolato Centre for Studies, Technical University, Graz, 159, 2001

Architektur + Bauforum, Mehrwert-Architektur, 05/06, 2001

The Architectural Review, 08, 2001

Mehrstimmiger Dialog Studienzentrum Inffeldgründe der TU-Graz, 2001, von Frank R. Werner, Verlag HdA, Graz, ISBN 3-901174-42-7

C3, Korea, 2002

St. Ulrich im Greith, *1999/00, Kulturhaus*

Architektur aktuell, Bauen für das Laubdorf, 04, 2001

l'ARCA "Fortemente riconscibile", Italien, 160, 06, 2001

Architektur & Bauforum, Kulturhaus St. Ulrich im Greith, Nr. 215, 06/2001

The Architectural Review, 11, 2001

Bildnachweis
Illustration credits

Archive de France / Institut français d'architecture, Paris; Atelier A-Josic, Paris 45

Gert von Bassewitz, Hamburg 40, 47, 60, 63 oben u. mitte, 65, 68, 73, 77, 101, 138, 139, 147, 150/151, 153–157, 161, 163, 176 rechts oben, 177, 178, 179 unten, 180, 181 unten

Achim Behn, Graz 24, 106 unten links, 107 oben links

Anna Blau, Wien 63 unten, 196, 204, 205 oben

Domenig & Huth, Graz 43

Luzia Ellert, Wien 30 links

Günter Hauer, Graz 12, 18, 41 rechts, 50, 55, 56, 66, 78, 88

Christian Kandzia, Stuttgart 27, 107 oben rechts, 118, 124, 126, 127, 129 unten

Behnisch & Partner, Christian Kandzia, Stuttgart 42

Andreas Lichtblau, Wien 29 oben, 128, 129 oben

Herbert Missoni, Graz 35 rechts, 110, 111, 113

Paul Ott, Graz 19, 57, 58, 62 links, 67, 69 links, 75, 171, 175, 176 links u. rechts unten, 179 oben u. mitte, 181 oben, 188, 189, 194, 195

B. Otte (Zeichnung), Bauhausarchiv Berlin, Museum für Gestaltung, Berlin (Repro) 32

Princeton Architectural Press, New York, Publikation „Adalberto Libera" 69

Georg Riha, Wien 71, 140, 141 unten, 144–146, 152

Michael Scholz, Gelsenkirchen 81

Michael Schuster, Graz 82

Harry Stuhlhofer, Graz 99

Gery Wolf, Graz 26

Gerald Zugmann, Wien 41 links, 62 rechts, 164, 165, 168, 169, 206, 207, 212

Alle übrigen Abbildungen:
Büro Szyszkowitz+Kowalski
All other illustrations:
office Szyszkowitz+Kowalski